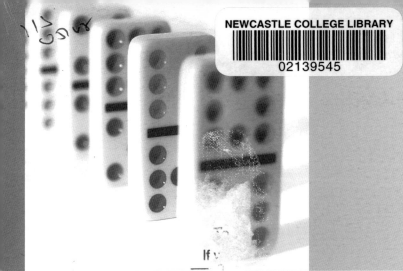

AUDITING

AUDITING

9TH EDITION

The late A H Millichamp
BA, MSocSc, FCA, FCCA, ATII

Alan Millichamp taught at the Universities of Wolverhampton and Birmingham, at the Open University Business School and in the private sector. He was a former examiner and assessor in auditing to the Association of Chartered Certified Accountants and was also a member of the examining panel of the ACCA.

J R Taylor
MA, FCA

John Taylor teaches at Leeds Metropolitan University on professional accounting courses. He was a professional auditor for many years and the former financial director of a PLC based in Leeds. He is the author of *Implementing Audit Procedures*, published by Osborne Books and *Business Finance* for the Institute of Chartered Secretaries and Administrators.

SOUTH-WESTERN
CENGAGE Learning

Australia • Brazil • Japan • Korea • Mexico • Singapore • Spain • United Kingdom • United States

SOUTH-WESTERN
CENGAGE Learning™

Auditing 9ᵗʰ edition
Alan Millichamp and John R. Taylor

Publishing Director: John Yates

Publisher: Pat Bond

Development Editor: Leandra Paoli

Content Project Editor: Lucy Mills

Manufacturing Manager: Helen Mason

Production Controller: Maeve Healy

Marketing Manager: Anne-Marie Scoones

Typesetter: KGL, India

Cover design: Adam Renvoize

Text design: Design Deluxe Ltd, UK

For product information and technology assistance, contact
emea.info@cengage.com

For permission to use material from this text or product, and for permission queries,
email **clsuk.permissions@cengage.com**

British Library Cataloguing-in-Publication Data
A catalogue record for this book is available from the British Library.

ISBN: 978-1-84480-940-0

Cengage Learning EMEA
High Holborn House, 50-51 Bedford Row
London WC1R 4LR

Cengage Learning products are represented in Canada by Nelson Education Ltd.

For your lifelong learning solutions, visit
www.cengage.co.uk

Purchase e-books or e-chapters at:
http://estore.bized.co.uk

Printed by Zrinski d.d., Croatia
1 2 3 4 5 6 7 8 9 10 – 10 09 08

BRIEF CONTENTS

v

FULL CONTENTS

ACKNOWLEDGEMENTS

The authors wish to express their thanks to the following for permission to reproduce past examination questions.

Association of Chartered Certified Accountants (ACCA)

Institute of Chartered Accountants in England and Wales (ICAEW)

PREFACE

AIMS OF THE BOOK

The primary aim of this book is to provide a simplified but thorough approach to the understanding of auditing theory and practice. It is intended for those with little or no knowledge of the subject. However, some knowledge of financial accounting, company law, and information technology would be an advantage.

Students who will find this book essential reading include:

- Students studying for the examinations of the UK and Irish Institutes of Chartered Accountants (ICAEW, ICAS, ICAI)
- The Association of Chartered Certified Accountants (Skills Level Paper F8 and Professional Level Paper P7)
- The Association of Accounting Technicians (Diploma Unit 17 Implementing Audit Procedures)
- Institute of Financial Accountants (Paper A4 Audit Techniques)
- The Association of International Accountants (Foundation Paper 5 and Professional Paper 7)
- Students studying auditing as a part of a Foundation Course in a college or university or as part of an Edexcel BTEC Higher National in Business (Unit on Financial Systems and Auditing).

The expansion of the basic core of knowledge required to pass the auditing papers of the professional bodies, has led to a need for a comprehensive, systematic book in one volume, aimed at the requirements of today's auditing examinations.

It is hoped that this book will provide the student with a clear and succinct exposition of the subject and be sufficiently interesting to encourage even the least conscientious student to proceed in easily digestible stages.

STRUCTURE OF THE BOOK

The book has been designed with several uses in mind:

- as a textbook, on its own, for specific examinations;
- for use with a lecture;
- as a revision text for those who are taking or retaking examinations.

The case studies, student self-testing questions and exam questions are particularly useful for those taking exams.

At the end of each chapter is found:

- Summary of the chapter.
- Points to note. These are used for emphasis and clarification of points which students often misunderstand.

- Short case studies. The objective of the case studies is to illuminate the material in the chapter. Readers may find it helpful to ponder on the case study while reading the chapter.
- Questions. These are a mixture of:
  - short questions to test comprehension and learning of the material of the chapter and as an aide-memoire;
  - exercises; and
  - examination standard questions where appropriate.

In addition, the case studies can be seen as questions. Answers to the exam questions are available on the website www.cengage.co.uk/millichamp.

WEBSITE

The website contains:

- additional questions and case studies;
- answers to the exam questions and some discussion on the case studies;
- additional material on matters of current interest;
- addenda and amendments to the text; and
- an opportunity to ask questions and make comments.

NOTES TO THE NINTH EDITION

The ninth edition now takes account of:

- The provision of the Companies Act 2006 relevant to the audit process.
- Relevant UK and International Auditing Standards and other official pronouncements, practice notes, bulletins and practice statements extant at the time of writing.
- The relevant accounting standards issued to date.

In addition, the opportunity has been taken to revise the text, rewrite some chapters completely and introduce new material. The test questions have also been updated.

CHAPTER ORDER

The chapter order follows a logical sequence.

The chapters are self-contained and can be read in any order, although some chapters do take account of what has gone before. If this is the case previous chapters have been referred to in the text.

PASSING AUDITING EXAMS

Many students have difficulty in passing auditing exams. Often this is simply due to a lack of preparation, but it can also be due to a lack of exam technique. We have begun the book with suggestions on how to pass auditing exams. This has been written from our experience as teachers and examiners in auditing. We hope it will be helpful!

HOW TO PASS AUDITING EXAMINATIONS

There is no simple formula for success, if there was everybody would be successful! However, there are many ways in which you can increase your chances of success.

These include:

- *Being well prepared* – there is no real substitute for hard work and application. However, reading is not enough. You must practice exam questions. At the end of each chapter there are student self-testing questions, exam questions and the case studies. The best way to learn is to write out answers to these in full. It is only by being faced with having to write things down, that you discover the gaps in your knowledge and understanding.
- *Knowing the syllabus and what you should know* – guidance on this is obtained by reading the relevant syllabus and any other information available from the examining body. Examples are the ACCA study guides. It is also essential to study past exam papers or pilot papers where the exam is a new one. Your study must be purposeful and directed and focused to specific goals. Most examining bodies publish official answers to their exam questions. These are far more comprehensive than expected student answers but they do give you a clear idea of what is expected.
- *Time in the exam room* – the time in the exam room should be used efficiently and profitably. Specific points here are:
  - Answer all the questions that you are asked to answer. Given a choice, never spend time finishing a question when there is still a question unanswered. The first few marks on a question are always easy but the last few are always hard to earn.
  - Give proper weight to each question and part of a question. There is no point in filling two sides of A4 on a part of a question which earns you 2 marks. Similarly writing two lines on a 20 mark question is clearly not enough. It is a good idea to consider how much time you can allocate to each task. For example in a three-hour, 100 mark exam, you should not spend any more than nine minutes per 5 marks.
  - Never omit parts of a question. Even if you do not know the answer, guess and write something – you never know it may get you a mark or two!

TACKLING A QUESTION

Here are some general points:

- *Plan the answer briefly.* Show your plan.
- *Answer the question asked.* This is a vital point. It is no good answering the question you would have preferred. Many examiners report that weak candidates simply write down everything they know about a topic rather than relating what they know to the question being asked. You do not get any marks for irrelevant detail. This means reading the question carefully and noting exactly what is required. A good way of doing this is to underline significant words in the question.

- *Don't waffle*. Questions are not marked by weight, so droning on with irrelevant detail will not get you any marks even if it fills up the page.

- *Make points*. This is the most important thing of all. Some questions say 'List four procedures . . .'. Obviously four points are wanted. Some say 'State the audit tests that you . . .'. What is wanted in such questions is as many tests as you can think of. It does not want long descriptions of two tests or a general answer. The marking scheme probably gives 1 mark per valid test.

- *Use all the data given in the question*. Many auditing questions have long scenarios before the requirement. This information is not just for idle reading. Then examiner expects you to use it in your answer. It probably contains lots of clues to the answer required.

- *Auditing examiners expect intelligent answers*. Try to see the implications in a question. For example a question about audit risk may want a general answer, and if so that is what it will ask for. Specific points about audit risk in the particular case will be in the scenario and these are what the examiner is looking for.

- *Keep the answers as short and succinct as possible*. When you have made a point using one sentence consider whether you really need more sentences. Write legibly and use short sentences and paragraphs. Tabulating and listing is usually acceptable, using bullet points, and this helps the marker see what you have said. Lengthy prose paragraphs are not normally the best approach.

- *Label each part of your answer*. If a question has four parts, a, b, etc., make sure each part is clearly labelled as such.

- *Explain your terms*. Suppose you are faced with a question like 'Explain why external auditors seek to rely on the proper operation of internal controls wherever possible'. First, briefly define 'external auditor' and 'internal controls'. You may get marks for it but in any case it will give you clues to how to answer it.

- *Apply lateral thinking*. In the internal controls example think about what an external auditor is trying to do or the context in which internal controls are designed or what they are designed to prevent or ensure.

READING THROUGH THE PAPER

Many students have a moment of panic when they first see the paper. This will pass when you realise how easy the paper really is! Most students read through all the questions briefly first, concentrating on the requirements of each question. As you do this note down any thoughts that occur to you as soon as you can, otherwise, if you find yourself under time pressure, you may spend fruitless time trying to remember a fact you had remembered but have now forgotten.

TACKLING A QUESTION – SPECIFIC IDEAS

With many questions, you may be faced with making points but not being able to think of many. Here are a few ideas which may trigger points you can make:

- What Auditing Standards are involved?
- What Accounting Standards are involved?
- What Companies Act accounting or auditing requirements are involved?

- Is business or audit risk relevant?
- Does the question have any relevance for the letter of engagement?
- Does the question have any relevance for the auditor's report?
- What assertions about a figure in the financial statements are implied?
- Does the question have any relevance to the idea of misstatements in the financial statements?
- Is materiality worth mentioning?
- Do ethics have any relevance?
- What types of audit tests may be applied?
- What working papers may be needed?
- What errors or frauds could occur?
- Is going concern an issue?
- Is internal audit involved?

HOW TO ANSWER A QUESTION

It all depends on the question but here are some general ideas:

- Read the question.
- Read it again.
- Underline important words in the question.
- Make sure you know exactly what the examiner requires you to do.
- Note down the points you want to make, add to these points others as you think of them even while writing the answer out.
- Stop and think for a moment.
- Draft an outline plan of your answer with the key points.
- Write your answer referring back continually to the requirements of the question. Take plenty of room, use short sentences and paragraphs. Number your points if you think it appropriate.

REVIEWING YOUR SCRIPT

Some students like to finish early and then proof read their scripts. This is unlikely to add many marks unless you think of new points. Polishing the grammar, spelling and punctuation is very unlikely to add many marks to your score and can waste time. If you finish very early either you are extremely able or you've not answered all the questions properly. Professional examinations are designed to put candidates under time pressure.

COMMON FAULTS IN AUDITING ANSWERS

Here are some common faults:

- *Not obeying the questioner's requirements*
  If it says set out, list, tabulate, to what extent, examine the truth of, state, state concisely, what are the principal matters, discuss, comment on, describe, write a short essay, then **do what it says!**
- *Not reading the question carefully*
  For example students on being asked to audit a partnership will refer to company-based information such as the Memorandum and Articles.
- *Not making enough points*
  This is very hard to overcome but one good technique is to try to break the question down into sections and list specific points relevant to each part of the question.
- *Not being specific*
  An audit test stating *'check sample transactions in the cash book'* will not often do; *'check a sample of the entries in the cash book with available supporting documents such as . . .'* might do.
- *Being irrelevant*
  Tied up with not obeying instructions and not reading the question carefully.
- *Lack of planning, coherence and logic*
  Planning an answer should cure this.
- *Lack of balance*
  If the examiner asks for five points he does not want four pages on point one and one line each on the others.
- *Handwriting, grammar, spelling, punctuation*
  Do not waste your time and opportunities by presenting your work badly or with avoidable errors.
- *Confusing the role of auditor with that of accountant, tax consultant, etc.*
  If asked what the auditor should do in certain circumstances, never say, for example, 'Alter the accounts' because producing accounts is not the auditor's function. Neither should you advise an action which would save your client tax, you must say what you would do as *auditor*.

LAYOUT AND WORDING OF ANSWER

- Use the wording of the question wherever you can.
- Answer the question in the sequence requested.
- Obey instructions on layout e.g. tabulate.
- State any assumptions you make in answering the question. However, do not make assumptions which change the question to suit your knowledge.

END OF EXAM PROCEDURE

- Have a very quick look at each answer, checking for grammatical errors and badly formed letters. Add any new points if you can think of them.
- Ensure each answer sheet has your number on it. Do not leave anything lying on the table.

CONCLUSIONS

Good technique plays a large part in examination success; this is a fact. Refuse to be panicked, keep your head, and with reasonable preparation you should make it.

Finally – remember – you don't have to score 100 per cent to pass.

I

Introduction to auditing – the why of auditing

INTRODUCTION

One of the most far-reaching consequences of the Industrial Revolution was the introduction of the limited liability company. The first such was registered at Companies House in 1856 and this, in essence, signalled the final, formal, split between ownership and control.

Prior to the Companies Act 1856 many ventures had been financed through the medium of the joint stock company – such as the Hudson's Bay Company formed in 1670 and the East India Company formed in 1600 – whereby a group of investors financed a venture using a joint stock company managed by an elected board of directors. However, to do this required a Royal Charter or an Act of Parliament. The great advantage of using these companies was, of course, limited liability, the great disadvantage being the cost and the ponderous process of setting them up. Only the wealthy could afford to do this.

The right of anyone to set up a company with limited liability, which was introduced in 1856, signified the creation of the modern company. The law and regulations which have grown up around it to regulate its actions and the actions of its members and managers stem from these nineteenth-century origins.

Whilst the modern company came into being in 1856, the audit profession came somewhat later, it was not until the Companies Act 1900 that an obligation to produce annual accounts was placed on the directors of companies.

AGENCY THEORY

Agency is the name given to the practice by which productive resources owned by one person or group are managed by another person or group of persons.

At it simplest agency theory is the recognition that the inclination of agents, in this case the directors or managers of the business, is to act rather more in their own interests than those of their employers, the shareholders.

The Institute of Chartered Accountants in England & Wales, in November 2006, put it this way:

> In principle the agency model assumes that no agents are trustworthy and if they can make themselves richer at the expense of their principals they will. The poor principal, so the argument goes, has no alternative but to compensate the agent well for their

endeavours so that they will not be tempted to go into business for themselves using the principal's assets to do so.

The origin of auditing goes back to times scarcely less remote than that of accounting . . . Whenever the advance of civilization brought about the necessity of one man being entrusted to some extent with the property of another the advisability of some kind of check upon the fidelity of the former would become apparent.

Clearly this is not universally true, but the extent to which principals don't trust their agents will tend to determine the level of the monitoring mechanisms created for the overview of agents' activities and the extent to which agents' compensations levels are determined to be acceptable.

Upon this principle rests the foundation of not only the auditing profession, but ultimately, in the latter part of the twentieth century and the early part of the twenty-first, the establishment of modern corporate governance.

FINANCIAL STATEMENTS

From 1900 the financial statements became the basic mechanism by which the activities of company managers were monitored, and, to some extent, this is still true today.

Once the directors were required by law to prepare annual financial statements shareholders then had access to financial information about the company they owned. However, this access is limited and the shareholders may come to believe that they are not getting all the information, or the right information to enable them to make investment decisions.

Thus the role of the auditor as agent for the shareholder becomes crucial and the costs of the audit are as nothing compared with the comfort and reassurance the audit affords the shareholders.

Owners who appoint managers to look after their property will be concerned to know what has happened to it. Reporting and accounting for their actions is usually done by means of financial statements which the managers must prepare, and it is through these that the owners of the business monitor the activities of their agents. The independent audit is a crucial part of this process to ensure that the financial statements faithfully represent the activities of the managers during the financial period.

Financial statements can take many forms. The best known are the profit and loss accounts and balance sheets of businesses. In the specific case of limited companies, financial statements are produced annually and take the form of an 'Annual Report and Accounts' which includes a Profit and Loss Account and Balance Sheet and also other statements including the Directors' Report and a cash flow statement.

Parties to financial statements

Historically, annual reports and accounts of companies are produced by the directors (as managers) to the shareholders (as owners), and other people were not expected to be interested in them. However, today, a much wider range of people are interested in the annual report and accounts of companies and other organisations.

The following people or groups of people are likely to want to see and use financial statements. These are often described as stakeholders:

- Actual or potential:

  - Owners or shareholders
  - Lenders or debenture holders

- Employees
- Customers
- Suppliers.

- People who advise the above – accountants, stockbrokers, credit rating agencies, financial journalists, trade unions, financial analysts.
- Competitors and people interested in mergers, amalgamations and takeovers.
- The government, including the tax authorities, and government bodies concerned with consumer protection and the control and regulation of business.
- The public, including those who are interested in consumer protection, environmental protection, and political and other pressure groups.
- Regulatory organisations for example those set up under the Financial Services and Markets Act 2000, principally the Financial Services Authority (FSA).

All these people must be sure that the financial statements can be relied upon.

WHY IS THERE A NEED FOR AN AUDIT?

As mentioned above in the section on Agency Theory, the problem which has always existed when managers report to owners is – can the owners believe the report?

The report may:

- contain errors;
- not disclose fraud;
- be inadvertently misleading;
- be deliberately misleading;
- fail to disclose relevant information;
- fail to conform to regulations.

The solution to this problem of credibility in reports and accounts lies in appointing independent professionals called auditors to investigate the report and report on their findings.

Only companies over a certain size need an audit.

These have:

- a turnover in excess of £5.6m;
- a net asset value of £2.8m; and/or
- employ more than 50 people.

Companies who do not fulfil two out of three of these criteria do not need what is known as a statutory audit.

Companies can be very large with multinational activities and comprising many subsidiaries.

The preparation of the accounts of such entities is a very complex operation involving the bringing together and summarising of accounts of subsidiaries with differing conventions, legal systems and accounting and control systems. The examination of such accounts by independent experts trained in the assessment of financial information is of benefit to those who control and operate such organisations as well as to owners and outsiders.

Financial statements must conform to statutory or other requirements. The most notable is that all company accounts have to conform to the requirements of the Companies Act

2006 but many other bodies (e.g. charities, building societies, financial services businesses etc.) also have detailed accounting requirements. In addition all accounts should conform to the requirements of Financial Reporting Standards (FRSs).

It is essential that an audit should be carried out on financial statements to ensure that they conform to these requirements.

OBJECTIVES OF AUDITING

The Auditing Practices Board (APB), which is the body responsible for issuing auditing standards and guidelines, states:

> *The objective of an audit of financial statements is to enable the auditor to express an opinion whether the financial statements are prepared, in all material respects, in accordance with an applicable financial reporting framework. The phrases used to express an auditors opinion are 'give a true and fair view' or 'present fairly in all material respects' which are equivalent terms.*
>
> *The 'applicable financial reporting framework' comprises those requirements of accounting standards, law and regulations applicable to the entity the determine the form and content of its financial statements.*

In the UK the financial reporting framework is the Companies Act 2006 together with all the associated accounting standards etc. which comprise UK Generally Accepted Accounting Principles (UK GAAP).

'Entity' is a general term embracing all types of business, enterprise or undertaking including companies, charities, local authorities, government agencies etc. Some are profit oriented and some are not.

'Present fairly' instead of 'true and fair' applies mainly to local authorities. A particular point is made of the fact that responsibility for the *preparation* of the financial statements and the presentation of the information included therein rests with the management of the enterprise (in the case of a company, the directors). The auditor's responsibility is to *report* on the financial statements as presented by management. We will come back to this key principle later.

The auditors should be an independent firm appointed to investigate the organisation, its records, and the financial statements prepared from them. The role of the auditors is to gather sufficient evidence so as to be able to form an opinion on the accuracy and correctness of the financial statements. The primary aim of an audit is to enable the auditors to say 'these accounts show a true and fair view' or, of course, to say that they do not.

The objectives of an audit are:

Primary

To produce a report by the auditors of their opinion of the truth and fairness of financial statements so that any person reading and using them can have belief in them.

Secondary

- To advise management of any defects or problems with their accounting systems and to suggest ways of improving it.
- To detect errors and fraud.
- To prevent errors and fraud by the deterrent and moral effect of the audit.

In addition to carrying out the audit auditors are able to assist their clients with accounting problems, accounting and financial reporting systems, taxation, financial risk management and other problems.

THE AUDITORS' REPORT

At the end of the audit, when they have examined the organisation, its records, and its financial statements, the auditors produce a report addressed to the owners in which they express their opinion of the truth and fairness, or otherwise, of the financial statements.

The auditors' opinion

Auditors, in their report, do not say that the financial statements *do* show a true and fair view. They can only say that *in their opinion* the financial statements show a true and fair view. The reader or user of financial statements will know from their knowledge of the auditor whether or not to rely on the auditors' opinion. If the auditors are known to be independent, honest, and competent, then their opinion will be relied upon.

True and fair

The expression 'true and fair' is central to auditing and yet it is an abstraction whose meaning is far from clear.

As we will see, the Companies Act states that every company balance sheet and profit and loss account must give a 'true and fair' view of the state of affairs and of the profit or loss of the company respectively, however, unhelpfully, it does not attempt to define what a 'true and fair view' might be.

Whatever the meaning might be the starting point is that a 'true and fair view' requires compliance with the legislation and with all the applicable accounting standards. However, there is an *override* (called, rather obviously, the 'true and fair override').

If the auditors consider that compliance with any particular standard may result in a true and fair view *not* being shown by the financial statements they may ignore it, *but* they have to explain and justify why they have done so. As might be imagined, this is quite rare.

Perhaps we can define what true and fair might mean by explaining what it does *not* mean. It does not mean 'correct in all respects' or 'free of all errors' or 'absolutely right'.

Truth, for accountants, is not absolute – it is not as a scientist would measure it, i.e. a truth which is fixed and never changes.

'True', in this case, means true in accordance with the facts that pertain at the time, either at the year end or at the time the auditors' report was signed. For example, the balance sheet records assets and liabilities at values which were considered to be true at the year end date. The day after the year end the values of those balances, or some of them, changes.

The concept of truth carries with it an understanding of the fundamental accounting concepts which underlay how the accounts are prepared, such as the accruals basis, historical cost etc., as well as all the accounting standards and rules which govern all the disclosures and presentation of the words and numbers.

'Fair' is an even more nebulous concept to grasp. Just as 'truth' carries with it the implication that the accounts have been prepared under generally understood accounting concepts and rules, so 'fair' implies that those rules have been applied impartially, objectively and with a view to presenting the facts of the financial situation of the company to readers of the accounts in as balanced, reasonable and unbiased way as is possible.

DIRECTORS' RESPONSIBILITY

Remember that it is the directors who are responsible for producing 'true and fair' accounts, the auditors simply express an opinion. The directors are the individuals who, collectively, have to struggle with presenting an accounting of their dealings with the shareholder's assets in as balanced and impartial a way as possible. It is their task to explain themselves in a way that can be understood and that represents what actually happened in the financial period.

Remember the principles of Agency Theory explained earlier – the directors are accounting to the shareholders (the owners of the business) for their actions during the financial year.

As with many seemingly simple tasks this can be quite complicated, hence the plethora of accounting standards, bulletins and guidelines!

AUDITORS' RESPONSIBILITY

The problems the auditors face are different from those of the directors. Their problems lie outside the area of simple bookkeeping and arise when the financial statements incorporate judgements, estimates and opinions.

For example, the accounts might contain an estimate – made by the directors to the best of their ability – of the potential loss on a contract – but is it too much? too little? shouldn't be there at all? – the auditors have to decide what they think, based on the evidence they can gather.

It is straightforward enough for a company to ensure that all the transactions in the books are properly processed (and, as we will see later in this book, there is an audit approach which doesn't even bother checking that this is so), but how do the auditors' know that:

- all the transactions that should be included have been included; and
- how do they know that all the transactions that are included are bona fide ones and not transactions invented by the directors to make the results look good?

They have to check the books and form an opinion.

So, because the auditors are expressing an opinion, they use a term of art – 'true and fair'. This carries with it implications of honesty, integrity, impartiality and objectivity in the telling of a story, which is what the accounts do, in as understandable a way as possible for the benefit of the people who, after all, own the business or have a significant vested interest in it.

ORGANISATION OF THE AUDITING PROFESSION

A vital part of auditing is that the auditors must be *independent* from the management who are responsible for the accounts and the owners who receive them.

In the case of companies, they must not be connected with either the directors or the shareholders. They must also be independent of government agencies or other groups who have contact with the business.

For these reasons auditors form themselves into independent firms willing to perform audits for a fee for whoever is able and willing to employ them. Some of these firms are very large with worldwide connections and employing thousands of people. Others are very small with sometimes only one or two principals and a very small number of staff.

Auditors have to conduct their audits, not only taking into account the relevant sections of the Companies Act 2006, or any appropriate legislation, but also as instructed by Auditing Standards, Guidelines and Bulletins issued by, in the United Kingdom, the Auditing Practices Board.

QUALITIES REQUIRED OF AUDITORS

Auditors need to possess the following qualities.

Independence

Auditors cannot give unbiased opinions unless they are independent of all the parties involved. There is a dilemma here in that auditors receive their fees from the client. Nonetheless, independence is very important. Not only must auditors be independent in fact and in attitude of mind but they must also be *seen* to be independent.

Competence

Auditors must be thoroughly trained and prove their competence before they can sign an audit report. Parliament has decreed that only members of certain professional bodies can become auditors of limited companies. These professional bodies (the three Institutes of Chartered Accountants and the Association of Chartered Certified Accountants) have developed competence in their members by using difficult examinations, and post-qualifying education. In addition, there are requirements before members can become and continue to be Registered Auditors.

Integrity

Qualified accountants are renowned for their honesty, discretion and tactfulness. Auditors authorised by their professional bodies to conduct audits are known as Registered Auditors. Registered Auditor firms are supervised and inspected by their professional bodies acting as recognised supervisory bodies.

TYPES OF AUDIT

There are three types of reporting assignment, of which an audit is the most common accountants carry out.

Statutory audits

These are audits carried out because the law requires them. Statutes which require audits to be done include the Companies Act 2006 and the Financial Services and Markets Act 2000.

Internal audits

Internal audits are conducted by employees of a business or by external auditors acting as subcontractors. They are becoming increasingly important because of the development of

Corporate Governance. These differ from statutory audits because the priorities are set by the management who, to some extent, control the work of internal auditors.

Other assurance assignments

These are enquiries into specific aspects of an enterprise – management, value for money, environmental matters etc. In recent years auditors have become involved with areas which take them away from their role as reporters on financial results. Two of the areas of emerging significance are Value for Money auditing and audits relating to Environmental and Social matters. We will discuss these further in Chapter 33.

In addition, auditors are asked to carry out specific 'one-off' assignments such as:

- Reporting on a prospectus for a share issue.
- Carrying out a fraud investigation.
- Reviewing systems and procedures.

This book is principally about the statutory audit, but we will look specifically at internal auditing and we will also review the auditors' duties with regard to assurance assignments other than the statutory audit.

Summary

- Agency involves the separation of ownership from control.
- Financial accounting is the means by which those who have day-to-day control report to the owners.
- The reports produced by those who control to the owners are used by many other people.
- All those who use the reports need to be able to believe in them.
- The audit is the means by which this belief is obtained.
- Auditing is concerned also with improving accounting systems and the detection and prevention of error and fraud.
- Auditors form independent firms and carry out numerous other services for their clients.
- There are statutory and internal audits and other types of assignment.

Points to note

- The individual auditor must be independent, a person of integrity and competent to carry out their work.
- Auditors give an opinion in their report. They do not certify or guarantee.
- A number of auditing issues are becoming subjects of debate and controversy at the time of writing. These include increased regulation of enterprises and the effect on auditors, increased regulation of auditors, the extent of auditors' responsibilities for the detection and prevention of fraud, auditors' responsibilities for ecological matters, the gap between the public's expectations of auditing and the legal position of auditors, risk management, corporate governance, auditor independence, and the whole future of auditing as a professional activity. The accounting press has many articles on these and other auditing issues and students should read as much as possible about them.

Case Study

Wren, Gibbs and Angelo are brothers who own 75 per cent of a firm of builders with a turnover of £7m, specialising in house alteration and improvements. The remaining 25 per cent of the business is owned by their sister Bertha who lives abroad and only comes over once a year. The books have been kept by Wren who has an HNC in Business Studies as well as in building and Wren has also prepared the accounts.

The company is profitable and the accounts have been filed regularly at Companies House. Although they have never had a proper audit the accounts prepared by Wren are reviewed by their financial advisor, Gibbons, a golfing friend of Angelo's who prepares and submits the tax computations. Gibbons does not give any form of opinion on the accounts.

The brothers now want to borrow a lot of money from the bank to acquire another local building company which is in financial difficulties. Bertha has also been told that the brothers seem to have a very affluent lifestyle, but she only receives a very small dividend each year.

Discussion
- What benefits would the company get from employing an independent auditor?
- Where would they find a suitable auditor?
- Would it benefit Bertha to insist on a proper audit?

Student self-testing questions

(Questions with answers apparent from the text)

a) List the people and groups of people who are likely to be interested in financial statements.

b) What other services do accountants provide in addition to auditing?

c) State the relationship between the Annual Accounts of a company, the shareholders, the directors, and the auditors.

d) What may be wrong with an annual report and accounts?

e) What is the primary objective of an audit?

f) What other benefits are obtained?

g) What are the objectives of an audit report?

h) What qualities are required in an auditor?

i) Distinguish statutory and internal audits and other assignments.

j) Define an audit.

2

Corporate governance

INTRODUCTION

The genesis of modern Corporate Governance can be dated to 1992 with the publication of the Cadbury Report.

During the 1980s there had been a prolonged period of economic growth which, by the early 1990s, was beginning to go into reverse.

Companies which had previously shown signs of spectacular success were shown to be built on sand, or at least very high borrowings, and the successive collapses, in the UK, of Coloroll, Polly Peck and Maxwell Communications Corporation, which took with it the pension fund of Mirror Group Newspapers, prompted public concern.

This was exacerbated by the £8bn collapse of the Bank of Credit and Commerce International, which was subsequently revealed to be a hotbed of fraud and illicit dealings, and the debacle of Delorean which took with it about £80m of public money. Thousands of individuals had lost their savings and public concern was mounting.

The City reacted quickly and commissioned Sir Peter Cadbury to come up with some good practice proposals which would:

- reinforce the responsibilities of executive directors;
- strengthen the role of the non-executive director;
- make the case for audit committees of the board;
- restate the principal responsibilities of auditors; and
- reinforce the links between shareholders, boards and auditors.

CADBURY AND AFTER

Cadbury was charged with creating a list of recommended changes. His 90-page report, *The Financial Aspects of Corporate Governance,* outlined a code of conduct for listed companies that attempted to address ethical as well as legal questions. These, ultimately, emerged as the basis for the Combined Code on Corporate Governance, which we will look at in the next section.

Cadbury's report was followed by several others. Students need to be aware of the basic principles of these reports:

Greenbury – 1995 – which looked at the question of directors pay, in particular the role of the Remuneration Committee in setting remuneration levels, guidelines on remuneration policy, the level of disclosure in financial statements and the question of terms of service contracts paying compensation when directors are dismissed for poor performance.

Hampel – 1998 – which reinforced points made in the original Cadbury Report, in particular the separation of the roles of Chairman and Managing Director and the balance of the composition of the Board between executive and non-executive directors.

Turnbull – 1999 – which offered guidance on how directors should comply with corporate governance, focusing on internal controls and risk management.

This report emphasised the importance of good internal and external reporting: '*This requires the maintenance of proper records and processes that generate a flow of timely, relevant and reliable information from within and outside the organisation,*' it stated. The report also noted the key role that IT plays in creating internal controls and in assessing accurately the risks faced by an organisation.

Higgs – 2003 – which set out measures designed to improve the structure and accountability of boardrooms in the UK. It argued that boards should be free to criticise company management, and suggested limiting the number of directors that hold managerial positions to no more than half the board – the remainder being non-executive directors.

This proved controversial and Higgs has since admitted that his recommendations were too harsh.

COMPANIES ACT 2006

The Companies Act 2006 incorporates within it specific duties of directors. Among other things s 172 lays down a specific duty on a company director to:

- *act in the way he considers, in good faith, would be most likely to promote the success of the company for the benefit of its members as a whole and to have regard to:*
- *the interests of the company's employees;*
- *the need to foster the company's business relationships with suppliers, customers and others;*
- *the desirability of the company maintaining a reputation for high standards of business conduct.*

For the first time there is a specific provision, in law, for the directors to have regard to the interests, not only of those who have invested in the company over which they have day-to-day control but also of others, employees, customers, suppliers and indeed – in its injunction to maintain a high standard of conduct – anyone the business comes into contact with in the course of its activities.

SARBANES OXLEY – 2002

The whole question of Corporate Governance was dominated by the financial scandals of the early part of the twenty-first century in the USA surrounding, in particular, Enron and the lesser, but no less shocking, scandals involving WorldCom, Tyco International, Global Crossing and many others. All of the major accounting firms had clients who were caught up in these scandals, the apotheosis being the destruction of the worldwide accounting firm of Arthur Andersen.

In 2002 this resulted in the USA publishing legislation known as The Sarbanes Oxley Act (often shortened to 'Sarbox').

It does not affect UK companies unless they are subsidiaries of US firms or are listed on US stock exchanges.

The Act is designed to enforce corporate accountability through new requirements, backed by stiff penalties. Under the Act, chief executives and chief financial officers must personally certify the accuracy of financial statements, with a maximum penalty of 20 years in jail and a $5m fine for false statements. In addition, and of great significance to auditors, under s 404 of the Act, executives have to certify and demonstrate that they have established and are maintaining an adequate internal control structure and procedures for financial reporting. This requires them to ensure that all the financial reporting systems, including the ancillary systems such as procurement and HR, are functioning in such a way as to prevent material misstatements appearing in the financial accounts - and it is a personal liability.

It should be pointed out that this legislation, passed in haste is, in the current climate, slowly being reassessed as being too prescriptive and too inhibiting of US business freedoms, so there may be further changes to come!

COMBINED CODE ON CORPORATE GOVERNANCE – 2003

The Financial Reporting Council drew up guidelines that were published in July 2003 as part of its Combined Code on Corporate Governance.

The Code incorporates the key provisions of the Cadbury Report and the subsequent reports detailed above. These, as they apply to directors are set out below in the section on 'Directors' duties'.

The Code is underpinned by a Financial Services Authority rule that requires companies listed on the London Stock Exchange to state, in their annual report, how they have complied with its provisions or to explain why they have not done so.

This is known as the 'comply or explain' basis and differs from the purely regulatory approach adopted in other countries, particularly the USA.

Directors' duties

The Combined Code sets out the key principles of good Corporate Governance. Listed companies are supposed to abide by this, but it is good practice for all companies to abide by as many of these principles as are practicable.

The main provisions, as set out in the Combined Code, are listed below.

Directors

- Every company should be headed by an effective board, which is *collectively* responsible for the success of the company.
- There should be a clear division of responsibilities at the head of the company between the running of the board and the executive responsibility for the running of the company's business. No one individual should have unfettered powers of decision. What this means, in practice, is that the Chairman of the Board should not be the same individual as the Managing Director or Chief Executive Officer.
- The board should include a balance of executive and non-executive directors (and, in particular, independent non-executive directors) such that no individual or small group of individuals can dominate the board's decision taking.
- There should be a formal, rigorous and transparent procedure for the appointment of new directors to the board.

- The board should be supplied in a timely manner with information in a form and of a quality appropriate to enable it to discharge its duties. This is a requirement to produce good-quality management information, both financial and non-financial, in a form the directors can understand and in a timely manner.
- All directors should receive induction on joining the board and should regularly update and refresh their skills and knowledge.
- The board should undertake a formal and rigorous annual evaluation of its own performance and that of its committees and individual directors.
- All directors should be submitted for re-election at regular intervals, subject to continued satisfactory performance. The board should ensure planned and progressive refreshing of the board.

Directors' remuneration

- Levels of remuneration should be sufficient to attract, retain and motivate directors of the quality required to run the company successfully.
- A company should avoid paying more than is necessary for this purpose.
- A significant proportion of executive directors' remuneration should be structured so as to link rewards to corporate and individual performance, i.e. incentive-based pay such as bonuses.
- There should be a formal and transparent procedure for developing policy on executive remuneration and for fixing the remuneration packages of individual directors. No director should be involved in deciding his or her own remuneration.

    In practice this usually takes the form of a Remuneration Committee of non-executive directors as recommended by Greenbury (see above).

Accountability and audit

- The board should present a balanced and understandable assessment of the company's position and prospects.
- The board should maintain a sound system of internal control to safeguard shareholders' investment and the company's assets.
- The board should establish formal and transparent arrangements for considering how they should apply the financial reporting and internal control principles and for maintaining an appropriate relationship with the company's auditors.

    This is should be carried out by an Audit Committee, comprising at least three non-executive directors.

The key point about good corporate governance is that its requirements should be met in the spirit of good governance and not just by observing the letter of the Code. 'Box ticking' should not be a substitute for clear thought and fair exposition.

This leads us into the fundamental doctrine of 'substance over form' which students need to understand so they can appreciate the theoretical framework on which Corporate Governance in the UK is built.

SUBSTANCE OVER FORM

The approach to regulating the activities of companies has been, at least in the UK, largely principles based; that is legislation is kept to a minimum and directors, managers and auditors are expected to conform to a standard of ethical behaviour rather than be dominated by detailed regulations.

In the USA the approach is quite the opposite. They tend to adopt a stringent regulatory approach, which has, in the past encouraged accountants and lawyers in the USA to devote a lot of time to trying to circumvent the rules!

As the UK does not have that many rules, other than those considered necessary, such as the Companies Act and the Accounting and Auditing Standards, accountants, and in particular auditors, tend to concentrate on nature of each type of transaction or activity rather than how it is described.

This is known as 'substance over form'.

For example:

The directors may have found a way to describe a small flightless bird with a beak and feathers as a chicken despite the noise it makes and the way it walks.

The auditor will look past the directors' description and say 'if it walks like a duck and it quacks like a duck – it's a duck!'

In other words the auditors look past the *form* of the transaction, i.e. what it appears to be or what it has been described as (chicken) to its *substance*, i.e. what it really is (duck).

This doctrine of substance over form is fundamental to corporate reporting but is also a fundamental aspect of corporate governance – it requires the directors to tell the truth about what has happened and not to attempt to present or disguise financial information, for whatever reason.

REPORT ON THE DIRECTORS' RESPONSIBILITIES FOR THE FINANCIAL STATEMENTS

This only applies to listed companies specifically, but it is good practice for all companies to include such a statement. The reasons for this are:

- the readers of the accounts can have a clear understanding of what the directors' are responsible for;
- it also helps remind the directors' of their responsibilities.

Here is an example of some wording. Note that includes references not only to the directors' responsibility for producing accounts but also responsibilities for:

- Consideration of the company's (and group's as applicable) ability to continue as a going concern – Chapter 24.
- The directors responsibility in respect of fraud and other irregularities – Chapter 20.

Example

Directors' responsibilities for the financial statements

The directors are required to prepare financial statements for each financial period which comply with the provisions of the Companies Act 2006 and give a true and fair view of the state of affairs of the company [and the group] as at the end of the accounting period and of the profit or loss for the period. Suitable accounting policies consistently applied and supported by reasonable and prudent judgements and estimates have been used in the preparation of the financial statements.

Applicable accounting standards have been followed and, as the directors have a reasonable expectation that the company [and the group] have adequate resources to continue in operational existence for the foreseeable future, the financial statements have been prepared on a going concern basis.

The directors are responsible for maintaining adequate accounting records, for safeguarding the assets of the company [and the group] and for taking reasonable steps for the prevention and detection of fraud and other irregularities.

The auditors are, of course, required to consider evidence to support an opinion on the truth and fairness of these statements made by the directors.

AUDITORS' RESPONSIBILITIES

The auditors' responsibilities are:

- To audit the financial statements. The auditors will give a 'true and fair' report on these – see Chapter 27.
- If it is a listed company – to review the company's compliance with the relevant parts of the Combined Code. The auditors will report negatively on this – i.e. they will only report if the company has *not complied* with the provisions of the Code (Chapter 27).
- To read all the rest of the Annual Report, which they are not auditing, in order to ensure that it is consistent with the audited parts and does not give a misleading impression. The auditors, again, will report negatively, i.e. only if it is not consistent with the financial accounts.

We look in detail at the forms of auditors' reports in Chapter 27.

AUDITORS' DUTIES IN RESPECT OF COMPLIANCE WITH THE COMBINED CODE

Here we will look specifically at the auditors' duties in considering whether or not the company has complied with the provisions of the Combined Code.

The requirements of the Code which are relevant to the auditors can be summarised as:

Requirement for UK listed companies	Auditor requirements
Principles of good Governance The directors have to disclose in a narrative statement in the Annual Report how they have applied the principles of good corporate governance	Read only
Statement of Compliance with Code provisions The directors must include in the annual report a statement as to whether or not they have complied throughout the period with the Combined Code provisions and if not, why not	Review certain specific matters, especially the internal control report – and read the rest
Directors' remuneration Inclusion in the Annual Report of a statement of directors' remuneration including details of the remuneration, pension contributions and benefits etc. for each named director	Audit and include in the audit report as if this was in the financial statements
Going concern The directors must include in the annual report a statement that the business is a going concern with supporting assumptions or qualifications as necessary	Review (see Chapter 24)

The auditors duties are covered by ISA 720 (Revised) *Section A – Other Information in Documents Containing Audited Financial Statements; Section B – The Auditor's Statutory Reporting Responsibility in Relation to Directors' Reports.*

These can be summarised as follows.

The 'read only' requirement for other information

Any apparent inconsistencies or any apparent misstatements in the corporate governance statements should be resolved and the directors should amend the inconsistency.

If this does not happen then the auditors should:

- If the financial statements are incorrect, qualify their report.
- If the financial statements are correct and the other information is incorrect or inadequate, make a statement in the auditor's report. This statement is however not a qualification.

Reviewing the statement of compliance with the provisions of the Code

The review should take the following form:

The auditors should obtain sufficient appropriate evidence to support the compliance statement made by the company.

Appropriate evidence can be gained by the following procedures:

- Reviewing the minutes of the meetings of the Board and of relevant board committees (audit, nomination, remuneration, risk management etc.).
- Reviewing relevant supporting documents prepared for the board or board committees.
- Making enquiries of the directors and the company secretary.
- Attending meetings of the audit committee (or other committee) when the annual report and accounts and statements of compliance are considered and approved for submission to the board.
- The auditors may ask for a letter of representation of any written or oral representations made in the course of the review (See Chapter 25).

If the auditors are not satisfied with the directors' compliance statement they will include an explanatory comment in their Auditors' Report (See Chapter 27).

DIRECTORS' REPORT ON INTERNAL CONTROLS

Listed companies have to include, in their financial statements, a narrative report from the directors which:

- Identifies the organisation's business objectives;
- Identifies and assesses risks which threaten achievement of those objectives;
- Reports on the design and operation of controls to manage those risks;
- Reports on the process of monitoring and reviewing those controls to ensure they are operating correctly.

We will be covering the detail of risk identification and management and the whole system of internal controls in this book – what we are concerned about now is simply the report the directors make.

ISA 720 requires the auditors only to read the report and comment on any inconsistencies *except that* part of the duties of the directors is to carry out a review of the internal controls and to report to the shareholders they have done so. The auditors have to verify that the directors have, in fact, carried out such a review.

The work the auditors carry out is:

- Enquire of the directors as to the process they use to carry out the review.
- Review the evidence gathered by the directors which they are going to use to support their statement to the shareholders and assess whether or not it is sufficient and appropriate.
- Match what the directors are saying with the evidence from other audit procedures and the auditors' own view of the internal control environment.

If the auditors are not satisfied with the directors' disclosure they will include an explanatory comment in their Auditors' Report (See Chapter 27).

DIRECTORS' REMUNERATION DISCLOSURE

The requirements of the Stock Exchange Listing Agreement go well beyond the requirements of the Companies Act insofar as the Listing Agreement requires full disclosure to be made of all amounts paid to or for the benefit of *named* directors. This includes salary, bonuses, pension contributions and benefits.

The auditor has to audit the required disclosure and should include this in their normal audit work and the Auditors' Report will include an opinion on the directors' remuneration statement.

For more detail on this see Chapter 27.

AUDIT COMMITTEES

The Combined Code requires that all listed companies set up an Audit Committee.
  Ideally:

- it should comprise at least three non-executive directors which are independent of management;
- the members should have a wide range of business and professional skills;
- the members should have a good understanding of the business yet should have had no recent involvement with direct management of the business;
- the committee should have clear written terms of reference setting out its authority and its duties.

Clearly this can sometimes be difficult to achieve. However, the object is to create a committee which is competent to carry out its role, is independent and is free from bias.

The key objectives associated with the setting up of Audit Committees, from the point of view of Corporate Governance generally, is:

- To increase public confidence in the credibility and objectivity of published financial information.
- To assist the directors in carrying out their responsibilities for financial reporting.
- To strengthen the position of the external auditors by providing a channel of communication at Board level without the constraint of any executive bias.

There are advantages to having an Audit Committee. These are:

- It can improve the quality of management accounting as they are able to criticise internal reporting, which is not necessarily the responsibility of the external auditors.
- It can facilitate communication between the directors, internal and external auditors and management.
- It can help minimise any conflicts between management and the auditors.
- It can facilitate the independence of the internal audit role if the internal auditors report to the Audit Committee directly.

However, there are some disadvantages which the members of the Audit Committee have to avoid:

- It can be seen that their purpose is to criticise or 'catch out' executive management.
- It can result in the perception, if not the reality, of a two-tier board.
- The non-executives can become too embroiled in detail and start to act like executive directors thus losing their independence.

In detail, the role of the Audit Committee can be summarised as:

- to review internal control procedures and processes;
- to review the Internal Audit function and act as a channel of communication to executive management;
- to review current accounting policies and the impact of any possible changes;
- review the usefulness and effectiveness of current management information;
- review the financial information presented to shareholders and other information issued by the company such as profit forecasts etc.;
- to liaise with external auditors and to consider their reports to management and any issues arising from the audit and ensure any audit recommendations are dealt with by executive management;
- to review the effectiveness and efficiency of the external audit;
- to consider the independence of the auditors from executive management. This can be particularly important where the audit firm is supplying substantial additional services to the client in addition to their role as external auditors;
- to recommend the nomination of external auditors and also to deal with their remuneration for carrying out the audit work;
- review compliance with the Combined Code on Corporate Governance.

In essence, the Audit Committee is designed to act as an independent voice on the Board of Directors with regard to audit and corporate governance issues and can be a valuable asset, particularly with respect to maintaining the independence and integrity of the internal audit function. Students need to be familiar with the composition and role of audit committees as it is a popular topic for examiners.

Summary

- Corporate governance has become an important issue and is a regular subject for examination questions.
- The Combined Code of the Committee on Corporate Governance should be complied with by all listed companies and represents good practice for non-listed ones.
- Directors of UK listed companies have duties both for procedures and for reporting actions.
- Auditors have some duties connected with the reports by the directors on their compliance with the requirements of the Code.
- These duties include reporting in true and fair terms re extensions to directors' remuneration disclosures, reviewing certain items and reading for consistency and misstatement all other corporate governance disclosures in the annual report.
- Auditors may need to report departures from the Code by means of a statement in the auditor's report.
- Audit Committees have a role to play in maintaining the standard of corporate governance within the company.

Points to note

- Had the audit committee of Enron done its job properly the auditors would not have been allowed to become so close to management that their independence was fatally compromised.
- It is advisable for students to read one or more complete annual reports of listed companies to see how these things work out in practice.
- In some circumstances there may be a departure from a Code provision specified for auditor review but there is a proper disclosure of this fact and the reasons for it. In such cases the auditors may not need to report the departure in their report.

Case Study

Bolington Ltd is a rapidly growing company presently owned by the Bolington family. It sells designer clothing and accessories which it sources from around the world and trading results are exceeding expectations.

The family are looking to cash in on the success of the business and also provide some capital for expansion so they have decided to float the company on the Stock Exchange.

At present the board of directors consists of Mark Bolington who is Chairman and Managing Director and his two sons Dave and Phil who are Sales and Buying directors respectively. They are going to appoint Bill Sticker, who is presently the chief accountant, as financial director just before the flotation.

The auditors, Tickitt & Run are a little concerned that the Stock Exchange will find the level of corporate governance unacceptably low, if not actually non-existent, and they think they should tell Mark Bolington, who is fairly dogmatic and not a man who like others interfering in his business, what he needs to do to comply with aspects of the Listing agreement.

> **Discussion**
> What will Bolington Ltd need to do in order to start complying with some of the key aspects of corporate governance?

Student self-testing questions

(*Questions with answers apparent from the text*)

a) What was the principal report from which most corporate governance requirements originate?

b) What are the duties of directors with regard to corporate governance?

c) How does the UK approach differ from that of the USA?

d) What is 'substance over form'?

e) What are the functions of the audit committee?

f) What specific reports do directors have to ensure are included in the accounts under the Combined Code?

g) What are the roles of non-executive directors in connection with corporate governance?

Examination questions

If there is a need for a uniform set of international accounting standards and international auditing standards, there is also a need for global corporate governance standards.

Required:

Discuss and reach a conclusion.

(ACCA)

3

The statutory framework for auditing

INTRODUCTION

The majority of audits performed in the UK are of companies which are regulated by the Companies Act. As we have seen there are other bodies, charities, financial service companies etc. where other regulations may apply but these are generally outside the scope of this book.

In this chapter we will concentrate on the legal foundation behind the audit of companies under the provisions of the Companies Act 2006, which is the statutory financial reporting framework for the UK.

We will look at the law as it applies to auditors, who is eligible, their professional bodies, the appointment and removal of the auditors and their rights and duties.

We haven't followed the sequence of sections in the Companies Act as we feel it is more useful to put the legislation in the context of the auditors and not simply follow a sequence devised for legal purposes.

Later chapters of this book return to these topics in detail and outline *how* directors and auditors carry out their duties and what form of words are used in reports etc. This chapter explains the legal reasons *why* directors and auditors have to report in the way they do. Much of this is technical and at first can appear quite daunting.

Examiners rarely expect students to be able to quote the law but they will expect students to have a good understanding of the legal framework which underpins the financial roles of auditors and directors in terms of corporate reporting. We have put it all in one chapter so that students can get a good grasp of the legal background before becoming embroiled in the detail of how to actually carry out an audit.

THE COMPANIES ACT 2006

The Companies Act contains detailed regulations on the conduct of an audit, the accounting records on which the auditor will work, the financial statements on which they will report and on the auditor's relations with the company. The next sections summarise the Companies Act rules in these areas.

The Companies Act 2006 is a codifying Act. Before this Act there were several Acts in force (those of 1948, 1967, 1976, 1980, 1981, 1985 and 2004). The 2006 Act effectively re-enacted all the parts of the previous Acts which were still in force, so all of the old Acts no longer apply, or at least won't when all of the provisions of the new Act finally come into force.

The Companies Act 2006 has been described as 'gargantuan' as it is now said to be the largest piece of legislation ever passed by Parliament, with 1300 sections and 16 schedules. We will deal only with the provisions that affect auditors and the financial statements of the entities they audit so many other parts of the legislation will not be covered by this book. Students wishing to immerse themselves in the detail should consult a specialised Company Law textbook.

All references are to the Companies Act 2006 unless otherwise stated.

REQUIREMENT TO HAVE AUDITORS

The basis of the audit requirement is set out in ss 485 and 489 which state that every company shall appoint an auditor if it is required to produce audited accounts i.e. if it is not dormant and is above a certain size.

Dormant companies (i.e. ones where no activity has taken place in the year) do not need an auditor.

Small companies are not required to prepare audited accounts and small company exemption is dealt with in the chapter on small companies (Chapter 30). For this purpose a small company is defined as having:

- A turnover less than £5.6m

- Net assets of less than £2.8m

- Employing less than 50 people.

If it fulfils *two out of three* of those criteria it does not have to have a statutory audit. It can still have an audit but it would be voluntary.

WHO CAN BE AN AUDITOR?

Anyone can check a set of books, and anyone can write a report, but to be a statutory auditor signing a report on a set of financial statements under the provisions of the Companies Act requires a specific accreditation. Anyone who does not have these specific qualifications and signs an Auditors' Report leaves themselves open to disciplinary proceedings, if they are a qualified accountant, or possible legal proceedings if they are not.

The definition of who can be an auditor is set out in s 1212 of the Companies Act 2006. Note that, under the Act, auditors are referred to as 'statutory auditors'. This is to confirm their legal status as properly qualified auditors eligible to audit a range of different organisations in addition to both quoted and unquoted companies.

Section 1212 says:

(1) *An individual or firm is eligible for appointment as a statutory auditor if the individual or firm–*

    (a) *is a member of a recognised supervisory body, and*

    (b) *is eligible for the appointment under the rules of that body.*

Note that the legislation refers to '*individual or firm*' so, generally, it is an audit firm who is appointed, not a named individual.

Section 1222 concerns auditors who are not members of professional bodies recognised by the Companies Act 1967.

These individuals retain rights to audit individual unquoted companies as a consequence of being in office when the Companies Act 1967 came into force. There are still some of these accountants around and many are now members of The Association of Authorised Public Accountants which is a recognised supervisory body (see below).

Note that there is no prohibition on corporate bodies (e.g. companies) being auditors. This has enabled many firms to incorporate as limited liability partnerships (LLPs). This protects the firm, as a whole, from being damaged by claims arising, for example due to the negligence of one partner. We will look at this further in Chapter 31.

Schedule 10, Companies Act 2006 (on the subject of supervisory bodies) requires that any firm appointed as auditors must be controlled by qualified persons. This means that firms of accountants may have unqualified members or differently qualified partners, but a majority of the individuals which form the controlling board or committee of the firm must be individuals qualified to act as statutory auditors. The Supervisory Bodies have complex rules to cover this point.

Ineligible persons who can't act as auditors

Section 1214 deals with people who are ineligible to act as a statutory auditor.
These persons are:

- officers and employees of the company;
- partners or employees of such persons or a partnership of which such a person is a partner;
- persons who have a connection with the company or where the company has a connection with an associate of his of any description specified in regulations made by the Secretary of State.

Note that:

- persons who are ineligible to act as auditor of a particular company are also ineligible to act as auditor of a parent, subsidiary, or fellow subsidiary of that company;
- the whole purpose of this section is to secure the *independence* of the auditor from the company.

Section 1215 makes it an offence for a statutory auditor to be a company auditor if their independence is lost because of the sorts of connections mentioned above. If the statutory auditor becomes compromised in that way they must resign immediately and notify the company that they are unable to continue because of their lack of independence.

Recognised Supervisory Bodies

Section 1217 deals with Recognised Supervisory Bodies (RSBs).

A Supervisory Body is a body established in the UK which maintains and enforces rules as to the eligibility of persons seeking appointments as statutory auditors and the conduct of audit work, rules which are binding on such persons because they are members of these supervisory bodies or subject to its control.

Recognition will only be given to a Supervisory Body if the body has rules on:

- holding of appropriate qualifications;
- professional integrity and independence;
- technical standards;
- investigation of complaints; and
- meeting of claims arising out of audit work.

There are currently five Recognised Supervisory Bodies:

- the three Institutes of Chartered Accountants, in England & Wales, Scotland and Ireland (ICAEW, ICAS, ICAI);
- the Association of Chartered Certified Accountants (ACCA); and
- the Association of Authorised Public Accountants (AAPA).

The last is responsible for regulating its members but, in fact, has subcontracted the actual monitoring to the Association of Chartered Certified Accountants.

Sections 1239 and 1240 require Supervisory Bodies to maintain a register of persons and firms which are eligible to be company auditors and to make the register available to the public.

Qualifying bodies

Section 1220 considers qualifying bodies. The Act recognises a distinction between supervisory bodies and qualifying bodies but in practice all bodies, except the AAPA, are both.

The currently recognised qualifying bodies are the three Institutes of Chartered Accountants (England & Wales, Scotland and Ireland) and the Association of Chartered Certified Accountants.

A qualifying body means a body established in the UK which offers a professional qualification in accountancy.

The body must have enforceable rules on:

- admission to or expulsion from a course of study leading to a qualification;
- the award or deprivation of a qualification;
- the approval of a person for the purposes of giving practical training or the withdrawal of such approval;
- entry requirements;
- courses of instruction;
- professional experience;
- examination and practical training.

Appropriate qualifications

Section 1219 sets out the persons who hold appropriate qualifications.

Essentially the only persons so qualified are members of the three Institutes of Chartered Accountants and the Association of Chartered Certified Accountants plus the pre-1967 auditors of certain unquoted companies mentioned earlier.

There are also some provisions regarding qualified accountants from EC countries who wish to conduct audits in the UK. The rules are set out in Section 1221 which deals with overseas qualifications generally.

What this means, in practice, is that to be an auditor you have to be a member of a qualifying body and accredited by that qualifying body, in its capacity as a Supervisory Body, to carry out statutory audits.

Professional body rules

All the professional bodies have strict rules on granting a licence to practise as a professional accountant, known as a practising certificate.

Members of the professional bodies cannot practise, i.e. sell their services to the public, unless they have a practising certificate. Obtaining a practising certificate is difficult and the rules about experience are strictly enforced. The precise rules change regularly and can be obtained by enquiry of the relevant professional body.

Professional bodies also require auditors to carry Professional Indemnity Insurance (PII). This is to indemnify clients from loss in the case of any errors, mistakes or, indeed, negligent behaviour by members so that, hopefully, the client is not made worse off.

In addition, all members of professional bodies have to keep themselves up to date with a programme of continuing professional education, to ensure that their skills remain up to date and relevant.

Disciplinary rules

Supervisory bodies must have a code of conduct and a disciplinary procedure to punish firms or individuals who have transgressed. Firms or individuals signing audit reports when not accredited to do so, breaches of independence requirements, failure to deal satisfactorily with clients, criminal convictions etc. will all result in the member or firm having to explain themselves to some form of disciplinary committee of the Supervisory Body.

The result could be fines, reprimands and, in extreme cases, expulsion from the professional body.

Investigations into members or audit firms which are considered to be 'in the public interest' are conducted by the independent Accountancy & Actuarial Discipline Board (AADB), which is part of the Financial Reporting Council. This is to reassure the public that high profile cases which might raise issues of real concern are not 'swept under the carpet' but are properly investigated. It has the power not only to have cases referred to it but also to intervene in cases which it decides are in the public interest.

In addition, another part of the Financial Reporting Council called the Professional Oversight Board (POB) provides independent oversight of the regulation of the auditing profession by the Recognised Supervisory and qualifying bodies. Its function includes:

- monitoring of the quality of the auditing function in relation to economically significant entities (very large companies); and
- independent oversight of the regulation of the accountancy profession by the professional accountancy bodies.

This regulation applies mostly to the audit of companies, however similar rules also apply to many other bodies.

These include bodies registered under other Acts of Parliament, e.g. Building Societies, Financial Service Companies, Clubs and Societies registered under the Friendly Societies Act, Associations registered under the Industrial and Provident Societies Act, Solicitors, etc. Special rules apply to Charities under the Charities Act 2006.

The object of all these rules and regulation is to:

- ensure all company auditors are fit and proper persons;
- ensure professional integrity and independence;
- maintain technical standards;
- have procedures to maintain competence;
- ensure practitioners have professional indemnity insurance;
- investigate complaints;
- maintain a register of eligible auditors;
- monitor and enforce the rules on individual members.

THE RIGHTS AND DUTIES OF AN AUDITOR UNDER THE COMPANIES ACT 2006

The law on the rights and duties of an auditor under the Companies Act is principally laid down in Section 475(1), and in Sections 495–507.

We will consider the relevant parts of each section as they affect the conduct of the audit and the duties, rights and powers of auditors.

Remember that you do not have to be able to quote the law, nor is it a general requirement that you remember section numbers of the various provisions of the Companies Act. However, it is useful for students, and practitioners, to read the actual law rather than just seeing an interpretation of it in a textbook so, for this reason, we quote it rather extensively in this Chapter. The Companies Act 2006 is rather more readable than its predecessors so you shouldn't find this unduly difficult!

We set out the law for the whole process ending with the auditor's report. The reason for this is to show the legal basis on which auditors carry out all their work. Without the legal requirement for an auditor to make a report, it could be argued that all the rest of this book, which deals with how they go about doing that, would be rather pointless!

APPOINTMENT OF AUDITORS

Public companies

Section 489 details how auditors of public companies are to be appointed.

- The company shall, at each general meeting at which Accounts are presented (usually at each Annual General Meeting (AGM)), appoint an auditor or auditors.
- Note that it is the company (i.e. the shareholders) who appoint the auditor.
- The appointment is for the period of time known as the tenure of office and that is from the conclusion of the meeting to the conclusion of the following general meeting at which accounts are laid (i.e. presented at the meeting) (s 491).
- On the commencement of a new company the directors may appoint the auditor at any time before the first AGM.

Private companies

Because private companies no longer have to hold an AGM (see page 34) the tenure of office of the auditor is slightly different for them.

Basically auditors must be appointed *before* the end of a 28-day period which starts either:

- nine months from the year end, the date accounts are sent to the shareholders; or
- the date the accounts are filed with the Registrar,

whichever is earlier.

The term of office technically ends at the end of the equivalent period for the following year.

Auditors are deemed to be automatically reappointed unless:

- shareholders holding a minimum of 5 per cent of the voting rights (or lower percentage if specified in the Articles) object and appoint another firm; or

- they are the first auditors and have not yet been approved by the members; or
- the Articles of Association of the company require the auditors to be re-elected each year.

In the event of a company, either public or private, not appointing an auditor as required, section 486 states that the company must inform the Secretary of State within one week of the end of the period allowed for appointing auditors. The Secretary of State may then make an appointment.

The directors have the power to appoint the first auditors of a company and to appoint auditors to fill a casual vacancy, perhaps caused by resignation of the existing auditors. In both these cases the appointment must be approved by the shareholders at the next opportunity e.g. at the next AGM.

REMUNERATION OF AUDITORS

Under section 492 the remuneration of the auditors is fixed by the person/persons appointing. If this is the company in General Meeting the company AGM agendas might include something like:

> To re-appoint the auditors Fussy & Co. as the company's auditors until the conclusion
> of the next AGM of the Company, and to authorise the Board to fix the auditors'
> remuneration.

You will notice that the independence of the auditors is made by an appointment by the members in general meeting. If you refer back to Chapter 1 on agency theory you may think that the auditors' independence is then compromised by the delegation of the fixing of their remuneration to the directors. This is one of the reasons why auditors must not only be independent of their client, but must be seen to be independent and not influenced by the size of any fees.

Section 493 requires that the remuneration of the auditors shall be stated in a note in the company's accounts.

Disclosure in the accounts must be made of all amounts (including benefits in kind) paid to the auditor for both audit and non-audit work (preparing accounts, tax, consultancy etc.). Inclusion must be made of the remuneration from non-audit work paid to associates of the audit firm (e.g. management consultancy firms which are connected with the auditors) and for work done for subsidiaries of the client. The auditors must supply the necessary information to the company.

Thus auditors' remuneration must be disclosed to members and other users of the accounts and cannot be hidden by including it in a global figure such as administration expenses. Look it up every time you see a copy of a company's Annual Report and Accounts.

THE REMOVAL OF AN AUDITOR

The Companies Act takes a serious view of the removal of an auditor and there are a number of special procedures and rules to go through in order to effect a change of auditor.

Suppose that the directors prepare the accounts with the inclusion of some unusual accounting policy in order to increase profits in a particular year. The auditors, Tickett & Run, being honourable people may feel that the unusual policy is not acceptable and inform the directors that they will qualify their report if the policy is not changed. The directors may decide to abandon the policy for this year and change the auditors to Flexible & Co. in order that, in future years, the unusual policy may be adopted. Flexible & Co. may privately indicate that the unusual policy is acceptable to them.

Company law takes the view that company auditors must be capable of being changed if the *members* wish it but is designed:

- to ensure that the reality of the usual company situation, where the appointment of the auditors is by the members, cannot be manipulated by the directors to change auditors who are doing their duty, but who do not please the directors;
- to ensure that maximum publicity is given to any proposed change of auditors so that members are aware of the matter and can make informed choices;
- to give the auditors, who the directors would like to remove, every opportunity to state their case.

The relevant Companies Act legislation is:

- Section 510 – which states that a company may remove its auditors by ordinary resolution (a simple majority) notwithstanding anything in any agreement between it and them.
- Section 511 – which requires that special notice (28 days) must be given to the company of intention to move a resolution to remove an auditor or appoint some person other than the retiring auditor. Most such resolutions are moved by the directors but occasionally shareholders may band together to remove an auditor who they may consider has become too complacent or pliable.

On receipt of such an intended resolution the company must immediately send a copy to the auditors who are to be removed. At least the removal cannot be done behind the auditors' back.

The auditors, proposed to be removed, may make representations in writing to the company and request their notification to members. Thus the auditors who do not wish to be removed can state their case and require it to be sent to the members. Note that representations may not exceed a reasonable length.

The company must do two things (unless the representations are received too late):

- state the fact of representations being received in any notice of the resolution; and
- send a copy to every member of the company to whom notice of the meeting has been or will be sent.

The auditors have a general right to speak at the meeting on the subject of their intended removal and, if the representations have *not* been sent to the members, they have the right to have them read out at the meeting.

Note:

- The object of these rules is not to prevent the auditors being removed, if the members wish to remove them, but to ensure that they have adequate opportunity to put their case to the members before they vote on the resolution.
- Section 511(6) allows the company to seek an injunction against the auditor to restrain him or her from using his or her representations as a vehicle for needless publicity for defamatory matter.
- Where a motion to remove the auditors from office is passed the company must give notice to the Registrar within 14 days.

RESIGNATION OF AUDITORS

Auditors can resign. There are two main reasons why they may wish to do so. These are:

- Operational reasons – for example the company has grown too large for a small audit firm, the fee is inadequate, there is a conflict of interest where the auditor is representing both parties in a dispute, the client may have been taken over by a larger firm with its own auditors, etc.

- Ethical reasons – where the auditors conclude that because of fraud or other irregularity the accounts do not show a true and fair view and there is no immediate opportunity to report to members. They would be unable to report to members if the company refused to issue its financial statements, or if, at another stage in the year, the auditor has considerable doubts about management's integrity.

The procedures are set out in the Act.

Section 516 states that an auditor may resign by depositing a notice in writing to that effect at the registered office. This is not effective unless accompanied by a statement of circumstances. This basically sets out the reasons for the auditors' resignation.

The statement of circumstances should contain a statement of any circumstances which they consider should be brought to the attention of members or creditors or if they consider that there are no such circumstances then a statement that there are none (s 519).

The company must send a copy of the notice of resignation to the Registrar of Companies within 14 days on pain of a fine (s 517). Thus any person searching the company's file will have notice of the resignation.

The auditors can cease to be auditors by simply not seeking re-election. However, in that case they must still deposit a statement of circumstances and there are time limits for this.

Statement of circumstances

If the statement of circumstances contains matters which the auditor considers should be brought to the attention of members or creditors then the company must, within 14 days of receipt of it, send a copy to all persons entitled to receive copies of the accounts (i.e. the shareholders) or must apply to the court.

The court may order that the statement may not be sent out if it thinks the statement is seeking needless publicity for defamatory matter but otherwise the statement must be sent out.

The auditors must send their statement to the Registrar.

Rights and duties of the resigning auditor

Section 518 gives specific rights and duties to the resigning auditor:

- the auditors may deposit, with their notice of resignation and statement of circumstances, a notice calling on the company to convene a general meeting for the purpose of receiving and considering the statement of circumstances and other explanations which the auditors wish to place before the meeting;

- the directors must call such a meeting within 21 days on pain of a fine and must send out copies of the statement and if they fail to do so the auditors can require that the statement be read at the meeting.

There are the usual caveats re the court and defamatory matters.

These provisions do give the auditors power to explain the circumstances of their resignation. Remember that the auditors are acting on behalf of the members who own the company.

If they are being forced out by the directors, for example, they have the right to call upon the shareholders to listen to their case.

This gives the auditors a very powerful tool in situations where they are in conflict with the directors and they feel that the rights of the shareholders are at risk, for example, in the case of a major fraud perpetrated by senior management.

AUDITORS' DUTIES

Section 498 reads:

(1) A company's auditor, in preparing his report, must carry out such investigations as will enable him to form an opinion as to–

(a) whether adequate accounting records have been kept by the company and returns adequate for their audit have been received from branches not visited by him, and

(b) whether the company's individual accounts are in agreement with the accounting records and returns, and

(c) in the case of a quoted company, whether the auditable part of the company's directors' remuneration report is in agreement with the accounting records and returns.

(2) If the auditor is of the opinion–

(a) that adequate accounting records have not been kept, or that returns adequate for their audit have not been received from branches not visited by him,

or

(b) that the company's individual accounts are not in agreement with the accounting records and returns, or

(c) in the case of a quoted company, that the auditable part of its directors' remuneration report is not in agreement with the accounting records and returns,
the auditor shall state that fact in his report.

(3) If the auditor fails to obtain all the information and explanations which, to the best of his knowledge and belief, are necessary for the purposes of his audit, he shall state that fact in his report.

Subsection 1 requires the auditors to carry out investigations to determine if proper accounting records have been kept and proper returns from branches (at least branches not visited by the auditors) have been received.

What 'proper accounting records' comprise is considered later.

The subsection also requires the auditors to investigate whether the Accounts are in agreement with the accounting records and with returns from branches.

Subsection 2 requires that if the investigations required by subsection 1 lead the auditors to form a negative opinion on whether or not proper accounting records have been kept or if the Financial Accounts do not agree to the underlying records then the auditors have to state the fact of their negative opinion in their report. If they form a positive opinion they need say nothing on the matter in their report. We will look at the wording of Auditors' Reports in more detail in Chapter 27.

Subsection 3 is another duty. If the auditors fail to get all the information and explanations which are necessary for the purposes of the audit they have to say so in their report. For example, if the auditors feel they need to know if the repairs expense account includes any capital expenditure and the invoices have been lost they have to say so in their report, or if they ask the directors if they have received any benefits in kind from the firm and they refuse to answer they have to say that in their report.

Auditors also have to report on disclosure in the financial statements in respect of director's remuneration and benefits. We will deal with this in detail in Chapter 27.

Subsection 5 of Section 498 requires the auditor to report adversely if the directors have prepared accounts as if the company was a small company when it is not.

AUDITORS' RIGHTS

Section 499 states:

(1)   *The auditor of a company–*

   (a)   *has a right of access at all times to the company's books, accounts and vouchers, (in whatever form they are held), and*
   (b)   *may require any of the following persons to provide him with such information and explanations as he thinks necessary for the performance of his duties as auditor.*

(2)   *Those persons are–*

   (a)   *any officer or employee of the company;*
   (b)   *any person holding or accountable for any of the company's books, accounts or vouchers;*
   (c)   *any subsidiary undertaking of the company which is a body corporate incorporated in the United Kingdom;*
   (d)   *any officer, employee or auditor of any such subsidiary undertaking or any person holding or accountable for any books, accounts or vouchers of any such subsidiary undertaking;*
   (e)   *any person who fell within any of paragraphs (a) to (d) at a time to which the information or explanations required by the auditor relates or relate.*

This section gives the auditors some very powerful rights. They have a right of access at all times to the company's books, accounts and vouchers in whatever format they are retained by the company. This recognises the fact that many companies maintain their books and records in electronic formats.

A whole range of people are put under an obligation by sub-s (2) to provide the auditors with information and explanations. These range from officers and employees of the company itself through officers and employees working for subsidiary companies, who either still work there or who have left the company but who worked there during the period for which the auditors are asking for information. This duty to disclose information also extends to anybody who doesn't work for the company directly but is concerned in maintaining the books and records.

This would cover a situation where, for example, a company has outsourced part of its accounting. The most common aspect of outsourcing is payroll and, in such a situation, the company which prepares the payroll is covered by this section and has to disclose information to the auditors.

In the same way s 500 gives the auditors similar rights to information from overseas subsidiaries, (i.e. a subsidiary company not incorporated in the United Kingdom), and persons connected with it as defined in sub-s (2) above.

Section 501 states (in Part):

A person commits an offence who knowingly or recklessly makes to an auditor of a company a statement (oral or written) that–

a) *conveys or purports to convey any information or explanations which the auditor requires, or is entitled to require, under section 499, and*

b) *is misleading, false or deceptive in a material particular.*

This Section is designed to punish individuals who deliberately set out to mislead the auditors and knowingly supply them with false information.

The penalties for doing so are set out in sub-s (2) and include a term of imprisonment and/or a substantial fine.

THE AUDITORS' REPORT

Section 495 states:

(1) *A company's auditor must make a report to the company's members on all annual accounts of the company of which copies are during his tenure of office–*

  (a) *in the case of a private company, to be sent out to members . . .*

  (b) *in the case of a public company to be laid before the company in general meeting . . .*

(2) *The auditors' report must include–*

  (a) *an introduction identifying the annual accounts that are the subject of the audit and the financial reporting framework that has been applied in their preparation,*

  (b) *a description of the scope of the audit identifying the auditing standards in accordance with which the audit was conducted.*

(3) *The report must state whether in the auditors' opinion the annual accounts–*

  (a) *give a true and fair view–*

   (i) *in the case of an individual balance sheet, of the state of affairs of the company as at the end of the financial year,*

   (ii) *in the case of an individual profit and loss account, of the profit or loss of the company for the financial year,*

   (iii) *in the case of group accounts, of the state of affairs as at the end of the financial year, and the profit or loss for the financial year, of the undertakings included in the consolidation as a whole, so far as concerns members of the company.*

  (b) *have been properly prepared in accordance with the relevant financial reporting framework, and*

  (c) *have been properly prepared in accordance with the requirements of this Act.*

(4) *The auditors report–*

  (a) *must be unqualified or qualified, and*

  (b) *must include reference to any matters to which the auditor wishes to draw attention by way of emphasis without qualifying the report.*

In addition to this *s 496* says:

The auditor must state in his report on the company's annual accounts whether in his opinion the information given in the directors' report for the financial year for which the accounts are prepared is consistent with those accounts.

What does all this mean?

A public company must hold an Annual General Meeting (AGM) of its members (i.e. shareholders) in each calendar year. Private companies can decide whether or not to hold an AGM, unless their Articles of Association (essentially the rules of company procedure) require them to do so.

If an AGM is held the Annual Report and Accounts, including the Balance Sheet and Profit and Loss Account (and, in the case of holding companies, group accounts), which comprise the financial statements, are presented to the meeting for approval by the members.

In the case of private companies which elect not to hold an AGM the report and accounts must be sent to the members within *nine months* of the year end or, if earlier, by the date it actually files its accounts with the Registrar of Companies.

Included in the Annual Report and Accounts, there must be a report by the auditors on the financial statements examined by them.

Auditors are appointed only for one financial year at a time. They are usually appointed at an AGM and hold office from the end of that meeting (say July 19th 20-7) till the end of the following AGM (say July 17th 20-8). That is their tenure of office. They report on the accounts presented at the AGM of 20-8, which is within their tenure of office.

Where a private company does not hold an AGM, generally, the auditor is deemed to be automatically reappointed, unless there is a provision in the company's Articles of Association that they must be physically re-elected by a vote at a meeting or unless disgruntled shareholders, holding at least 5 per cent of the shares, object to automatic re-appointment.

The auditors' report has very specific content viz:

- The Act contains very detailed requirements on the form and contents of Accounts. The auditor has to say whether in his opinion the Accounts have been prepared in accordance with the Act.

- The Act requires, in s 396, that the Accounts must give a true and fair view of the state of affairs of the Company (i.e. by the Balance Sheet) and of its profit or loss (i.e. by the Profit and Loss Account).

The auditors must say in their report whether, in their opinion, the financial statements give a '*true and fair*' view.

The idea of 'true and fair' is a difficult one and we will consider it in a later chapter. At this stage assume that it means that the accounts are free from any significant errors or misstatements.

Finally, s 496 requires the auditors to consider whether there is any inconsistency between the information given in the Directors' Report and the Annual Accounts.

We will deal with this in more detail latter in the book but for the moment you should understand that auditors are not being asked to give an opinion on the Directors' Report as a whole; they are only asked to review the Directors' Report and to consider whether the statutory disclosures which the directors have to make are properly stated and whether, taken as a whole, the Report is consistent with the Accounts. If the auditors form an opinion that there is an inconsistency they have to say so in their audit report.

For example, suppose the Directors' Report states that 'production at the Bilston Factory has ceased and that the plant there will be sold for scrap', but the Accounts include the Bilston plant at full cost. There is an inconsistency in that the directors' report shows the Bilston plant to have no further use and the Accounts assume further use. If the matter was material (i.e. of significant size) then the auditors would have to detail this inconsistency in their report.

Publication of the auditors' report

The Companies Act has a number of rules for publicising the auditors' report. However, the Companies Act treats small companies and large quoted companies rather differently. These are a summary of the regulations designed to set out the basic principles. A lot of the detailed provisions have been left out in the interests of clarity, and brevity.

Students should be aware from their studies in Financial Accounting of the form and content of company accounts and the various dates for filing these with the Registrar of Companies, so much of that detail is omitted from the following paragraphs.

These are the main provisions:

a) Firstly, s 423:

> **(1)** *Every company must send a copy of its annual accounts and reports for each financial year to–*
>
> (a) *every member of the company,*
> (b) *every holder of the company's debentures, and*
> (c) *every person who is entitled to receive notice of general meetings.*

b) Secondly s 430, which is *new* and only applies to quoted companies:

> **(1)** *A quoted company must ensure that its annual accounts and reports–*
>
> (a) *are made available on a website, and*
> (b) *remain so available until the annual accounts and reports for the company's next financial year are made available in accordance with this section.*
>
> **(2)** *The annual accounts and reports must be made available on a website that–*
>
> (a) *is maintained by or on behalf of the company, and*
> (b) *identifies the company in question.*

Sections 431 and 432 are also relevant.
Section 431 states:

> **(1)** *A member of or a holder of debentures of an unquoted company is entitled to be provided, on demand and without charge, with a copy of–*
>
> (a) *the company's last annual accounts,*
> (b) *the last directors' report, and*
> (c) *the auditors' report on those accounts.*

Section 432 says the same thing in respect of quoted companies. The auditors' reports must include any additional reports the auditors make, including those in respect of the Directors' Remuneration Report and the Directors' Report. We will discuss these in more detail in Chapter 27.

And Section 434:

> **(1)** *If a company publishes any of its statutory accounts, they must be accompanied by the auditor's report on those accounts (unless the company is exempt from audit and the directors have taken advantage of that exemption).*

finally Section 437:

> **(1)** *The directors of a public company must lay before the company in general meeting copies of its annual accounts and reports.*

Remember that this section applies only to public companies.

The reason for this is that private companies no longer have to hold Annual General Meetings unless they wish to do so. However, as we saw above, s 424 requires a private company to send a copy of its annual report and accounts to its shareholders within nine months of the year end, (s 442) or the date it files its accounts with the Registrar of Companies, if earlier.

Section 441 requires each company to deliver to the Registrar each year a set of reports and accounts in the prescribed format within a set period after the financial year end. There are various requirements dependent upon the size of the company and whether it is quoted or unquoted. These are too detailed to be set out here but interested students should refer to ss 442 to 447 of the Act.

Thus, whenever the full or summary financial statements are sent to members and other entitled persons, published, put onto a website, laid before the company in general meeting, or delivered to the Registrar of Companies then the Auditors' Report has to be included.

Every company has a file at Companies House and the accounts sent to the Registrar are included in the file. The file is open to inspection by members of the public. Thus, any interested person has access to the file without the company being aware of the enquiry.

AUDITORS' RIGHTS TO ATTEND MEETINGS

Section 502 establishes the right of an auditor to receive notice of and to attend at meetings:

(2) *A company's auditor is entitled–*

   (a) *to receive all notices of, and other communications relating to, any general meeting which a member of the company is entitled to receive;*
   (b) *to attend any general meeting of the company; and*
   (c) *to be heard at any general meeting which they attend on any part of the business of the meeting which concerns him as auditor.*

In the case of private companies which are no longer required to hold Annual General Meetings, unless they wish to, s 502(1) requires a private company to send to the auditors a copy of any written resolution to which a member is entitled. Written resolutions can be used by private companies and circulated to members instead of having meetings.

POWERS OF AN AUDITOR

Auditors of limited companies are given burdensome duties by the Companies Act. They are required to make a report on, amongst other things, the truth and fairness of the Annual Accounts. If they are negligent in any way and fail to discover that the Accounts contain an untruth or do not fairly present the position they may be sued by the company and have to compensate it for any loss arising as a result of the 'false' Accounts.

Because of these responsibilities the Act has given the auditors extensive rights and powers. In practice however, whilst the Act lies down provisions requiring directors and employees of a company to provide the auditor with information and insists that that information is true and correct, this is something which cannot really be enforced. The main power the auditors have lies in the reports they write and we will discuss this further in Chapters 27 and 28.

Case Study

Mainbrace Ltd is a book publisher and retailer which trades via the Internet. The company was formed using a kit bought from a legal stationers, start up capital was provided by the major shareholder, Bertie Bracewell's father, another friend and co-owner Angela Main also provided some capital. Bertie's father owns 10 per cent of the company but doesn't take any part in its activities.

When it was set up Angela and Bertie didn't want to get too 'tied up in paper-work' so they put on the forms that Bertie's father and Angela's mother, who just signed the form because she was asked to, were the first directors.

Since it started the company has done exceptionally well and, some 18 months after it started up it is now turning over approximately half a million pounds per month, employs 60 people in three offices and has recently entered into a contract to buy a huge distribution warehouse valued at over £3m.

The company has Angela and Bertie to run the business and make all the decisions between them, with occasional advice from the company accountant Ron Whistler. He produces monthly management accounts but the company has never had an audit and has never filed any accounts with the Registrar of Companies.

Ron is getting a little concerned, particularly as he has just received an envelope from 'Companies House'. He daren't open it because he thinks it will be bad news.

Discussion

- What provisions of the Companies Act are Bertie, Angela and Mainbrace Ltd not complying with?
- What should they do as a matter of urgency to correct the situation?

Student self-testing questions

(Questions with answers apparent from the text)

a) What is the main piece of legislation regulating companies?

b) What are the limits for the statutory audit to apply to a company?

c) What is the role of a Recognised Supervisory Body?

d) Which are the RSBs in the UK?

e) Who can be an auditor?

f) What should the Auditors' Report state?

g) List the main rights of auditors

h) How are auditors appointed?

i) What should auditors do on resigning their office?

4

Accounting requirements of the Companies Act

INTRODUCTION

This section details the requirements on the keeping of accounting records by companies. The basis for this is, as might be anticipated, set out in the Companies Act 2006. This lays down the minimum requirements for the books and records a company has to keep.

Auditors must know these rules because, as you will remember from a previous chapter, one of the duties of the auditors is to carry out investigations to enable them to form an opinion on whether the company has kept proper accounting records and has proper returns from any branches not visited by the auditors.

Further, if they form an opinion that the company have not kept proper accounting records, they have to say so in their report. The word 'proper' here means in accordance with custom or appropriate to the circumstances.

ACCOUNTING AND ACCOUNTING RECORDS

It is important to understand that that the responsibility for keeping proper accounting records lies *wholly* with the directors.

The Companies Act 2006 sets out the company's responsibilities towards maintaining proper accounting records. Once again we must quote extracts from the Act but we think it important that students understand the legal framework within which they have to operate as auditors.

Section 386 states:

(1) *Every company must keep adequate accounting records;*

(2) *Adequate accounting records means records that are sufficient–*

    (a) *to show and explain the company's transactions,*

    (b) *to disclose with reasonable accuracy, at any time, the financial position of the company at that time, and*

    (c) *to enable the directors to ensure that any accounts required to be prepared comply with the requirements of this Act.*

(3) *The accounting records must in particular contain–*

(a) *entries from day-to-day of all sums of money received and expended by the company, and the matters in respect of which the receipt and expenditure takes place, and*

(b) *a record of the assets and liabilities of the company.*

(4) *If the company's business involves dealing in goods, the accounting records must contain–*

(a) *statements of stock held by the company at the end of each financial year of the company,*

(b) *all statements of stocktakings from which any statement of stock as is mentioned in paragraph (a) has been or is to be prepared, and*

(c) *except in the case of goods sold by way of ordinary retail trade, statements of all goods sold and purchased, showing the goods and the buyers and sellers in sufficient detail to enable all these to be identified.*

(5) *A parent company which has a subsidiary undertaking in relation to which the above requirements do not apply must take reasonable steps to secure that the undertaking keeps such accounting records as to enable the directors of the parent company to ensure that any accounts required to be prepared under this Part complies with the requirements of this Act.*

Section 387 deals with the failure of a company to comply with these requirements. It states:

(1) *If a company fails to comply with any provision of Section 386, (duty to keep accounting records) an offence is committed by every officer of the company who is in default.*

(2) *It is a defence for a person charged with such an offence to show that he acted honestly and that in the circumstances in which the company's business was carried on the default was excusable.*

A person guilty of an offence under this section is liable to a term of imprisonment or a fine, or both.

What are accounting records?

The Act says that the accounting records must be sufficient to disclose,

- with reasonable accuracy,
- at any time,

the financial position of the company at that time.

In practice, with computerised accounting systems, this should not present any difficulty.

The company's accounting records must also record all the information the directors need in order to ensure that any financial accounts they prepare for presentation to the shareholders comply with the Act.

Note that most companies of any size produce detailed accounts regularly as part of their management processes. These management accounts will not be in a statutory format but do provide, as we will see in a later chapter, a good source of information for the auditor.

In detail, *as a minimum*, the accounting records have to include:

- A cash book to record sums of money received and expended and the matters about which the receipts or payments took place.
- A record of assets and liabilities – which includes sales and purchase ledgers recording debtors and creditors balances.

- Except for ordinary retail sales (i.e. cash sales over the counter) statements of all goods purchased and sold, showing the buyers and sellers and identifying them which means retention, in some form, of invoices, or copy invoices.
- Sales and purchase day books.
- Where the company deals in goods then:
  - Statements of stock held at each year or, where perhaps the company carries out a rolling inventory or perpetual stocktaking,
  - Statements of stock takings from which the year end stock figure is to be calculated.

Subsection (5) is concerned with subsidiary undertakings abroad. The directors must ensure that they can obtain the information they need from the accounting records of subsidiary companies. This may present a difficulty in the case of companies incorporated in countries where the accounting regime is not a strict as it is in the UK, and don't forget these will be in a foreign currency and a foreign language so will require translation.

The company's accounting records can be kept wherever the directors think fit.

There are some special rules relating to accounting records kept outside the UK. Accounts and returns in respect of such business must be sent to the UK.

These accounts and returns sent to the UK must be such as to:

- Disclose with reasonable accuracy the financial position of the overseas business at intervals not exceeding six months.
- Enable the directors to ensure that Accounts comply with the Act as to form and content.

STATUTORY BOOKS

The Companies Act requires a company to keep the following books, in addition to the accounting records as described above.

- A register of directors – (s 162).
- A register of charges (fixed and floating) – (s 876).
- Minute books of meetings of the company, including meetings of its directors and meetings of its managers – (s 248).
- A register of members – (s 113). If it has more than 50 members the register must be indexed – (s 115).
- Public companies must keep a register of information received from any person to whom they have sent a notice requiring them to disclose whether or not they have an interest in the company's voting shares – (s 808).

The auditor's interest

The auditor is interested in the statutory books being properly maintained because:

- They are directly concerned with the accounts.
- They are audit evidence to be used in verifying detailed items in the accounts; for example the total share capital shown by the sum of the individual share holdings in the register of members must agree with the share capital recorded in the books of account.

Failure to maintain proper records of any sort casts doubt upon the accuracy and reliability of the records generally.

Particular problems that may cause the auditor to reflect on whether proper accounting records have been kept include:

- delays in writing up the records;
- frequent alterations in records;
- exceptionally large numbers of errors found by the auditor;
- audit trail difficulties (audit trail is the ability to follow a transaction through the records and documentation);
- computer problems including failure of software, chaos, hardware breakdowns, changes of computer staff, viruses, loss of data etc.

We will look at these in more detail as we look at the process whereby the auditors gather their evidence by probing the company's books and records in their search for the truth. But before that we must consider the accounting requirements of the Act.

ACCOUNTING REQUIREMENTS

This section deals with the Companies Act requirements on:

- the accounting reference date,
- the form and content of company accounts,
- the procedure on the completion of the accounts,
- modified accounts, and
- the publication of full and abridged accounts.

An auditor must know these rules because:

- The majority of audits are company audits.
- The principal objective of the audit is to report on the truth and fairness of the financial statements.
- Section 495 requires the auditors to state in their report whether, in their opinion, the accounts have been properly prepared in accordance with the Act.
- Examiners in auditing require this knowledge in students.

Some of this you will know from your studies into Financial Accounting and Financial Reporting, nevertheless we include them here because it is a part of the auditors' role to ensure that all the financial rules have been complied with. It is outside the scope of this book to detail all the various disclosure requirements for a set of financial statements etc. but knowledge of the fundamental accounting principles is vital to sound understanding of audit work.

Remember also that the responsibility for preparing financial statements, laying them before the company (i.e. presenting them to shareholders) and delivering them to Companies House lies wholly with the directors.

Accounting reference date

Every company has to have a period end and the profit and loss account is for the period ending on that date and the balance sheet is made up as at that date. A company's period end is known as the Accounting Reference Date and the financial statements are made up for the accounting reference periods ending on that date.

Sections 390 to 392 give the law on this matter in unbelievable length. In short:

- the company can give notice to the Registrar of its chosen date.
- if this is not done then the Accounting Reference Date is either:
  - the last day of the month in which the anniversary of its incorporation falls or,
  - if the company was formed before 1 April 1990, it is automatically 31 March.

  The date can be changed by going through the prescribed procedures.
  The company must prepare accounts for each and every accounting reference period.
  The actual date used may be up to seven days either side of the accounting reference date.

Financial statements required

The following financial statements must be prepared:

- A Profit and Loss account for each accounting reference period – (s 396).
- A Balance Sheet as at the accounting reference date – (s 396).
- If the company is a holding company then group accounts must also be prepared – (s 399). It is permissible and is the common practice not to publish the company's own profit and loss account but to publish a consolidated profit and loss account which shows how much of the consolidated profit or loss for the financial year is dealt with in the company's individual accounts – (s 408).
- Notes attached to and forming part of the Accounts:
  - Giving the detailed information required by the Act and various accounting standards without cluttering the financial statements.
  - Giving certain required additional information – (ss 409–413).
- A Directors' Report – (ss 415–418).
- A Directors' Remuneration Report – (s 420).

This is the minimum required by law. Most public companies, particularly those listed on the Stock Exchange, include a lot more in their annual accounts. These may take the form of a chairman's statement, a review of operations, a five year summary of accounts etc.

The auditors are not responsible for auditing these as they are not part of the statutory minimum accounts but, as we will see in a later chapter, the auditors must make sure that these extraneous pages are consistent with the statutory accounts.

Form of company accounts

The financial statements must follow the formats specified by the Act. In addition to the Companies Act requirements there are International Financial Reporting Standards (IFRS) and Generally Accepted Accounting Principles (GAAP), which contain the various rules relating to disclosure and reporting in company accounts.

Section 395 allows a company to prepare accounts either in accordance with the Companies Act or in accordance with International Accounting Standards (IAS individual accounts).

Auditors must be familiar with the principles which lie behind the preparation of, and disclosures required in, company accounts.

In practice, checklists will be used to ensure that nothing vital has been missed. However, many examination bodies set questions which require a knowledge of accounting disclosures so students must have in mind their studies in financial accounting when answering auditing questions.

ACCOUNTING PRINCIPLES

Accounts are prepared under four fundamental accounting principles. These constitute the underlying framework for all the items to be included in the accounts and all the specific disclosures required either by the Act or the various accounting standards.

The fundamental accounting principles are listed here.

Going concern
The company is be presumed to be carrying on business as a going concern. What this means, in practice, is that the company will have the ability to continue to trade in substantially the same way as it does in the financial period being reported on for the forseeable future. This particular principle is very important to the auditors and we will look at it in more detail in Chapter 24.

Consistency
Accounting policies will be applied consistently within the same accounts and from one financial year to the next.

Prudence
The amount of any item reported on the financial statements will be determined on a prudent basis, and in particular:

(a) only profits realised at the balance sheet date shall be included in the profit and loss account; and

(b) all liabilities and losses which have arisen or are likely to arise in respect of the financial year to which the accounts relate or a previous financial year shall be taken into account, including those which only become apparent between the balance sheet date and the date on which it is signed on behalf of the board of directors.

Accruals basis
All income and charges relating to the financial year to which the accounts relate will be taken into account, irrespective of the actual date of receipt or payment.

Departure from the accounting principles

If it appears to the directors of a company that there are special reasons for departing from any of the principles stated above in preparing the company's accounts in respect of any financial year they may do so, but particulars of the departure, the reasons for it and its effect must be given in a note to the accounts.

CONTENT – DISCLOSURE REQUIREMENTS

The Act and associated financial reporting standards give extensive detailed rules on the *minimum* information which must be given in the accounts or in notes attached to them.

There is no objection to accounts giving more information than the minimum, but in practice most accounts, particularly of private companies, just disclose the minimum required by the law.

Companies are required to state, with their statement of accounting policies, whether the accounts have been prepared in accordance with applicable accounting standards and give particulars of any material departure from those standards and the reasons for any such departure.

TRUE AND FAIR OVERRIDE

The Act requires that the accounts show give a true and fair view. This means that when they are prepared they must be prepared giving full recognition to all the relevant accounting principles and the requirements of the statutory reporting framework. This is the responsibility of the directors.

In the event that compliance with the law meant that the accounts did not show a true and fair view s 396 has the answer:

(1) If compliance with the regulations, and any other provisions made by or under this Act as to the matters to be included in a company's individual accounts or in notes to those accounts, would not be sufficient to give a true and fair view, the necessary additional information must be given in the accounts or in a note to them.

(2) If in special circumstances compliance with any of those provisions is inconsistent with the requirement to give a true and fair view, the directors must depart from that provision to the extent necessary to give a true and fair view.
Particulars of any such departure, the reasons for it and its effect must be given in a note to the accounts.

In other words this, admittedly somewhat nebulous concept of a 'true and fair view' takes precedence over the strict legal requirements of the reporting rules. This is closely tied to the doctrine of 'substance over form' which we looked at in Chapter 1 and students should be familiar with these ideas.

However this so-called 'true and fair' override is not a licence for non-compliance and it should be used only in exceptional circumstances and with a full explanation.

PROCEDURE ON COMPLETION OF THE FINANCIAL STATEMENTS

The financial statements comprising:

- the balance sheet
- the profit and loss account
- the directors' report
- the directors remuneration report
- the auditor's report
- group accounts, where required

must be approved by the board of directors and then the balance sheet must be signed by at least one director of the company on behalf of the board – (s 414).

For a public company required to hold an AGM:

- A copy of the Accounts must be sent to all persons entitled at least 21 days before the AGM – (s 424).

- Copies of the Accounts must be laid before the company in general meeting (usually the AGM) – (s 437).
- A copy of the Accounts must be delivered to the Registrar of Companies – (s 441).

For a private company not holding an AGM the shareholders must be sent the accounts not later than nine months from the year end, or the date the company files them with the Registrar if earlier – (s 424).

PERIOD ALLOWED FOR FILING ACCOUNTS

The directors of a company are required by the Act (s 441) to file the accounts with the Registrar of Companies in accordance with a timescale as:

- Private companies – within *nine months* after the end of the accounting reference period.
- Public companies – within *six months* after the end of the accounting reference period.

ABBREVIATED ACCOUNTS

Sections 444 and 445 gives a number of exemptions to small and medium-sized companies. These are, broadly:

- small companies are exempt from some filing requirements.

  They need only file an abbreviated Balance Sheet and need not include many of the notes to the accounts. They do not need to file a profit and loss account or the directors' report.

- medium-sized companies can file a set of financial statements which can include a slightly abbreviated profit and loss account and exemption from certain disclosures of information.

  Small and medium-sized companies are defined as companies which satisfy *two or more* of the following:

	Small-sized	Medium-sized
Turnover does not exceed	£5.6 million	£22.8 million
Balance Sheet total does not exceed	£2.8 million	£11.4 million
Average number of employees does not exceed	50	250

These exemptions apply to groups of companies where *the whole group* falls within these limits.

The exemptions do not apply to a company if, in the year, it is:

- a public company;
- an insurance company; or
- a company carrying on a regulated activity under the Financial Services and Markets Act 2000, which, basically, includes banks, building societies, investment and pension advisors, friendly societies, credit unions etc.;
- a group where one of its members is also a public company or regulated under the Financial Services and Markets Act 2000.

Auditors have to give special reports where small and medium-sized companies file abbreviated accounts. We will deal with this in Chapter 27 when we discuss forms of audit report.

PUBLICATION OF ACCOUNTS

Sections 434–436 contain some rules on the publication of accounts.

A company may publish its statutory accounts and if it does so, it must also publish its auditors' report. Statutory accounts means the full accounts or the reduced accounts allowed to small or medium-sized companies described above.

Companies may also publish non-statutory accounts, i.e. accounts containing more than the statutory minimum or extracts (s 435). If it does, then it must also publish a statement:

- that the accounts are not statutory accounts;
- whether statutory accounts have been delivered to the Registrar;
- whether the auditors have made a report;
- whether any such report has been qualified.

In addition the Companies Act brought in a new provision.

Quoted companies must publish accounts on a website and must maintain them on that website until accounts for the next period are available (s 430).

These must be freely available to anyone logging on and not restricted unless there is a legal requirement to do so. The website must clearly identify the company and be maintained by it.

This gives auditors some special problems which we will cover later.

SUMMARY ACCOUNTS

Section 426 contains the option for a company to provide its shareholders with summary accounts if the shareholders so wish. This is to reduce the burden of sending full accounts to shareholders who may only be interested in certain parts of them. The company's shareholders can pass a resolution allowing the company to send summary accounts to all shareholders except those who insist on having the full accounts.

Sections 427 and 428 contain detailed rules as to the form and content of these summary accounts for both quoted and unquoted companies. Insofar as these rules affect auditors the key aspect is that they must contain a statement from the auditors that:

- the summary accounts are consistent with the full accounts;
- the information in the summary accounts is derived from the full accounts, including the Directors Report;
- the summary accounts comply with the Act;
- whether or not their report on the full accounts was qualified and, if it was;
- details of the qualification.

DORMANT COMPANIES

Section 1169 has some rules on dormant companies:

A company is dormant in a period if during the period no significant accounting transaction occurred. Such companies need not appoint an auditor but must still file accounts.

Summary

- The Companies Act lays down rules for keeping of proper accounting records and for proper returns from branches including those overseas.
- The Companies Act also requires a company to keep a range of additional records called the statutory books.
- The directors are wholly responsible for the maintenance of accounting records and statutory books.
- The auditor has a duty to investigate and form an opinion on whether proper accounting records have been kept.
- The Companies Act lays down rules for the keeping of proper accounting records and proper returns from branches overseas and the directors have the responsibility for seeing that the company obeys the rules.
- Failure to obey the rules may mean that:

  - Proper books of account have not been kept.
  - Proper returns have not been received.

- Sufficient information has to be available for the proper disclosure of matters of which the Companies Act requires detailed disclosure.
- The Companies Acts lay down very detailed rules on:

  - What financial statements are required.
  - The form of the financial statements.
  - The accounting principles to be followed.
  - Detailed information to be disclosed.

- Auditors must know the rules because their duties laid down by the Act include a requirement to report on the true and fair view and compliance with statute of the Accounts.
- There are accounting period and time limits for laying and delivering accounts.
- Specified exemptions from these rules are given to small and medium-sized companies.
- Listed companies may send out summary financial statements.
- Quoted companies must publish accounts on a website.

Points to note

- Returns in the context of this chapter are of two types:

  - Those from branches in the UK. The auditors must see that proper returns have been received by head office when they have not visited the branches. Some companies have numerous branches, e.g. Tesco. The auditors cannot be expected to visit them all.
  - Those from branches overseas. These are subject to special statutory requirements but the auditors have the same duty to satisfy themselves on overseas branch matters as they do for UK branches.

- There are penalties for failing to keep proper accounting records or statutory books.
- Organisations other than companies may have specific statutory requirements re accounting records (e.g. financial service companies) and the auditor needs to ensure that these have been complied with.

- Note the requirement in Section 386 to be able to prepare financial statements 'at any time'.
- Auditing students are sometimes required to show specific and detailed knowledge of the rules in exams.
- In addition to the Companies Act requirements on accounts, there are also two other sets of requirements to be fulfilled. These are:
  - Financial reporting standards.
  - Stock Exchange requirements for quoted companies.
- Shareholders are entitled to a full set of accounts which contains all the disclosures required by the Companies Act and various accounting standards.

Case Study

Cicero Ltd has now realised that it needs to improve its financial records and send some accounts to Companies House. So far it has managed with a series of spread-sheets devised by the company accountant, Eric Chopper, who is not a qualified accountant, which records incoming cash and cheques, payments and outstanding invoices. There are no ledgers and no double entry system. Eric does, however, rec-oncile his bank spreadsheets with the bank statements each month. He claims that all the company needs to know to run the business is how much money is in the bank.

The business consists of four small supermarkets and two clothes shops. The company has never prepared audited accounts, even though it has traded for three years. Stocktakes are held annually at each of the shops, and when the total figure is calculated the stock sheets are thrown away as they are only rough counts.

Discussion
- What does Cicero Ltd need to do to rectify the situation?
- Who is responsible for ensuring this is properly dealt with?
- What advantages will improving the position bring to Cicero Ltd?
- Why might Eric Chopper not be keen to rectify the position?

Student self-testing questions

Questions with answers apparent from the text

a) What must appear in books of account?

b) List the statutory books.

c) Who are responsible for maintaining the books of account and the statutory books?

d) What is the auditor's interest in these documents?

e) What financial statements must be prepared?

f) What are the time limits for laying and delivery of accounts?

g) Define small and medium-sized companies.

h) What exemptions are available to them?

i) What is the true and fair override?

j) What are the rules on publishing accounts in abridged form?

k) What are the rules on sending out accounts in summary form?

l) What additional reports are required from an auditor?

5

Auditing and accounting standards and guidelines

INTRODUCTION

The professional accounting bodies are very anxious to improve and maintain high standards in the conduct of audits and to that end they set up the Auditing Practices Board (APB). This authoritative body, which is part of the Financial Reporting Council issues:

- International Standards on Auditing (ISA) which are mandatory and which we will be dealing with at length in this book;
- Practice Notes which are helpful and indicative of good practice; and
- Bulletins which comment on items of current interest.

These standards are derived from generic International standards issued by the International Auditing and Assurance Standards Board (IAASB) which is a committee of the International Federation of Accountants (IFAC).

INTERNATIONAL STANDARDS ON AUDITING

Each ISA contains two types of material:

- *Basic principles and essential procedures* with which auditors are required to comply.
- *Explanatory and other material* which, rather than being prescriptive is designed to assist auditors in interpreting and applying auditing standards.

Auditors must comply with the International Standards on Auditing. Apparent failure to comply leads to disciplinary or regulatory action against the auditor. In addition the courts may take into account the ISAs when considering if audit work was adequate in negligence cases. The explanatory and other material has less authority in theory but not much less in practice.

Current ISAs issued by the APB are:

200	Objective and general principles governing an audit of financial statements
210	Terms of Audit Engagements
220	Quality Control for Audits of Historical Financial Information
230	Documentation

Both the APB and the International Accounting Standards Board (IASB) have glossaries of terms used.

PRACTICE NOTES

The APB also issues Practice Notes which are designed to assist auditors in applying Auditing Standards of general application to particular circumstances and industries.

They are persuasive rather than prescriptive and have similar status to the explanatory material in the ISAs. Practice Notes may later be developed into or be included in ISAs.

Current ones of importance are:

PN08   Reports by Auditors under Company Legislation in the United Kingdom
            August 1994
PN10   (Revised) Audit of Financial Statements of Public Sector Bodies in the
            United Kingdom (Revised) *January 2006*

PN11	The Audit of Charities in the United Kingdom (Revised) *April 2002*
PN12	(Revised) Money laundering – Interim guidance for auditors in the United Kingdom *January 2007*
PN13	The Audit of Small Businesses *July 1997*
PN14	The Audit of Registered Social Landlords in the United Kingdom (Revised) *March 2006*
PN15	The Audit of Occupational Pension Schemes in the United Kingdom (Revised) *March 2007*
PN16	Bank reports for audit purposes (Revised): Interim guidance *October 2006*
PN19	The Audit of Banks and Building Societies in the United Kingdom (Revised) *January 2007*
PN20	The Audit of Insurers in the United Kingdom (Revised) *January 2007*
PN21	The Audit of Investment Businesses in the United Kingdom *June 2000*
PN22	The Auditors' Consideration of FRS 17 'Retirement Benefits' - Defined Benefit Schemes *April 2002*
PN23	Auditing Derivative Financial Instruments *April 2002*
PN24	The Audit of Friendly Societies in the United Kingdom (Revised) *January 2007*
PN25	Attendance at Stocktaking

The IAASB also issues *International Auditing Practice Statements* which provide practical assistance to auditors on implementing the ISAs.

In addition the IAASB is also responsible for issuing the International Standards on Quality Control (ISQCs), ISQC 1 having been adopted by the APB, and also the International Framework for Assurance Engagements (IFAE). We will refer to these in later chapters.

BULLETINS

The APB also issues bulletins which provide auditors with timely advice on new or emerging issues which, like Practice Notes, are persuasive rather than prescriptive.

Some of the current bulletins include:

2000/03	Departure from Statements of Recommended Practice for the Preparation of Financial Statements: Guidance for Auditors *December 2000*
2001/01	The Electronic Publication of Auditors' Reports *January 2001*
2001/03	E-Business: Identifying Financial Statement Risks *April 2001*
2004/01	The Auditors' Association with Preliminary Announcements *January 2004*
2005/01	Audit Risk and Fraud – Supplementary Guidance for Auditors of Charities *February 2005*
2005/02	Audit Risk and Fraud – Supplementary Guidance for Auditors of Investment Businesses *April 2005*
2005/03	Guidance for Auditors on First-time Application of IFRSs in the United Kingdom and the Republic of Ireland *November 2005*
2006/2	Illustrative Auditor's Reports on Public Sector Financial Statements in the United Kingdom *January 2006*
2006/3	The Special Auditor's Report on Abbreviated Accounts in the United Kingdom
2006/5	The Combined Code on Corporate Governance: Requirements of Auditors under the Listing Rules of the Financial Services Authority and the Irish Stock Exchange *September 2006*

2006/6   Auditor's Reports on Financial Statements in the United Kingdom
            September 2006
2007/1   Example Reports by Auditors under Company Legislation in Great Britain
            January 2007

Other APB documents

Other APB documents include The Scope and Authority of APB pronouncements and the APB Ethical Standards which we will deal with in Chapter 6.

ACCOUNTING STANDARDS

Introduction

In general, published accounts are required to conform to the relevant financial reporting standards. Part of the auditor's duty is to assess whether or not the financial statements they are auditing do comply in general and in detail with financial standards. This book is about auditing and cannot include a detailed description of all the accounting standards. For a detailed understanding readers will need to consult an accounting textbook.

Accounting standard setting

The financial reporting standards are issued by the Accounting Standards Board (ASB) which is a subsidiary of the Financial Reporting Council (FRC).

A subcommittee of the ASB is the Urgent Issues Task Force (UITF) which issues UITF Abstracts. These abstracts are regarded as accepted practice in the area in question and financial statements should generally conform to them. There is another subsidiary of the FRC – the Financial Reporting Review Panel (FRRP) which examines departures (when referred to them) from the accounting standards.

Some areas, particularly charities and public sector bodies have Statements of Recommended Practice (SORPs), which are also approved by the ASB. The financial statements of organisations within the relevant sectors would normally comply with the appropriate SORP. The best known of these is probably the SORP which relates to the accounts of charities.

The ASB issues a Financial Reporting Exposure Draft (FRED) on matters on which a new FRS is intended and sometimes a discussion paper before the FRED. The FREDs have no standing but often give an understanding of current best practice.

Current accounting standards

Auditing students should be aware of and familiar with the financial reporting standards required for the syllabuses they are studying. They should also be aware that new standards are being issued all the time and the up-to-date situation must be known.

Small companies and the accounting standards

The accounting standards are on a continuum from basic accounting, for example IAS2 (SSAP9) – which affects all companies who carry stock, to arcane issues, such as FRS13 – *Derivates and Other Financial Instruments – Disclosures*, which is likely only to affect large companies.

For small companies (i.e. those that are classed as small under the Companies Act 2006) the ASB has issued the Financial Reporting Standard for Smaller Entities (FRSSE) which considerably reduces the volume of accounting standards such companies have to comply with.

Students should also be aware of the Statement of Principles for Financial Reporting (ASB) and/or the Framework for the Preparation and Presentation of Financial Statements (IASB).

The relevance of accounting standards to auditing

As we have seen from the previous chapter auditors must include in their reports, their opinion on whether the financial statements they report on give a true and fair view.

Accounts, to show a true and fair view, must comply with these financial reporting standards, unless circumstances are exceptional. The Companies Act 2006 formally recognised the financial reporting standards and required that accounts should include a statement confirming that the accounts have been prepared in accordance with applicable accounting standards.

Thus auditors are, in effect, being asked to give an opinion on whether all accounting standards have been complied with in the preparation of the accounts they are auditing – which means that auditors must know and understand the accounting standards in detail.

Auditing students are expected to know the main accounting standards in detail. Many auditing questions in examinations require this knowledge and examinees are advised to quote from the accounting standards and state which of the accounting standards are relevant to their answer.

Summary

- The Auditing Practices Board issues ISAs, Practice Notes, Bulletins and other pronouncements.
- The CCAB bodies have undertaken to adopt all ISAs promulgated by the APB.
- Apparent failures by auditors in the UK to comply with the Auditing Standards contained in the ISAs may be investigated and may lead to penalties. The penalties may ultimately include withdrawal of registration in the worst cases.
- The Auditing Standards are likely to be taken into account in a court of law where the adequacy of an auditor's work is being considered, for example if auditors are being proceeded against for the recovery of damages caused by their alleged negligence. All the APB pronouncements are in practice likely to be taken into account in this way.
- The ISAs contain numbered Auditing Standards which are mandatory and also explanatory and other material which is persuasive.
- Accounting standards are essential knowledge for auditing students.
- Amongst the requirements for a true and fair view is compliance with the relevant accounting standards.
- The UITF abstracts are also relevant to auditing students.

Points to note

- Departures from the accounting standards are rare and have to be fully explained.
- SORPs are normally issued with regard to the accounts of specialised bodies (e.g. universities, pension schemes, charities). SORPs are not mandatory but accounts for a body where a relevant SORP exists are unlikely to show a true and fair view if the SORP is not followed. Examiners do not normally expect students to know the SORPs.
- Accounting standards are mandatory except where a true and fair view would not be given which is very unlikely. FREDs and Discussion documents are not mandatory until they have become FRSs but the discussion in them may indicate what present opinion is on what is a true and fair view. However, a present accounting standard must be complied with until it is superseded.

Case Study

Both Cicero Ltd, (from Chapter 4) and Mainbrace Ltd (from Chapter 3) have realised that things cannot go on as they are. They have approached audit firm Tickitt & Run who have agreed to act and are currently setting up a meeting with each company to explain the legal and audit situation.

Discussion
- What will be the key points Tickitt & Run will have to explain to them about auditing standards?
- How will accounting standards, broadly, affect these businesses?
- How would you go about explaining to entrepreneurial management the need for all these auditing and accounting rules?

Student self-testing questions

(Questions with answers apparent from the text)

a) What documents are issued by the APB?

b) What material is contained in a Statement of Auditing Standards?

c) What is a SORP?

d) What is the relevance of FREDs for auditors?

e) In the audit of small companies what accounting standard is specially important?

f) Why are accounting standards important to auditors?

Examination questions

I The profession has been criticised by politicians for its role in monitoring potential corporate failure. Radical reforms have been called for in the way the audit is regulated. For example, politicians have stated there should be a change of legislation in the following ways:

- *Auditing standards*
  Auditing standards should be set and enforced independently from the accounting profession.
- *Fraud*
  Auditing firms should have a duty to detect and report fraud.
- *Non audit services*
  Non auditing services supplied to a client should be stopped.
- *The duration of the appointment of auditors*
  The appointment of auditors should be for a maximum period of seven years.

Required:

a) Describe the current regulatory and professional requirements relating to each of the headings listed above.

b) Discuss the reasons why you feel that the audit profession has been criticised over the current regulation in the above areas.

(ACCA)

6

Rules of professional conduct

INTRODUCTION

Auditing is carried out by accountants in public practice. Accountancy is a profession and professions have certain characteristics including an ethical code and rules of conduct.

This chapter is concerned with the rules of conduct prescribed by the professional accounting bodies.

Questions on professional standards are frequently found in auditing examinations, as examiners see auditing papers as a suitable vehicle for examining ethics, even when they do not specifically relate to auditing.

The rules are found in the handbooks issued to all members of their professional body. Students should be aware of the Ethical Rules of the professional body they are trying to join as these apply to registered students as well as qualified members. In any case there are some generic ethical standards which are included in the ethical codes of all the professional accountancy bodies.

In this chapter we will look at the fundamental ethical principles which underpin the auditor's day-to-day work. Certain specific topics, principally fraud, changes in professional appointments (professional etiquette) and professional liability will be dealt with in separate chapters. Some of these principles are based on the APB Ethical Standard 1 Integrity, Objectivity and Independence.

FUNDAMENTAL PRINCIPLES

These fundamental principles apply to all members of the professional bodies in some form and are the basis for the way auditors carry out their work and in their dealings with other people. Students must have a full understanding of these principles and should conduct their work in accordance with them.

The five Fundamental Principles are:

Integrity

Auditors should behave with integrity in all professional, business and personal financial relationships. Integrity includes not merely honesty but fair dealing, truthfulness, courage, and confidentiality. It is important that directors and management of an audit client can rely on the auditors to treat the information obtained during the audit as confidential, unless they have authorised its disclosure or it is already known to a third party or the auditors have a legal right to disclose it.

Objectivity

Auditors should strive for objectivity in all professional and business judgements.

Objectivity is the state of mind which has regard to all considerations relevant to the task in hand but no other. It presupposes intellectual honesty and excludes bias, prejudice and compromise. Auditors must give fair and impartial consideration to all matters relevant to their task and disregard all those that are not. Objectivity must not be impaired by conflicts of interest.

Independence

Auditors should try and ensure at all times that they do not put themselves in a position where their objectivity might be impaired or be seen to be impaired. It is important that the relationships auditors develop with their clients do not become such that their judgement becomes impaired or, most importantly, a third party may gain the impression that the auditor's objectivity has become compromised.

Competency

Auditors should not accept or perform work which they are not competent to undertake unless they obtain such advice and assistance as will enable them competently to carry out the work. Members should carry out their professional work with due skill, care, diligence and expedition and with proper regard for the technical and professional standards expected of them as members.

Courtesy and consideration

Members should behave with courtesy and consideration to all with whom they come into contact during the course of performing their work.

ETHICS – GENERAL RULES

Professional accountants are required to observe proper standards of professional conduct whether or not the standards required are written in the rules or are unwritten.

Apart from the ethical rules each professional body has for its members the Auditing Practices Board (APB) issues its own ethical standards. These cover broadly the same areas as set out above and also include standards applicable to auditors of smaller companies, which we will refer to in Chapter 30.

Auditors are specifically required to refrain from misconduct, which is difficult to define precisely, but which includes any act or default which is likely to bring discredit on themselves, their professional body or the profession generally.

Several general points can be made:

- Professional independence is exceedingly important. This is very much an attitude of mind rather than a set of rules but there are many rules which we will describe later.
- Integrity is vital. Synonyms for integrity include honesty, uprightness, probity, moral soundness, rectitude. Auditors are required to have the intellectual honesty to come to

their own conclusions and the courage to defend their opinions in the case of any dispute. As we have seen an important aspect of integrity is confidentiality.

- Accountants must not only be people of integrity and independence; they must also be seen to be so. Any interest (e.g. owning shares in a client company) which might diminish an accountant's objectivity of approach or which might appear to, must be avoided.
- When auditors have ethical difficulties or are unsure of what course of conduct to follow, they should consult their professional body or take legal advice. If in doubt always seek advice.

THREATS

Compliance with these fundamental principles may potentially be threatened by a broad range of circumstances. Many threats fall into the following categories:

- Self-interest threats, which may occur as a result of the financial or other interests of a professional accountant or of an immediate or close family member.
- Self-review threats, which may occur when a previous judgement needs to be re-evaluated by the accountant originally responsible for that judgement.
- Advocacy threats, which may occur when an accountant promotes a position or opinion to the point that subsequent objectivity may be compromised.
- Familiarity threats, which may occur when, because of a close relationship, a professional accountant becomes too sympathetic to the interests of others.
- Intimidation threats, which may occur when a professional accountant may be deterred from acting objectively by threats, actual or perceived.

  Safeguards that may eliminate or reduce these sorts of threats to an acceptable level fall into two broad categories:

(a) Safeguards created by the profession, legislation or regulation; and

(b) Safeguards in the work environment.

  Safeguards created by the profession, legislation or regulation include, but are not restricted to:

- Educational, training and experience requirements for entry into the profession.
- Continuing Professional Development.
- Corporate governance regulations.
- Professional standards.
- Professional or regulatory monitoring and disciplinary procedures.

  Safeguards in the work environment include generally avoiding or minimising threats to auditor objectivity and independence. We discuss these in more detail below.

INDEPENDENCE

The auditors' objectivity must be beyond question when conducting an audit. Auditors must always approach their work with integrity and objectivity. The approach must be in a spirit of independence of mind.

There are a number of matters which may threaten or appear to threaten the independence of an auditor. These include:

Undue dependence on an audit client

Public perception of independence may be put in jeopardy if the fees from any one client or group of connected clients exceed 15 per cent of gross practice income or 10 per cent in the case of listed or other public interest companies. This general observation needs modifying in the cases of new practices.

Family or other personal relationships

It is desirable to avoid professional relationships where personal relationships exist. Examples of personal relationships include mutual business interests with members of the group comprising the client, the audit firm, officers or employees of the client, partners or members of staff of the audit firm.

Beneficial interests in shares and other investments

Partners, their spouses, and minor children should not hold shares in or have other investments in client companies. An audit staff member should not be employed on an audit if the staff member or some person connected with him or her has a beneficial interest in the audit client.

Loans to and from clients

An auditing practice or anyone closely connected with it should not make loans to its clients. Overdue fees may in some circumstances constitute a loan. They should not receive loans from clients, unless they are on the same terms as an ordinary member of the public, i.e. on an arm's-length commercial basis. The same applies to guarantees.

Acceptance of goods and services

Goods and services should not be accepted by an audit practice or by anyone closely connected with it unless the value of any benefit is modest. Acceptance of undue corporate hospitality poses a similar threat; a box of chocolates as a gift is probably acceptable, but a weekend in Paris would not be. Acceptance of continuing or excessive corporate hospitality, for example regular attendance at football matches with a client, may well lead to the perception that the auditor's objectivity has been compromised.

Actual or threatened litigation

Litigation or threatened litigation (e.g. on auditor negligence) between a client company and an audit firm would mean the parties being placed in an adversarial situation which clearly undermines the auditor's objectivity.

Influences outside the practice

There is a risk of loss of objectivity due to pressures from associated practices, bankers, solicitors, government or those introducing business.

Provision of other services

This is acceptable in principle, but care must be taken to ensure that the quality of audit work is not compromised because of the urge to cross sell other, more lucrative, services to the client. This topic is continually under review by the professional bodies. It was a contributory factor in several recent financial scandals where the audit firms in question seemed to lose their objectivity and become unnecessarily involved in the affairs of their clients.

COMMISSIONS AND FEES

Auditors should not allow their judgement to be swayed by the receipt of a commission, fee or other reward from a third party as a result of advising a client to pursue one course rather than another. If a commission is to be received the accountant should either give it to the client or, with the client's express or implied consent, retain it. If it is to be retained then the fact of a payment of commission, and the amount or how it is to be calculated, should be disclosed to the client. The client must assent to its retention.

Audit firms should review their relationship with every client on an annual basis to determine if it is proper to accept or continue an audit engagement, bearing in mind actual or apparent threats to audit objectivity.

Warnings are included in the ethical guides of the professional bodies of the risks to objectivity in performing non audit services, but these all fall a long way short of prohibition. The real question is whether an audit firm can offer a totally dispassionate opinion if it and/or an associated firm are supplying services like:

- bookkeeping;
- preparing the annual accounts;
- taxation;
- advice on company secretarial matters;
- management consultancy;
- obtaining staff;
- selecting computer systems;
- litigation support;
- corporate financial advice e.g. on capital raising or takeovers.

Generally the rules require a separation of the staff providing advisory services from those carrying out the audit. There should be a system of what have become known as 'chinese walls' within the accounting firm to ensure that information disclosed in an advisory capacity is not revealed to audit staff and vice versa.

This may seem perverse, but it retains the independence of each set of staff to carry out their defined roles as if they were from separate firms and not merely different departments of the same firm.

This does pose difficulties to very small firms, but they have to find a way of abiding by these principles and retaining their objectivity and independence. In most cases small firms carry out little or no statutory audit work because of the size limits on firms which no longer have to have a statutory audit.

It is understood that the nature of preparing complex accounts must necessarily require that some services (e.g. finalising the financial statements) should be performed by the auditors. However, any such assistance should be solely of a technical or mechanical nature and any advice given must be of an informative nature only.

The auditor can advise on issues but must not take part in making any management decisions. The overriding rule is that the auditor should not be involved in decision-making and, where there is a threat to independence, the risk has to be reduced to an acceptable level.

CONFLICTS OF INTEREST

Conflicts of interest can arise between accountants and their client. Conflicts of interest can also arise between a client and another client, and accountants should not act for both parties if the parties are in dispute.

For example, the accountants may be called upon to advise two clients who are tendering for the same contract; or they may be advising a company and also one of its directors who are in dispute. In all such cases the accountants should not accept assignments where they are put in a position where they are being asked to advise both sides. On the other hand they may well be able to put forward proposals to settle the dispute.

Specific examples of conflict of interest include:

- Provision of other services to audit clients. It is customary for auditors in many cases to provide other services as well as the audit, for example preparing tax computations. This is perfectly acceptable providing the service does not involve performing executive functions or making executive decisions. For example, discussing the annual dividend decision with the board would be an executive action and hence unacceptable.

- Preparation of accounting records. Care should be taken that the client takes responsibility for the work done and that objectivity in auditing is not impaired. The accounting records of public company clients should not be prepared by the auditor.

- A practice should not report on a company if a company associated with the practice is the company secretary to the client. However, it is acceptable to provide assistance to the company secretary.

- No person in an accounting firm should take part in the audit of a company if he or she has, in the accounting period or, it is recommended, in the previous two years been an officer or employee of that company.

  There is no similar rule regarding a senior member of the audit staff or a partner joining an audit client, however, where an individual is indicating an intention to join a client they should be taken away from any involvement with that client's affairs as soon as practicable. Again it is recommended that a 'cooling-off' period be instituted where the individual who proposes to join an audit client is taken away both from the audit and from any possibility of influencing the course of the audit or the audit firm's approach to the audit. The more senior the individual the more problematic this becomes.

  If it is not possible to have any sort of cooling-off period, the audit team should be changed and, if possible, a new audit approach instituted with a different team. The involvement of the former employee should be monitored to ensure there is no question of undue influence being brought to bear on the audit work.

- Receivership, liquidation and audits. In general auditors should not accept receiverships or appointment as a liquidator of client companies without a three year gap between the assignments. Clearly a liquidator of a company would be inhibited from taking a negligence action against the auditor if he had himself been the auditor.

ADVERTISING AND PUBLICITY

There are still considerable restrictions on advertising. Any advertisement should not:

- bring into disrepute themselves, any member of the professional body, the firm or the accountancy profession generally;
- discredit the services of others by for example claiming superiority;
- contain comparisons with other members or firms;
- be misleading, either directly or by implication;
- fall short of the Advertising Standards Authority as to legality, decency, honesty and truthfulness.

Adverts may refer to the basis on which fees are calculated, but this is often best avoided.

Firms must be careful about comparisons with other audit firms to avoid being misleading. Under certain circumstances they may offer free consultations and possibly discounts, but this has to be handled very carefully. Audits may not be carried out free of charge or at a discount!

None of this means that accountants' advertisements need be dull or unimaginative; many firms have put out exciting adverts but whether they are also 'attractive' is a different matter.

Enterprises in all sectors of the economy have sought to reduce costs in recent years. A major cost is the audit fee and other fees paid to the auditor for other work. Many enterprises have asked several firms to tender for the audit and other work. This has led to the practice of 'lowballing' or tendering low to get the work, with the intention to gain extra income by charging the client for additional services.

The practice of 'lowballing' is, generally, prohibited by the regulatory bodies and auditors must be prepared to justify the fees charged to the client in terms of work done, hours spent and rates at which staff are charged out.

There is no evidence that 'lowballing' compromises audit quality as the regulations and the fear of litigation generally ensures that auditors try and deliver a quality service to their client irrespective of the size of the fee charged.

There is a general prohibition on any publicity which would bring accountants, their professional body or the profession, into disrepute.

Accountants may advertise for work and engage in other forms of publicity, for example, by posters or hoardings or on motor vehicles, on sportswear or by sports sponsorship providing that the advertising itself is considered concomitant with the dignity of the profession. Accountants may not make any unflattering references to, or comparisons, with competitors or other professional service providers.

Accountants may pay an introductory commission, fee or reward to a third party for introducing clients, however, it is advisable that such payments are declared to the client.

REMUNERATION

The normal basis for charging for professional work, is on the time spent on the work calculated at appropriate hourly rates for principals, senior and other staff. The hourly rate may vary according to the difficulty or complexity of the work involved. It is up to the accountants to decide upon their hourly rates depending on cost structures, the complexity of the work, the timetable for completion, market conditions, etc.

It is not permissible to charge on a percentage basis except where statute or custom allows, e.g. in liquidation and receivership work, nor should audits be carried out on a contingency fee basis.

A contingency fee is one based on the achievement of some goal or target, for example, a fee based on the successful raising of finance.

It is possible for accountants to charge for non-audit services on a contingency fee basis, however, the basis of charging such fees must be notified to the client in writing and agreed by the client.

Accountants who receive commissions from stockbrokers, insurance brokers, etc. for transactions effected for clients or for trusts of which the accountant is a trustee should either:

- pass on the commissions to the client or trust by deducting the amounts received from their fees and showing the deduction on the invoice; or

- keep the commissions if specifically authorised to do so by the client.

INSIDER DEALING

Insider dealing is illegal. It is also contrary to the ethical rules. People who during the course of their work come across 'unpublished price-sensitive information' are prohibited from dealing in securities to which that information relates.

Unpublished price-sensitive information covers specific matters not generally known to those who normally deal on the Stock Exchange but which, if it were known to them, would alter the prices of those securities to which the information relates.

The prohibition applies to anyone who has a connection at present or had one at any time in the previous six months and to any third person whom the insider may wish to instruct.

Auditors with their close connection with the accounts of a public company client are often in possession of insider information. For example, they may know that the profit is £12 million when the market is expecting only £10 million. They must not take advantage of this information by buying shares in the company on the expectation of a rise in the price when the accounts are published.

MONEY LAUNDERING

Money laundering is the process by which criminals try to conceal the true nature of proceeds of illegal activities. The term includes possessing, in any way dealing with or concealing the proceeds of any crime.

This includes monies generated through tax evasion, bribery and corruption or the operation of gangs involved in more conventional criminal activities, such as drug or people smuggling, illegal arms trading, theft and robbery etc.

The regulations have been extended considerably since the rules on Money Laundering were first introduced by the Criminal Justice Act 1993. In particular, the financing of terrorism has focused government attention internationally and governments are setting in place initiatives whereby they can co-operate globally in an effort to track monies being used to fund terrorist groups.

At present the legislation relating to Money Laundering includes:

- the Criminal Justice Act 1993;

- the Terrorism Act 2000;
- the Proceeds of Crime Act 2002;
- the Money Laundering Regulations 2003.

Firms must appoint a 'Money Laundering Reporting Officer' (MLRO) to deal with the whole matter. The job of the MLRO is to receive and assess reports about suspicious transactions from partners and staff and to make reports to the Serious and Organised Crime Agency (SOCA). The reports must give full details of the suspicious transactions and the identities of the persons involved.

In addition, firms must put in place systems and procedures which fundamentally ensure that staff are aware of their responsibilities under the legislation and that the firm itself has procedures and internal controls which will enable suspicious transactions to be identified and reported in accordance with the regulations.

In particular these should include procedures which ensure that:

- Before accepting an assignment they take all necessary steps to establish that their potential new client is who it claims to be. This can include proof of identity for individual clients and inspecting the company certificate of incorporation.
- If they handle clients' money accountants have controls which ensure that the identity of the client, the commercial purpose of the transaction, the source of the funds and their destination are known and verifiable.
- Staff have training in the regulations and how to identify suspicious transactions.
- The firm has procedures to review client's activities on an ongoing basis.
- 'Suspicious transaction reports' are made to the MLRO should they be identified.
- The MLRO reports these to the SOCA.

Generally firms commit an offence under the regulations if they fail to implement these procedures.

In addition, there are some other offences which can be committed under the regulations which the student should be aware of. These are:

- Attempting, conspiring with or inciting someone to commit an offence.
- Aiding or abetting an offence or advising on the commission of an offence.
- Obtaining, concealing or investing funds or property knowing or suspecting that they are the proceeds of crime or funds for terrorist activity.
- Doing or disclosing anything that might prejudice an investigation into money laundering activities – this is known as 'Tipping off'.
- Proceeding with a transaction without the consent of the relevant authority after having submitted a Suspicious Transaction Report.

SUSPICIOUS TRANSACTIONS

Whilst carrying out their work auditors are expected to be on the alert for suspicious transactions (see Chapter 20). Risk factors which can be associated with such transactions are:

- 'Secret' or 'confidential' transactions which are dealt with outside the main accounting systems, possibly by one individual or a small group. Be aware, however, that secrecy can be associated with commercial confidentiality and be perfectly innocent.

- Routing transactions through tax havens or countries with lax fiscal rules.
- Routing transactions through several countries or institutions.
- Routing transactions through a country different from the one from which the underlying transaction is sourced e.g. services are purported to be bought from Country A but payment is made to a bank in Country B. Note that there may be underlying commercial reasons for this such as foreign currency hedging or even tax evasion by the supplier, but it is suspicious and should be investigated.
- Frequent use of wire transfers or money transfers which do not disclose details of the ultimate recipients of the funds e.g. transfers to overseas lawyers or nominee bank accounts.
- Transactions which involve the use of large amounts of currency or 'bearer' financial instruments (financial instruments which can be cashed by the person who has physical possession of them).
- Large movements of funds in and out of an account on the same day without any apparent commercial reason.
- High value deposits or withdrawals which don't fit the normal patterns of the movement of funds through an account, especially in cash.
- Movement of funds 'through' (i.e. in and straight out again) an account by electronic transfer.

There are two important things for auditors to bear in mind:

- Reporting suspicious transactions to the authorities does not necessarily breach the auditor's duty of confidentiality to their client. Auditors may have a statutory defence under these circumstances.
- Auditors encountering what they think might be a suspicious transaction are in a difficult position. Having knowledge of a transaction may include:
  - actual knowledge;
  - refraining from making enquiries;
  - deterring someone else from making enquiries;
  - closing one's mind to what is obvious and ignoring it.

So auditors should make the sort of reasonable enquiries about a transaction which might be expected of a careful and conscientious professional auditor and carefully note the client's response to their questions.

Having said that auditors must be careful when making enquiries not to 'tip off' their client that they have detected what they think is a suspicious transaction and are going to report it the MLRO and thus, ultimately, to SOCA, as they could be charged with an offence.

As noted 5 above the APB have revised their practice note PN12 in relation to money laundering and the auditor which is a useful source of further advice and information on this topic.

WHISTLEBLOWING

Whistleblowing means informing the proper authorities of some significant breach of law or regulation. It is an issue for employees who feel compelled to tell the proper authorities of some wrong doing by their employers, but fears being dismissed if they do. In this case employees are protected under the Public Interest Disclosure Act 1988.

Employees of companies, who are also members of professional accountancy bodies, may be required by their ethical code, particularly the aspects of it relating to integrity and objectivity, to make reports.

Protections are available if reports are made:

- in the public interest;
- to the proper authority;
- without malice.

Reports to an outside body, such as a regulatory authority, by professional accountants, be they auditors or employees, can be defended against any accusation of breaching client confidentiality as the matter would be in the public interest.

There are additional issues for auditors:

- If auditors become aware of a significant non-compliance they should report it to the directors in the first instance with a recommendation that it be disclosed to the proper authority.
- If the directors don't do that then the auditors should report it, relying on the public interest defence to guard them against accusations of breach of client confidence.
- Breaches of law or regulation may have an impact on the financial statements and the auditors should assess what this effect might be and the disclosures which might be required. This may have an influence on their audit report if suitable disclosures are not made in the financial statements. We will look at this sort of issue later in Chapter 27.

Summary

- The professional bodies require their members and students to behave in an ethical manner.
- There are significant threats to auditor independence. These can be countered by adherence to professional standards and the regulatory regimes of the professional bodies.
- Codes of ethics and conduct are spelt out in detail both by professional bodies and the Auditing Practices Board.
- Independence is of particular importance and detailed guidance is issued to members.
- Auditors become privy to all sorts of information in the course of their work, about both the organisations they audit and the individuals who work for it. Audit staff must regard all such information as totally privileged and not disclose it to third parties except in circumstances where there is a legal right or duty to disclose it. They may not also use such information for personal gain, e.g. by insider trading.
- Partners and staff of audit firms can become so familiar with the management or staff of a client company that they lose their objectivity. This must be avoided, perhaps by rotating the partners and staff involved.

Points to note

- The ethical codes are mandatory, particularly in the area of dealing with clients and the designatory letters accountants may use to describe the services they offer.
- In some areas they give guidance only. For example, in the independence ethical guide, the 15 per cent fees rule is for guidance only, a client giving 10 per cent of gross fees may influence auditors who fear the loss of income if they lose the client.
- In all these ethical matters, accountants must not only behave correctly, they *must be seen* to be behaving correctly.
- Ethics is taken very seriously by professional accountants.
- Professional accountants are not allowed to give investment advice or conduct investment business unless they are authorised to do so by their professional body under the Financial Services Act 1986.
- Independence is a big issue and the practice of accounting firms performing other services for their audit clients is constantly under review, particularly since the collapse of Enron in the USA which revealed the extremely close links the auditors, Arthur Andersen, had with their client and the balance of audit and non-audit fees charged by Andersen to Enron.
- These matters are frequently tested in examinations.

Case Study

Tickitt & Run are auditors of McColl Holdings PLC, a chemical manufacturer. The financial director has left the company recently to take up another post and McColl have so far been unable to find a suitable replacement. They have therefore asked

Tickitt & Run to be responsible for the preparation of the financial statements for the year ending 31 December 20x7 as part of the audit.

McColl have also asked Tickitt & Run to:

- help them help in designing and selecting a new computerised management accounting system;
- assist in finding a new financial director; and
- discuss at a board meeting the dividend to be paid.

The company is also subject to a probable takeover bid and wants Tickitt & Run to act for them in rebutting statements made by the takeover bidder.

During the audit, the audit team find that the company are systematically breaching safety guidelines on chemicals shipped to a developing country and they suspect some bank transactions with an offshore based bank.

Discussion

- What are the ethical implications for Tickitt & Run?
- How far can they ethically go in assisting their client?

Student self-testing questions

a) List the fundamental principles?

b) What general ethical rules are there?

c) What should an accountant do if faced with an ethical dilemma?

d) Enumerate the guidelines to independence.

e) What should an accountant do about commissions?

f) Give examples of areas where conflicts of interest may occur.

g) What restrictions are there on advertising?

h) How can an accountant obtain publicity in an ethical manner?

i) What are the rules on accountants' remuneration?

j) What is insider dealing? What does an audit team member do when they know their mother has shares in Risky PLC and that, whilst on the audit of Risky, they discover that company's new pharmaceutical product of which the market expects much, has been banned as unsafe? An announcement of the ban will be made next week.

k) What is money laundering?

l) What is whistleblowing? When may an auditor inform the proper authorities of a breach of the law?

m) What criteria apply to the decision of auditors as to whether they can assist their client in non-audit ways?

Examination questions

I The objectivity of the external auditor may be threatened or appear to be threatened where:

   (i)   There is undue dependence on any audit client or group of clients.

   (ii)   The firm, its partners or staff have any financial interest in an audit client.

   (iii)   There are family or other close personal or business relationships between the firm, its partners or staff and the audit client.

   (iv)   The firm provides other services to audit clients.

Required:

(a) For each of the four examples given above, explain why the objectivity of the external auditor may be threatened, or appear to be threatened, and why the threat is important.

(b) Describe the ethical requirements that reduce the threats to auditor objectivity for each of the four examples given above.

(ACCA)

2 A waste disposal company has breached tax regulations, environmental regulations and health and safety regulations. The auditor has been approached by the tax authorities, the government body supervising the award of licences to such companies and a trade union representative. All of them have asked the auditor to provide them with information about the company. The auditor has also been approached by the police. They are investigating a suspected fraud perpetrated by the managing director of the company and they wish to ask the auditor certain questions about him.

Required:

Describe how the auditor should respond to these types of request.

(ACCA)

7

Quality control in audit firms

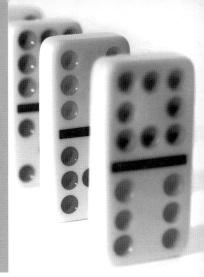

INTRODUCTION

It is of primary importance to the business world in general and to the auditing profession in particular that an audit should be a quality product. Audits should be extremely well done and yet be completed expeditiously and economically.

There is an ISA 220 *Quality Control for Audits of Historical Financial Information.*

This requires that, in all firms, quality control procedures should be introduced that are applicable to the individual audit engagement.

ISA 220 places the responsibility specifically on the audit or engagement partner, who is in charge of the audit, to ensure that all matters in respect of the audit are dealt with properly.

In addition to ISA 220 there is the snappily titled International Standard on Quality Control (ISQC 1) *'Quality Control for Firms that Perform Audits and Reviews of Historical Financial Information and Other Assurance and Related Services Engagements'.* This creates an obligation for the firm to establish a system of quality control to provide reasonable assurance that professional standards and legal requirements are complied with and that any reports issued are appropriate.

All firms issuing reports to clients, whether they are audit reports or reports on other types of assurance engagements, are exposed to risk, i.e. the risk of giving an incorrect or inappropriate opinion in the report. The result of that could be legal action against the firm for damages, adverse publicity and loss of reputation and certainly the loss of the client.

Consequently it is in the interests of the firm to ensure that there are the highest standards of ethical behaviour and full compliance with reporting standards within it.

This chapter deals with quality control under three heads:

- Audit firm organisation.
- Planning, controlling and recording individual audits.
- Reviews of audit firms' procedures in general and of particular audits.

AUDIT FIRM ORGANISATION

It is recognised that each firm has its own needs depending on size, geographical spread, special expertise, etc., but all firms must organise quality control policy and procedures.

These procedures should include:

- Clear designation of leadership responsibilities – to ensure that quality is part of the culture of the firm. This should be the managing or senior partner's responsibility.
- Ethical requirements – ensure that the firm complies with relevant ethical requirements such as those involving audit independence and involvement with clients.
- Acceptance and continuation of relationships with clients – considering the integrity of the clients and whether the firm can continue to supply services at the appropriate level.
- Human resource policies – to ensure that the firm has sufficient staff, of the right levels of competence and commitment to ethical principles to carry out the work required and also to ensure a continuing programme of training and development. These policies should also include performance evaluation, promotion and training needs for individual staff members at all levels.
- Engagement partners should be assigned to each client. They are responsible for quality at the audit or engagement level. Their job is to ensure that there is:
  - a system of written procedures for engagements; and
  - that these are complied with;
  - that each engagement or audit is supervised;
  - all audit work is reviewed; and
  - quality control reviews for each assignment are carried out as appropriate.
- A monitoring system to ensure that quality procedures within the firm are reviewed and that there is a process for recommending improvements. This will include such things as evaluation of standard procedures and reviews of completed assignments (known as 'cold' reviews).

In practical terms this will involve:

- *Control policies and procedures* – each firm should establish and monitor control policies and procedures and communicate these to all partners and staff. Larger firms employ printed manuals but smaller firms may have to rely on verbal instructions and handouts.
- *Acceptance and reappointments as auditor* – there should be a procedure for evaluating prospective clients with consideration of the firm's ability to meet the client's needs and for making the decision on acceptance which may be made by an individual partner, or by a committee.
- *Professional ethics* – procedures to ensure all partners and staff are aware of and adhere to the principles of independence, objectivity, integrity and confidentiality. It is important to instruct staff who are not members of professional bodies and to monitor observance of ethical standards. For example, staff might not be aware of the prohibition on ownership of shares in client companies or may be unwilling to sell them if they are so aware. Consideration should be given to the auditor's independence and ability to serve the client properly and to the integrity of the client's management.
- *Skills and competence* – the object is to have a fully competent and skilled set of partners and staff. Procedures include:
  - *Recruitment* – only of suitably qualified and expert staff. Staffing needs should be planned ahead.
  - *Technical training and updating* – all partners and staff should be encouraged to learn, and to keep up-to-date with technical matters. The firm could provide literature, maintain a technical library, send people on courses and hold courses themselves. Some firms produce a special newsletter at intervals to update staff with

technical developments. All qualified staff should be up to date with Continuing
Professional Development (CPD) requirements.

- *On-the-job training and professional development* – planning, controlling and recording
  emphasises the importance of relating staff abilities to client needs but opportunities should
  also be provided for staff to have adequate experience on a range of clients as on-the-job
  training. Performance of staff should be evaluated and discussed with staff concerned.

- *Consultation* – individual members of the firm should not take decisions on problem
  areas without consultation with others. Problem areas might be technical (e.g. computers
  where expert members of staff should be consulted) or matter of risk evaluation. Sole
  practitioners are advised to consult with other firms or with professional advisory services.

- *Monitoring the firm's quality control procedures* – suitable procedures should be introduced to
  ensure that all procedures are working adequately. This is dealt with in the review section.

INDIVIDUAL AUDITS

ISA 220 deals with quality issues in respect of individual audits. Its purpose is to ensure
audit procedures take into account many of the firm-wide points mentioned above such as:

- Leadership – the audit partner is responsible for quality at the audit level.
- Ethical requirements are met.
- That the client has been reviewed to ensure its integrity.
- That the audit has been planned and performed properly, all procedures documented, all
  work reviewed, staff properly supervised, etc. and that sufficient appropriate evidence
  has been obtained to support the audit opinion.
- That any disputes with the client have been resolved.
- That any consultation on technical issues has been carried out.
- That any 'hot' reviews needed have been carried out (see below).

  The control procedures to be applied to individual audits or assignments include:

- *Allocation of staff* – staff should have appropriate training, experience, proficiency and, if
  required, special skills (e.g. in computing).
- *Proper briefing of staff* – staff should be properly informed on:
    - the nature of the client, its industry and the client's place in it;
    - objectives of the audit;
    - timing;
    - the overall plan of the audit;
    - significant accounting and auditing risk areas;
    - related parties (see Chapter 21);
    - the need to bring problems and enquiry situations to more experienced staff, the
      audit manager or audit partner.
- *Audit completion checklists* – with sections for completion by staff and reporting partner.
  It is a common experience that, in the rush to complete an audit on time, matters of
  importance can be overlooked.
- *Contentious matters* – all problems, special difficulties, and potential qualifications must
  be identified, recorded and discussed by the reporting partner with colleagues or even
  another practitioner.

- *Documentation* – all audit work and conclusions reached must be fully recorded in the working papers – the rule is always 'if it's not documented it doesn't exist'. Recording can be either paper-based records or, of course computer files (see Chapter 18).
- *Reviews* – all audit work must be fully reviewed. This is dealt with in the next section.
- *Sign* – all audit work and review action should be acknowledged in writing by the performer by initialling or signing the working paper.
- *Supervision* – personnel with supervisory responsibilities should monitor the progress of the audit to consider whether:

  - assistants have the necessary skills and competence to carry out their assigned tasks;
  - assistants understand the audit directions; and
  - the work is carried out in accordance with the overall audit plan and the audit programme.

REVIEWS

Hot reviews

Firms should ensure that an independent review (by a partner who is not the engagement partner) is undertaken for all listed company audits. These are known as 'hot' reviews. A hot review should be carried out *during the course of the engagement or audit* (hence the use of 'hot') by a second partner not connected with the audit or assignment and should be applied to all audits of listed companies and a selection of other assignments.

In addition, firms should establish policies setting out the circumstances in which an independent review should be performed for other audits or assignments, whether on the grounds of the public interest or particular audit risk.

The independent review should take place before the audit report is signed so as to provide an objective, independent assessment of the quality of the audit. The policies should set out in detail the manner in which the review is to be performed.

The independent review involves consideration of the following matters in order to assess the quality of the audit.

- the objectivity of the audit engagement partner and key audit staff and the independence of the firm;
- the rigour of the planning process including the analysis of the key components of audit risk identified by the audit team and the adequacy of the planned responses to those risks;
- the results of audit work and the appropriateness of the key judgements made, particularly in high-risk areas;
- the significance of any potential changes to the financial statements that the firm is aware of but which the management of the audited entity has declined to make;
- whether all matters which may reasonably be judged by the auditors to be important and relevant to the directors, identified during the course of the audit, have been considered for reporting to the board of directors and/or the audit committee (or their equivalents); and
- the appropriateness of the draft auditors' report.

Monitoring

Firms should appoint a senior audit partner to take responsibility for monitoring the quality of audits carried out by the firm by means of 'cold reviews' as referred to earlier.

Summary

- Audit work must be planned and controlled.
- This control is implicit in an audit firm's systems and procedures for carrying out audits.
- Audit work must be subject to review before the report is signed.
- Reviews are carried out in practice by a variety of categories of person from inside and, in the case of small firms, outside the firm.
- Reviewers must be independent and objective.

Points to note

- Auditors are under pressure to ensure that audit standards are high because:
    - Publicly aired failure is bad for business.
    - Failure to live up to standards can lead to expensive litigation.
    - Inefficiency is unprofitable.
- Independent review by persons unconnected with the detail of an audit can lead to the discovery that:
    - The firm's procedures are not always followed.
    - There are gaps in the procedures.
    - There are technical matters of general interest which need investigation.
    - There are deficiencies in the quality of the staff or in their training.
- Quality control can be seen in several stages:
    - Proper organisation of the firm and its procedures.
    - Planning for each audit.
    - Control of each audit.
    - Working papers.
    - Review of work done.
    - Review of organisation and procedures.
- It is important to distinguish between procedures designed to ensure the firm, as a whole, provides a high standard product in all professional engagements and procedures to ensure that each individual engagement is properly carried out. A review of an audit may be to sample the effectiveness of the overall procedures or may be to ensure that a particular audit was performed effectively.
- In order to ensure that all that needed to be done on an audit was done, any review should be conducted on the basis of a checklist.
- Drivers of quality include individual responsibilities, collective responsibilities, a quality culture, the collective wisdom of the audit team in resolving difficult or contentious matters, building quality into processes and monitoring the results.

Case Study

In Newtown there are three small firms of qualified accountants and registered auditors who, between them, have most of the large businesses, farmers and landowners and other service providers as clients.

They have heard a rumour that one of the 'Big 4' firms want to set up an office in the town with a view to taking over all their best clients and expanding into the adjacent area.

As a defensive measure they decide to amalgamate their practices and set up as one firm under the name of Tickitt & Run. This will mean merging their offices into one new building and rationalising all their administrative staff and systems, but this can be done relatively painlessly.

Angela Goodbody is one of the senior partners and has been asked to look at the quality standards in the new firm. Previously, as they had all been small firms, they hadn't bothered with formal systems, and if they had an ethical dilemma they had contacted their institute.

Now they feel they have to introduce a new regime.

Discussion

– How should Angela convince her fellow partners this is a good idea and will not just be a costly waste of time?
– What procedures should Angela introduce:

- In the short term?
- Over a longer period?

Student self-testing questions

Questions with answers apparent from the text

a) What are the key aspects of good organisation in an audit firm to ensure quality?
b) What are the responsibilities of the audit partner?
c) What is the difference between a hot review and a cold review and when is each one carried out?
d) What control procedures should be applied to individual audits?

Examination questions

1 'Quality control policies and procedures should be implemented at both the level of the audit firm and on individual audits' – ISA 220 'Quality control for audit work'.

Required:

Describe the nature and explain the purpose of quality control procedures appropriate to the individual audit.

(ACCA)

2 You are an audit manager in Ebony, a firm of Chartered Certified Accountants. Your specific responsibilities include planning the allocation of professional staff to audit assignments. The following matters have arisen in connection with the audits of three client companies:

(a) The Finance Director of Almond, a private limited company, has requested that only certain staff are to be included on the audit team to prevent unnecessary disruption to Almond's accounting department during the conduct of the audit. In particular, that Xavier be assigned as Accountant In Charge (AIC) of the audit and that no new trainees be included in the audit team. Xavier has been the AIC for this client for the last two years.

(b) Alex was one of the audit trainees assigned to the audit of Phantom, a private limited company, for the year ended 31 March 20x7. Alex resigned from Ebony with effect from 30 November 20x7 to pursue a career in medicine. Kurt, another AIC, has just told you that on the day Alex left he told Kurt that he had ticked schedules of audit work as having been performed when he had not actually carried out the tests.

(c) During the recent interim audit of Magenta, a private limited company, the AIC, Jamie, has discovered a material error in the prior year financial statements for the year ended 31 December 20x7. These financial statements had disclosed an unquantifiable contingent liability for pending litigation. However, the matter was settled out of court for $4·5 million on 14 March 20x8. The auditor's report on the financial statements for the year ended 31 December 20x7 was signed on 19 March 20x8. Jamie believes that Magenta's management is not aware of the error and has not drawn it to their attention.

Required:

Comment on the ethical, quality control and other professional issues raised by each of the above matters and their implications, if any, for Ebony's staff planning.

(ACCA)

8

Accepting appointment as auditors

INTRODUCTION

Before accepting an audit engagement accountants should first consider whether or not they can take on the work from an ethical, legal and practical point of view.

Ethical considerations have been dealt with in Chapter 6. For example, an audit firm cannot accept a client where the total value of fees would exceed 15 per cent of the firm's total fee income or where a partner in the firm is closely related to a director of the proposed audit client.

Assuming there are no ethical problems around independence and objectivity there are practical considerations to take into account.

CLIENT SCREENING

When a firm is approached to take over an existing audit from another firm, or is to be appointed as the first auditors they must make some investigations before they accept the appointment.

The ISA 315 *Obtaining an Understanding of the Entity and Assessing the Risks of a Material Misstatement,* requires the auditors to obtain a thorough understanding of the client, its industry and its business environment. We look at this in more detail in Chapter 10.

However, this process begins *before* the client is accepted.

It is incumbent on the incoming auditor to discover all they can about their potential client. This will include:

- Establishing the potential client's business, its products and customer base – what does it actually do?
- Consideration of the potential client's position in its industry and its reputation – is it a reputable company or is it seen as being a bit dubious?
- Consideration of the potential client's management and their ability – is it a new company with inexperienced, perhaps unqualified management or have the senior management long experience in the industry – do they have a successful track record?
- Consideration of the strength of the finance function – does the company have a qualified financial director, is the finance function a part of the business or is it seen as a necessary evil by the operational directors?

- Reviewing the client's financing and capital structure – how is it financed, are there any potential problem areas looming involving repayment of loans or debentures?
- Consideration of any particular legal or special reporting requirements – is it in a highly regulated industry where additional certificates may be required or special reports prepared?

  Sources of information will include:

- Previously published accounts.
- Trade literature and brochures.
- Press and magazine articles.
- The Internet.
- Local knowledge.
- Discussions with the potential client and any detailed information provided by the client in response to enquiries, e.g. management information.

Other considerations

The auditors have to consider:

- Whether or not they have the physical resources to carry out the audit satisfactorily. This includes not only physical locations and availability of staff, but also whether or not any specific expertise, e.g. computer auditing is required.
- Any potential conflicts of interest – does the firm represent any other client connected with the potential new one?
- If there are any considerations which must be taken into account in connection with possibilities of money laundering, insider dealing or any other dubious activities.

PROFESSIONAL ETIQUETTE

If the organisation already has an auditor who is ceasing to act, i.e. one firm is replacing another, the professional bodies require the new auditor to communicate with the previous auditor.

The professional bodies have specific rules which their members must follow.
These are:

- A member (of a professional body) on being asked to act as auditor should request the client's permission to communicate with the previous auditor (if there is one).
- If this permission is refused, the firm must refuse the appointment as auditor.
- If permission is given the firm should request, in writing:
  - confirmation that there is no professional reason why the appointment may not be accepted;
  - any information required to enable them to decide whether or not they are prepared to accept the appointment.
- Members receiving such a request should, in turn, request the client's permission to discuss the client's affairs with the proposed new auditor.
  - If this permission is refused, the outgoing auditor will inform the new auditor who will then refuse the appointment.

- If permission is given then the old auditor:

  - Confirms that there is no professional reason why the appointment cannot be accepted
  - Discloses to the proposed auditor all information which they will need to decide whether or not to accept the appointment.
  - Discusses freely with the new auditor all matters relevant to the appointment which the new auditor will need to know.

The reasons for this are:

- It is a matter of courtesy between professionals.
- It enables the proposed auditors to know if it is proper for them to accept the appointment. If, for example, the outgoing auditors are in dispute with the client over unpaid fees, or they feel they are being dumped in favour of a new firm which might be more amenable to signing an audit report and asking fewer questions, this is the opportunity for the outgoing auditors to say so.
- It safeguards the position of the retiring auditors who can express any reservations they may have.
- It protects the shareholders and others interested in the final accounts.

The next step, assuming all the formalities are completed and there are no problems regarding the appointment, is to agree a letter of engagement with the client. This sets out the agreement between the auditor and the client. We look at these in a later section of this chapter.

The new auditors must also confirm that they have been properly and legally appointed. They do this by examining the minute books of meetings at which they were appointed and placing a copy of the appropriate minute on a new Permanent File (Chapter 18). In companies these minutes will be of the company in general meeting, if they were appointed at the AGM or meetings of the directors if the appointment is to fill a casual vacancy or is between AGMs – see Chapter 3.

LETTERS OF ENGAGEMENT

Before commencing any professional work, an accountant should agree, in writing, the precise scope and nature of the work to be undertaken. This is done through the medium of an Engagement Letter.

The Engagement Letter forms the basis of a legally binding contract between the auditors and their client. If the auditors carry out their work in a negligent manner it is on the basis of this letter that the client may well sue them.

There is an International Standard on Auditing (ISA210) '*Terms of Audit Engagements*' which governs the form and content of such letters.

This states:

The auditor and the client should agree on the terms of the engagement. The agreed terms should be recorded in an audit engagement letter or other suitable form of contract.

Purposes

The purpose of the Engagement Letter is:

- to set out the basis on which the firm is to act as auditors and the respective responsibilities of the auditors and the directors;

- to minimise misunderstandings between auditor firm and client;
- to set out the scope of the work to be carried out and the nature and extent of the audit procedures to be carried out;
- to set out details of any other services the audit firm is to carry out, e.g. preparation of tax computations;
- to set out the basis on which fees will be charged;
- to set out which legal jurisdiction the agreement is made under and the process of arbitration of any disputes;
- to confirm acceptance by both the client and the auditor of the terms of the engagement.

When to send an Engagement Letter

Engagement letters should be sent:

- To all new clients *before* any professional work has been started.
- To all existing clients who have not previously had such a letter.
- Whenever there is a change of circumstances (e.g. extra duties to be performed or a major change in ownership or management of the client) or any change in the audit firm (e.g. merger, change of name). The engagement letter should be reviewed every year to see if there is a need for a revised letter.
- In the case of groups an engagement letter should be sent to each member company of the group that is to be audited by the firm. If a standard letter is satisfactory, then a letter can be sent to the group board requesting that it be copied to all group members to be audited by the firm and that acknowledgement be received from all of them.

   This should be carried out before any audit work is commenced in the case of a new client or before the current audit starts in the case of an existing client.
   Auditors must:

- On or before acceptance of a new client, discuss the precise terms with the directors and review the draft of the letter with the client.
- Sign the letter before commencing any part of the assignment and send two copies to the client. One copy has an acceptance confirmation which the client is required to sign and return to the auditors.
- Acceptance of the audit appointment should be confirmed by the directors at a formal meeting and the signing of the acceptance of the terms of the Engagement Letter should be minuted.
- When the signed letter is returned by the client the auditor should keep it safely and place a copy of it on the Permanent File.
- Every year review the letter and consider if revision is necessary.

Principal contents

The letter should outline the clients' statutory duties (e.g. on accounting records) and the auditors' statutory (e.g. to report) and professional responsibilities (e.g. to follow the auditing standards).

The sections may include:

- The Board's responsibilities regarding proper accounting records and for financial statements to show a true and fair view and comply with the Act. Also the Board's responsibility to make available to the auditors all the accounting records, other relevant records and related information and minutes of meetings.
- The auditor's responsibility to report on the financial statements and on the consistency of the directors' report.
- the auditors' planning of the audit to have a reasonable expectation of discovering fraud or material misstatements in the accounts, including a statement in respect of non-reliance on the auditor to uncover irregularities and frauds.
- The scope of the auditor's work including reference to:

  - auditing standards;
  - accounting systems review;
  - collection of audit evidence;
  - tests and reliance on internal controls;
  - the sending of a letter of weakness to the management (Chapter 28).

- Any special factors:

  - relations with the internal auditors; if any
  - audit of divisions or branches;
  - any overseas location problems;
  - relationships with other auditors if any.

- Significant reliance on supervision of the directors in small proprietary companies.
- The need for a letter of representation (Chapter 25) from the management.
- Any agreement for the auditor to provide taxation services or work of a bookkeeping or accounting nature – this could also be a separate letter.
- The fees and the basis on which they are charged.

An example of an Engagement Letter is included in Appendix 1

Summary

- Apart from ethical considerations auditors must ensure they have the resources to carry out the work for the proposed client and the fee charged is not excessive.
- Potential auditors should attempt to find out all they can about their client before accepting the assignment.
- There is a procedure involving communication with any outgoing auditors which must be followed.
- All assignments given to accountants should be subject to an Engagement Letter agreeing the terms of the assignment with the client.
- ISA 210 governs this subject.

Points to note

- The letter of engagement is central to agreeing the basis on which audit firms act for their clients and all services which auditors perform for clients should be on the basis of detailed, written instructions.
- Students should look for opportunities to put 'agree a letter of engagement' in many answers.

Case Study

Juliet B a partner in Tickitt & Run, Registered Auditors, receives a telephone call from the managing director of Chateaubriand Ltd which runs a chain of restaurants and bars. They wish to appoint Tickitt & Run as auditors as they have a disagreement with the existing auditors. The audit would be due to commence in about two months time.

Discussion
- What should Juliet B consider before accepting the appointment?
- What matters should be discussed at the meeting?
- In the light of the first question draft an engagement letter.
- What might be the consequences of omissions from the letter?

Student self-testing questions

Questions with answers apparent from the text

(a) List the purposes of an engagement letter.

(b) What are the procedures connected with engagement letters?

(c) List the principal contents.

(d) Write out an engagement letter for a public company client.

Examination question

1 Viswa is a company that provides call centre services for a variety of organisations. It operates in a medium-sized city and your firm is the largest audit firm in the city. Viswa is owned and run by two entrepreneurs with experience in this sector and has been in existence for five years. It is expanding rapidly in terms of its client base, the number of staff it employs and its profits. It is now 15 June 20x7 and you have been approached to perform the audit for the year ending 30 June 20x7. Your firm has not audited this company before. Viswa has had three different firms of auditors since its incorporation.

Viswa's directors have indicated to you informally that the reason they wish to change auditors is because of a disagreement about certain disclosures in the financial statements in the previous year. The directors consider that the disagreement is a trivial matter and have indicated that the company accountant will be able to provide you with the details once the audit has commenced. Your firm has explained that before accepting the appointment, there are various matters to be considered within the firm and other procedures to be undertaken, some of which will require the co-operation of the directors.

Your firm has other clients that operate call centres. The directors have asked your firm to commence the audit immediately because audited accounts are needed by the bank by 30 July 20x7. Your firm is very busy at this time of year.

Required:

(a) Describe the matters to consider within your firm and the other procedures that must be undertaken before accepting the appointment as auditor to Viswa.

(b) Explain why it would be inappropriate to commence the audit before consideration of the matters and the procedures referred to in (a) above have been completed.

(c) Explain the purpose of an engagement letter and list its contents.

(ACCA)

9

Accounting systems and internal controls

ACCOUNTING SYSTEMS

Introduction

The management of an enterprise needs complete and accurate accounting and other records because:

- the business cannot otherwise be controlled;
- day-to-day records of debtors and creditors are indispensable;
- assets can only be safeguarded if a proper record of them is made;
- financial statements which are required for numerous purposes can only be prepared if adequate primary records exist;
- statutes (e.g. the Companies Act) often have specific requirements on record keeping for specific types of business;
- record keeping for PAYE, NI, VAT, statutory sick pay and statutory maternity pay is a statutory requirement.

What constitutes an adequate system of accounting depends on the circumstances. A small company may use a bespoke accounting package from one of the many suppliers of accounting software but a large international company clearly needs rather more sophisticated records.

The basic need of a system is that it provides for the orderly assembly of accounting information to enable the financial statements to be prepared but all the other requirements of an accounting system must be borne in mind.

For auditing purposes we tend to concentrate on the financial accounting systems, the cash book, sales, purchase and nominal ledgers etc. but auditors should be aware that organisations often combine their financial accounting with management accounting, which includes budget and costing information etc.

This enables auditors to obtain much more detailed information about the business, its financial performance, its weak areas and its strong, than the financial accounts alone may be able to provide. In addition, cost information and management accounts will assist not simply with audit tasks such as stock valuation but also in the carrying out of analytical procedures (Chapter 12).

The need for controls over the system

A system of accounting and record keeping will not succeed in completely and accurately processing all transactions unless controls, known as internal controls, are built into the system. The purposes of such internal controls are:

- to ensure transactions are executed in accordance with proper general or specific authorisation;
- to ensure all transactions are promptly recorded at the correct amount, in the appropriate accounts and in the proper accounting period so as to permit preparation of financial statements in accordance with relevant legislation and accounting standards;
- to ensure access to assets is permitted only in accordance with proper authorisation;
- to ensure recorded assets are compared with the existing assets at reasonable intervals and appropriate action is taken with regard to any differences;
- to ensure errors and irregularities are avoided or made apparent.

INTERNAL CONTROLS

Introduction

This part considers the auditors' approach to internal control systems as outlined in ISA 315 'Understanding the Entity and its Environment and Assessing the Risks of a Material Misstatement' and then considers what internal control is and gives a detailed review of internal control in specific areas. At the end we take a look at the ideas on control environment and control procedures and consider the limitations of internal control.

The auditor and internal control

As we have seen, ISA 315 requires auditors to obtain an understanding of the internal control sufficient to plan the audit and develop an effective audit approach.
   This includes:

- using the understanding of internal control to identify types of potential misstatements;
- considering factors that affect the risks of potential misstatements; and
- designing the nature, timing and extent of audit procedures.

   ISA 315 is based on the idea that internal control is not simply a set of procedures and checks but instead includes a whole range of activities and attitudes.
   Internal control consists of the following:

- The control environment.
- The risk assessment processes.
- The information system, including the related business processes, relevant to financial reporting and communication.
- Control activities.
- Monitoring of controls.

   We will look at these, individually, in more detail later.
   Clearly smaller and less complex organisations will have less complex systems. They may not, for example, have detailed written procedures, or formal risk assessment policies;

in owner managed businesses the owner/manager may well be directly involved in internal control matters which, in larger organisations, would be the responsibility of accountants, managers or internal auditors.

Within the organisation there will be many and various controls of many and various aspects of the organisation's activities. It is important to understand that the ones the auditor is interested in are the ones which relate to the objective of preparing accounts which are true and fair. This will, primarily, centre around the financial system and the control of assets and liabilities as well as some of the controls involved in the risk management processes of the organisation.

Some internal controls used for management control purposes are not immediately relevant to the audit. For example, a company may have controls designed to prevent excessive use of materials in production, or controls designed to make operations efficient, such as an airline's automated controls to maintain flight schedules. These are not directly relevant to a financial statement audit.

The auditor must exercise professional judgement in deciding whether a control, or series of controls, are relevant and should be tested. Included in that decision-making process will be judgements which involve

- the size of the business;
- its nature, including its ownership and how it is organised;
- how diverse and complex its operations are;
- the legal and regulatory framework it operates within;
- the nature and complexity of the financial and management systems;
- the level of materiality or significance of the transactions being controlled (Chapter 10) – which the auditor will have set at the planning stage.

What the auditors are trying to do is to make judgements about the efficiency and reliability of the internal control systems and the risks involved should it fail, so that the audit effort can be concentrated in areas of highest risk and where the systems are most vulnerable.

The auditor has to obtain a full understanding of how the controls work and how effective they are in preventing misstatements and detecting errors. They do this by:

- asking questions of managers and staff;
- observing controls in operation;
- inspecting documents and reports;
- tracing transactions thorough the system.

We deal with this in detail in Chapter 10. However, one important thing for the student to understand is that *understanding* the controls is not the same as *testing* the controls. Auditors use their knowledge of the systems and controls to design their audit procedures for the testing of the system and its controls.

Students need to understand the integrated nature of the accounting system and the internal controls which are built into it.

There are five key aspects to internal control:

The control environment

This includes the attitudes, awareness and actions of the directors and senior managers of the organisation. It is, in effect, the culture of the organisation insofar as it relates to internal control and is part of the Corporate Governance framework (Chapter 2).

It includes:

- The fostering and communication of a culture of honesty and ethical behaviour throughout the organisation.
- A commitment to competence – to training and maintaining the appropriate levels of skill and knowledge.
- Management's philosophy and operating style, their approach to risk and attitudes toward correct financial reporting.
- The organisation structure.
- The involvement of non-executive directors in the audit process – we discuss this further in Chapter 2.
- The human resource policies – recruitment, training, evaluation, promotion, and rewarding of staff.

The auditor must assess the control environment, and ensure that the policies and procedures which are part of it are actively being implemented. This will form part of the routine audit tests which we will look at later.

The risk assessment process

We look at this in more detail in Chapter 14 when we discuss business risk and the business risk approach to auditing. Suffice to say now that the auditor should review the organisation's approach to business risk, or at least those relevant to financial reporting and assess what, if any, impact these are likely to have on the financial accounts.

The auditor will look at:

- How management identifies business risks relevant to financial reporting.
- How management estimates the significance of those risks.
- How management assesses the likelihood of their occurrence.
- What actions they decide to take in respect of the risks they have identified.

Once again we are only concerned with the risks which affect financial reporting.

Operational risks, for example, the risk of loss of customers due to competition or risks posed by the potential loss of a key supplier, are not directly relevant to the audit of the financial statements; however, the risk of fraud or the risk of non-compliance with laws and regulations is directly relevant so how management identifies and deals with these types of risk is something the auditors have to review.

The information system

The auditor has to obtain a full understanding of the information system and the related business processes.

This includes:

- The classes of transaction in the organisation's operations which are significant to the financial systems.
- The procedures, both IT and manual, which are used to record those transactions.
- The related accounting records, whether electronic or manual and the supporting information used to initiate, record, process and report transactions.
- How the systems work.
- The process by which the organisation prepares its financial statements.

We look at auditing using IT in more detail in Chapter 17.

Control activities

These are the detailed policies and procedures that help ensure that management directives are carried out, for example, that necessary actions are taken to address the risks that threaten achievement of the organisation's objectives.

Monitoring of controls

It is important to understand that the management should not be using the external auditors as the vehicle for monitoring the effectiveness or otherwise of their system of internal control.

They should have their own procedures which might take the form of:

- Internal audit – carried out by specialist internal auditors.
- Senior management review – where senior managers perform audit-type tests on selected parts of the system.
- Analysis of the results by applying analytical procedures to, say, monthly management accounts and detecting anomalies or areas for investigation.

CONTROL PROCEDURES

This is a critical part of auditing which the student must fully understand. These are frequently the basis of examination questions and a failure to understand what constitutes good control procedures will undermine your work in the rest of this book.

Examples of specific control procedures are:

- **S**egregation of duties
- **O**rganisational controls
- **A**uthorisation and approval
- **P**hysical controls
- **S**upervision
- **P**ersonnel
- **A**rithmetical procedures
- **M**anagement.

You can remember these through the mnemonic *SOAPSPAM.*
Let's look at these in more detail.

Segregation of duties

- This is the most important single control activity and is the key to good system and procedure design. What it means is that *no one person should be responsible for the recording and processing of a complete transaction.*
- The involvement of several people reduces the risk of intentional manipulation or accidental error and increases the element of checking of work.
- An example of how a given transaction should be separated is:
  - initiation (e.g. the works foreman decides the firm needs more lubricating oil);
  - authorisation (the works manager approves the purchase);

- execution (the buying department order the oil);
- receipt (on arrival the oil is taken in by the goods-in section and passed with appropriate goods-in documentation to the stores department);
- recording (the arrival is documented by the goods inward section and the invoice is compared with the original order and goods-in note by the accounts department, and recorded by them in the books).

- Another example is the area of sales where initiation is by a sales executive, authorisation by credit control and the sales manager, execution is by the finished goods warehouse staff who physically send the goods, custody is transferred from the warehouse staff to the transport department, and the transaction is recorded by the goods outward section, the invoicing section and the accounts department.

Organisational controls

An enterprise should have a plan of organisation which should:

- Define and allocate responsibilities – every function should be in the charge of a specified person who might be called the responsible official. Thus, the administration of the accounts department should be entrusted to a particular person who is then responsible (and hence answerable) for that function.
- Identify lines of reporting both upwards and downward through the organisation, and where appropriate, across it as well.

  In all cases, the delegation of authority and responsibility should be clearly specified. Employees should always know the precise powers delegated to them, the extent of their authority and to whom they should report. Two examples:

  - Responsibility for approving the purchase of items of plant may be retained by the directors for items over £X and within the competence of the works manager for a budgeted amount agreed by the board up to a total less than this.
  - Responsibility for the correct operation of internal controls may be delegated by the board to specific management personnel and to the internal audit department.

Authorisation and approval

All transactions should require authorisation or approval by an appropriate person. The limits to these authorisations should be specified.
  Examples of such procedures are:

- All credit sales must be approved by the credit control department.
- All overtime must be approved by the factory manager.
- All individual office stationery purchases may be approved by the office manager up to a limit of £x. Higher purchases must be approved by the chief accountant.

  Remembering the principle of segregation of duties outlined earlier it should not, for example, be the case that the individual who has authority to say, set up a new supplier's account in the purchase ledger is also responsible for authorising invoices from that supplier and approving payment to them.
  That opens the door to a particular kind of fraud – the creation of a fictitious supplier. Auditors should always, when reviewing use of authorisations and authorities as system controls, also look at what else those individuals are allowed to do and how they do it.

Physical controls

These are such things as physical custody of assets and involves procedures designed to limit access to assets and systems to authorised personnel only.

These controls are especially important in the case of valuable, portable, exchangeable or desirable assets. Examples of physical controls are:

- use of passes to restrict access to a warehouse;
- locks or keypads on doors;
- use of passwords to restrict access to particular computer files;
- hierarchical menus for computer operators.

Supervision

All actions by all levels of staff should be supervised. The responsibility for supervision should be clearly laid down and communicated to the person being supervised.

Personnel

Procedures should be designed to ensure that personnel operating a system are competent and motivated to carry out the tasks assigned to them, as the proper functioning of a system depends upon the competence and integrity of the operating personnel.

Measures include appropriate remuneration and promotion and career development prospects, selection of people with appropriate personal characteristics and training, and assignment to tasks of the right level.

Arithmetical procedures

These are the controls in the recording function which check that the transactions are all included and that they are correctly recorded and accurately processed.

Procedures include checking the arithmetical accuracy of the records, the maintenance and checking of totals, reconciliations, control accounts, trial balances, accounting for documents (sometimes known as sequence checks or continuity checks). Examples include:

- bank reconciliations;
- control accounts;
- reconciliations of suppliers statements with purchase ledger accounts;
- checking the calculations on purchase invoices.

Management

These are controls, exercised by management, which are outside and over and above the day-to-day routine of the system. They include overall supervisory controls, review of management accounts, comparisons with budgets, internal audit and any other special review procedures.

Examples are:

- Senior management must be aware of day-to-day activities and be seen by staff to be so. Glaring failures of control (stock thefts, excess stocking, unnecessary overtime) will become apparent and staff will be motivated to perform well.

- Management accounts should be designed to summarise performance in detail. Any anomalies (cost overruns, higher than budgeted wastage levels) should become apparent.
- Budgeting and variance analysis is a management tool which should prevent or at least detect departure from management's intended plans.

Individuals performing control activities should acknowledge their checking by means of signatures, initials, rubber stamps, etc. For example, if invoice calculations have to be checked, the checker should initial some kind of posting slip attached to the invoice to indicate that this check has been carried out.

If a control procedure is not evidenced it cannot be proved to have been performed. Auditors will look for this evidence of performance as part of their audit procedures.

CONTROL ACTIVITIES IN SPECIFIC AREAS OF A BUSINESS

This section is divided up into the areas of activity usually found in a business. We look at the *control objectives* in each area and some example of control procedures which will enable the organisation to achieve those objectives.

Students should be familiar with the term 'control objectives' which is fairly self explanatory and simply refers to what the control procedure is designed to do.

Internal control generally
Control objectives
- to carry on the business in an orderly and efficient manner;
- to ensure adherence to management policies;
- safeguard its assets; and
- secure the accuracy and reliability of the records.

Control procedures
- An appropriate and integrated system of accounts and records.
- Internal controls over those accounts and records.
- Financial supervision and control by management, including budgetary control, management accounting reports, and interim accounts.
- Safeguarding and, if necessary, duplicating records.
- Engaging, training, allocating to specific duties staff who are capable of fulfilling their responsibilities. Rotation of duties and cover for absences.

Purchases and creditors system
Control objectives
- To ensure that goods and services are only ordered in the quantity, of the quality, and at the best terms available after appropriate requisition and approval.
- To ensure that goods and services received are inspected and only acceptable items are accepted.

- To ensure that all invoices are checked against authorised orders and receipt of the goods and services in good condition.
- To ensure that all goods and services invoiced are properly recorded in the books.

Control procedures

- There should be procedures for the requisitioning of goods and services only by specified personnel on specified forms with space for acknowledgement of performance.
- Order forms should be pre-numbered and kept in safe custody. Issue of blank order form books should be controlled and recorded.
- Order procedures should include requirements for obtaining tenders, estimates or competitive bids.
- Sequence checks of order forms should be performed regularly by a senior official and missing items investigated.
- All goods received should be recorded on goods received notes (preferably pre-numbered) or in a special book.
- All goods should be inspected for condition and agreement with order and counted on receipt. The inspection should be acknowledged. Procedures for dealing with rejected goods or services should include the creation of debit notes (pre-numbered) with subsequent sequence checks and follow-up of receipt of suppliers' credit notes.
- At intervals, a listing of unfulfilled orders should be made and investigated.
- Invoices should be checked for arithmetical accuracy, pricing, correct treatment of VAT and trade discount, and agreement with order and goods-in records.
- These checks should be acknowledged by the performer preferably on spaces marked by a rubber stamp on the invoices.
- Invoices should have consecutive numbers put on them and batches should be pre-listed.
- Purchase invoices should be pre-listed before entry into the accounting system and the pre-list total compared independently with the total of the invoices entered into the system.
- Totals of entries in the invoice register or day book should be regularly checked with the pre-lists.
- Responsibility for purchase ledger entries should be vested in personnel separate from personnel responsible for ordering, receipt of goods and the invoice register.
- The purchase ledger should be subject to frequent reconciliations in total by, or be checked by, an independent senior official.
- Ledger account balances should be regularly compared with suppliers' statements of account.
- All goods and service procurement should be controlled by budgetary techniques.
- Orders should only be placed that are within budget limits. There should be frequent comparisons of actual purchases with budgets and investigation into variances.
- Cut-off procedures at the year end are essential.
- A proper coding system is required for purchase of goods and services so that the correct nominal accounts are debited.

Payments

Control objective

To prevent unauthorised payments being made from bank accounts.

Control activities

- Control over custody and issue of unused cheques. A register should be kept if necessary.
- Individuals responsible for the preparation of cheques or credit transfers should be different to the individuals who process invoices and enter them into the purchase ledger system.
- Rules should be established for the presentation of supporting documents before cheques, cheque requisitions or payment lists are to be signed. Such supporting documents may include invoices, a copy of the payroll, purchase account reconciliations, aged creditors listings, etc.
- Establishment of who can sign cheques. All cheques should be signed by at least two persons, with no person being permitted to sign if they are a payee.
- All cheques should be restrictively crossed.
- The signing of blank cheques must be prohibited.
- Special safeguards should be implemented where cheques have pre-printed signatures including controls over unused and spoilt cheques.
- Rules to ensure prompt despatch and to prevent interception or misappropriation.
- Special rules for authorising and checking direct debits and standing orders.

Wages and salaries

Objectives

- To ensure that wages and salaries are paid only to actual employees at authorised rates of pay.
- To ensure that all wages and salaries are computed in accordance with records of work performed whether in respect of time, output, sales made or other criteria.
- To ensure that payrolls are correctly calculated.
- To ensure that payments are made only to the correct employees.
- To ensure that payroll deductions are correctly accounted for and paid over to the appropriate third parties.
- To ensure that all transactions are correctly recorded in the books of account.

Control procedures

- There should be separate records kept for each employee. The records should contain such matters as date of employment, age, next of kin, agreed deductions, skills, department, and specimen signature. Ideally these records should be maintained by a separate HR department.
- Procedures for employment, retirements, dismissals, fixing and changing rates of pay. Procedures should be laid down for notification of these matters to the personnel and payroll preparation departments.
- Time records should be kept for hourly paid staff or staff on time based payments (e.g. part-time staff) as opposed to a regular monthly salary. These can take the form of clock

cards or electronic swipe cards. There should be supervision of the time recording system to ensure that staff do not abuse the system by getting other staff to clock them in or out.

- Time records should be approved before preparation of salaries and wages. All overtime should be authorised.

- Output or piecework records should be properly controlled and authorised and procedures should exist for reconciling output or piecework records with production records.

- Procedures should be established for dealing with advances, holiday pay, lay-off pay, new employees, employees leaving, sickness and other absences and bonuses.

- Starters and leavers should be dealt with by the HR department and details passed to payroll separately. These should be followed up to ensure that leavers have been removed from the payroll and starters brought on at the correct time for the correct amount.

- The payroll should be approved by a senior official prior to wages being paid. If this is not practical arrangements should be made for managers to confirm the employees entered on the payroll at fixed dates to ensure only bona fide employees are being paid.

- Deductions such as PAYE, National Insurance, pension contributions and other authorised deductions should be subject to prompt payment over to the institutions concerned. Control totals subject to frequent review should be kept.

- Regular independent comparisons should be made between personnel records and wages records, in particular direct bank transfer (such as BACS payments) lists.

- Regular independent comparisons of payrolls at different dates and reconciliation of numbers.

- Regular independent comparisons of wages paid with budgets and investigation of variances.

- Surprise investigation of wage records and procedures by internal audit or senior officials.

- A wages supervisor should be appointed to be responsible for settling queries and dealing with some control procedures.

Sales and debtors

Control objectives

- To ensure that all customers orders are promptly executed.

- To ensure that sales on credit are made only to bona fide good credit risks.

- To ensure that all sales on credit are invoiced, that authorised prices are charged and that before issue all invoices are completed and checked as regards price, trade discounts and VAT.

- To ensure that all invoices raised are entered in the books.

- To ensure that all customers' claims are fully investigated before credit notes are issued.

- To ensure that every effort is made to collect all debts.

- To ensure that no unauthorised credits are made to debtors accounts.

Control procedures

- Incoming orders should be recorded, and if necessary, acknowledged, on pre-numbered order forms. Orders should be matched with invoices and lists prepared at intervals of outstanding orders for management action. Sequence checks should be made regularly to ensure no orders are missing.

- Credit control. There should be procedures laid down for verifying the credit worthiness of all persons or institutions requesting goods on credit. For existing customers, credit worthiness data should be kept up-to-date and checks made that outstanding balances plus a new sale does not cause the pre-set credit limit to be exceeded. For new customers, investigative techniques should be applied including enquiry of trade protection organisations, credit rating agencies, referees, the company's file with the Registrar of Companies, etc. A credit limit should be established. This may be fixed at two levels, a higher one such that further sales are not made and a lower one such that management are informed and a judgement made on granting credit.

- Selling prices should be prescribed. Policies on credit terms, trade and cash discounts, and special prices should be established and communicated to all the relevant staff in writing.

- Despatch of goods should only be on properly evidenced authority. Goods out should be recorded by using pre-numbered despatch notes.

- Unissued sets of despatch notes should be safeguarded and issues of sets recorded.

- Sequence checks of despatch notes should be made regularly by a senior official.

- Acknowledgement of receipt of goods should be made by customers on copy despatch notes and these should be retained as proof of delivery.

- Invoicing should be carried out by a department or staff separate from the department processing invoices and collecting sales receipts.

- Invoices should be pre-numbered and the custody and issue of unused invoices controlled and recorded. Sequence checks should be regularly made and missing or spoiled invoices investigated.

- All invoices should be independently checked for agreement with customer order, with the goods despatched record, for pricing, discounts, VAT and other details. All actions should be acknowledged by signature or initials.

- Accounting for sales and debtors should be segregated by employing different staff for sales receipts, from those responsible for invoices, sales ledger entries and statement preparation.

- Sales invoices should be pre-listed before entry into the accounting system and the pre-list total independently compared with the total of the invoices entered into the system.

- Customer claims should be recorded and investigated. Similar controls (e.g. pre-numbering) should be applied to credit notes. At the year end, uncleared claims should be carefully investigated and assessed. All credit notes should be subject to acknowledged approval by a senior official.

- A control account should be regularly and independently prepared.

- Procedures must exist for identifying and chasing slow payers. This is normally done via an aged debtors listing. Very overdue balances should be brought to the attention of management for legal or other action to be taken.

- All balances must be reviewed regularly to identify and investigate overdue accounts, debtors paying by instalments or round sums, and accounts where payments do not match invoices.

- Bad debts should only be written off after due investigation and acknowledged authorisation by senior management.

- Also at the year end, cut off procedures will be required. Particular attention will be paid to orders despatched but not invoiced.

Cash sales and collections

Control objectives

- To ensure that all cash, to which the enterprise is entitled, is received.
- To ensure that all such cash is properly accounted for and entered in the records.
- To ensure that all such cash is deposited promptly and intact in the bank.

Control activities

- Prescribe and limit the number of persons who are authorised to receive cash, e.g. sales assistants, cashiers, collectors, sales representatives, etc.
- Establish a means of evidencing cash receipts, e.g. pre-numbered duplicate receipt forms, cash registers with sealed till rolls. Any duplicate receipt form books should be securely held and issue controlled.
- Ensure that customers are aware that they must receive a receipt form or ensuring that the amount rung up on the cash register is clearly visible to the customer.
- Appoint persons with responsibility for emptying cash registers at prescribed intervals, and agreeing the amount present with till roll totals or internal registers. Such collections should be evidenced in writing and be initialled by the assistant and the supervisor.
- Immediate and intact banking. Payments out should be from funds drawn from the bank using an imprest system.
- Investigation of 'shorts' and 'overs' in excess of an agreed limit should be carried out promptly.
- Independent comparison of agreed till roll totals with subsequent banking records.
- Persons handling cash should not have access to other cash funds or to purchase or sales ledger records.
- Rotation of duties and cover for holidays (which should be compulsory) and sickness.
- Collections by collectors and sales representatives should be banked intact daily. There should be independent comparison of the amounts banked with records (e.g. duplicate receipt books) of the collectors and sales staff.

Payments into bank

Control objectives

- To ensure that all cash and cheques received are banked intact.
- To ensure that all cash and cheques received are banked without delay at prescribed intervals, preferably daily.
- To ensure that all cash and cheques received are accounted for and recorded accurately.

Control procedures

- Cash and cheques should be banked intact.
- Cash and cheques should be banked without undue delay.
- The bank paying-in slip should be prepared by an individual with no access to cash collection points, purchase or sales ledgers.

- Bankings should be made with security in mind, e.g. for large cash sums, security guards should be used.
- There should be independent comparison of paying-in slips with collection records, post lists and sales ledger records.

Cash and cheques received by post

Control objectives

To ensure that all cash and cheques received by post are accounted for and accurately recorded in the books.

To ensure all such receipts are deposited in the bank promptly and intact.

Control procedures

- Measures to prevent interception of mail between receipt and opening.
- Two persons to be present at the opening of the post.
- All cheques and other negotiable instruments to be immediately given a restrictive crossing, e.g. account payee only, not negotiable.
- Immediate entry of the details of the receipts (date, payer, amount, cash, cheque, or other) in a 'rough cash book' or post list of money received. The list should be signed by both parties present.
- Regular independent comparison of the post list with banking records. The tests should be of total, detail and dating to detect teeming and lading (Chapter 20) at a later stage in the processing.

LIMITATIONS OF INTERNAL CONTROLS

Internal controls are essential features of any organisation that is run efficiently.

However, it is important to realise (especially for an auditor) that internal controls have inherent limitations which include:

- A requirement that the cost of an internal control is not disproportionate to the potential loss which may result from its absence.
- Internal controls tend to be directed at routine transactions. The one-off or unusual transaction tends not to be the subject of internal control.
- Potential human error caused by stress of workload, alcohol, carelessness, distraction, mistakes of judgement, apathy and the misunderstanding of instructions.
- The possibility of circumvention of controls either alone or through collusion with parties outside or inside the entity.
- Abuse of responsibility by senior managers resulting in management override of controls.
- Fraud.
- Changes in environment making controls inadequate.

The IAS 315 requires that auditors must always perform some substantive tests of material items as well as relying on internal controls. The inherent limitations of internal controls are the reason.

Summary

- The Control Environment means the overall attitude, awareness and actions of directors and management regarding internal controls and their importance in the entity. The control environment encompasses the management style, and corporate culture and values shared by all employees.

- Control activities are those policies and procedures in addition to the control environment which are established to achieve the entity's specific objectives. They include in particular procedures designed to prevent or detect and correct errors.

- Specific control procedures can be recognised by the mnemonic SOAPSPAM.

- Auditors are expected to make an assessment of the control environment in a client. A good control environment may well mean that the commitment to internal control is strong, but nonetheless actual control procedures may be weak or ineffective. It is generally felt that a poor control environment will mean unreliable control procedures.

- Internal control procedures have limitations insofar as, for example, they may not be operated properly but by inadequately trained or demotivated staff, they may be overridden by management or be evaded by deliberate fraud.

Points to note

- The definitions of 'Control Environment' and 'Control Procedures' should be memorised.

- All entities have some sort of accounting system with some internal controls over the transactions. Indeed listed companies are required to have systems and report on them in accordance with the Combined Code on Corporate Governance (see Chapter 2). Auditors may rely on these controls as evidence of prevention or detection and correction of errors and irregularities, but whether or not they do so depends on their assessment of the risks attached. In any event some substantive tests must be performed on all material balances and classes of transaction.

Case Study

Skye Antiques Ltd operates a large shop in the centre of North Bromwich and two smaller shops in adjacent towns. They sell expensive reproduction antique furniture. Normally customers see the furniture in the shop and place an order for delivery in the company van within four weeks. The delay occurs because each sale results in a purchase order for one of the suppliers. On placing the order the customer pays by cash, cheque, credit card or signs a hire purchase agreement. There are four sales assistants, a van driver and a cashier in the shop.

The smaller shops have a shop manager who deals with all the paperwork and part-time staff who assist at busy times. Customer orders are sent through to the main shop for sending to suppliers. Receipts from customers are banked daily – weekend receipts being banked on the Monday – and duplicate sales invoices are also sent to head office. Tills for any cash sales are cashed up daily and cash sheets agreed to till rolls. Managers have to sign the record of receipts.

Accounting and purchasing is done centrally by the manager and a part-time bookkeeper.

The three directors all have other businesses and review the company operations once a month at an all-day board meeting.

Discussion
- Devise an internal control system for the shops.
- Relate your system to the definition of internal control.
- Identify the types of internal controls in your system.

Student self-testing questions

Questions with answers apparent from the text

a) Define internal control and control risk and tests of control.

b) List the types of internal controls.

c) What categories of internal controls are comprised in the term 'organisation'?

d) What functions should be segregated so that no two are under the control of one person?

e) What kinds of access to assets and records are there?

f) What types of arithmetical and accounting controls are possible?

g) What are the internal control objectives of personnel policies?

h) What personnel policies achieve these ends?

i) List some management controls.

j) What budgeting benefits have internal control implications?

k) When are physical controls especially important?

l) List some physical controls.

m) List suitable controls over a petty cash system.

n) How can the issue of fraudulent cheques be prevented?

o) List some possible wages frauds.

p) What is a control environment?

q) List some limitations of internal control.

Examination questions

1 Flowers Anytime sells flowers wholesale. Customers telephone the company and their orders are taken by clerks who take details of the flowers to be delivered, the address to which they are to be delivered, and account details of the customer. The clerks input these details into the company's computer system (whilst the order is being taken) which is integrated with the company's stock control system. The company's standard credit terms are payment one month from the order (all orders are despatched within 48 hours) and most customers pay by bank transfer. A sales ledger is maintained and statements are sent to customers once a month. Credit limits are set by the sales ledger controller according to a standard formula and are automatically applied by the computer system, as are the prices of flowers.

Required:

Describe and explain the purpose of the internal controls you might expect to see in the sales system at Flowers Anytime over the:

(i) Receipt, processing and recording of orders.
(ii) Collection of cash.

(*ACCA*)

2 A proper understanding of internal controls is essential to auditors in order that they understand the business and are able to effectively plan and execute tests of controls and an appropriate level of substantive procedures.

You are the auditor of a small manufacturing company, Dinko, that pays its staff in cash and by bank transfer and maintains its payroll on a small stand-alone computer.

Required:

(a) For the payroll department at Dinko, describe the:

(i) internal control *objectives* that should be in place;
(ii) internal control *environment* and internal control *procedures* that should be in place to achieve the internal control objectives.

(b) For the payroll charges and payroll balances (including cash) in the financial statements of Dinko:

(i) describe the external auditor *audit objectives;* ·
(ii) list the *tests of control* and *substantive procedures* that will be applied in order to achieve the audit objectives identified in (b) (i) above.

(*ACCA*)

10

Audit planning, audit risk and materiality

INTRODUCTION

Before delving into the technical details of how to plan, conduct and report on an audit it is useful to consider the objective of an audit and the general principles which underlie the auditor's work. Unless this is fully understood the planning process may become a mere mechanical exercise based on previous period's audits perhaps. Instead, if the objective and role of auditors is fully appreciated, the planning process can be directed and unnecessary or ill-directed work avoided.

This section is based on ISA 200 'Objectives and General Principles Governing an Audit of Financial Statements'.

OBJECTIVES

ISA 200 begins with a statement of the objectives of an audit. The primary objective of an audit of financial statements is to enable the auditor to express an opinion whether the financial statements are prepared, in all material (i.e. significant) respects in accordance with an applicable financial reporting framework. The phrases used to express the auditor's opinion are 'give a true and fair view' or 'present fairly in all material respects' which are equivalent terms.

The financial reporting framework is the law and accounting standards applicable to the organisation being audited which determine the form and content of the financial accounts. In the UK this is based on the Companies Act 2006 and all the applicable financial reporting standards issued by the Accounting Standards Board.

Let us look at three key phrases.

- *opinion* – is not a guarantee or a certificate, just an opinion – see Chapter 27. ISA 200 goes on to point out that although the auditor's opinion enhances the credibility of the financial statements the user of the accounts cannot assume that the audit opinion is an assurance as to the future viability of the entity nor of the efficiency or effectiveness with which management have conducted its affairs.

- *in all material respects* – this is a difficult point. Essentially there is a degree of imprecision in all but the very simplest of financial statements because they contain accounting estimates about uncertainties and unresolved transactions. There may even be some non-material misstatements in some of the individual items. However, the objective is that the auditor's work will provide evidence to support an opinion that the *overall* view given by the financial statements is a true and fair one (or that it is not).

- *true and fair* – this too is a difficult concept which we discuss in more detail in Chapter 27. Broadly, it means that the financial statements show the financial position of the entity in as fair and accurate a way as is reasonably possible.

REQUIRED PROCEDURES

ISA 200 requires that, in undertaking an audit of financial statements, auditors should:

- conduct their audit in accordance with ISAs.
- plan and perform the audit with an attitude of professional scepticism recognising that circumstances may exist that cause the financial statements to be materially misstated. This requires the auditor to make a critical assessment with a questioning mind as to the validity of the audit evidence obtained, and to be alert to any audit evidence that contradicts or brings into question the reliability of documents or management information.

    This is a critical component of the way that auditors are expected to conduct themselves during the course of the audit and is designed to:

  - reduce the likelihood of auditors ignoring or turning away from suspicious circumstances;
  - drawing *general* conclusions from *specific* events;
  - using faulty assumptions when carrying out audit procedures.

    This is not to say that auditors should assume that management is intrinsically dishonest, or indeed that they are totally honest. Accordingly representations from management are not a substitute for auditors obtaining sufficient reliable evidence on which to base their conclusions.

- Carry out procedures designed to obtain sufficient appropriate audit evidence, in accordance with Auditing Standards, to determine, with reasonable assurance, whether the financial statements are free from material misstatement.
- Plan and perform the audit so as to reduce audit risk to an acceptably low level. We will examine the concept of audit risk in more detail later. It is the risk that the auditor will give an inappropriate opinion on the financial statements, i.e. by saying they are 'true and fair' when they are not, or alternatively, by saying they are not 'true and fair' when they are.
- ISA 200 also makes the important point, which the student must fully appreciate, that the responsibility for preparing and presenting the financial statements rests with the management of the entity and that the audit does not relieve them of that responsibility.

    It is appropriate to make some comment about phrases which you will find repeated throughout this book. It is important you become familiar with them and fully understand what they mean.

'Sufficient, appropriate audit evidence'

This is a phrase to be committed to memory. Audit evidence is the subject of Chapter 11. The gathering of evidence is a matter of judgement in deciding on the nature, timing and extent of audit procedures. Even when evidence has been gathered it is a matter of judgement as to what conclusions are drawn from the evidence. For example, the auditors may gather much evidence on the future useful life of some plant and machinery – its natural life, the possibility of obsolescence, the cost of repairs as against replacement, etc. but still have to determine whether they think the life selected by the directors is reasonable in the circumstances.

'Reasonable assurance'

This is a difficult concept and, to some extent, can be rather subjective. It relates to the accumulation of evidence throughout the audit process which allows the auditor to conclude that the financial statements, taken as a whole, are free from material misstatements. It relates to the whole audit process.

Absolute assurance is not possible because:

- auditors carry out their work based on sampling of transactions;
- internal controls can be overridden by management or defeated by collusion; and
- most audit evidence is persuasive rather than conclusive.

For example, the auditors might test a sample of two hundred sales invoices out of a total population of one hundred thousand in order to verify the operation of an internal control in the sales system. If they find no errors, or even an acceptable number of errors, they may reasonably conclude that the remaining ninety-nine thousand eight hundred invoices contain the same level of errors – but they don't know for sure that they do. They draw the conclusion, based on their audit test, which persuades them that it is more likely to be true than not true.

'Free of material misstatement'

Materiality is discussed in detail in Chapter 10. It relates to the significance, or otherwise, of errors or misstatements in the context of either the accounts as a whole or in the context of individual transactions and balances. Misstatement is usually in terms of fact, for example if creditors do not include a significant accrual or the valuation of stock does not comply with IAS 2 (SSAP 9), or the requirements of the Companies Act re fixed assets have not been fully complied with. In those cases the auditor has to consider the effect of the error or omission on the accounts and recommend appropriate action.

INFLUENCES ON AN AUDIT

There are many influences on how an actual audit is conducted. These include:

- International Standards on Auditing. These have to be complied with – see Chapter 5.
- Professional body rules – (see Chapter 6) these are now very extensive.
- Legislation – for companies this is the Companies Act 2006 but most enterprises seem to be affected by some legislation or other. We live in a very regulated age.
- The terms of the engagement – see Chapter 8.
- Codes of practice – some audits are influenced by codes of practice, local authorities are an example.

- The level of Audit Risk. Risk permeates all auditing. Risk arises due the nature of the organisation and its management, the quality of the internal controls within the organisation and the ability of the auditor to perform the audit in such a way that any material errors or misstatements which evade the company's procedures will be detected by the audit work performed. We explore this in more detail later.
- The possibility of some fraud or misrepresentation which is committed with collusion by staff or management.
- The quality of audit evidence.
- Fear of litigation – Actions under the law of tort to recover losses alleged to be caused by the negligence of auditors, if successful can be very expensive for auditors in terms of cost, time and loss of clients and reputation. See Chapter 31.
- Ethics – ISA 200 requires that in the conduct of any audit of financial statements auditors should comply with the ethical guidance issued by their relevant professional bodies. These guides are now fairly extensive – see Chapter 5. Relevant matters include integrity, objectivity, independence, professional competence, due care, professional behaviour and confidentiality.
- The individual auditing manual of the firm of auditors. These may be influenced by quality control standards – see Chapter 7.

STAGES IN THE AUDIT

The stages in the audit can be summarised as:

1 The planning phase:

- know your client;
- internal control system review;
- planning the audit;
- evaluation of Audit Risk;
- develop the audit programme.

2 The operational phase:

- audit testing;
- analytical review techniques;
- analytical review of financial statements.

3 The reporting phase:

- preparation and signing of the audit report;
- the management letter or letter of weakness.

We will deal with each of these as this book progresses. For now we will deal with the planning phase.

PLANNING THE AUDIT

An audit can be carried out on enterprises both large and small, and both new and well established. The audit of smaller enterprises has special features that are dealt with in Chapter 30.

This chapter describes the stages in the audit of an established client enterprise which is big enough to have a comprehensive system of accounting and record keeping and a system of controls over those records.

Know your client

ISA 315 *'Obtaining an Understanding of the Entity and its Environment and Assessing the Risks of a Material Misstatement'* sets out the matters the auditor should consider before commencing the audit planning process and certainly before starting work.

ISA 315 requires the auditors to:

- obtain a knowledge of the business which is sufficient to enable them to identify and understand the events, transactions and practices that may have a significant effect on the financial statements and the audit of them.
- use the knowledge gained to:
  - assess the risks of fraud and error (Chapter 20);
  - plan the nature, timing and extent of audit procedures; and
  - consider the consistency and reliability of financial statements.

As we saw in Chapter 8, before commencing the audit proper the auditor must get to know their client i.e. discover as much as possible about:

- The present condition and future prospects of the industry of which the client is a part, including the competition.
- The past history and the present condition and future prospects of the client itself.
- The client's:
  - products and services;
  - important customers;
  - key suppliers; and
  - details of significant contracts.
- The management and key personnel of the client and any recent changes.
- The products and manufacturing and trading processes of the client and any recent changes.
- The locations of all the client's operations.
- Any difficulties encountered by the client in:
  - manufacturing;
  - trading;
  - expanding or contracting the business;
  - labour relations;
  - financing the continuing operations.
- Any problems in accounting or in internal control systems.
- Any problems in accounting measurement e.g. in stock valuation or income recognition.
- Any problems likely to lead to increased audit risk e.g. the difficulty of assessing the value of long-term contracts in a civil engineering business.
- Any problems likely to be met in carrying out the audit e.g. distant geographical locations, tight timing problems, specialist staff requirements e.g. IT auditors.
- Any changes in law or accounting practice which may affect the client.

This background research will involve research, which will include reading:

- Previous years' audit files.
- Published material concerning the client company and the industry.
- Internet searches.
- The company's interim, internal and management accounts, if these can be obtained.

and holding discussions with:

- The management of the enterprise.
- Audit staff who have been previously engaged on the audit.

In order to carry out a comprehensive and effective audit which is nevertheless efficient in terms of time spent, the auditor must focus the audit on areas of particular difficulty and risk. In addition, the evaluation of many areas in the financial statements must entail a consideration of the whole circumstances of a client.

As simple examples, the evaluation of the life of fixed assets liable to obsolescence or the value of the investment in a subsidiary company can only be effected by a knowledge of all factors having a bearing on the matter and many of these factors are external to the company.

Case Study 1

Metalbash Pressings Ltd

Jane is the audit manager of Tickitt & Run and is about to start to plan the audit of Metalbash Pressings Ltd, a company which manufactures parts for UK lorry manufacturers. She will need to research the background of:

- The industry

  She finds that UK lorry output is 75 per cent of normal levels. This reduces the market demand for components and stimulates greater competition between component manufacturers, resulting in lower prices for component suppliers. Companies with high manufacturing costs could find their market share declining rapidly.

- The company

  The company is suffering from price and cost squeezes, plant closures and redundancies. She finds that a factory has closed and 50 workers have been made redundant. However, the company have purchased for cash (with a bank loan) the business of a company in receivership which is in a related industry. This new company will require a cash injection, some new plant and new management before it can start trading profitably. It has a factory in a neighbouring town and Jane has to plan visits there and interviews with management and personnel. Metalbash itself has gone through an administrative reorganisation during the year and some experienced office staff have left. Any significant changes to operations may weaken controls, change policies or worsen accounting records. Jane finds that there is now a new chief accountant who is not familiar with the components business.

- Products and processes

  New production processes have been introduced and some new machinery installed. Jane does not know what has happened to the old machines. Changes in costs of manufacture may have possible consequences to stock values and there is the value of redundant equipment to consider.

- Locations

Closures may involve closure costs with disclosure problems from FRS3.

- Client's difficulties

Difficulties experienced by the client (e.g. on labour relations or cost and quality control) may impact on internal controls. Jane finds that the new accountant has streamlined several accounting processes and controls may have changed and be weaker.

- Systems changes

Accounting systems change frequently nowadays as a consequence of the need to improve management information systems. The accounting records of the new business have been incorporated into new systems and some teething problems have occurred. A new computer system has been installed.

- Accounting issues

Accounting measurement problems may arise in product costs, redundant stocks, closure costs, redundancy costs, lives of fixed assets, etc.

- Key risk areas

Some lorry makers have gone into receivership and there is a risk of Metalbash losing its business or incurring fatal bad debts. Jane will need to concentrate consequently upon the value of debtors and whether or not the business is going to survive the next few years. In addition, any changes to systems and personnel all have to be evaluated.

- Key audit issues

New systems will need to be documented, the audit programmes amended for the new business and additional audit procedures thought through to take account of the changed circumstances of the business.

- Planning

In planning the audit, Jane will need to consider locations, timing problems, staff requirements, and the quality of audit staff needed for some of the risky areas including a possible need to look into and assess new systems.

- Sources of information

Jane will do all this by:

- reading the previous years' files;
- talking to the staff member responsible for last year's audit;
- discussing the impact of all the changes with the management;
- discussing audit timings and the access to records with the new chief accountant;
- reading the minutes of directors' and senior management meetings;
- reviewing the management accounts;
- reading any newspaper and magazine articles;
- looking at the company's website and surfing the net for information about the industry generally and any comments about her client from third party sources.

INTERNAL CONTROL SYSTEM REVIEW

Internal controls are the client's procedures which ensure that all transactions, assets and liabilities are recorded correctly.

In essence, what auditors need to do when faced with a new system or a system that has changed significantly is:

- ascertain the system;
- record it;
- corroborate that record with the client;
- review the overall system for reliability;
- test the system with some sample checks;
- evaluate its reliability; and
- form a conclusion on the adequacy of the client's system of internal control.

The objectives of investigations and recording of the accounting and internal control systems are to enable the auditor to have evidence that:

- The client maintains adequate books and records – don't forget this is a secondary objective of the audit.
- The client has a system of internal controls over the processing and recording of transactions such that all transactions are recorded correctly both numerically and in principle.
- The books of account can be relied on to form a reliable basis for the preparation of the financial statements.

The auditors are primarily looking to rely upon the system. If the system is satisfactory then they can substitute an investigation and test of the system for a lot of detailed tests of individual transactions and balances.

Only by examining the system can they gather evidence to prove that all the transactions are recorded correctly and in the right accounting period.

If, in some areas of the business, internal controls do not exist or are weak the auditors cannot rely on the controls and other evidence needs to be sought for the completeness and accuracy of the records.

There are three basic techniques used when documenting client's systems.

These are:

- Use of Internal Control Questionnaires (ICQs).
- Flow charting and documenting the system.
- Use of Internal Control Evaluation Questionnaires (ICEQs).

Internal control questionnaires (ICQs)

These documents can have several functions:

- A method of ascertainment of the system.
- Enabling the auditors to review and assess the adequacy of the system.
- Enabling the auditors to identify areas of weakness.

- Enabling the auditors to design a series of tests; in effect this means enabling the auditors to draw up their audit programme.
- Enabling audit staff to familiarise themselves with the system quickly and comprehensively.

The advantages of using ICQs are implicit in the functions just stated but in addition they include:

- The use of standardised ICQs ensures that all the important questions are asked and the important characteristics of a system are brought out.
- The ICQ is a comprehensive, all in, inclusive method of ascertaining, recording, and evaluating a system of internal control.

Next follows an example of a part of an ICQ. Note the separate columns for:

- Questions.
- Answers – Yes/No.
- Reviewer's comment which can identify systems weaknesses.

Internal control questionnaire (extract)

Client name: **METALBASH LTD** Prepared by **JT** Date **19/7/20-8**
Period to **31 December 2-07** Reviewed by **DB** Date **22/8/20-8**

Subject area: PURCHASE ORDERING

Process	Yes	No	Comments
Are all purchases made as a result of written orders?	√		
Are all orders sequentially numbered?	√		
Are all numbers accounted for?		√	**Spoiled orders destroyed**
Do orders have to be authorised by a senior manager?	√		**CEO or purchasing manager**
Are orders only sent to approved suppliers?	√		
If there are no approved suppliers, is the procedure for approving a supplier carried out before the order is placed?	√		**Only approved suppliers used**
Do all purchase orders show quantities?	√		
Prices?	√		
Terms?	√		
Initials of authoriser?	√		
Date?	√		
Is there a limit to individual order values?	√		**CEO – no limit** **Purchasing manager – limit £50,000**
Are copies of the purchase order sent to Purchase ledger department?	√		
Stores?	√		
Are purchase orders matched to invoices?	√		
Are copies of all orders retained in the purchasing department?	√		

The auditor is looking for **'NO'** answers as these indicate a possible systems weakness which must be followed up and evaluated.

Flow charts

Flow charts are a method of recording internal control systems from the auditor's stand-point. There are two methods of flowcharting – charting of processes and charting of document flows. Auditors find it more useful to chart document flows as documents form the basis of their checking work.

The *advantages* of flow charts are as follows:

- Narrative notes can be lengthy and confusing. Changes in the system usually require the whole of the notes to be re-written. Flow charts provide a visual representation of a system which is much more easily appreciated than a lengthy written note.
- Flow charts enable the system to be recorded in such a way that it can be understood by:

  - New staff coming to the audit.
  - Supervisors, managers and partners.
  - Client staff, who can have weaknesses pointed out more easily.

- The overall picture of a firm can be seen, and in particular the auditor can be assured they have the whole picture. Flow lines going nowhere can easily be spotted.
- Flow charting is a consistent system of recording.
- Flow charting is a disciplined method of recording. Full understanding must be gained to draw them.
- Flow charting highlights the relationships between different parts of a system. By linking charts together even complex systems can be described easily.
- Weaknesses are easier to spot.
- Superfluous forms and bottlenecks are easily spotted. Auditors can help their clients improve efficiencies in this area.
- Flow charts are a permanent record but are relatively easily updated.
- In complex cases, flow charting is the only way to gain an understanding of a system.
- There are computerised flow charting packages available to simplify the process.

The *disadvantages* of flow charting are:

- They can become overcomplicated or confusing if badly drawn.
- They have to be redrawn if the system changes even to a limited extent.
- They are fine for describing accounting processes where documents are moving through a system, but once documents stop moving they cannot describe controls, e.g. flow charts can describe procedures for controlling goods inward and outward but not the controls over stock in the stores.

When preparing flow charts the following points should be borne in mind:

- An organisation chart is an essential concomitant.
- Simplicity and clarity are fundamental.
- Flow charts must not be congested. Use separate charts for sub-procedures, exceptional procedures etc. Small congested charts can be misleading.

- Use only horizontal and vertical lines and standard flow charting symbols.
- Start at the top left and finish at the bottom right.
- Charts must show:

  - Initiation of each document and operation.
  - Sequence of all operations on documents and all copies of documents, especially operations of control, inspecting, checking, comparing and approving.
  - The sections or individuals who perform operations.
  - The ultimate destination, i.e. where is it filed?
  - Explanatory narrative notes where required.

- Specimens of documents could be attached and cross referenced.

The objective of a flow chart is that it is complete in itself and can be read and understood quickly and comprehensibly. However, this takes practice.

Case Study 2

Metalbash Ltd Sales Order and invoicing system
A narrative description of the system might be:

- The company has a number of separate departments (e.g. sales, credit control). This is important for separation of duties.
- Orders are received from customers in various forms.
- All orders are transcribed onto pre-numbered official 'sales order forms'. Pre-numbering ensures all orders will be fulfilled or discovered as unfulfilled.
- The blank order forms are kept locked in the manager's safe. Order forms are important as they key the release of goods.
- The sales order forms are in duplicate. One copy is attached to the original customer order and filed in a temporary file.
- The second copy is sent to credit control. Credit control check that the customer is credit worthy by reference to their records and the customer's ledger account printout (to see the customer is not overdue or has not exceeded their credit limit).
- If credit is not approved then a credit approval sub-routine applies. (The sub-routine is on another flow chart which is not included).
- The order is then sent to the warehouse. There, the goods on the order are checked for availability. If the goods are not available then a routine is operated (to order more from the supplier).
- A despatch note in triplicate is made out from the details in the sales order form. This despatch note is pre-numbered.
- One copy of the despatch note is put with the goods (which are picked off the shelves and packed) and signed by the goods-out foreman who compares the goods with the despatch note.
- This copy is attached to the sales order form and filed in despatch note number order in the warehouse.

- The second copy of the despatch note is checked against the goods and sent with the goods to the customer.
- The third copy is used to make out the invoice. It is subsequently attached to a copy of the invoice and filed in invoice number order in the invoice section. But before being so attached it is checked for sequence (to see none are missing, meaning goods were despatched but not invoiced) by the invoice section manager.
- The invoice has three copies. The top copy is sent to the customer.
- The second copy has been dealt with (see above).
- This copy is checked for accuracy and initialled by the checker. The second copy is batched daily. From the batch a prelist is made out in duplicate. The top copy of the prelist is filed in numerical sequence in the invoice department.
- The second copy of the prelist is sent with the batch of copy invoices daily to computer input (this is yet another flow chart, not included).
- The third copy of the sales invoice is sent to the sales department.
- From the order forms and the invoice copies, a schedule of outstanding orders is made out weekly in duplicate.
- The matched order forms and invoices are attached to each other and filed monthly in alphabetical order of customer.
- The top copy of the schedule is filed. The second copy is sent to the managing director.

You may well feel that a flow chart explains the system in a much more digestible manner than the narrative notes above which are lengthy and difficult to retain.

The same system can be described in a flow chart. The symbols used are explained below and the internal control features listed.

Flow Chart for audit purposes

Metalbash Ltd – Flow Chart of Sales Orders and Invoicing Procedures

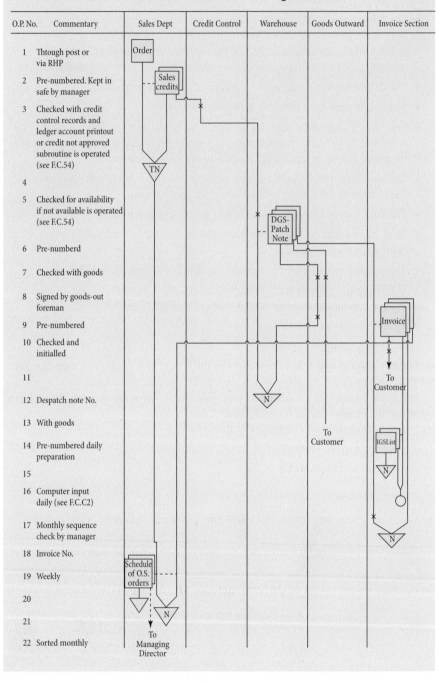

O.P. No.	Commentary
1	Thtough post or via RHP
2	Pre-numbered. Kept in safe by manager
3	Checked with credit control records and ledger account printout or credit not approved subroutine is operated (see F.C.54)
4	
5	Checked for availability if not available is operated (see F.C.54)
6	Pre-numberd
7	Checked with goods
8	Signed by goods-out foreman
9	Pre-numbered
10	Checked and initialled
11	
12	Despatch note No.
13	With goods
14	Pre-numbered daily preparation
15	
16	Computer input daily (see F.C.C2)
17	Monthly sequence check by manager
18	Invoice No.
19	Weekly
20	
21	
22	Sorted monthly

Notes to flow chart

1. Symbols used are:

Document	☐
Prepared using details in	- - - - -
Action or Check	✕
File	▽

T   Temporary
A   Alphabetical order
N   Numerical order
D   Date order

To another flow chart	◯

Note incidence of:

- Separation of duties:

    - initiation (by customer);
    - authorisation (credit control);
    - custody (warehouse);
    - documentation and recording.

- Specified organisation structure.
- Proof measures (prelist).
- Acknowledgement of performance (invoice checking).
- Protective devices (blank sales order forms kept in safe).
- Formal transfer of goods (warehouse to goods out).
- Pre-review (by credit control).
- Post review (sequence checks).

Notes to students:

1   This is, of course, incomplete. The warehouse, goods-out section etc., have not been included.
2   Further detail could be included if desired, e.g. actual names of officials, their location, etc.

Internal control evaluation questionnaires (ICEQs)

ICQs and flow charts are used to ascertain and record the system.

However, it is also necessary to evaluate the system's strengths and weaknesses. An ideal method of doing this is by means of an internal control evaluation questionnaire. This is a standardised set of questions which has the advantage, like the ICQ, of ensuring all the right questions are asked and the strengths and weaknesses of a system are brought out.

The basic questions in an ICEQ are called control questions. An example from the sales area is 'Can sales be invoiced but not recorded in the books?'. Each control question requires a 'NO' answer.

You will recall that for an ICQ the auditors were looking for 'YES' answers because they were trying to confirm that controls were operating. Here they are looking for 'NO' answers as the purpose of the ICEQ is to see if it is possible to get round the controls in the system. A 'NO' answer confirms it is not possible.

Example Internal Control Evaluation Questionnaire – Extract

Client name: **METALBASH LTD**   Prepared by **JT**   Date **19/7/20-8**
Period to   **31 December 2-07**   Reviewed by **DB**   Date **22/8/20-8**

Subject area: Goods Inward

Control Question	Yes	No	Comments
Can goods be accepted without being inspected for damage?		√	Damaged goods report
Can goods be delivered without being signed for?		√	
Can goods be delivered without a goods received note being prepared?		√	Invoices not paid without copy GRN attached
Are the individuals who deal with goods inward the same as those who deal with the security and recording of stock?	√		Stores staff deal with goods inward
Are the individuals who deal with goods inward the same as those who deal with the security and recording of purchase ordering?		√	
Is it possible for invoices to be paid without goods having been received?		√	Invoices not paid without copy GRN attached
Is it possible for goods to be accepted without having been ordered?		√	Copy order sent to stores
Are damaged goods stored in the same part of the warehouse as accepted goods?		√	Quarantine area

In this case the '**YES**' answer should be followed up to see if it has any internal control implications

Walk-through tests

Once the system has been documented, flow charts and notes prepared and reviewed and ICQs and ICEQs completed, the final step is to 'walk through' the system to ensure that what is noted on the audit files actually happens in practice.

The auditor will take a small number, say two or three only, of actual transactions and trace them through the system following the system notes as they go. This is called a 'walk-through test' and ties the system notes to the actual live system. These tests will be documented on the audit files as they form part of the compliance testing of the company's internal control procedures.

PLANNING THE AUDIT WORK

It is of great importance that an audit is planned in advance because:

• The intended means of achieving the audit objectives must be established.

• The audit can be controlled and directed.

- Attention can be focused on to critical and high-risk areas.
- Any potential problem areas can be identified as early as possible.
- The work can then be completed economically and to timescale requirements.

The Relevant ISAs are ISA 300 *Planning an Audit of Financial Statements* and ISA 315 *Obtaining an Understanding of the Entity and its Environment and Assessing the Risks of a Material Misstatement.*

The planning process

Before the audit is commenced an audit plan must be drawn up. This will normally be contained in a document known as an *Audit Planning Memorandum.*

It is important that auditors document the planning process as they have included in their audit report a confirmation that they have done so, and this memorandum is the evidence for that process.

The planning process will normally involve:

- Reviewing last year's working papers for key issues and problem areas.
- Considering the impact of any changes in legislation (e.g. Companies Act 2006) or auditing or accounting standards.
- Considering the background of the client and the nature of any changes in the industry or issues which may affect the audit work.
- Considering the impact of changes in the business itself or its management or ownership.
- Reviewing the effect on the audit of changes in systems or accounting procedures.
- Carrying out an analytical review of management accounts.
- Consulting with management on any key issues which have arisen in the financial period.
- Deciding on the audit strategy, for example, how much reliance could be placed on the client's own internal controls so a systems-based approach could be adopted, which areas may need detailed substantive testing or whether a risk-based audit strategy could be used.
- Agreeing the timing of the audit work – is there to be an interim audit followed by a final visit?
- Agreeing the extent of preparation by the client of analyses and summaries.
- Deciding on the degree of reliance to be placed on internal audit reports and whether this will reduce the amount of audit work carried out by the external auditors.
- Considering the use of any experts, e.g. computer audit specialists or third party experts such as valuers of stock or property.
- Liaising with joint auditors, if any, and, in the case of group audits, liaison with any auditors of subsidiary companies.
- Planning the rotational testing where there are multiple locations or branches so the ones to be visited this year can be agreed and visits scheduled.
- Working out the time budget.
- Planning and arranging staffing requirements.
- Considering the budget in the light of the likely fee to be charged.
- Organising liaison with the company's Audit Committee, if any.

Case Study 3

Steps in planning the audit

Metalbash

In order to illustrate the process of audit planning we will use an example in order to illustrate the process.

Let us consider the case of Metalbash again, and the auditors who are Tickitt & Run. The December 20-8 audit plan is to be prepared by audit manager Jane. She has to consider all the matters mentioned above and finds the following matters require attention:

- A special report has to be prepared for the Lorry Part Manufacturers' Association on the cost structures in the company.

- As Jane is new to the audit she needs to read previous years' papers especially carefully as her predecessor has left Tickitt & Run and the audit partner, to whom she reports, has also changed as old Mr Tick has retired and gone to live in the Bahamas.

- The 20-7 audit was completed in May 20-7 and the time is now July 20-8.

- There are several new FRSs and ISAs and some new relevant legislation. Happily all these are summarised in Tickitt & Run's internal updating and Jane is sent on courses regularly.

- The client produces monthly accounts internally and Jane finds that turnover increased substantially after March as a new branch was opened in Wigan and two major new products began manufacture. These two products are new technology and the company have taken a risk in introducing them at this time. Substantial capital expenditure throughout the first part of the year has already led to liquidity problems and this has been added to by increases in stock and debtors and the acquisition of the new company.

- A structural review of the company consequent on the items mentioned above has led to three senior directors and managers being retired early and new appointments made in June. There is a new Chief Accountant and new Sales and Production Directors.

- A completely new networked computer system was installed in April and is working well.

- The directors have expressed a wish for the audit to be completed by the end of March 20x9 and they promise to have the accounts ready by mid February.

- Every conceivable schedule is available from the computer system. Jane feels she should think up analyses which will help her prepare her analytical review procedures.

- The company have no internal audit function.

- The company relies heavily on internal controls to control its day-to-day transaction processing. Jane thinks that once the controls have been properly documented it may well be possible to rely on them to a significant extent.

- There are no joint auditors.

- Metalbash is based in one location except for the branch in Wigan and the new company which is based in Essex.

Deciding an audit strategy

ISA 210 states that there should be an overall audit plan, set out in the Audit Planning Memorandum, which outlines the general strategy and a detailed approach specified in the Audit Programme.

As stated above, before the detailed audit planning work commences Jane must ensure that she has a good understanding of the client, the industry in which it operates and its products and processes.

Before deciding on an audit strategy she must go through the following steps:

1 *Understand the client and its background* – history, products, locations, especially noting factors like the new directors and chief accountant, a new computer system, new products and the new subsidiary. In particular she must review and update the records on:

- The management structure;
- The products and processes;
- The financial accounting system;
- The abilities of the management to control the business;
- The operating style (e.g. direction from the top or disseminated decision-making);
- The attitude of directors and management towards internal control.

2 *Select an audit strategy*
The audit strategy will be take into account the following:

- The terms of the engagement with the client, i.e. what work is to be done. This will obviously include the audit but will also include any accounting work to be done for the client (i.e. drafting the final accounts, tax computations, etc.) and preparing any reports to third parties, e.g. The Lorry Parts Manufacturers Association.
- Important figures and ratios – from previous years and, if available, from relevant management and draft accounts. This will form the basis of a preliminary analytical review which may highlight audit problem areas.
- Identification and consideration of key risk areas to the financial statements as a whole – these might include stock and asset valuations, work in progress, or liquidity.
- Going concern issues (see Chapter 24).
- The effect of information technology on the audit, in particular the new systems.
- There is no internal audit so no help there!
- Any requirement for involvement of specialists. These may be from within the audit firm, e.g. computer audit or external specialists such as valuers.
- Setting of preliminary materiality levels.
- Agreeing the timing and extent of client responsibilities. The responsibilities of the client to provide draft accounts, supporting schedules and analyses, and to provide computer time, arranging visits to branches, etc. If the deadline is to be met the client has to fulfil its part of the arrangement.
- Deciding the overall audit approach. The extent of reliance on internal control, the use of substantive tests and analytical review procedures. We will discuss these in more detail in later chapters.

> - Timetable – dates of interim, year end and final audits and of deadlines to meet, e.g. AGM of company.
> - Staffing requirements.
> - Budget and fee.
> - Possibilities of material error or fraud.
> - Any specific regulatory requirements (especially important in some types of company, e.g. those in financial services).
>
> Once all these factors have been evaluated the general audit strategy will have to be decided upon.

AUDIT STRATEGIES

Basically there are three approaches:

(i) Substantive approach

This is usually adopted for the audit of small organisations where the internal systems are weak and there are a limited number of staff. For example, a small charity or perhaps a small family company requiring an audit might have a simple proprietary computer based bookkeeping system and a part-time bookkeeper who does all the accounting work.

There are no real controls within the system and the auditor has little choice but to test a large number of transactions. Clearly this approach is not practicable in any but the smallest organisations. We look at the audit of small organisations in Chapter 30.

(ii) Systems-based auditing

This approach is used on larger organisations where there is a proper accounting system and sufficient staff to constitute a proper system of internal control. We look at this in detail in Chapter 13.

This is an approach to auditing which relies on the controls contained within the client's financial systems to validate the accounting records. The auditors test *the controls* by means of testing a sample of transactions and extrapolating the results of those sample tests to the population as a whole. In this way they can draw conclusions as to the reliability of the accounting records.

Note that the individual transactions are only chosen because they are representative of the types of transaction checked by the particular control or set of controls the auditors are testing.

The auditors will carry out detailed testing (known as substantive testing) on balance sheet items or unusual transactions which haven't gone through the normal accounting system.

(iii) Risk-based auditing

We will look at this specifically in Chapter 14. Basically this is used to audit very large organisations or those with excellent internal control systems. The auditors carry out a limited amount of testing of transactions and balances and concentrate their efforts on analysing the business risks faced by the organisation. These then become the subject of the auditors' attention.

This approach requires the auditors to use experienced and competent staff and to have faith in the client's underlying systems. It is, however, an efficient way of auditing very large organisations where errors or misstatements have to be fairly huge to have any impact on the financial statements. The audit logic is that these will not arise from wrongly recorded day-to-day transactions, but will have their source in an identified area of risk. The risks can be either actual operational risks arising from the nature of the business (e.g. oil exploration) or from the complexity of the accounting required (e.g. derivatives trading).

Case Study 4

Prepare a plan and a budget

Jane will have to choose one of these approaches. Clearly for a company such as Metalbash a systems-based approach is likely to be the most appropriate. She could consider moving to a more risk-based approach once she is confident the new systems are working properly and the new financial controller is competent and understands the business.

The overall plan which Jane needs to prepare takes into account:

- An amendment of the Letter of Engagement to include the report to the Lorry Parts Manufacturers' Association and the visit to Wigan and the new company.
- Assessment of the impact of new directors staff and managers and the need for Jane to meet all the relevant staff and tour the works.
- Extra time needed to audit capital expenditure and consider the impact of all the changes on the organisation as a whole.
- Identification of audit risk areas. These include:
  - going concern;
  - capital/revenue identification on new plant;
  - the branch in Wigan;
  - new company in Essex, formerly insolvent;
  - increased stocks and debtors;
  - identification of all creditors especially as payment is likely to be slower;
  - the new computer system even though this is apparently going well;
  - the viability of the new products.
- Need to plan year-end presence at stocktaking at all locations.
- Need to spend time evaluating the new computer system and the changes in internal controls which have been introduced.
- Identification of areas which are not material and setting preliminary materiality levels.
- The making of a list of all assets and liabilities, revenues and expenses so that detailed schedules of these can be requested from the client. For example, she may request a breakdown of sales by product in order to examine the success/failure of the new products.
- Need to identify and test, at the interim audit, internal controls which she may wish to rely on.
- Need to audit assets and liabilities as much as possible before the year end in view of the short time available after the year end.
- Jane will need staff for the interim (which is flexibly dated), at the year-end stock take (at an awkward time and in widely separated locations), and at the final audit which will be rapid and therefore may need extra staff.

- Extra work is required this year (capital expenditure, new computer system, faster audit, Wigan, new company in Essex, liquidity problems) and the fee will need to reflect this.

Discuss the specific audit areas, the timing and the work the client will undertake in terms of providing draft accounts and supporting schedules.

ANALYTICAL REVIEW PROCEDURES

We discuss analytical review procedures in more detail in Chapter 12. For now it is sufficient to say that, as part of the initial planning process, it is important that the planner obtains a reasonable ideas of what has happened in the period so far and obtains a preliminary view of any possible problem areas at which audit work can be directed.

Apart from discussions with management, etc. one way of doing this is by carrying out a preliminary analytical review of the latest management accounts.

Analysis of key ratios, for example, Gross profit %, Net profit %, Stock turn, Debtor and creditor days, liquidity and quick ratios, etc. can give an indication of possible problem areas, which can be discussed further with management and investigated. It also aids the planner's understanding of the client and its activities.

THE TIMING OF AUDIT WORK

Audit work on the records and financial statements relating to a financial year are carried out at various times during, at the end and after the end of the financial period.

Audit visits

Audit work will be carried on at the client's premises. Where the client has branches, this can create problems of travelling for the auditor but in such cases some branches are visited as samples or all the branches are visited by rotation.

In the majority of cases, three extended visits are made by the auditor to the client's premises to carry out audit work:

- During the year – the interim audit.
- At the year end.
- After the year end – the final audit.

Clearly on audits of very large organisations there may be almost a permanent audit presence at the client. For example, the audit of a very large multinational may warrant almost a full-time presence on site.

If this is the case it is important that the staff be rotated regularly. The reason for this is that it is very easy for audit staff who are almost permanently in contact with their client to lose their objectivity and to begin to feel that they are, in fact, part of the client and not its auditors. The most notorious case of this was audit of Enron in the USA by Arthur Andersen, where it was noted that visitors to Enron could not tell the difference between Arthur Andersen staff and Enron personnel.

Interim audit

The interim audit will be carried out during the financial year. Very often the interim audit will be about two-thirds of the way through the year, e.g. September or October for a December year end.

The work done includes:

- Ascertain the system of accounting and internal control or review any changes from the previous year.
- Record the system or update systems records using flow charts or other methods.
- Evaluate the systems for adequacy and presence of apparent weaknesses.
- Design and carry out compliance tests to determine if the system is operated at all times in accordance with the description of the system evaluated by the auditor.
- Design and carry out tests to determine if, in areas where controls are weak or non-existent, the records can be relied upon.
- Draw conclusions on the adequacy of the systems and hence of the reliability of the books of account and other records.
- Seek evidence, by substantive tests, that unusual or one-off transactions have been fully and correctly recorded.
- Where possible carry out tests on assets and liabilities. Tests on assets and liabilities should be carried out after the year end but with clients with strong systems, some verification can be done at the interim stage. Examples are physical verification of stock records and debtors circularisation.

Year-end work

On the last day of the client's year end it will be possible to verify some year-end assets and liabilities in a way impossible at any other time. Thus attendance will be required for:

- Observation and testing of any stock count. This is now mandatory under ISA 501 *Audit Evidence – Additional Considerations for Specific Items.*
- Observation and testing of cut-off procedures.
- Counting of cash balances where these are a material figure on the Balance Sheet.

Final audit

The final audit will take place after the year end and is designed to seek evidence that financial statements give a true and fair view and comply with statutory and other requirements.

The timing of the final audit varies from client to client. Some final audits are commenced within days of the year end and the financial statements are published within as short a period as two months after the year end. Others are commenced many months after the year end. The advantage of an early audit and early publication of the accounts is that the information given to members and others is up to date.

From the audit point of view, transactions in progress at the year end are often not resolved and estimates of outcome have to be made and evaluated. The advantage of a late audit is that transactions in progress at the year end are often resolved and fewer estimates need to be made. For example, after a few months it will have become clear whether or not a doubtful debt is in fact bad. The disadvantage of a late audit is that information reaching members and others is out of date. The accounts will have become truly historical.

The work carried out after the year end will be:

- Updating of the auditor's review of the systems of accounting and internal control.

  This will involve:

  - Determining if the systems changed between the interim audit and the year end by interviewing officials and a few 'walk-through' tests.
  - Thoroughly testing new systems.
  - Compliance tests of the unchanged systems from the interim audit to the year end.
  - Drafting a Letter of Weakness for management regarding any weaknesses found in the control systems (Chapter 28).

- Drawing conclusions on:

  - Adequacy of the accounting system and the system of internal controls thereon.
  - Whether proper books of account have been kept.
  - Whether the book of account and other records form a reliable base for the preparation of the financial statements.

- Comparing the financial statements with the underlying records and books of account to see that they correspond.
- Performing substantive tests on assets and liabilities.
- Performing the final analytical review.
- Preparing and signing the auditor's report.

Audit Planning Memorandum

This records, in a standard format, all the decisions Jane has taken and the reasons why she has taken them. This will then have to be agreed with and signed off by the audit engagement partner.

An example of an Audit Planning Memorandum is included in Appendix 2.

AUDIT RISK

Audit Risk is the risk that the auditor might give an incorrect or inappropriate opinion on the financial statements.

A wrong audit opinion means, for example, saying that the financial statements show a true and fair view when in fact they do not or saying they do not show a true and fair view when, in fact, they do.

This can result in damage to the audit firm for giving a negligent opinion if the audit has not been performed properly. Damage to the audit firm may be in the form of monetary damages paid to a client or third party as compensation for loss caused by the conduct (e.g. negligence) of the audit firm or simply loss of reputation with the client and the business community.

ISA 200 *Objective and General Principles Governing an Audit of Financial Statements* and ISA 315 *Obtaining an Understanding of the Entity and its Environment and Assessing the Risks of a Material Misstatement*, set out the basis of how auditors should approach assessing Audit Risk.

It is important for the student to appreciate that Audit Risk is *not* the same as business risk, although there are some common features. Audit risk is the risk auditors have to assess, business risks are the totality of risks faced by a business or organisation carrying on its everyday activities.

Audit Risk is not business risk and nor is it the sort of areas of audit difficulty (i.e. new subsidiary, branch in Wigan, new staff, etc.) identified in our Metalbash example above – although these contribute to the auditors overall assessment of Audit Risk, but as part of a much wider consideration.

Audit Risk must be assessed at both the organisational level, i.e. looking at the financial statements as a whole, and at the transaction level where the auditor is seeking to verify disclosure of individual components of the financial statements, e.g. the value of stock and work in progress or the turnover figure. However, the general approach to assessing audit risk is the same whether it is being considered at the organisational level or at the transaction level.

Audit risk is calculated by using a formula which is:

$$AR = IR \times CR \times DR$$

AR is *Audit Risk* – the risk that the auditor will draw an invalid conclusion.

Inherent Risk (IR)

IR is *Inherent Risk* – risk which derives from the nature of the entity itself, its business and of its environment, or at the transaction level it is the susceptibility of the transactions to possible misstatement due to their nature or complexity.

Factors influencing Inherent Risk are:

- The nature of the entity's business, e.g. a construction company is a more volatile business than a fruit importing business.
- The quality and experience of the management.
- The level of competition in its market.
- The complexity of its operations.
- The cash situation of the business.
- The trading history of the business.

At the transaction level inherent risk is affected by:

- The susceptibility to misappropriation.
- The complexity of the transactions.
- The degree of judgement involved.

Control Risk (CR)

CR is *Control Risk* – this is the risk that the client's Internal Control procedures will fail to detect a material error or misstatement.

Control Risk is influenced by:

- The attitude of the directors and management towards internal control – what is known as the 'control environment'.
- The level of supervision in the business.
- The integrity of the staff and management.
- The strength of the individual controls in each area of the system.

The ICQs, flow charts and ICEQs will all influence the assessment of control risk, as will some of the areas of audit difficulty such as those described in the Metalbash example above:

- New and inexperienced staff.
- Changes in accounting systems.
- Additional locations.
- New products.

Detection Risk (DR)

DR is *Detection Risk* – the risk that the auditor's own procedures and review of the financial statements will not detect material errors or misstatements.

Evaluating Audit Risk

The auditor will make a preliminary assessment of the levels of inherent and control risk.

This can be done either by a simple subjective judgement, assessing risk as 'high', 'medium' or 'low' or by applying a value weighting or a statistical technique.

Auditors generally aim to have no more than a 5 per cent risk that the financial statements are materially incorrect – in other words they would be 95 per cent certain that their opinion is the correct one. This is known as the *confidence level*.

The important thing for the student to appreciate is that Detection Risk is the variable in the equation. The higher the level of Inherent and Control Risk, the more checking work the auditor has to do.

This can be illustrated by using an arithmetical example.

Suppose the auditors estimate the level of Inherent Risk to be 50 per cent and the level of Control Risk to be 20 per cent, i.e. that there is an 80 per cent chance that an error or mistake would be detected by the internal control system.

By rearranging the equation we can determine the level of Detection Risk:

$$DR = AR \div (IR \times CR)$$

With Audit Risk at 5 per cent, the equation becomes:

$$DR = 0.05 \div (0.5 \times 0.2) = 0.5 \text{ or } 50\%$$

Auditors would then have to consider the level of audit work they would have to do to maintain Detection Risk at the 50 per cent level.

Care must be taken to weigh the risk from each source of evidence as it is gathered and then to avoid over auditing in the remaining evidence gathering. For example, if adequate weight is given to inherent factors and analytical review it may be that minimal internal control evaluation and/or detailed testing will be required.

In order to properly evaluate the levels of Inherent and Control Risk auditors need to carry out the investigatory procedures described above, namely:

- get to know their client – as part of their planning procedures; and
- review the client's internal control systems by documenting them thoroughly and by the use of questionnaires.

It cannot be stressed enough that without this preliminary review of the client's business and its systems and thorough documentation the audit may be seriously flawed.

Auditors base all of their checking work, indeed their whole audit strategy, on their opinion of the client's financial capabilities and the business risks involved in the client's activities. All the auditors' subsequent activity stems from this preliminary investigation and discovery work which, if it is incomplete or flawed may well lead to:

- Inadequate testing of key areas.
- Being misled by managers because of incomplete knowledge of the business.
- Failing to identify areas where frauds could be committed.

MATERIALITY

Materiality is often an matter of judgement and can be a particularly difficult matter in practice but is of great importance. Great care should be taken before coming to a conclusion on matters of materiality.

ISA 320 *Audit Materiality* states:

Information is material if its omission or misstatement could influence the economic decisions of users taken on the basis of the financial statements. . . .

The assessment of what is material is a matter of professional judgement.

In addition to that, the Companies Act is full of references to materiality. For example, there must be shown separately in the profit and loss account the amount, *if material*, charged to revenue in respect of sums payable for the hire of plant and machinery.

Materiality is a matter of professional judgement and it has both quantitative (amount) and qualitative (nature) dimensions.

Quantitative estimates

For example a figure might be material purely because of its size relative to other amounts in the accounts. Auditors often set some form of percentage values on errors which will decide if they are material or not, for example:

- 5–10% of pre-tax profits;
- 1% of turnover;
- 5% of net asset value.

However, this should not be taken as being prescriptive – the actual amount decided on will be a matter of professional judgement.

For example, a sum might be quite small but is sufficient to turn a pre-tax profit into a pre-tax loss. This would almost certainly be material as it would be likely to influence the economic decisions of a reader of the accounts. There are some methods by which auditors can assess whether or not items are material:

- Compare the magnitude of the item with the overall view presented by the accounts.
- Compare the magnitude of the item with the magnitude of the same item in previous years.
- Compare the magnitude of the item with the total of which it forms a part (e.g. 'debtors' may include employee loans but if employee loans become large, i.e. material, then, the description 'debtors' may be inadequate).
- Some items are always material, e.g. directors' remuneration.

Qualitative estimates

Materiality also has qualitative aspects and these relate to the nature of the error or misstatement detected, regardless of its financial value.

For example, errors which are material by virtue of their nature would include:

- Omission of a disclosure required by the Companies Act or accounting standards.
- An item which is misstated in the accounts – e.g. a short-term loan classified as a long-term loan.
- An item which might affect the accounts but which has been omitted because it cannot be quantified with a reasonable degree of certainty, e.g. the outcome of a court case.

In these cases the auditors should remind the directors of their duty to comply with the Companies Act and the accounting standards and rectify omissions or misstatements.

Materiality and audit procedures

Auditors should take materiality into account when considering the nature, timing and extent of audit procedures.

Materiality should be taken into account at the planning stage and reconsidered if the outcome of tests, enquiries or examinations differs from expectation.

In evaluating whether the financial statements give a true and fair view, auditors should assess the materiality of the *aggregate* or total of uncorrected errors. These may be those identified during the audit and the best estimate of others which the auditors have not quantified specifically. Examples might be numerous small errors in the sales ledger or in coding expense invoices. If the directors adjust the financial statements for these all may be well, but if not the aggregate misstatement may be material when each individual misstatement is not.

Summary

- The audit can be seen as having the following stages:

  - Background research into the client's place in the economy generally and its industry in particular, the client's constitution, history, operations and personnel.
  - Evaluation of audit risk.
  - Documentation of the client's systems.
  - Preparation of an audit plan.
  - Accounting and internal control system review.
  - Audit testing including analytical review procedures.
  - Analytical review of financial statements at both the planning and final stages.
  - Audit work is usually accomplished on several visits to the client's premises.

- The work is usually distributed between:

  - An interim audit during the financial year.
  - A year-end attendance.
  - A final audit after the year end.

- The interim audit is principally for the investigation and testing of the systems of recording and internal control.

- The year-end work is mainly for the observation and testing of the stock count but also the examination of cash balances where these are material.

- The final audit is all the rest of the work and includes:

  - testing systems for the period from the interim audit to the year end;
  - substantive testing of transactions and balances;
  - final analytical review;
  - preparation and signing of the report.

- Audit risk involves consideration of the levels of inherent and control risk. The higher these are the more audit work has to be done to reduce Detection Risk.

- Audit risk is not business risk.

- Materiality has both quantitative and qualitative aspects and is a matter of judgement.

Points to note

- The auditors are not concerned with individual routine transactions but with the system for documenting and recording them. They are still concerned with material non-routine transactions.

- It is important to remember that the system of accounting is not separate from the system of internal controls over the books and records.

- Audit firms have sought greater effectiveness in their audit procedures together with greater efficiency. This has led to:

  - Greater use of risk-based techniques.
  - Greater reliance on analytical review.

The timing of audit work depends upon many factors including:

- Deadlines fixed by the client. For example, the client may arrange an AGM for three months after the year end.

- The organisation of the accountant's office. For example, bunching of client year ends around certain dates (e.g. 31 December) can create severe problems.
- The extent to and the time in which the client can provide schedules and analyses. If these are not available more time is required on the final audit.
- The extent to which the client has very strong systems in routine areas such as debtors, creditors, stock control, fixed asset registers. Where the systems are very reliable substantive tests can sometimes be performed at the interim instead of the final audit. For example, debtors and creditors circularisation and comparison of physical stock or fixed assets with records could be performed at the interim with only small samples being tested at the final.
- When an audit is carried out for the first time on a new client, additional visits may be necessary, in order that the auditor may obtain knowledge of the client, its background, personnel, accounting problems, audit risk areas, etc. Following the visits the audit plan can be prepared.
- In some large audits with very highly computerised records, audit evidence is sometimes available on a temporary basis only. For example, where internal control (say over the credit worthiness of customers) is operated by a computer program which is changed at intervals. Then the auditor needs to be present at fairly frequent intervals to test the functioning of the controls on which he wishes to rely.

Case Study 5

You are working on the audit of your client Sweetie Ltd for the year ended 31 March 20x8.

The company employs one hundred workers in a doughnut manufacturing plant. Wages are paid weekly.

The following procedures are carried out:

- Employees clock cards are signed by supervisors and brought to the wages office every Monday morning.
- Hours are taken from the cards. Overtime hours are calculated and entered on an overtime sheet which is then used to calculate overtime payments.
- The overtime sheet is authorised by the production manager.
- Wages are prepared using a standard computerised wages software package – Sage.
- Standard hours and overtime hours are entered into the payroll using the input screen.
- Any amendments to employees' details, e.g. changes of address or tax code, are entered on each employee's computer file.
- Details of any new starters are entered into the system.
- Leavers are removed from the system once their final week's wages have been calculated.
- The payroll is processed and then authorised by the production manager.
- It is then passed to the accounts department who prepare BACs payments for each employee.
- Wages are paid on Friday so the payroll has to be prepared in time to ensure employees are paid promptly.

Internal Control Questionnaire

Client name _____

Prepared by _____
Date _____
Reviewed by _____
Date _____

Period to _____

WAGES SYSTEM
Control procedures

Process	Yes	No	N/A	Comments
Is there an individual file recording each employees details?				
Are rates of pay authorised by a responsible official?				
Are there procedures to remove leavers from the payroll as soon as they have been paid their final wages?				
Are there procedures to ensure new starters are included on the payroll correctly?				
Are there procedures to ensure that changes in employees' details are properly recorded?				
Is the payroll software a standard package? (Record details)				
Is there a wages preparation timetable?				
Do employees have to record start and finish times?				
Are overtime rates approved by a responsible official?				
Are hours worked authorised by a responsible official of the company? (record details)				
Is the payroll approved by a responsible official before wages are paid?				
Are employees paid by bank transfer?				
Are the people involved in making the payments different to those who prepare the payroll?				

Discussion

- The audit manager has asked you to complete the ICQ based on the payroll system details set out above.

Case Study 6

One of your junior staff has prepared some slides for a presentation to a client on the practical procedures involved in auditing. The slides contain the following statements:

a) Materiality is generally defined as being about 5 per cent of gross profit or 10 per cent of net profit.

b) Audit sampling depends on the level of materiality – the higher the level the less work you need to do.

c) Vouching is a test of transactions between books of original entry.

d) Analytical procedures should be used as a final procedure at the end of the audit just to check the figures look OK.

e) Auditors need to select samples which represent the population as a whole.

f) Providing the financial statements comply with the law auditors have to accept them.

Discussion

– Which of these should you remove from the slides before the presentation is given and why?

Student self-testing questions

(Questions with answers apparent from the text)

a) Outline the key stages of the audit.

b) What is the difference between an ICQ and an ICEQ?

c) Give three advantages of flow charting a client's system.

d) What is a walk-through test?

e) What are the components of audit risk?

f) Define materiality.

g) What is inherent risk?

h) What are the three main audit strategies?

i) What sort of work can be carried out at an interim audit?

j) What would be the main components of an audit plan?

k) How would an audit plan be recorded?

Examination question

1 You have been presented with the following draft financial information about Hivex, a very successful company that develops and licences specialist computer software and hardware. Its fixed assets mainly consist of property, computer hardware and investments, and there have been additions to these during the year. The company is

experiencing increasing competition from rival companies, most of which specialise in hardware or software, but not both. There is pressure to advertise and to cut prices.

You are the audit manager. You are planning the audit and you are conducting a preliminary analytical review and associated risk analysis for this client for the year ended 31 May 20x8. You have been provided with a summarised draft profit and loss account, which has been produced very quickly, and certain accounting ratios and percentages.

You have been informed that the company accounts for research and development costs in accordance with SSAP 13 *Accounting for Research and Development*.

PROFIT AND LOSS ACCOUNT

Year ended 31 May

	20x8	20x7
	£000s	£000s
Sales	15 206	13 524
Cost of sales	3 009	3 007
Gross profit	12 197	10 517
Distribution costs	3 006	1 996
Administrative expenses	994	1 768
Selling expenses	3 002	274
Profit from operations	5 195	6 479
Net interest receivable	995	395
Profit before tax	6 190	6 874
Corporation tax	3 104	1 452
Net profit	3 086	5 422
Dividends paid	1 469	1 439
Retained profits	1 617	3 983
Accounting ratios and percentages		
Earnings per share	0·43	1·04
Performance ratios include the following:		
Gross margin	0·80	0·78
Expenses as a percentage of sales:		
Distribution costs	0·20	0·15
Administrative expenses	0·07	0·13
Selling expenses	0·20	0·02
Operating profit	0·34	0·48

Required:

(a) Using the information above, comment briefly on the performance of the company for the two years.

(b) Use your answer to part (a) to identify the areas that are subject to increased audit risk and describe the further audit work you would perform in response to those risks.

(ACCA)

11

Audit evidence and using the work of an expert

INTRODUCTION

ISA 500 *Audit Evidence* sets out the standards and guidelines as to what constitutes suitable audit evidence. It will be apparent by now that the purpose of all the auditor's planning and testing work is the gathering of *sufficient appropriate* evidence which can be used to substantiate the audit opinion.

It says:

> The auditor should obtain sufficient appropriate evidence to be able to draw reasonable conclusions on which to base the audit opinion.
>
> "Audit evidence" is all the information used by the auditor in arriving at the conclusions on which the audit opinion is based, and includes all the information contained in the accounting records underlying the financial statements and other information. Auditors are not expected to address all the information that may exist.

This extract from the international standard tells us two things:

- evidence has to be 'sufficient' and 'appropriate';
- that auditors do not have to look at everything.

Sufficiency is the measure of the *amount* of evidence gathered and *appropriateness* is a measure of its *quality*, its fitness for purpose.

For example, an auditor looking at fixed assets verification may go and inspect the relevant assets. This may be sufficient evidence if the auditor can inspect a significant number of the relevant assets and it may be appropriate – but only as far as existence of the assets are concerned. An inspection of assets can prove they exist, but it doesn't prove the client owns them – another test has to be done for that.

FINANCIAL STATEMENTS AND ASSERTIONS

Directors produce or cause to be produced financial statements. In doing so they are *asserting* that:

- The individual items are:

  - Correctly described.
  - Show figures which are arithmetically correct or fairly estimated.

- The accounts as a whole show a true and fair view.

ISA 500 splits the assertions into three categories, as follows:

1 Assertions about classes of transactions and events for the period under review

Occurrence	Transactions and events that have been recorded relate to the company being audited and not to another organisation.
Completeness	All transactions and events that should have been recorded have been recorded.
Accuracy	Amounts and all other data relating to recorded transactions have been recorded appropriately.
Cut-off	Transactions and events have been recorded in the correct accounting period.
Classification	Transactions and events have been recorded in the proper accounts (in the books and records).

2 Assertions about account balances at the period end

Existence	Assets, liabilities and equity interests (shareholdings) exist.
Rights and obligations	The company holds or controls the rights to assets, and all liabilities are those of the company.
Completeness	All assets, liabilities and equity interests that should have been recorded have been recorded.
Valuation and allocation	Assets, liabilities and equity interests (shareholdings) are included in the financial statements at appropriate amounts and any resulting valuation or allocation adjustments are properly recorded.

3 Assertions about presentation and disclosure

Occurrence and rights and obligations	Disclosed events, transactions and other matters have occurred and pertain to the company.
Completeness	All disclosures that should have been included in the financial statements have been included.
Classification and understandability	Financial information is appropriately presented and described and disclosures are clearly expressed.
Accuracy and valuation	Financial and other information is disclosed fairly and at appropriate amounts.

The assertions are set down in this way but, as you can see, some of them are the same in each category. Auditors are allowed to combine them together so, for example, evidence validating assertions about transactions in (1) can also be used to validate assertions about balances in (2).

Providing auditors gather sufficient evidence of the right type to validate these assertions they will have enough to support their audit opinion.

The auditor's attitude to each item in the accounts will be as follows:

- Identify the express and implied assertions made by the directors in including (or excluding) the item in the accounts.
- Evaluate each assertion for relative importance to assess the quality and quantity of evidence required.
- Collect information and evidence.
- Assess the evidence for:
    i. Appropriateness. Appropriateness subsumes the ideas of quality and reliability of a particular piece of audit evidence and its relevance to a particular assertion.
    ii. Sufficiency – more of this in a later paragraph.

It is important to note that audit evidence tends to be *persuasive* rather than absolute. Consequently, like a good detective, auditors tend to seek evidence from several different sources or of a different nature to support the same assertion.

Note also that auditors only have to provide *reasonable* assurance that the financial statements are free from a material misstatement, they don't have to prove the assertions beyond doubt – although if they can do it is very reassuring.

Having formulated judgement on each individual item in (or omitted from) the accounts, the auditors must formulate a judgement on the truth and fairness of accounts as a whole.

To do this they will need other evidence in addition to the judgements they have made on the individual items. As an extreme example, they may need evidence of the directors' implied assertion that the accounts should be drawn up on the going concern principle.

SOURCES OF EVIDENCE

The evidence an auditor collects can be from many different sources.

1 Auditor-derived evidence
    The best evidence is evidence derived by the auditors as a result of their own tests and procedures. These can include:

- Compliance tests of controls.
- Substantive tests of transactions and balances.
- Observation of company procedures, e.g. stocktakes.
- Inspection of documents, assets, etc. These include:
    - Authoritative documents prepared *outside* the firm, e.g. title deeds, share and loan certificates, leases, contracts, franchises, invoices.
    - Authoritative documents prepared *inside* the firm, e.g. minutes, copy invoices.

2 Independent third-party evidence
    The next most reliable form of evidence is that provided by independent third parties. Examples of this include:

- bank letters;
- debtors circularisation;
- suppliers statements.

3 Representations made by directors and officers of the company.

In many ways this is the least reliable form of evidence. Auditors should not accept the unsupported testimony of directors or staff without any other form of corroboration unless there is absolutely no other evidence available. We discuss this in Chapter 25 in connection with the Letter of Representation.

This type of evidence may be formal, for example, the Letter of Representation, or informal, for example, in replies to ICQ questions.

BASIC TECHNIQUES FOR COLLECTING EVIDENCE

There are several ways the auditors can gather sufficient appropriate evidence. The main methodologies are:

- Inspection of documents, procedures and tangible assets.
- Observation. Seeing for oneself is the best possible confirmation especially in connection with internal control systems.
- Enquiry. Asking questions. This is a necessary and valid technique. The reliability of the evidence depends on the qualification and integrity of its source. A good example is the circulation of debtors at the year end to confirm balances in the sales ledger.
- Confirmations. These should be in writing, external sources being preferable to internal sources; for example, a supplier's statement can be used to confirm a purchase ledger balance.
- Computation – additions, calculations, reconciliations, etc.
- Re-performance – testing controls by re-performing them, for example, checking the bank reconciliation.
- Sample testing.

This subject is explored in more detail in Chapter 12 but needs some consideration here. Auditors obtain evidence about each type of transaction by examining a representative sample of each type. This is called sample testing and is applied as much to assets and liabilities as to routine transactions.

The size of the sample to be tested depends on:

- the strength of the internal control system;
- the materiality of the items;
- the number of items involved;
- the nature of the item;
- the Audit Risk attached.

Sources of audit evidence

Sources of audit evidence include from within:

- accounting systems;
- accounting records;
- documents;
- management and staff.

and from without:

- customers;
- suppliers;
- lenders;
- professional advisers, etc.

The sources and amount of evidence required will depend on:

- materiality;
- relevance; and
- reliability

of the evidence available from a source.

Remember that auditors have to provide evidence that is *appropriate* to the assertion being validated, it must be *reliable* evidence, i.e. not flawed by a wrongly performed or invalid test or evidenced by a copy document rather than an original and there must be enough of it to make a valid test, so it must be *sufficient*.

Appropriateness

The appropriateness of audit evidence depends upon whether it assists the auditors in forming an opinion on some aspect of the assertions on which the financial statements are based. For example, evidence that indicates that a recorded asset exists is relevant to audit objectives.

Reliability

The reliability of audit evidence can be assessed to some extent on the following presumptions:

- Documentary evidence is more reliable than oral evidence.
- Evidence from outside the enterprise (e.g. a confirmation bank letter) is more reliable than that secured solely from within the enterprise.
- Evidence originated by the auditor by such means as analysis, audit testing and physical inspection is more reliable than evidence obtained from others.
- Evidence for a figure in the accounts is usually obtained from several sources. For example, to verify debtors auditors could provide evidence from:

  - verifying that there is a good sales system with strong internal controls;
  - performing a debtors circularisation;
  - carrying out ratio analysis;
  - checking payment of balances after date, etc.

- The cumulative effect of several evidential sources which give a consistent view is greater than that from a single source (i.e. in this case $2 + 2 = 5$).
- Original documents are more reliable than photocopies or facsimiles.

Sufficiency

Sufficiency is the great problem. The auditors' judgement will be influenced by:

- Their knowledge of the business and its industry.
- The degree of audit risk.

Assessment of this is helped by considering:

- Nature and materiality of items of account (e.g. provisions for liabilities may be material but may be difficult to measure accurately because of the assumptions involved).
- The auditor's experience of the reliability of the management and staff and the records.
- The financial position of the enterprise (in a failing enterprise, directors may wish to bolster profits by over-valuing assets or suppressing liabilities).
- Possible management bias (as above) but also the management may wish to 'even out' profits for stock market image or taxation reasons.
- The persuasiveness of the evidence.
- The nature of the accounting and internal control systems and the control environment.

USING THE WORK OF AN EXPERT

Introduction

IAS 620 *Using the Work of an Expert* states:

> *When using work performed by an expert, the auditor should obtain sufficient appropriate audit evidence that such work is adequate for the purposes of the audit.*

In other words it is up to the auditors to confirm whether or not the work performed by the expert is 'adequate' for the audit – the responsibility remains, as always, with them.

In general the auditors programme of work will provide them with sufficient reliable relevant evidence to enable them to substantiate their opinion. However, there can be circumstances where the auditor's knowledge is insufficient and they may then need to rely on the opinions of experts or specialists to help them form an opinion.

What is an expert?

What is an expert, in this context?

IAS 620 defines an expert as:

> *A person or firm possessing special skill, knowledge and experience in a particular field other than accounting or auditing.*

Examples of specialists whose work may be relied upon by auditors include:

- Valuers – on the value of fixed assets such as freehold and leasehold property or more rarely plant and machinery and on the value of specialist stock in trade such as beers, wines and spirits or specialist stock such as jewellery.
- Quantity surveyors – on the value of work done on long-term contracts.
- Actuaries – on the liability to be included for pension scheme liabilities.
- Geologists – on the quantity and quality of mineral reserves.
- Stockbrokers – on the value of stock exchanges securities.
- Lawyers – on the legal interpretation of contracts and agreements, or the outcome of disputes and litigation.

Points to consider

In general, in deciding whether the auditors needs to have specialist opinions they will consider:

- The knowledge and abilities of the audit team – does it have the expertise to deal with the issue itself? If not an expert may have to be called in.
- The risk of a material misstatement based on the nature, complexity and materiality of the material being considered.
- The quantity and quality of other audit evidence which can be obtained.

Often auditors have little other evidence on which to base their opinion on such values. Property companies incorporate values of properties in their accounts, the source of such valuations being specialist commercial valuers. The auditors may have little other reliable evidence except the specialist valuer's opinion.

The expert can be hired either by the auditor or the client – either way the client is likely to end up paying – so cost considerations are important. The auditor should involve experts *only* when no other sufficient appropriate evidence is available.

Factors which may influence the auditor to rely upon or not to rely upon the work of a specialist include:

- *The competence of the specialist* –This may be indicated by technical qualifications, certification and licensing or membership of professional bodies. The expert also should have some level of reputation or standing in the area of their expertise.
- *The experience of the specialist* – The expert should have the appropriate experience to carry out the work. For example, if the matter involves a valuation of commercial property it would not be appropriate to engage an expert whose experience was only that of valuing domestic property, however well-qualified technically that person was.
- *The independence of the specialist* – The degree of relationship with the client may be the key factor. Any specialist who is related to the directors or employees of the client or who has financial interest (other than his fee) with the client is clearly less than wholly independent. Apparent dependence may be mitigated by professional body disciplinary and ethical codes.

Process

If it is the intention of the auditor to place reliance on the work of a specialist, it is important to hold a consultation between auditor, client and specialist, at the time the specialist is appointed, to reach agreement on the work to be performed. The agreement should cover:

- Objectives, scope and subject matter of the specialist's work.
- Assumptions upon which the specialist's report depends and their compatibility with the accounts. For example, are going concern or market values to be taken?
- A statement of the bases used in previous years and any change to be made.
- The use to be made of the specialist's findings. (They may need this for professional indemnity insurance purposes.)
- The form and content of the specialist's report or opinion.
- The sources of information to be provided to the specialist.

- The identification of any relationship which may affect the specialist's objectivity. An example of this may be the case of an architect who, though in private practice, obtains most of his commissions from the client who is subject to audit.

It is possible to use a specialist's opinion without this process but it is desirable to go through this procedure.

Evaluation of the specialist evidence

As we have seen the sufficiency and appropriateness of such evidence will depend upon:

- the nature of the evidence required;
- the materiality of the items being evidenced;
- the auditor's assessment of the competence of the specialist;
- their independence from the client.

The auditors have to review the findings of the experts and draw their own conclusions. In particular they will look at:

- The source data used i.e. what has the expert based their opinion on?
- The assumptions and methods used – and their consistency with previous periods.
- When the expert's work was carried out – i.e. were valuations carried out at the year end or some other date and does it matter?
- An overall evaluation of the expert's work in the light of the auditors' overall knowledge of the business and the industry and the results of other audit procedures, which may go some way towards corroborating the expert's opinion.

The auditors may well want to:

- review the sources themselves to ascertain whether or not they are reliable;
- review the specialists procedures; and
- review any data used by the expert for themselves

in order to satisfy themselves that the work the expert has done can be relied on.

Clearly the auditor does not have the same level of expertise and experience as an expert and the expert's opinion can be difficult to challenge.

The key point is this:

- the expert's opinion is their responsibility – they have to carry out the work they do to the best of their ability;
- whether that work provides sufficient appropriate evidence for the auditor is the *auditors'* responsibility – and that is what they alone can decide.

If the auditors are not happy with the expert's work they have some options:

- Try again with another expert – cost considerations are important and there is no guarantee the outcome will be any different.
- Discuss the situation with the client and the expert together to see if difficulties can be resolved.
- Apply additional audit procedures.
- As a last resort it may be necessary to modify (qualify) the auditors' report on the grounds of lack of evidence.

Summary

- When the directors prepare accounts they are making assertions about the items in the accounts, items omitted from the accounts, and the accounts as a whole.
- The auditor conducts an audit by:
  - Identifying the assertions made.
  - Considering the information and evidence needed.
  - Collecting the evidence and information.
  - Evaluating the evidence.
  - Formulating a judgement.
- There are many different varieties of evidence. Some varieties are of more value than others.
- There are several techniques for collecting evidence and auditors should endeavour to collect evidence from a variety of different sources.
- An established method of collecting evidence is sampling.
- Some legal decisions have appeared to guide the auditor in assessing what evidence is needed. We will look at this in a later chapter.
- IAS 500 on Audit Evidence discusses relevance, reliability and sufficiency and gives some criteria for assessing these qualities in audit evidence.
- An expert should be suitably qualified and appropriately experienced for the task.
- The specialist should have their terms of agreement drawn up after consultation with the auditors.
- It is up to the auditors whether or not to accept that the evidence produced by the expert is sufficient and appropriate for their purposes.
- The opinion of a specialist could be essential evidence to the auditors so they should review the bases on which the expert's opinion is founded.

Points to note

- It is a very good idea both in practice and in examinations to identify what express and implied assertions are being made when an item appears in accounts or does not appear. You should get into the habit of doing this as often as possible.
- A mental review of the varieties of evidence and the techniques of evidence collection as shown above will often suggest a comprehensive answer to practical and examination problems of verification.
- There is a distinction made in the more theoretical books on auditing between evidential matter and audit evidence. The auditor gathers immense quantities of evidential matter from the business records and management and staff and from third parties. This evidential matter is evaluated by the auditor. If it is relevant to the audit objectives (e.g. ownership of an asset or completeness of a revenue total) and it is reliable to any extent, it becomes audit evidence.
- An expert may be engaged by or employed by the entity or the auditor. When the expert is employed by the auditor then ISA 220 *Quality Control for Audits of Historical Financial Information* will apply to the work.

- Auditors should never uncritically accept the opinion of a specialist. Corroborative evidence should always be sought.
- In all cases, the auditors have to consider whether they have relevant and reliable audit evidence which is sufficient to enable them to draw reasonable conclusions.

Case Study 1

Down Market Department Stores PLC sell a high proportion of their merchandise on hire purchase (HP). The system for dealing with HP sales is highly organised and well controlled. The HP debtors ledger is kept on a specially designed computer system. The HP debtors of the company at 30.9.-X7 appear in the accounts at £4.6 million out of gross assets of £19.3 million.

Discussion
- What assertions are the directors implying in stating the HP debtors at £4.6 million?
- What possible misstatements could occur?
- What varieties of evidence may be collected re this current asset?
- What basic techniques for collecting evidence can be applied to the item?

Case Study 2

Archaic Manufacturing PLC have a freehold factory which has been used to make the company's heavy metal products for generations. The factory was revalued ten years ago and is being depreciated over 50 years from that value. The company made a product for many years which has now been shown to be toxic and legal actions against the company have been expected. No mention occurs in the financial statements of these possible actions.

Discussion
- What are the assertions relevant to these matters?
- What FRSs and/or International Accounting Standards are relevant here?
- What kind of evidence might be collected?

Case Study 3

Hermit Galleries PLC are international art dealers with a turnover of £30 million a year.

They specialise in Impressionist paintings and have a stock valued at £10 million.

Recently it has been rumoured that some £4 million worth of their stock may be the work of a particularly brilliant forger.

Towards the end of the financial year the company have agreed with the auditor to commission a report on the authenticity of the stock from a well-known academic expert.

Discussion

- Draw up the terms of reference for the expert.
- Draft a checklist to examine the expert's report as audit evidence.
- The actual expert's opinion was certainty on the authenticity of £1.1 million worth, certainty on the forged nature of £1.6 m worth and doubt about the remainder.
- What should the auditor do?

Student self-testing questions

(Questions with answers apparent from the text)

a) What are the main classes of Assertions about items in accounts?

b) What varieties of audit evidence are there?

c) What basic techniques for obtaining audit evidence are there?

d) What criteria are there for determining the size of a sample to be used in test checking?

e) What criteria are there for assessing reliability?

f) What criteria are there for assessing sufficiency?

g) List sources of audit evidence.

h) What might influence an auditor's judgement on sufficiency of audit evidence?

i) Give examples of reliance by auditors on the evidence supplied by specialists.

j) In what conditions may such reliance be required?

k) What factors indicate the reliability of the specialist?

l) What terms should appear in the agreement?

m) How should the auditor evaluate the evidence?

12

Audit testing, sampling and analytical procedures

INTRODUCTION

In order to gather the evidence they need auditors carry out audit testing on the transactions and balances which are represented in the financial statements presented to them.

They also have to look for possible transactions which may not be included in the accounts and transactions which occur after the period end but which might have a bearing on the accounts, but we will deal with these elsewhere.

FORMS OF AUDIT TESTING

The form of testing the auditors carry out is divided into *compliance tests* of the system of controls and *substantive testing* of transactions and balances.

Compliance tests

Compliance tests are tests to obtain audit evidence about the effective operation of the control environment, in particular the operation of control procedures.

The auditor will review the answers from:

- the internal control evaluation questionnaires which will highlight any particular areas of weakness;
- previous period's audit files to identify any problem areas encountered in previous years;
- the Letter of Weakness (see Chapter 28) sent to management at the conclusion of the previous period's audit identifying any areas of weakness in the control environment which management was being asked to address.

In areas where the system appears to be particularly defective or weak then the auditor may need to abandon a systems-based approach and apply more detailed *substantive tests*. These would normally be applied more at the period end than at the interim audit.

Two points must be made about compliance testing:

- It is very important for the student to understand that it is the application of the control procedure that is being tested, *not* the transaction itself, although the testing is through the medium of the transactions. When designing audit tests emphasis must be placed on designing tests which check the operation of the *control*. The actual transaction is, to this extent, not relevant as long as it is representative of the entire population being tested.

- If the auditors discover that the control procedures were not functioning correctly in a particular way then:
  - they may need to revise the system description and re-appraise its effectiveness;
  - they will need to determine if the failure of compliance was an isolated instance or was symptomatic of a larger failure;
  - it may be that a larger sample needs to be taken.

We discuss audit sampling later in this Chapter.

As an example of a test of control procedures, suppose that a system provided that all credit notes issued by the client had to be approved by the sales manager and that a space was provided on each credit note for his initials. The auditor would inspect a sample of the credit notes to determine if all of them had been initialled. This is testing that the *control* is operating – and the details of the credit note aren't relevant to the test being performed.

Substantive testing

Substantive procedures are detailed tests of transactions and balances. They are designed to obtain audit evidence to detect material misstatements in the financial statements and are required to be used in Balance Sheet testing in particular.

They are generally of two types:

- analytical procedures – see later in this Chapter.
- other substantive procedures, such as tests of details of transactions and balances, reviews of minutes of directors' meetings and enquiries.

From this definition, you may deduce that *all* audit work comes within the definition of substantive testing. However, the term 'substantive testing' is usually used to mean all tests other than tests of controls. A substantive test is any test which seeks *direct evidence* of the correct treatment of a transaction, a balance, an asset, a liability, or any item in the books or the accounts.

Analytical review is also seen as a separate type of test.

Some examples:

- Of a transaction – the sale of a piece of plant will require the auditor to examine the copy invoice, the authorisation, the entry in the plant register and other books, the accounting treatment and some evidence that the price obtained was reasonable.
- Of a balance – direct confirmation of the balance in a deposit account obtained from the bank.
- Analytical review – evidence of the correctness of cut-off by examining the gross profit ratio.
- Completeness of information – obtaining confirmation from a client's legal adviser that all potential payments from current litigation had been considered.
- Accuracy of information – obtaining from each director a confirmation that an accurate statement of remuneration and expenses had been obtained.
- Validity of information – validity means based on evidence that can be supported. For example, a provision for future warranty claims may be extremely difficult to estimate in precise monetary terms. If such a provision is made in the Financial Statements, the auditor would need to apply substantive tests to determine its validity, i.e. that it was supported by adequate evidence.

IAS 500 'Audit Evidence' states:

When substantive procedures alone do not provide sufficient appropriate audit evidence the auditor is required to perform tests of controls to obtain audit evidence about their operating effectiveness. . . .

. . . substantive procedures for material classes of transactions, account balances and disclosures are always required to obtain sufficient appropriate audit evidence.

Auditors must therefore use both these types of tests in order to provide the evidence they need.

The tests set out below comprise a mixture of compliance and substantive approaches, as it is really not necessary when designing audit tests to decide which test falls into which category.

Remember though that the *amount* of testing carried out and the *emphasis* of the tests is very much geared to the assessment of Audit Risk (see Chapter 10). If audit risk is considered to be high samples will be larger and the audit will focus on testing a larger number of transactions and balances than if the risk assessment is low and the audit approach can be one based on the successful operation of the company's internal control procedures.

Audit tests comprise a combination of:

- inspecting for evidence that a control has been operated;
- re-performing the accounting procedure on a sample of transactions, in either direction, to demonstrate that they have been carried out correctly;
- carrying out substantive tests on balances and reconciliations including obtaining independent evidence and analytical review procedures.

AUDIT SAMPLING

Introduction

Clearly it is impossible, in all but the very smallest organisations, for auditors to check every transaction. In the case of the largest companies there may be millions of items of data which the auditor would have to consider. Oddly the general public often has the perception that auditors check everything, which is why, when some form of financial scandal surfaces, uninformed speculation often tries to attach blame to the auditors because they are supposed to have checked everything.

The sheer impossibility of this, not to mention the prohibitive cost if it were to be even attempted, is why auditors adopt a either a systems-based approach to auditing or a risk-based approach, which we look at in Chapters 13 and 14, both of which require the auditors to select samples of transactions for testing.

Note, however, that the auditors expect to gain audit evidence about a population from sampling it but wise auditors will use sampling tests only in conjunction with other available evidence, in addition to the evidence from the sample.

Sampling is only one method of gathering evidence by audit testing and students should be familiar with other methods of evidence gathering, as discussed in Chapter 11.

Basis of sampling

Central to any form of systems-based auditing is the concept of audit sampling.

The objective in all sampling is to draw conclusions about a large volume of data, known as the population, based on examination of a sample taken from that population. The population for this purpose is a category of transactions e.g. all the sales invoices or all the PAYE calculations or all the goods received notes.

Note that for sampling purposes every item in the population must be of the same type. There is an auditing standard ISA 530 *Audit Sampling and Other Means of Testing.* ISA 530 states:

When designing audit procedures the auditor should determine appropriate means for selecting items for testing so as to gather sufficient appropriate audit evidence to meet the objectives of the audit procedures.

What this means is the application of audit procedures to less than 100 per cent of items within a class or type of transactions such that each individual item within that class has an equal chance of selection. This enables the auditors to draw conclusions, based on the results of those tests, about the population as a whole.

Sampling is most often used in compliance testing of client's internal controls, but can also be applied to tests of balance sheet items such as stocks, debtor and creditor ledger balances, or fixed assets.

There are two key issues fundamental to all sampling techniques.

1 The population has to be homogeneous – i.e. each item in the population has to be the same as the next one.

For example, sampling test on sales invoices cannot include credit notes; a sampling test on finished goods stock items cannot include raw material stocks. Each class of transaction has to be sampled separately – which may mean lots of tests!

2 Every item in the population must have an equal chance of selection.

This means that, for example, block sampling – where auditors pick a block of transactions to test, e.g. all Goods Returned Notes in May – is not actually a very good basis for testing as, in this case, the Goods Returned Notes for January to April and June to December have no chance of being selected.

When sampling is not appropriate

Note that sampling may *not* be appropriate in certain circumstances. These are primarily:

- When the auditor has already been advised of a high level of errors or systems failures or in connection with a possible fraud.
- Where populations are too small for a valid conclusion – it may be quicker to check them all!
- Where all the transactions in a population are material, e.g. a manufacturer of aeroplanes – they may only sell 20 in a year but each contract is worth several hundred million pounds.
- Where data is required to be fully disclosed in the financial statements, e.g. directors' emoluments.
- Where the population is not homogeneous.

Points to consider before sampling

Auditors should consider:

Objective of the test
Why is this test being carried out? What contribution does it make to the overall assessment of a true and fair view?

What is the population from which the sample will be taken?

The population has to be defined precisely. This may be, for example, all sales credit notes.

The sampling unit

Note that in compliance testing it is the operation of the control on a transaction which is being tested, not the transaction. It is the transaction which is the sampling unit used to test the control.

The definition of error

The auditors have to define what constitutes an error. Some 'errors' may not be material or not considered to be significant – auditors have to decide what it is they are looking for.

Sampling risk

Because they do not check the entire population there is a risk that the sample, however well chosen, will not be representative of the population as a whole. This is called 'sampling risk'.

If the basis for choosing the sample is a rational one and planning, testing and evaluation procedures are properly carried out then sampling risk can be minimised to an acceptable level.

Note that auditors have to deal with sampling risk both in compliance and substantive testing. For example, in compliance testing, there is a risk that the auditor will place a higher estimate of the effectiveness of a control, and therefore a lower estimate of control risk, during compliance testing because the error in the sample used in testing the control is less than the error in the population as a whole.

In substantive testing the sampling risk relates to the relationship between the sample and the population described above.

Bases of sampling

There are two approaches to selecting samples:

- Non-statistical or 'judgement' sampling.
- Statistical sampling.

Non-statistical sampling

This means selecting a sample of appropriate size on the basis of the auditors' judgement of what is desirable.

This approach has some advantages:

- The approach has been used for many years. It is well understood and refined by experience.
- The auditors can bring their judgement and expertise into play.
- No special knowledge of statistics is required.
- No time is spent on struggling with mathematics.

There are, however, some serious disadvantages:

- It is unscientific.
- Often sample sizes are too large, which can be wasteful, or too small, which renders the test invalid.

- There is no consistency of results – two different auditors will produce two different samples.
- No quantitative results are obtained.
- Personal bias in the selection of samples is unavoidable.
- There is no real logic to the selection of the sample or its size.
- The sample selection can be slanted to the auditor's needs, e.g. selection of items near the year end to help with cut-off evaluation, but it may invalidate the test.

Overall, judgement sampling is considered difficult to defend in court and far too subjective to have any real validity so is rarely used.

Statistical sampling

Statistical sampling requires the use of mathematical procedures, but it still requires the exercise of judgement, for example, in deciding what constitutes an error and what the materiality level is.

Statistical sampling

Drawing inferences about a large volume of data by an examination of a sample is a highly developed part of the discipline of statistics. It seems only common sense for the auditors to draw upon this body of knowledge in their own work. In practice, a certain level of mathematical competence is required if valid conclusions are to be drawn from sample evidence.

The advantages of using statistical sampling are:

- It is scientific.
- It is defensible.
- It provides precise mathematical statements about probabilities of being correct.
- It can be used by all levels of staff.
- It is efficient – overlarge sample sizes are not taken.
- It tends to result in a uniform standard of testing.

Its primary disadvantages are:

- that it is a mathematical process, which needs to be understood; and
- the principles of testing have to be applied properly in order for the tests to be valid.

Designing the sample

Auditors need to consider:

Population

As already stated the population is the data set from which the sample will be chosen. The essential feature of the population is that it be homogeneous. Care has to be taken to ensure this is the case. For example – suppose the population to be tested is all credit sales invoices, but that, part way through the year, the company replaced its old invoice recording system with a new one. In this case there are, in fact, two populations, the old system and the new system and both have to be tested.

Note also that testing the sample of a population does not test that population for completeness – it only tests what is actually there. To test for completeness tests have to be performed from source documents (sometimes called the *reciprocal population*) into the population.

Level of confidence

Auditors work to levels of confidence which can be expressed precisely. For example, a 5 per cent confidence level means that there are 19 chances out of 20 that the sample is representative of the population as a whole. The converse view is that there is one chance in 20 that the sample, on which the auditor draws conclusions, is non-representative of the population as a whole.

Precision

From a sample it is not possible to say that the auditors are 95 per cent certain that, for example, the error rate in a population of stock calculations is $x\%$, but only that the error rate is $x\% \pm y\%$ where $\pm y\%$ is the precision interval. Clearly the level of confidence and the precision interval are related, in that for a given sample size higher confidence can be expressed in a wider precision interval and vice versa.

Tolerable error

Tolerable error is the maximum error in the population that auditors are willing to accept and still conclude that audit objectives have been achieved. The tolerable error in a population is usually determined in the planning stage. It is related to and affected by:

- materiality considerations;
- assessment of control risk;
- results of other audit procedures.

The essential procedure is to set a tolerable error rate then to project the error rate in the population implied by the sampling results and to compare the two. If the projected error is larger than the tolerable error then further auditing procedures will be necessary in the area.

Expected error

This is the level of error the auditors might expect to find in the population. Sample sizes need to be larger in populations where a high level of error is expected than if the population is expected to be error free. This is because it is necessary to prove that the actual level of error is greater than the expected error.

Materiality

This is really a subset of risk. Materiality is fundamental to auditing and with all populations being sampled, materiality should be considered in fixing the sample size because populations that are material to the overall audit opinion (e.g. stock) must be sampled with smaller precision intervals and higher confidence levels.

Sampling methods

In auditing, a sample should be:

- Random – a random sample is one where each item of the population has an equal (or specified) chance of being selected. Statistical inferences may not be valid unless the sample is truly random.
- Representative – the sample should be representative of the items in the whole population. For example, it should contain a similar proportion of high- and low-value items to the population.

- Protective – protective, that is, of the auditor. More intensive auditing should occur on high-value items known to be high risk.

- Unpredictable – client should not be able to know or guess which items will be examined.

There are several methods available to an auditor for selecting items. These include:

Random sampling

This is simply choosing items subjectively but trying to avoid bias. Bias might come in by tendency to favour items in a particular location or in an accessible file or conversely in picking items because they appear unusual. This method is acceptable for non-statistical sampling but is insufficiently rigorous for statistical sampling.

Simple random

All items in the population have (or are given) a number. Numbers are selected by a means which gives every number an equal chance of being selected.

This is done using random number tables or computer- or calculator-generated random numbers.

Stratified sampling

This means dividing the population into subpopulations (strata = layers) and is useful when parts of the population have higher than normal risk (e.g. high-value items, overseas debtors). Frequently high-value items form a small part of the population and are 100 per cent checked and the remainder are sampled.

The information can be produced by a report generator from the management information system and used by the auditor to design the test.

For example:

	Number of items in stratum	Value of stratum	Test size
Above £1m	10	£38m	10
£750 000 – £1m	30	£28m	20
£500 000 – £750 000	50	£42m	20
£250 000 – £500 000	100	£28m	15
£50 000 – £250 000	1000	£93m	50
£10 000 – £50 000	4000	£65m	40
Under £10 000	8000	£12m	15

As can be seen, the sample chosen is weighted towards the high-value transactions because they are the most material. If one of the transactions in excess of £1m is in error it may be material to the accounts, an error in a transaction totalling £50 000 may not be.

Systematic selection

This method involves making a random start and then taking every nth item thereafter. The sampling interval is decided by dividing the population size by the sample size, i.e. if the population is 1000 and the number to be sampled is 10 the sampling interval will be every tenth transaction. The starting point can be determined randomly.

This method is useful when sampling non-monetary items, e.g. despatch notes.

However, the sample may not be representative as the population may have some serial properties, for example, there may be a pattern in the way documents are filed so that say, every tenth despatch note is for Hull. If this is the case the sample will be distorted.

Multi-stage sampling

This method is appropriate when data is stored in two or more levels. For example, stock in a retail chain of shops. The first stage is to randomly select a sample of shops and the second stage is to randomly select stock items from the chosen shops.

Block sampling

Choosing at random one block of items, e.g. all June invoices.

This common sampling method has none of the desired characteristics and is not recommended. Analogous to this is Cluster Sampling where data is maintained in clusters (= groups or bunches), as wage records are kept in weeks or sales invoices in months. The idea is to select a cluster randomly and then to examine all the items in the cluster chosen. The problem with this method is that the sample may not be representative as the month or cluster chosen may have unique characteristics.

Value weighted selection

This method uses the currency unit value rather than the items as the sampling population and is sometimes called *Monetary Unit Sampling* (MUS).

- Its application is appropriate with large variance populations. Large variance populations are those like debtors or stocks where the individual members of the population are of widely different sizes.
- The method is suited to populations where errors are not expected.
- It implicitly takes into account the auditor's concept of materiality.

Procedures are:

1 Determine sample size. This will take into account:

- the size of the population;
- the minimum unacceptable error rate (related to materiality);
- the assurance level required.

2 List the items in the population (we will use debtors) e.g., here is a list of debtors:

Debtor name	Balance	Cumulative	Selected
	£	£	
Jones	**6201**	6 201	**yes**
Brown & Co	474	6 675	no
XY Co Ltd	**1320**	7 995	**yes**
JB	1220	9 215	no
RS Acne	**4197**	13 412	**yes**
and so on . . .	. . .	. . .	. . .
	384 200	384 200	

If the sample size were 100 items the sampling interval will be every 3842nd pound (£384 200/100) thereafter.

If we start from £0, the first balance, Jones, has within it the first sampling interval of £3842, this next arrives in the balance belonging to XY & Co and finally (in our list) in the balance belonging to RS Acne.

Note that, using this method, the larger balances have a greater chance of being selected which is protective for the auditor.

MUS has some disadvantages:

- It does not cope easily with errors of understatement. A debtors balance which is underestimated will have a smaller chance of being selected than if it was correctly valued. Hence there is a reduced chance of selecting that balance and discovering the error.
- It can be difficult to select samples if a computer cannot be used as manual selection will involve adding cumulatively through the population.
- It is not possible to extend a sample if the error rate turns out to be higher than expected. In such cases an entirely new sample must be selected and evaluated.

MUS is especially useful in testing for overstatement where significant understatements are not expected. Examples of applications include debtors, fixed assets and stock. It may not be suitable for testing creditors balances where understatement is a primary characteristic to be tested.

At the end of the process, auditors should evaluate the result, which might be a conclusion that the auditor is 95 per cent confident that the debtors are not overstated by more than £x. £x is the materiality factor chosen.

If the conclusion is that the auditors find that the debtors appear to be overstated by more than £x then they may take a larger sample and/or investigate the debtors more fully.

Additional aspects of sampling

These include the following.

Estimation sampling for variables

This method seeks to estimate (with a chosen level of confidence and precision interval) the total value of some population. For example, the auditor might be 95 per cent confident that the total value of debtors, stock or loose tools, might lie between £58.3m and £59.4m and the best estimate is £59m.

The procedure is to extrapolate from a sample to an estimate of the total value. However, the calculations involved in carrying this out scientifically are complex and can only be performed easily using a computer application.

Attribute sampling

This provides results based on two possible attributes, i.e. correct/not correct and is used primarily in connection with the testing of internal controls, i.e. non-monetary testing.

It is generally used in compliance testing where the extent of application of a control is to be determined, i.e. the test is 'complies/does not comply'. Each deviation from a control procedure is given an equal weight in the final evaluation of results.

MUS is an attribute sampling technique as it measures monetary deviations.

Projecting the error into the population

Once errors have been identified they should be projected into the population.

This is relatively straightforward.

Suppose out of a population of £100 000 errors of £450 are discovered based on a sample size of transactions totalling £25 000.

The error in the population would then be expected to be (within the confidence levels).

$$\frac{£450}{£25\ 000} \times £100\ 000 = £1\ 800$$

The auditor would have to take a view as to whether this was material if it exceeds the level of tolerable error. If it does the auditors may well perform additional tests to ensure that the level of error they have discovered is constant.

This may, of course, only serve to demonstrate that the population is materially incorrect, which would result in a degree of substantive testing if the figures were material to the financial statements.

Working papers

As in all audit work, the work done in audit sampling situations should be fully documented in the working papers. In particular the documentation in the working papers should show:

- Planning the sample;

  - Stating the audit objectives.
  - Definition of error or deviation.
  - The means of determining the sample size.
  - The tolerable error rate.

- Selecting the items to be tested;

  - The selection method used.
  - Details of the items selected.

- Testing the items;

  - The tests carried out.
  - The errors or deviations noted.

- Evaluating the results of the tests;

  - Explanations of the causes of the errors or deviations.
  - The projection of errors or deviations.
  - The auditor's assessment of the assurance obtained as to the possible size of actual error or deviation rate.
  - The nature and details of the conclusions drawn from the sample results.
  - Details of further action taken where required (e.g. a larger sample or other forms of evidence gathering).

ANALYTICAL PROCEDURES

As we have seen auditors, are required to carry out procedures designed to obtain sufficient appropriate audit evidence to determine with reasonable confidence whether the financial statements are free of material misstatement. They are also required to evaluate the overall presentation of the financial statements, in order to ascertain whether they have been prepared in accordance with relevant legislation and accounting standards. The auditors have to give an opinion on whether the accounts give a true and fair view and comply with regulations.

One of the key ways of gathering such evidence is the use of analytical procedures at each stage of the audit.

There is the standard ISA 520 '*Analytical Procedures*'. This standard requires that auditors should apply analytical procedures at the planning and overall review stages of the audit.

It also suggests that analytical procedures can be applied as substantive procedures designed to obtain audit evidence directly.

Definition

Analytical procedures can be defined as:

The study of plausible relationships between elements of financial information expected to conform to a predictable pattern based on the organisation's experience and between financial information and non-financial information. Information is compared with comparable information for a prior period or periods, with anticipated results and with information relating to similar organisations.

In addition, analytical procedures involve:

- Investigating unexpected variations identified by the use of analytical procedures.
- Obtaining and substantiating explanations for such variations.
- Evaluating the results of an analytical review with other audit evidence obtained.

In an actual case the procedures might involve:

- increases in magnitude corresponding to inflation or in excess of inflation;
- changes in amounts arising from changes in output levels;
- comparisons with previous periods;
- trends and ratios;
- comparisons with budgets and forecasts;
- comparisons with other, similar, organisations, e.g. by inter-firm comparison.

Similar techniques are also applied by management, investment analysts and internal auditors to provide information on the performance of an entity, the efficiency of its operations or the quality of its management. Remember that, in performing these procedures, an auditor has a quite different purpose.

Analytical procedures can be simple tests comparing absolute magnitudes of different years, comparing ratios with earlier years, budgets and industry averages but also:

- using computer audit software;
- using advanced statistical techniques, e.g. multiple regression analysis.

Timing

Analytical procedures will be applied throughout the audit but specific occasions include:

- *At the planning stage.* The auditors will hope to identify areas of potential risk or new developments so that they can plan their other audit procedures in these areas. As a simple example, the auditors might discover that the gross profit ratio in a retail organisation had changed from the 28–30 per cent of previous years to 24 per cent. Or they might discover that a sales analysis revealed that exports had increased from 3 per cent to 26 per cent of turnover. This will lead to a direction of the emphasis of audit testing in order to investigate these apparent anomalies.
- *During the audit* as a form of gathering audit evidence. Audits with their emphasis on efficiency and economy depend heavily on analytical procedures as a valid audit

technique either used alone or in conjunction with internal control reliance and substantive testing.

It can be as reasonable to obtain assurance of the completeness, accuracy and validity of the transactions and balances by analytical procedures as by other types of audit evidence. For example, if the relative amounts under different expense headings repeat the pattern of previous years the auditor has evidence of the accuracy of expense invoice coding.

- *At the final review stage* of the audit. Analytical procedures can provide support for the conclusions arrived at as a result of other work. The techniques are also used to assess the overall reasonableness of the financial statements as a whole.

Extent of use

Factors which might influence the extent of use of analytical review include:

- The nature of the entity and its operations. A long-established manufacturing company which has changed little in the period under review will offer many opportunities for analytical procedures to be used as a primary source of audit evidence. Conversely a newly established manufacturer of high-tech products will not.

- Knowledge gained in previous audits of the enterprise. The auditors will have experience of those areas where errors and difficulties arose and of those areas of greatest audit risk.

- Management's own use of analytical procedures. If management has a reliable system of budgetary control then the auditors will have a ready made source of explanation for variances. Also the reliability of information prepared for management will be a factor. Information subject to internal audit will be an example of reliable information.

- Availability of non-financial information to back up financial information. Many companies record non-financial statistics (e.g. on production, input mixes, etc.). Some companies have to make returns of output (e.g. newspapers on circulation, dairies on gallonage, etc.). All this data can be used as evidence by auditors.

- The reliability, relevance and comparability of the information available. Clients that take part in inter-firm comparison exercises will be especially appropriate for analytical review evidence.

- The cost-effectiveness of the use of analytical procedures in relation to other forms of evidence. In general using analytical procedures is cheap but requires high-quality (and therefore expensive) staff. Some analytical procedures can be relatively expensive if for example they involve complex statistical techniques (e.g. multiple regression) and computer audit software where experienced or specialised staff are required.

Procedures

The following points can be made:

- Analytical review procedures can best be carried out on particular segments of the organisation, e.g. the branch at Walsall or the paint division or the subsidiary in France. They can also be used on individual account areas such as creditors or fixed asset depreciation.

- Analytical procedures are a breaking down of data into subdivisions for analysis over time, by product, by location, by management responsibility, etc.

- Analytical procedures are not effective in reviewing an entity as a whole unless it is very small. The greater the disaggregation the better.

- One approach is to identify the factors likely to have an effect on items in the accounts; to ascertain or assess the probable relationship with these factors and items; and then to predict the value of the items in the light of the factors. The predicted value of the items can then be compared with the actual recorded amounts. As an example, gas consumption is a function of temperature. A knowledge of daily temperature will permit the auditors to estimate gas consumption. If actual consumption is similar to that expected the auditor has evidence of the correctness of the sales value of gas.

- The auditors should consider the implications of significant fluctuations, unusual items or relationships that are unexpected or inconsistent with evidence from other sources. Similarly they should consider the implications of predicted fluctuations that fail to occur.
- Any significant variations should be discussed with management. Independent evidence must then be sought to validate management's explanations.
- The auditor's reactions to significant fluctuations or unexpected values will vary according to the stage of the audit:
  - at the planning stage, the auditor will plan suitable tests;
  - at the testing stage of the audit, further tests and other techniques will be indicated;
  - at the final stage the unexpected should not happen!
- All fluctuations and unexpected values must be fully investigated and sufficient appropriate audit evidence obtained.
- As with all audit work, analytical procedures should be fully documented in the working papers. The files should include:
  - the information examined, the sources of that information and the factors considered in establishing the reliability of the information;
  - the extent and nature of material variations found;
  - the sources and level of management from which explanations were sought and obtained;
  - the verification of those explanations;
  - any further action taken, e.g. further audit testing;
  - the conclusions drawn by the auditor.

Case Study 1

Example of use of analytical techniques

Zilpha Fashion Shops PLC own a chain of high fashion shops in major towns. Each shop is operated by a separate subsidiary company. All subsidiaries buy from the parent. The auditors of the Covhampton shop are reviewing the accounts for the year ending 31.1.X7 before starting the audit.

These reveal (in extract):

(all in £'000)	20-6	20-7	budget 20-8
turnover	600	638	640
cost of sales	400	459	425
gross profit	200	179	215
wages	78	71	70
overheads	70	75	74
net profit	52	33	71
stock	58	53	62
creditors	71	79	74

External data known to the auditors includes:

- rate of inflation – 5 per cent;
- a university survey, found on the Internet, of the traders in the precinct in which the shop is situated indicates a 5 per cent growth in real terms;
- the rate of gross profit achieved by other shops in the group was 34 per cent and average stock was 45 days' worth;
- creditor days in three other shops averaged 65 days;
- wages in the other shops averaged 13 per cent of turnover.

From all this data, the auditors could:

- Compute estimated turnover as $600 \times 1.05 \times 1.05 = 661$. The actual turnover is significantly less. The difference must be investigated.
- Gross profit from the turnover could be estimated as $638 \times 0.34 = 217$. Actual rate of gross profit is only 28 per cent, resulting in a profit of only 179. This might be explained by the drop in sales.
- Stock should be about 45 days' worth – $459 \times 45/365 = 56$. Actual is lower but not materially so.
- Creditors should be $459 \times 65/365 = 82$. This confirms the figure as the actual level of creditors is not materially different.
- Wages perhaps ought to be $638 \times 0.13 = 83$. If the direction of causation was reversed turnover should be $71 \times 100/13 = 546$. Wages do agree with budget and should be confirmable by considering the numbers on the staff.
- Other expenses should perhaps have risen by 5 per cent but they should be reviewed after disaggregation.

Conclusions:

- Stock and creditors are in line with expectations.
- Globally other overheads are out of line and disaggregation is required.
- Sales are lower than expected. Causes may be misappropriation of stock or cash or a reduction in selling price which might explain the reduced gross profit also. Close investigation is required.
- Gross profit is way out of line. This does not appear to be cut-off errors as stock and creditors seem to be about right. Debtors are negligible in this type of retail business.
- If customers pay by cash, cheque or credit card it might be that misappropriation of stock or cash has occurred. Further investigation is required. It may be of course that the management have other explanations – burglary losses, excessive shoplifting, price competition, sales of old stock at low prices etc.

Summary

- Traditionally, auditors have relied upon test checks or samples in forming conclusions about populations of data.
- The size and composition of samples can be determined by the judgement of the auditor but this is considered too subjective and unreliable.
- Statistical methods are used. These have the advantage of enabling the auditor to draw conclusions like 'I am 95 per cent certain that the error rate in the wage calculations is 1.4% ± 0.3%'.
- Samples should be random, representative, protective and unpredictable.
- Sample selection methods include random, stratified, random systematic, block, and value weighted or monetary unit sampling (MUS).
- Sample sizes are a function of population size, confidence levels and precision limits.
- Confidence levels and precision limits are a function of risk assessment, materiality and other subjective factors relating to other forms of audit evidence (internal control, analytical review, knowledge of the business, correlative factors).
- Statistical sampling can be used in all areas of an audit and with both compliance and substantive tests.
- Sampling methods include estimation sampling for variables and attribute sampling.
- Amongst the methods for obtaining audit evidence available to an auditor are analytical review procedures.
- Analytical review can be and should be carried out at all stages of the audit from planning to final review.
- The extent of use of analytical review depends on many factors but must be capable of generating sufficient reliable evidence relevant to the assertion being validated.
- Procedures include:
  - disaggregation;
  - concentration on segments or single areas;
  - identifying influences, assessing mathematical relationships, predicting values, comparing predictions with actual;
  - examining unexpected values and seeking explanations which must be fully verified.

Points to note

- The design of the sampling techniques is a technical matter and needs understanding of statistics.
- Examiners do not require a knowledge of the technical aspects of sampling beyond that given in this chapter.
- Materiality is very important in auditing. In sampling, materiality manifests itself in the term 'tolerable error' which is related to the statistical term 'precision interval'.
- Risk is important. In statistical sampling this is related to the level of confidence required.
- The nature of analytical procedures includes a comparison over time and the use of past experience on the audit. Therefore, it is desirable to build up a picture of the organisation and the relationship between magnitudes in the permanent files.

- There is a relationship between the use of analytical review and the reliability of the information being reviewed. Information which is subject to good control procedures is clearly more susceptible to analytical review techniques than other information.
- Analytical review is especially useful in obtaining evidence of completeness of accounting magnitudes.
- If anomalies are found and inadequate explanations are received then further audit work will be necessary.

Case Study 2

Hoopoe PLC are an old established large food processing company mainly buying poultry from local farmers, freezing them and selling them to retailers on credit terms.

Assets employed total £6 million, turnover £15 million, profits are £1.8 million and debtors are £3 million. The company have excellent internal controls which the auditor has evaluated at the interim audit. The auditor is examining the debtors schedule. He finds that there are 3900 items upon it. Four balances are over £100 000, being to large supermarket chains; 162 balances totalling £114 000 are for customers overseas.

Discussion
- Discuss the tolerable error that might be acceptable in the case of debtors.
- What audit risk factors are relevant? What substantive tests and analytical review techniques will enable the audit to reduce the detection risk?
- Outline the stages of a suitable audit sampling approach to the debtors in this case, determining the audit objectives, the population, the sampling unit, the definition of error, the sample selection method, and the sampling method. In each area, discuss the difficulties which might be encountered.

Case Study 3

Sheek Clothing PLC is a retailer with 200 branches throughout the UK. Most of the branches are small. The stock is a very significant item in the financial statements.

Stock is counted physically at all branches on the nearest Sunday to 31 March and that Sunday becomes the year end. Each branch buys some stock on its own initiative and some from the company's central buying department in Birmingham.

Discussion
- The auditors, Tickitt & Run, are planning the audit of stock in March 20x8. How might they use statistical or other sampling methods?

Case Study 4

Tickitt & Run are about to embark on the audit of Hosiah Wholesale Health Foods Ltd. The company have been established for five years and have been modestly successful. The auditors have not encountered many problems in the past except for debt collection problems and bad debts. A feature of the accounts each year has been the large amount of stock. The management is good and monthly accounts are prepared by Hortensia Goodbody FCCA who was headhunted from the auditors. The accounts are disaggregated for management purposes into dried goods, tinned goods and specialty imports.

Discussion

- To what extent can Tickitt & Run engage in analytical techniques?
- Devise analytical techniques using financial and non-financial data for verifying the expense 'motor van running expenses'. The company have 20 vans.
- Devise analytical techniques for verifying sales figures. The auditors are particularly worried that they have no systems assurance that all sales have been invoiced.

Student self-testing questions

Questions with answers apparent from the text

a) Why is a 100 per cent check not usual in auditing?

b) Where is a 100 per cent check likely to be applied?

c) What is the difference between a compliance test and a substantive test?

d) What is meant by: representative, population; sampling units?

e) What is 'tolerable error' and how is it related to materiality?

f) What factors are relevant in considering whether to sample?

g) List the stages in sampling.

h) Auditors are looking at purchases. Should they see the population to be sampled as all goods entered in the goods received book or all purchase invoices?

i) Auditors are sampling (statistically) purchase invoices to ensure that all are checked against goods inwards notes. Such checks are evidenced by the signature of a member of staff in a grid. Given the population size (25 000), the sample size (500) and that 24 items carried no signature, what should the auditors do? What conclusions can be drawn?

j) List the sampling methods available.

k) List the advantages and disadvantages of judgement sampling and of statistical sampling.

l) List some sample selection methods.

m) Distinguish level of confidence from precision interval.

n) List some statistical sampling techniques.

o) Explain monetary unit sampling.

p) Why is MUS not good for testing understatement?

q) What is tolerable error?

r) Define analytical procedures.

s) When should analytical procedures be used?

t) What factors influence the extent of use of analytical procedures?

u) List some analytical review procedures.

v) What actions can auditors take if they find fluctuations or unexpected magnitudes?

Examination questions

1 There are a number of different methods of obtaining audit evidence. Methods include:

    (i)   analytical procedures;
    (ii) audit sampling;
    (iii) tests of controls;
    (iv) detailed testing of transactions and balances;

These methods overlap and may be used for different purposes during an audit of financial statements.

   Required:

   (a) Explain the advantages and disadvantages of each of the methods of evidence-gathering listed above.
   NB: You are not required to describe the methods listed above.

   (b) Describe the relationship between the five methods of evidence-gathering described above.

   (ACCA)

2   (a) Explain how analytical review procedures can contribute to an audit.

   (b) Explain how the results of analytical review can influence the nature and extent of other audit work.

   (c) Give THREE specific examples of analytical review procedures that might be carried out as part of the audit of a company that operates a chain of departmental stores.

   (ICAEW)

13

Systems-based auditing

INTRODUCTION

Systems-based auditing is a technique whereby the auditors review, by testing, the operation of internal control procedures within the client's accounting system.

The objective is to gather sufficient appropriate audit evidence to demonstrate that the controls are functioning well enough to give the auditors confidence that they will discover any material error or misstatement which might affect the financial reports.

Systems-based auditing was, at one time, the universally accepted method of carrying out audit work, but auditors are increasingly adopting a business risk-based approach. We will look at this in the next chapter.

Students should familiarise themselves with the principles of systems-based auditing because;

- It is still tested in examinations and is likely to be for the foreseeable future.
- At some point – even using risk-based techniques – some investigation of the reliability of internal controls has to be carried out.
- Auditors should develop the skills of understanding financial systems in order to identify areas of potential problems and studying systems-based auditing is a good way to develop that understanding.

In this chapter we look at the systems-based approach to the most common processing cycles which are tested by examiners.

These are:

- Purchases and creditors;
- Sales and debtors;
- Wages.

This chapter will pull together the internal controls outlined in Chapter 9, the assertions, detailed in Chapter 11, and will provide a list of tests whereby internal controls can be evaluated.

It is important for the student to relate the audit tests described to the internal controls and the Assertions so that a proper understanding of systems-based auditing can be obtained.

Students will, however, also need to refer to later chapters where we look specifically at testing balance sheet items because, whether the audit approach is systems- or risk-based, the balance sheet still needs to be verified by substantive testing at some level.

TESTING SYSTEM COMPONENTS

Every system can be broken into a series of component parts which, when linked together form the entire system.

For example, in the case of the purchases system the system can be subdivided into

- ordering;
- goods received and invoice processing;
- accounting.

Auditors need to test every part of the system. They need to provide evidence that the Assertions (see Chapter 11), which apply to the purchases system, have been properly tested and that there is evidence to justify the audit conclusions.

However, you will be reassured to know that, in order to do this, audit tests can be combined so that one test will provide evidence for more than one Assertion in more than one part of the system. This means that auditors don't have to create a single test for every Assertion for every part of the system, thus repeating work unnecessarily.

You will need to be familiar with some of the principles of audit sampling explained in Chapter 12 when designing audit tests.

The reasons for this are:

- you will need to be able to justify the sizes of the samples and the method chosen for selecting the sample in order to conclude that the work done meets the audit objectives;
- by selecting the direction of testing more than one assertion can be tested at the same time.

Directional testing

It is important to understand, when carrying out testing, that the direction in which the test is carried out can provide evidence – but only up to a point. Consider a basic sales transaction, very much simplified!

Order from customer — goods despatched — invoice sent — sales day book — sales ledger

The auditors might be testing that invoices have been properly checked for:

- a valid customer order;
- that the goods have been sent; and
- that they have been properly entered into the sales day book with the right codes for the right customer and nominal ledger account, and from there, logically, into the sales ledger.

The obvious thing to do is to select a sample of invoices from the sales day book and check them against the source documents – a test known as *vouching*.

This is a valid test and will confirm, or otherwise, that the controls within the system are operating.

However, the test fails as a test of completeness. How do we know that all the orders issued resulted in a supply of goods? How do we know that goods haven't been sent without an invoice? In other words how do the auditors confirm that all the transactions are entered in the books?

The only way to do this is to take a sample of source documents – goods despatched notes or sales orders and test them *in the other direction* – i.e. towards the books of account.

This will validate the assertion for completeness *and* the other assertions tested.

Case Study 1

Bobo Ltd – directional testing

You are the audit senior of Bobo Ltd, a manufacturer of electrical goods. You have been asked to design audit tests for part of the purchases system.

Key aspects of the system you are reviewing are:

1 All purchases are ordered by means of an official order signed by the purchasing manager.
2 All goods received are evidenced by a goods received note raised by the stores.
3 Purchase invoices are matched with purchase orders and goods received notes before being entered in the purchase ledger.

Required:
Design audit tests to evidence the relevant assertions in the most efficient way.
Solution:
There are two ways of carrying out these tests:

A) Select a sample of purchase invoices and test to the relevant purchase orders and goods received notes.

This will help to validate the assertions of:
Occurrence – the fact Bobo ordered the goods mean the purchases and the liability to pay for them belong to them.
Accuracy (part) – the goods ordered have been delivered and, combined with other audit tests on prices and a test to trace them into the purchase ledger the auditors could use this to validate the accuracy of the suppliers account. Or the auditors could do it the other way round.

B) Select a sample of goods received notes including the goods received notes at the year end and compare them with purchase orders and invoices.

By testing in this direction they can evidence:
Occurrence – they can evidence that Bobo both ordered and received the goods so they and the liability to pay for them belong to Bobo.
Accuracy – as in test A).
Completeness – by selecting a sample of goods received notes the auditors can evidence whether Bobo has received any goods which haven't been invoiced yet.
Cut-off – including in this test the goods received notes around the year end means the auditors can evidence that the transactions are included in the correct accounting period.

Obviously there are more tests to do to evidence these assertions, for example, the auditors might want to support a test of completeness by selecting a sample of purchase orders but this example shows how a good deal of audit time can be saved by intelligent design of audit tests.

Purpose of audit tests

Remember that you are testing two things:

- the functioning of the internal control procedures and activities;
- that the company's financial procedures have been complied with.

Some of the tests which are carried out are not simply about whether transactions have been accurately recorded in the books; they are about discovering whether the staff involved are obeying company rules and procedures.

For example, there may be a company rule that goods can only be ordered from approved suppliers. This rule has got nothing to do with the accuracy of the underlying records but has everything to do with the business's approach to risk and the operation of its control environment.

Therefore, when designing an audit test or carrying out the work auditors should be aware of the purpose for which the test has been designed and the implications for the organisations if they discover errors or misstatements.

Bearing all these aspects of audit testing in mind, let us look at specific approaches to the testing of the purchases, sales and payroll systems.

THE PURCHASES AND EXPENSES SYSTEM

The first point to consider is the objectives of the audit of the purchases and expenses system. The objectives are based on the assertions set out in Chapter 11.

Audit objectives – purchases and expenses system

The audit objective is to carry out audit work so as to gather sufficient appropriate evidence to validate the assertions about the purchases system. These can be summarised as:

- purchases of goods and services relate to the company being audited (occurrence);
- all purchases of goods and services that should have been recorded have been recorded (completeness);
- purchases of goods and services have been recorded at the correct amounts (accuracy);
- all the relevant transactions have been recorded in the correct accounting period (cut-off);
- purchases of goods and services have been recorded in the correct accounts in the nominal and purchase ledgers and any other related records, e.g. stock or costing records (classification).

System objectives – purchases and expenses system

The purchases and expenses system has objectives which are the basis for the internal controls designed into the system.

We can consider the purchases system in three sections:

- ordering;
- receipt of goods and invoicing;
- accounting.

These objectives, together with the assertions they relate to, can be summarised as:

Ordering

- All orders for goods and services are properly authorised, are for goods and services that are actually received and are for the company (occurrence).
- Orders are made only to authorised suppliers (accuracy).

Receipt of goods and invoicing

- All goods and services received are for the purposes of the business and not for the private purposes of any individual (occurrence).
- Goods and services are accepted only if they have been ordered (completeness).
- All receipts of goods and services are accurately recorded (accuracy).
- Liabilities are recognised for all goods and services received (accuracy).
- Any credits due to the business for faulty goods and services have been claimed (completeness).
- It is not possible to record a liability for goods or services which haven't been received (completeness).

Accounting

- All payments have been properly authorised (occurrence).
- All payments are for goods and services which have been received (completeness).
- All expenditure has been recorded correctly in the books and records of the business (accuracy).
- All credit notes have been properly recorded in the books and records of the business (accuracy).
- All entries in the purchase ledger are to the correct supplier's accounts (classification).
- All entries in the nominal ledger are to the correct account (classification).
- Cut-off has been applied correctly (cut-off).

System controls – purchases and expenses system

The purchases and expenses system will have within controls and procedures which are designed to:

- achieve the system objectives;
- minimise the possibility of fraud and error;

You should be familiar with the principles of internal control from Chapter 9 but if not you should review them before reading further.

Ordering

organisational controls	• written procedures
	• policy on ordering from approved suppliers
	• authority levels for order limits
	• defined structure of who can order what
segregation of duties	• separation of staff responsible for raising orders from those involved in processing and paying invoices
physical controls	• safeguarding blank order forms
authorisation	• all orders to be authorised by a responsible person
arithmetical and accounting checks	• pre-numbered order forms
	• review of orders placed but not delivered or invoiced

Delivery of goods and invoicing

organisational controls	• written procedures
	• authority limits for approving invoices
	• procedures for obtaining credit notes from suppliers
segregation of duties	• separation of staff responsible for checking goods received from those responsible for checking purchase and posting invoices
physical controls	• monitoring quantity and condition of goods received
	• recording arrival and acceptance of goods (pre-numbered goods received notes)
	• recording return of goods (pre-numbered goods returned notes)
authorisation and approval	• matching of invoices with orders and goods received notes
	• matching suppliers' credit notes with goods returned notes
	• confirmation that invoices have been checked with orders and goods received notes

Accounting

organisational controls	• written procedures
	• authority limits for making payments
	• cheque signatories (usually minimum two)
segregation of duties	• separation of staff responsible for checking and posting invoices from those responsible for payment
physical controls	• numbering supplier invoices consecutively
	• controls on processing invoices, e.g. batch totals
	• control over blank cheques
	• restriction of access to parts of accounting system not relating to purchases
authorisation and approval	• authorisation of invoices for payment
arithmetical and accounting checks	• checking of invoices for:
	– prices
	– calculations
	– quantities

- invoices and credit notes entered into accounting records promptly
- regular reconciliations of suppliers' statements with purchase ledger balances
- reconciliation of purchase ledger control account with purchase ledger balances
- cut off checks and accrual of goods received notes not matched by purchase invoices at the year end

Audit testing – purchases and expenses system

The auditor's objective is to test that the controls are functioning properly.

Audit work to be carried out

The key areas of audit testing for the purchases and expenses system are:

- Check evidence that invoices are supported by:
    - Goods received notes;
    - Purchase orders.

- Check evidence that invoices are:
    - Checked for arithmetic, prices and calculations;
    - Correctly coded with supplier and nominal codes;
    - Entered in day books, ledgers and stock records.

- Test numerical sequences and enquire into missing numbers (including unused copies) of:
    - Invoices;
    - Purchase orders;
    - Goods received notes;
    - Goods returned notes.

- Obtain explanations for items outstanding for a long time – e.g. unmatched orders and goods received notes or unprocessed invoices.
- Check authorisation of invoices approved for payment.
- Check goods returned:
    - Supported by goods returned note;
    - Evidence of correspondence with supplier;
    - Credit note entered in ledgers;
    - Invoices for faulty or defective goods or services cancelled;

- Check postings between day books, cash book and ledger.
- Check analysis in purchase day books.
- Check payments to suppliers are debited in full to correct account in purchase ledger.
- Check additions where appropriate.
- Check entries in stock records.
- Check cut-off procedures at period end.
- Check purchase ledger control account reconciliations.

- Check evidence of reconciliation of purchase ledger balances with suppliers' statements.
- Check explanations for contra and journal entries in purchase ledgers.
- Examine all records for particularly large or unusual entries or transactions.

These tests can be used in different combinations and different ways to audit virtually any kind of purchases and expenses system. It is the skill of the auditor in using combinations of these tests to provide the sufficient appropriate evidence needed.

THE SALES SYSTEM

Audit testing – the sales system

The first point to consider is the objectives of the audit of the sales system. The objectives are, again, based on the assertions set out above.

Audit objectives – sales system

The audit objective is to carry out audit work so as to gather sufficient appropriate evidence to validate the assertions about the sales system. These can be summarised as:

- sales of goods and services relate to the company being audited (occurrence);
- all sales of goods and services that should have been recorded have been recorded (completeness);
- sales of goods and services have been recorded at the correct amounts (accuracy);
- all the relevant transactions have been recorded in the correct accounting period (cut-off);
- sales of goods and services have been recorded in the correct accounts in the nominal and sales ledgers and any other related records, e.g. stock records (classification).

System objectives – sales system

The sales systems can be considered in three sections:

- ordering and granting of credit;
- despatch and invoicing;
- accounting.

Ordering and granting of credit
- goods and services are supplied to customers with good credit ratings (occurrence);
- orders are recorded correctly (accuracy);
- customer orders are fulfilled (occurrence);
- goods and services returned by customers are recorded (goods returned notes) and the reasons investigated (completeness).

Despatch and invoicing
- all invoices raised relate to goods and services supplied by the business (occurrence)

- all despatches of goods and services are accurately recorded (accuracy)
- all despatches of goods or provision of services are invoiced correctly (completeness and accuracy)
- any credit notes are only given for a valid reason (completeness)
- cut off is applied to the recording of despatch of goods stock records (cut-off).

Accounting

- all invoices and credit notes are properly recorded in the books and records (completeness and accuracy)
- all receipts from customers have been properly recorded (accuracy)
- all payments are for goods and services which have been supplied (completeness)
- all credit notes given have been properly recorded in the books and records of the business (accuracy)
- all entries in the sales ledger are to the correct customer's accounts (accuracy)
- potential or actual bad debts are identified (accuracy)
- all entries in the nominal ledger are to the correct account (classification)
- cut-off has been applied correctly (cut-off).

System controls – sales system

As with the purchases and expenses system, the sales system will have within it controls and procedures which are designed to:

- achieve the system objectives;
- minimise the possibility of fraud and error.

This second objective is considered to be of increasing significance to auditors who are required to approach audits with an attitude of professional scepticism.

In businesses where sales income may be vulnerable, e.g. businesses which involve a lot of cash transactions, there is an increased risk of fraud and auditors have to be very much aware of this when they are designing their procedures.

The controls built into each part of the system will include:

Ordering and granting of credit

organisational controls	• written procedures
	• authority for approving new customers
	• procedures to be adopted for credit checking customers
segregation of duties	• separation of staff responsible for despatching goods or supplying services from those involved in processing invoices or collecting monies
physical controls	• pre-numbered sales order forms
	• safeguarding blank sales order forms
authorisation	• authorisation for changes in customer data (e.g. discount allowed)
	• authorisation for customer credit limits

arithmetical and accounting checks	• correct prices quoted to customers' discounts calculated correctly • VAT correctly calculated • matching of customer orders to despatch notes and queries over orders not matched

Despatches and invoicing

organisational controls	• written procedures • authority levels for selling prices and discount arrangements • authority for issuing credit notes to customers
segregation of duties	• separation of staff responsible for despatching goods received from those responsible for processing sales invoices

physical controls	• monitoring quantity and condition of goods and services supplied
	• pre-numbering of:
	  – delivery notes
	  – sales invoices
	  – good returned notes
	• safeguarding blank forms
	• recording delivery of goods to customer (signed delivery notes)
	• recording return of goods by customer (pre-numbered goods returned notes)

authorisation and approval	• authorisation of selling prices • authorisation of discounts • special authorisation of goods on special terms or free of charge • matching of sales invoices with despatch and delivery notes • matching credit notes with goods returned notes

Accounting

organisational controls	• written procedures • authority to write off debts
segregation of duties	• separation of staff responsible for posting invoices and maintaining customer accounts from those responsible for receipts from customers
physical controls	• numbering sales invoices consecutively • controls on processing invoices e.g. batch totals • control over unused invoice sets • control over spoilt invoices • restriction of access to parts of accounting system not relating to sales
authorisation and approval	• authorisation to implement credit control procedures

arithmetical and accounting checks	• checking of invoices for:
	  – prices
	  – calculations
	• invoices and credit notes entered into accounting records promptly

- sending statements to debtors
- production of aged debtor reports and credit control procedures
- reconciliation of sales ledger control account with sales ledger balances
- cut off checks to ensure goods despatched but not invoiced are dealt with in the correct period
- analytical review of sales ledger and profit margins

Audit testing – sales system

As we've already outlined, in the section above on purchases and expenses, auditors must use a mixture of compliance and substantive procedures in order to obtain the evidence they need.

The key areas of audit testing are procedures to:

- Check new customer credit procedures are operating.
- Check new accounts and credit limits are properly authorised.
- Check orders only accepted from customers within credit limits.
- Check evidence that sales invoices are supported by:

  - customer orders;
  - signed delivery note or evidence of supply of goods or services.

- Check evidence that invoices are:

  - checked for arithmetic, prices and calculations, particularly of VAT;
  - correctly coded with customer and nominal codes;
  - entered in day books, ledgers and stock records.

- Test numerical sequences and enquire into missing numbers (including unused or cancelled copies) of:

  - invoices;
  - sales orders;
  - delivery notes;
  - goods returned notes.

- Check goods returned:

  - supported by goods returned note;
  - evidence of correspondence with customer;
  - credit note authorised.

- Check non-routine sales, e.g. scrap, sales of fixed assets:

  - check authorisation for sale;
  - check evidence of arrangements for sale;
  - check assets removed from plant register.

- Check postings between day books, cash book and ledgers:

  - ensure receipts from customers posted to correct accounts;
  - investigate payments on account or round sum amounts;
  - investigate sums received where no invoice has been issued.

- Check analysis in sales day books.
- Check additions where appropriate.
- Check entries in stock records for despatches of goods.
- Check cut-off procedures at period end.
- Check sales ledger control account reconciliations.
- Check remittances from customers are credited in full to the correct account in sales ledger.
- Check aged debtor analysis and evidence of credit control procedures such as follow-up of overdue debts.
- Check explanations for contra and journal entries in sales ledgers.
- Examine records for particularly large or unusual receipts or transactions.

These tests can be used in different combinations and different ways to audit virtually any kind of sales system. It is the skill of the auditor in using combinations of these tests to provide the sufficient appropriate evidence needed.

CASH SALES

Special procedures – cash sales

There are some types of business where a significant proportion of trading activity is carried out in cash.

Examples of such types of business are:

- shops and supermarkets;
- bars, cafés and restaurants;
- taxi firms.

Auditors therefore have not only to be aware of the correct procedures for verifying that sales income has been recorded correctly but of the increased likelihood of fraud.

Audit procedures will also include:

- Review of procedures for recording cash sales – e.g. tills, cash sheets etc.
- Review and sample testing of reconciliations of cash taken with an independent record, e.g. a till roll.
- Review and sample testing of banking procedures.
  - ensure cash sales banked intact, i.e. money is not taken from cash sales to pay small bills or top up petty cash floats;
  - ensure reconciliation and banking of cash sales is carried out by persons not responsible for sales;
  - ensure takings banked the same day to reduce cash retained on client's premises by checking paying in slip dates;
  - check entries in cash book with bankings and till receipts or cash sheets.

It is often very difficult to obtain conclusive proof that all cash sales have been recorded and auditors should be alert to opportunities for recommending improvements to the client's systems wherever possible.

THE PAYROLL SYSTEM

Audit testing – the payroll system

The objectives of the payroll system are similar to those of the purchases and expenses system insofar as the business only wants to pay for work done and at the correct rate.

Although wages and salaries are often mentioned separately there are many common features from an audit point of view.

The principal differences are that wages tend to be paid weekly and often vary from week to week with overtime or piecework payments. Piecework is based on the amount of work an employee completes rather than the length of time they spend at work. Salaries on the other hand tend to be paid monthly, be the same amount each month and only vary with, say, commission payments or bonuses.

In some businesses wages are paid weekly in cash. Nowadays this tends to be quite rare in all but the smallest businesses, mainly for reasons of security, but we will mention a few points relating to wages paid in cash so you can understand the special issues involved in that situation.

The common features when considering both wages and salaries are:

- all employees have to have a contract of employment setting out terms and conditions of employment;
- rates of pay have to be agreed;
- all deductions either have to be statutory (e.g. PAYE and NI) or authorised by the employee (e.g. pension contributions);
- calculations of tax and NI are basically the same for monthly paid and weekly paid workers;
- they have to be paid on time.

Where businesses have a mixture of weekly and monthly paid employees there may be two payrolls. The weekly payroll may be prepared by specialised staff in a separate department whereas the monthly payroll may be prepared by a senior official of the company, particularly if it includes salary payments for senior managers and directors. It may be outsourced to an independent body in which case the auditors will have to adopt some separate procedures as outlined in Chapter 22.

In that case the auditor will have to carry out separate tests on each payroll to ensure both are being operated correctly.

It is possible that some of the work that auditors do can be used to validate both types of payment. For convenience we will cover both wages and salaries together and highlight areas which relate only to one type of payment.

Audit objectives – payroll system

The audit objective is to carry out audit work so as to gather sufficient appropriate evidence to validate the assertions about the payroll system. These can be summarised as:

- payment for wages and salaries relate to work done for the company being audited (occurrence);
- all payments of wages and salaries that should have been recorded have been recorded (completeness);

- wages and salaries and any deductions relating to them have been calculated and recorded at the correct amounts (accuracy);
- all the relevant payments and liabilities have been recorded in the correct accounting period (cut-off);
- payments of wages and salaries have been recorded in the correct accounts in the nominal ledger and any other related records, e.g. costing records (classification).

There are businesses where payroll can be a particularly difficult area such as those involving a lot of casual workers where sums are paid in cash often with little documentation. Where there is a risk of fraud it is the practice that auditors have to be very much aware of this when they are designing their procedures.

Confidentiality – payroll

As we've already discussed in Chapter 6 auditors have to treat all the information they gather from dealing with a client's affairs as totally confidential. This is very much the case when dealing with payroll as matters such as the rate of pay between individuals can be a very sensitive subject.

The payroll system contains a lot of personal data about employees including:

- rate of pay;
- deductions;
- home address;
- bank details;
- birth date;
- National Insurance number;

all of which is confidential information and can be used by unscrupulous individuals as raw material for 'identity theft'.

The auditor should be very much aware of this and it is quite often the case that only the more senior members of the audit team are allowed access to payroll data.

Care also has to be taken when documenting tests on the audit files so confidential information about individual employees should be kept to a minimum. The important thing is to meet the audit objectives from a company-wide point of view so employees can be identified by a work number, payroll number or clock number rather than by name.

System controls – payroll

As with the purchases and sales systems the payroll system will have within it controls and procedures which are designed to:

- achieve the system objectives;
- minimise the possibility of fraud and error.

The payroll system can be subdivided into two parts:

- basis of payroll calculation;
- payment of wages and salaries and accounting.

Basis of payroll calculation

organisational controls	• written procedures • approved wage and salary rate lists • procedures to be adopted for starters and leavers
segregation of duties	• separation of staff responsible for preparing payroll from those involved in payment • separation of staff involved in personnel administration from staff involved with payroll
physical controls	• restriction of access to payroll office • restriction of access to parts of accounting/computer system not relating to relevant payroll
authorisation	• authorisation for changes in rates • employee authorisation for non-statutory deduction • authorisation of hours worked • authorisation of bonuses • authorisation of commission payments • authorisation of piece work payments
arithmetical and accounting checks	• correct basic rates set as basis for calculation of gross pay • correct overtime rates applied • piecework payments reconciled to completed quantities • tax codes applied for correct tax years as notified by Inland Revenue • computerised payroll upgrades received and applied following tax rate changes

Calculation and payment of wages

organisational controls	• written procedures • separate payroll department from personnel department • individual personnel file for each employee
segregation of duties	• separation of staff responsible for preparation of wages from those authorising payment
physical controls	• filling of pay packets by staff not involved with preparing payroll • general security of cash in transit and on premises • distribution of wage packets by staff not involved with preparing payroll • controls for security of unclaimed cash wages
authorisation	• payroll authorised by responsible official before payment • wages cheques signed by two senior officers of the company not connected with payroll preparation • BACS transfer signed by two senior officers of the company not involved in wages preparation
arithmetical and accounting checks	• wages control account • reconciliation of payroll between dates • payment of PAYE and NI to HM Revenue and Customs • comparison and reconciliation with budget figures

Audit testing – payroll

The test performed on payroll are basically designed to ensure that:

- internal controls are working;
- the scope for fraud is limited.

Payroll has often been a vulnerable area to fraud but the decline in the payment of cash wages has limited the opportunities open to the fraudster and the use of reliable payroll software has further eroded the possibility of falsifying payroll details in order to defraud the business.

However, this does not reduce the auditor's responsibility to ensure that the systems are functioning correctly.

The key areas of audit testing are designed to test that:

- all employees exist;
- all employees are paid at the correct rate;
- all deductions from wages are properly calculated;
- net pay and deductions are accounted for correctly.

Again the audit work will consist of a mixture of compliance and substantive tests. The main procedures are:

- check authorised rates of pay are being used;
- confirm authorisation procedures operating with regard to:
  - clock cards, job cards, time sheets or other evidence of time worked;
  - production records for payments based on productivity;
  - signed lists for bonuses;
  - approved lists for commission payments to sales staff.
- check calculations of gross to net pay for a sample of employees verifying authorisation for and calculation of:
  - gross pay;
  - overtime payments;
  - piecework payments;
  - PAYE and NI using HM Revenue and Customs documents, e.g. coding notices;
  - holiday pay.
- inspect authorised payment lists for BACS transfers;
- obtain cancelled cheques from bank and compare to payroll;
- test non-statutory deductions from payroll authorised by employee;
- test holiday pay calculations;
- observe delivery of pay advice to employees;
- ascertain reason for any pay advice not delivered;
- check additions and calculations on payroll;
- reconcile movements in payroll for two different periods;
- test starters and leavers procedures applied to payroll, i.e. ensure leavers removed at correct date and starters started on correct date;

- check payroll summary to payroll;
- check payroll summary to nominal ledger;
- check any cost analysis reconciles to payroll;
- check salary payments are in accordance with contracts of employment;
- ensure payments made to HM Revenue and Customs within permitted period to clear tax and NI creditor.

For payment of cash wages:

- check the packets to the payroll to ensure each employee has a packet;
- attend wages payout and observe procedures;
- check procedures are secure from point of view of staff paying out;
- ensure all wage packets signed for by recipients;
- check no employee receives more than one packet;
- check unclaimed wages entered in unclaimed wages book;
- check unclaimed wages details with payroll;
- ascertain reason for unclaimed wages.

Most payroll systems operate on broadly the same principles, although there are frequently special arrangements for calculating such things as overtime or commission. Auditors can apply the principles outlined above to their audit of both weekly and monthly payrolls, adapting them to suit the particular circumstances of each client.

Summary

- A system can be broken down into its component parts and each part tested separately.
- Directional tests should be used especially for testing completeness.
- It is necessary to link audit testing to control objectives and assertions.
- Tests can be combined to validate more than one assertion simultaneously.
- Tests must be relevant to the assertion being evidenced.
- Tests are designed to ensure control objectives are being achieved.

Points to note

- Fraud is an issue in auditing and auditors must be aware of the possibilities of fraud or the potential for misstatement.
- Systems-based auditing is often tested in examinations as it still the basis for many audits.

Case Study 2

Tickitt & Run are in the process of completing the audit of their client Fredbare Ltd, a manufacture of swimwear and sports clothing.

They have just carried out the interim audit and have discovered the following.

The audit team have discovered that the purchases system has changed. They have provided the following description of the purchasing system. No other controls exist apart from those described.

Fredbare has no specific buying department so employees can place orders with suppliers in their own area of responsibility. A three-part order form is used; copy 1 is retained by the originator, copy 2 is sent to the goods inward department and copy 3 is sent to the supplier.

Goods are received, but not checked, by the warehouse personnel who also deal with stock control and dispatches. Once received, the advice note and purchase order for those goods are sent to the purchase ledger clerk.

When the supplier's invoice is received the purchase ledger clerk checks the calculations on it, initials it and staples the advice note and purchase order to it. She enters the invoice on to the purchase ledger.

The invoice is then sent to the manager responsible for the employee who ordered the goods. The manager codes the invoice and returns it to the purchase ledger clerk. Purchase invoices are coded, entered on an analysis sheet and posted to the nominal ledger monthly by journal entry.

The cashier pays suppliers monthly on instructions from the purchase ledger clerk. The purchase ledger control account is reconciled monthly by the purchase ledger clerk who also reconciles suppliers' statements.

On a number of occasions goods have been delivered to customers but no invoice raised.

In the wages department the wages for staff are based on clock cards for factory staff which are passed to the wages department on Monday morning by the night watchman whose job it is to put new cards out ready for the staff. Weekly paid office staff are paid the same every week so don't need to complete any form of time sheet.

Wages are made up by Mrs Bobbin with assistance from one part-time member of staff and occasional secondment from the office. Mrs Bobbin calculates the wages, adjusts for any starters and leavers, and any other changes and produces the payroll.

You are required

To list any weaknesses you can identify in the above systems. You should amplify the weakness as appropriate, explain its implications and suggest recommendations for improvement.

Student self-testing questions

Questions with answers apparent from the text

a) What is the basis of systems-based auditing?

b) What are control objectives?

c) List control objectives for a purchasing system.

d) What types of control would there be in a sales credit system?

e) What types of control would there be in a wages system?

f) What audit tests would be performed on purchase invoices?

g) When would cash balances not be audited?

h) What is the main principle of segregation of duties?

i) Why is it important?

j) List other forms of internal controls.

k) How would you verify the existence of an arithmetical control?

Examination questions

1 Your firm is the external auditor of Bestwood Engineering Ltd which manufactures components for motor vehicles and sells them to motor vehicle manufacturers and wholesalers. It has a turnover of around £20m and a profit before tax of £800 000.

The company has a new financial director who has asked you for advice on controls in the company's purchasing system.

Bestwood Engineering has separate accounts, purchasing and goods received departments. Most purchases are required by the production department but other departments are able to raise requisitions for goods and services. The purchasing department is responsible for obtaining goods and services at the lowest price which is consistent with the required delivery date and quality and for ensuring their prompt delivery.

The accounts department is responsible for obtaining authorisation of purchase invoices before they input to the computer which posts them to the purchase ledger and the nominal ledger. The accounting records are kept on a computer and the standard accounting software was obtained from an independent supplier. The accounting software maintains the sales ledger, the purchase ledger, nominal ledger and payroll. The company does not maintain stock records as it believes the cost of maintaining these records outweighs the benefits.

The financial director has explained that services include gas, electricity, telephone repairs, and short-term hire of equipment and vehicles.

Required:

a) Describe the procedures which should be in operation in the purchasing department to control the purchase and receipt of goods.

b) Describe the controls the accounts department should exercise over obtaining authorisation of purchase invoices before posting them to the purchase ledger.

c) Explain how controls over the purchase of services, from raising the purchase requisition to posting the invoice to the purchase ledger might differ from the procedures for the purchase of goods described in your answers to parts a) and b).

(ACCA)

2 You are responsible for the statutory audit of Servit Ltd (Servit) for the year ended 30 November 2007. Servit provides industrial maintenance services to companies operating in the engineering sector. Customers sign a standard contract for each job which can last between 1 and 15 days. The company charges for its services hourly and all claims for work done have to be submitted to customers for approval before invoicing.

Historically only the receivables (debtors) ledger was computerised and the company experienced a number of invoicing errors, including failure to invoice, which had a detrimental effect on the cash collection. In order to reduce errors and speed up the invoicing and cash collection process the company has upgraded its computer system.

A new system which integrates job costing, payroll, invoicing and ledger processing was implemented during the year ended 30 November 20x7.

Under the new system each job is logged on the computer and the software automatically allocates a sequential job number and produces time logs to be completed by each contract manager. Each contract manager inputs daily the hours worked by each employee and the system generates a copy of the time log to be approved by the customer. At the end of each week, or on completion of a job if less than a week, an invoice is generated from the information stored on the system and details are automatically posted to the receivables ledger and sales account in the nominal ledger. Customers are required to pay within 30 days of invoice date.

In addition to the time logs and invoices, the system routinely produces statements of customer balances and reports detailing:

- standing data amendments;
- age analysis of receivables; and
- list of customer balances.

Required:

(a) State the responsibilities of external auditors and directors in relation to the design and operation of internal control systems.

(b) Describe the control procedures that should be in place in the receivables system to:

    (i) reduce the risk of invoicing errors, including failure to invoice promptly or at all; and

    (ii) speed up the cash collection process.

(c) Outline the audit procedures you would undertake in order to ensure that receivables are fairly stated in the financial statements of Servit for the year ended 30 November 20x7.

(ICAEW)

14

Business risk approach to auditing

INTRODUCTION

The definition of business risk is:

The threat that an event or action will adversely affect a business's ability to achieve its ongoing objectives.

It can be split between external and internal factors.

The business risk approach to auditing involves:

- looking at the business in its entirety;
- evaluating the various risks the business faces; and
- considering the impact, if any, that those risks might have on the financial statements.

The idea is that businesses face risks and an understanding of these risks requires the auditor to have a thorough understanding of the client's business, which will suggest where misstatements may occur in the financial statements.

Relevant auditing standards here are ISA 315 *Obtaining an Understanding of the Entity and its Environment and Assessing the Risks of a Material Misstatement* and ISA 330 *The Auditor's Procedures in Response to Assessed Risk.*

EXTERNAL RISKS

Risks arising from outside the organisation include:

Political risk

Risk arising from changes in government policy and also risks arising from changes in the political climate. This may be particularly relevant to companies operating globally where, in some countries, the political situation may suffer sudden and often violent change. This may bring with it, for example, the threat of nationalisation of assets or actions against foreign ownership. In more stable countries a change in the political climate may have an effect on economic policy which, in turn could affect such things as inflation and interest rates.

Example

Nationalisation of oil company assets in Venezuela following the election of a socialist government.

Economic risk

This is the risk caused by changes in the economic situation of the county which might result in changes in anticipated levels of inflation, higher or lower unemployment, interest rate movements, etc. It may also result in increased competition from low-cost producers from abroad. Again auditors have to consider the risks applicable in all the countries in which the business operates.

Example

The effect on UK manufacturing of competition from low-cost producers in eastern Europe, India and China.

Legislative risk

Changes in legislation may result in restrictions to operations or increased costs of compliance. Environmental legislation has increased 'clean up' costs and businesses are increasingly having to provide information to government bodies.

Example

Clean up costs and damages paid arising from asbestos-related claims.

Compliance risk

This is the risk arising from non-compliance with laws and regulations. Most organisations are capable of ensuring compliance with tax or VAT rules but many still have, judging by the number of cases still coming before the courts and tribunals, inadequate procedures for complying with employment law or health and safety legislation.

It is particularly relevant in the area where the law and finance interact, in particular with reference to such matters as money laundering, insider dealing and tax or VAT fraud.

Example

Damages for constructive dismissal arising from sexual harassment awarded against financial institutions in the City of London.

Physical risk

Evaluation of physical risk includes consideration of natural hazards such as floods, fires, tornados and the effects of global warming. It includes problems caused to organisations because of loss of power or water supplies, deliberate damage to machinery or equipment, key component failures, etc. It also includes the risk of problems caused to the business or its employees because of direct or implied terrorist action, particularly where companies operate in some of the more volatile parts of the world.

Example

The damage caused to local businesses as a result of Hurricane Katrina in 2006.

Technological risk

Many businesses, and not only those involved in so called 'hi-tech' operations, face risks from new and developing technologies. Businesses which fail to spot the potential or the risks to their existing operations presented by new and emerging technologies may well find themselves overtaken by competition or find their markets so radically changed they are no longer able to compete in them.

Developments in computing are an obvious area for most businesses but more scientific developments such as developments in biotechnologies may well lead to developments which will have a major impact on current businesses.

Example

The rise of Internet-based trading which has forced huge changes in business practices in many sectors, e.g. banking, insurance, clothes retailing, bookselling.

Market risk

Risks arising from sudden or unexpected changes in the company's market, e.g. increased competition, price wars, new products, etc.

Example

The development of Internet-based music downloads threatens the high street record retailer.

Financial risk

This is probably the biggest single area affecting businesses and is very wide ranging. It includes:

- Credit risk – the risks arising from non payment of debts due either due to insolvency of customers, fraud or unresolved disputes.
- Foreign exchange risk – risks caused by trading in foreign currencies.
- Interest rate risks – risks to business financing caused by unexpected movements in interest rates.

Examples

Many businesses have examples of losses arising from unpaid debts – insolvency causes many defaults in payments. Several high profile insolvency cases also involve some element of fraud, e.g. Enron and WorldCom in the USA, others were as a result of trading problems, e.g. BenQ in Germany, Railtrack and ITV Digital in the UK.

Problems caused by foreign exchange trading, also coupled with some element of fraud and a failure of internal systems, caused the collapse of Barings Bank.

Note that organisations often face a combination of risks so auditors should avoid the temptation of adopting a 'tick list' approach and consider the possibility of what might be perceived to be a number of low-level risks combining to produce a very serious problem.

An understanding of the risks facing a client adds to an auditor's understanding of the client. The auditors also need to extrapolate their risk analysis into a consideration of how some of these may affect the financial statements. Some may affect the value of assets and some may affect the going concern concept for all or part of the enterprise.

INTERNAL RISKS

These are risks arising from inside the company and include the following.

Strategic risk

Management making a set of bad strategic decisions which define the company's objectives wrongly and result in trading losses and, in the worse cases, insolvency.

Strategic risk includes:

- emphasis on the wrong products;
- attempting to break in to unfamiliar markets without adequate expertise;
- inappropriate acquisitions;
- poor planning processes;
- lack of focus by on key objectives by senior management;
- lack of key performance indicators;
- poor monitoring procedures;
- inadequate management information systems.

Operational risk

These are risks caused by underlying flaws in the way the business is carried on, its processes and systems. These are not confined to manufacturing industry: the failure to correct poor processes affecting customer service has adversely affected many service-based organisations.

Operational risk includes:

- failure to modernise products and processes;
- poor labour relations;
- weak marketing;
- loss of key employees;
- breakdown of relationships with key suppliers or customers;
- reliance on a few products, customers, suppliers;
- lack of research and development of new products.

Governance risk

Risks to the organisation can be created by poor or inadequate Corporate Governance (see Chapter 2). This includes problems arising from inappropriate board structures, poor communications within the business and no support for a strong internal control environment.

Governance risk includes:

- excessive reliance on a dominant chief executive;
- weak or non-existent non-executive directors;
- poor internal control environment;
- failure to communicate goals and objectives;

- inefficient feedback mechanisms and poor corporate communications;
- lack of, or ineffective, internal audit function.

Financial risks

These include risks arising both from the structure and financing of the business and the operation of financial systems. Auditors have to consider not only the detail of the financial processes within the business but the appropriateness of its structure and the ability to finance its operations so as to achieve its objectives for the foreseeable future.

Financial risks includes:

- inadequate finance for future operations or development of new products and markets;
- high levels of gearing at a time of rising interest rates;
- overtrading resulting in cash flow difficulties;
- related parties involved in the business with no obvious commercial motive or inappropriate terms of trading;
- systems failures and loss of records;
- internal control weaknesses;
- fraud.

Any of these risks can damage a company and may impact on the financial statements. The auditor thus has to consider two things:

- How well do I know my client and all aspects of its operations?
- Will my audit procedures identify all the potential risks my client faces and can I, from that, anticipate the key risks which may result in a serious error or misstatement in the financial statements?

THE CLIENT'S APPROACH TO RISK

Many smaller companies do not have a formal risk assessment process and their goals and objectives may not be incorporated into detailed plans. Such companies though are often very flexible, know their markets and can respond quickly to threats and changes.

Larger organisations often have a hierarchy of plans involving:

- *Strategic planning* – longer term planning (often incorporating a Mission Statement or Statement of Goals).
- *Detailed tactical planning* – shorter term operational planning in order to achieve milestones or goals as part of the achievement of the wider strategic plan.
- *Budgets and forecasts* – in detail for shorter term tactical plans and sometimes on a wider scale to consider financing implications as part of strategy planning.

Auditors need to be familiar with the plans and the processes which are used to derive the plans. In other words they need to be assured that both strategic and operational planning, and the financial information derived from it, is based on an ordered and systematic consideration of the business' future carried out by experienced and competent senior management.

As part of the development of these plans the organisation should carry out risk assessments from which the auditors can begin to derive their audit planning.

Risk assessment

This has two components:

- Risk identification.
- Risk evaluation.

Risk identification requires the organisation to carry out a systematic review of:

- itself;
- its place in its industry;
- its industry's place in the wider economic context.

This encompasses consideration of all the forms of risk highlighted above. It is not appropriate for the company simply to identify all its internal risks, it must look at the factors affecting its own industry, and the wider economic and social factors which might have an impact on its industry.

Example

A good example of this need for wider considerations is retail banking in the UK.

As late as the 1980s retail banking was very much the same as it had been for a hundred years. Banks dealt with retail customers on the High Street and maintained a network of branches to service the public. Some of these were relatively small and serviced a local community. Building Societies were mutual organisations (i.e. owned by their members) which were lenders in the home buying market.

The development of the Internet and deregulation by government meant that competition for banking services increased, consumer credit expanded and customers had new and, to them, better ways of contacting their bank, i.e. after hours and a weekends when traditional bank branches were shut. Building Societies de-mutualised in order to raise cash for expansion and moved into retail banking at the same time as banks moved into the home loans market.

The result of this was a wave of mergers, of bank branch closures, the loss of thousands of jobs from the banking sector, adoption of electronic banking (once customers could be persuaded to trust it), amalgamation of banks in order to meet the threats from overseas banking giants seeking to enter the lucrative UK market and banks and building societies competing to sell a range of financial products including insurance, credit cards and pensions.

By the present century the operation of retail banking had became completely different to what it was less than 30 years previously, i.e. in less than a working lifetime. Not only had individual companies either expanded hugely or disappeared completely, but legislative changes had created new opportunities, and risks, for those organisations which had survived and prospered.

Risk evaluation

Once risks are identified they should be evaluated.

There are many ways of doing this but the least complicated is a simple matrix.

Here is an example based on a company selling specialist skateboarding clothing over the Internet.

	High likelihood	Low likelihood
High impact	• Distribution difficulties with parcel delivery based on present supplier. • Small parcels and low order quantities are expensive	• Loss of computer systems due to software failure • Loss of consumer trust due to breakdown in security of payments system
Low impact	• Competition from new entrants into market. We have dominant position at this time and are well known to customers	• Loss of popularity of skateboarding – clothing may not suffer

As can be seen risks can be categorised into:

High impact/High likelihood

High impact/Low likelihood

Low impact/High likelihood

Low impact/Low likelihood

Organisations can use some form of analysis to attribute probabilities of identified risks occurring and also evaluate the impact in financial terms. They can thus calculate the possible risk impact to their organisation by:

Financial cost of risk occurring × probability it will occur

Clearly a lot of this is subjective, particularly the estimate of the likelihood, or probability, of the risk crystallising which is why it requires involvement of senior, experienced management and staff.

ACTIONS TO MITIGATE RISK

Once risks are identified and evaluated the organisation is faced with a range of actions. Options are:

- Accept the risk – do nothing and hope for the best – not really recommended except for low-impact/low-likelihood risks which are classed as *Residual Risks.*
- Manage the risk – reduce the risk – by, for example:

  - raising staff awareness of risk;
  - establishing physical measures such as improved security;
  - diversifying computer systems instead of having one complex one;
  - active development of new products and markets;
  - strengthening internal controls;
  - developing quality controls over production of goods, production of services;
  - good staff recruitment and training policies.

- Transfer the risk – by insurance, subcontracting, outsourcing.
- Avoid the risk – don't allow the organisation to engage in high-risk activities. For example, if trading in a volatile country where there is a risk of government interference, instead of funding the operation from say the UK or the USA use local finance and local management and suppliers wherever possible, thus mitigating the effects of possible nationalisation, import controls, etc.

WHY USE A BUSINESS RISK APPROACH TO AUDITING?

By evaluating the organisation's risk management processes and studying the outcomes of the risk identification and evaluation the auditors can reduce their workload considerably and, it is argued, carry out an audit which is more directly relevant to the client's day-to-day activities and more likely to identify the possibility of significant errors or misstatements arising.

There are, as might be expected, both advantages and disadvantages to adopting a business risk approach.

Advantages

- Research shows that processing errors are rarely a cause of major audit problems. Major audit problems (e.g. companies failing shortly after receiving an unqualified audit report) arise out of issues such as going concern, major fraud by top management, larger-scale systems breakdown, failure to modernise products, lack of response to market forces, etc.

- Investigation of business risk enables the auditor to have a profound knowledge of the business (as required by ISA 310) and focuses the audit on the high-risk areas.

- The approach tends to involve partners and senior managers much more in the planning stages of an audit.

- The approach adds value to the audit and enables the auditor to offer some commercial benefits to the client.

- Using a systems-based audit approach is impractical, expensive and uneconomic in large company audits where the internal control environment is strong.

- The pace of change in business and in computing and communications means that companies are much more at risk of failure than ever before. The global economy is more competitive and more unforgiving than the national economy.

- Audit firms wish to be in the forefront of innovation in order to attract clients.

- The business risk evaluation may show up areas where the audit firm can suggest that its other services can be offered to the client.

- The business, environmental, corporate governance issues and the nature of management control are all now more significant for businesses. They also translate more quickly into the financial statements.

Disadvantages

There are some important disadvantages which have to be considered:

- The approach increases the level of risk to the audit firm. This requires the firm to have strong quality control procedures and to document all its processes thoroughly.

- The process requires highly qualified and competent staff both at the planning stage and during the audit itself which negates some of the efficiency gains.

- Audit firms must be careful to maintain their objectivity and independence. The assessment of risk will undoubtedly require a close relationship with senior management and the development of mutual trust. Auditors may come to discover facts which the management may not wish to disclose and auditors may have to take hard decisions which may cause a rift in that relationship. However, the destruction of Arthur Andersen following the collapse of Enron is a salutary lesson in what happens to audit firms who get too close to their client.

UNDERSTANDING THE BUSINESS RISK APPROACH

Students need to obtain a clear understanding of the business risk approach and of the difference between *business risk* and *audit risk*.

There is still a lack of clarity in the articulation between business risk and audit risk, however the ideas of inherent risk and control risk have tended to merge into the larger idea of business risk. To simplify the position:

- Audit risk (see Chapter 10) is the risk the *audit firm* has to consider.
- Business risks are the risks facing the *client.*

The interaction between the two is that audit risk includes assessment of inherent and control risk, which include some of the components of business risk.

Some other key features of the business risk approach are:

- The direction of the audit is from the risks to the financial statements. Earlier approaches to auditing tended to start with the financial statements.
- The approach is very much a strategic one – much less of the *'can wages be paid to non-employees?'* and much more of *'could the client close its Bristol factory and manufacture in China and what are the possible consequences for the company and its financial statements if it did?'*
- Because of the better understanding of the client's business it is possible to use analytical review more frequently as a verification of Assertions procedure.
- It is an aid to the client acceptance and continuation procedures (*'Do we want this client?'*).
- Going concern considerations (see Chapter 24) are a natural by-product of business risk investigation and separate consideration of going concern may be unnecessary.
- The audit needs to be tailor-made and a generalised approach to audits is neither productive nor economical; however this needs well trained and experienced staff.
- Auditors need more understanding of business and to that end the larger firms set up large databases of information about the economy and the business world.
- The concept implies a continuing relationship with the client rather than a one-off, each year separate, view.

'Top-down' approach

Auditors can adopt what has become known as the 'top-down approach'.

In this the general risks are assessed first and then specific risks are evaluated. The auditor must gain a understanding of the business' strategies, both current and future, as well as the risks associated with business operations and the controls in place to deal with them.

The auditor can then assess the expectations developed from this assessment of the business with what is shown by the accounts. The approach is known as a 'top-down' approach because it begins with management discussions and evaluations of controls at the highest level in the business and then cascades down as specific issues are addressed. It attempts to look at the accounts holistically, as a part of the ongoing business and its processes, tackling say, materiality on the basis of the financial statements as a whole and looking at the control environment from the point of view of the highest level of control, i.e. senior management level, downwards through the organisation.

THE IMPLICATIONS OF THE BUSINESS RISK APPROACH FOR THE AUDIT

Planning

The auditor needs to plan the audit (ISA 300) and needs to develop a thorough understanding of the business.

The planning process still needs an assessment of audit risk (Chapter 10).

The effects on planning may include:

- A consideration of the control environment. Is the control environment strong – if it is not the business risk approach may not be appropriate.

- Does the management manage risk effectively? Do they have in place procedures which can identify and evaluate the business risks faced by the organisation? This should be evaluated at all levels of management.

- Is the Management Information System adequate to provide the information needed to manage the business effectively?

- Do any risks threaten the going concern status of the company?

- Do any of the risks have implications for cash flow?

- Is there a high risk of fraud – e.g. poor controls, management override, egotistical ambition and arrogance in the chief executive?

- Are there related parties with different agendas?

- Is the business under threat of being taken over with the risk of management misstating financial statements?

- Is there a risk of litigation against the company?

- Is there any risk of withdrawal of support by loan or trade creditors?

Audit procedures

Although detailed systems-based audit checking work may be eliminated altogether because the auditor is relying on the strength of the company's own internal controls this does not mean that the auditor does not have to carry out any detailed checking work.

Key features are:

- The auditors must be sure that the internal control processes are strong. This will require them to validate that assumption – perhaps by considering the internal audit function and the effectiveness of corporate governance within the organisation. These tests need to be carried out and documented.

- Auditors cannot escape some level of substantive testing of balance sheet items. Whilst they may consider issues such as fixed asset recording, debtors and purchase ledger balances and possibly even stocks to be within the internal control system and therefore not subject to detailed testing such matters as provisions, contingent liabilities and analytical review cannot be overlooked.
- The amount of testing carried out will depend on the risk of each item in the balance sheet being likely to be seriously misstated and of the financial statements as a whole not showing a true and fair view. This assessment will be carried out in the context of the business risks identified and evaluated by the auditors.

In the end many of the audit risks come down to:

- Possible misstatements due to inadequate of controls or weak corporate governance. Recent company failures have been caused by overvaluations of stocks or under-provisions for bad debts or situations where senior management have overridden controls and procedures.
- Working capital shortage leading to cash flow difficulties and technical insolvency (inability to pay debts as they fall due), often due to too rapid expansion.
- Inappropriate accounting policies. These can often lead to overstatement of assets or understatement of liabilities. Compliance with accounting standards is essential.
- Deliberate suppression or concealment of liabilities.
- Fraud by management.
- Activities of related parties.
- Computer systems failures.
- Litigation and regulatory issues and attempts by management to subvert disclosures.

Summary

- Business risk is the threat that an event or action will adversely affect a business's ability to achieve its ongoing objectives.
- Business risk relates to all risks faced by the business, including both internal and external risks.
- Businesses should have procedures for identifying risks and evaluating their impact on the business.
- Auditors need to develop a thorough understanding of their client and the risk management process.
- Auditors can considerably reduce the amount of checking work they carry out by auditing the risks rather than carrying out systems audits.
- Business risk and audit risk are not the same, however the evaluation of both types of risk includes some common components.
- Auditors need to carry out substantive tests on high-risk items in the financial statements.

Points to note

- This area is becoming increasingly popular with examiners and students must be clear on how this works and the advantages and disadvantages of the business risk approach.
- Don't make the mistake of confusing audit risk and business risk.
- Remember that this approach is only really appropriate for the best run companies. Any problems with internal controls will make this approach far too risky for the auditor.

Case Study

You are the manager responsible for prospective new clients and you have visited Bolington Publishing PLC which publishes a small range of fiction paperbacks. The chief executive is Daniel Dunbar and he has asked your firm to make a proposal for the company's audit and other services.

During the initial meeting you have ascertained the following:

- The company's turnover has increased by about 20 per cent a year for the last three years.
- Daniel is a dominating personality who is very ambitious.
- The company has recently paid very large sums to two relatively unknown authors for new books which Daniel thinks will be highly successful.
- Bolington has borrowed heavily from its bank and a major repayment of the loan is due shortly. The company is already on its overdraft limit as a result of the advances to the new authors. Daniel is in negotiation with a foreign bank for further finance.
- Many of the company's books are printed in a country with an exchange rate which is very favourable to the UK. The financial press have lately suggested that this rate may change in the near future.

- The company recently purchased a very large and very complex computer system to control all its affairs. The IT manager has just left and gone to Australia.
- The company have agreed to sponsor a sailor who is racing round the world single-handedly and the cost of this is not yet clear. The company has a racing yacht which Daniel sails.
- The company have received a writ from a person who alleges he has been wronged by a book published by the company. The company has large stocks of this book and is contesting the issue.
- The company have no formal management accounting system but the new IT system, when it is working, will supply this.
- Daniel wishes to maintain the company's high share price so that he can use the shares to take over a competitor.
- The company recently took over an ailing printing firm. Daniel reckons he can turn it round.

Discussion

- Identify and describe the principal business risks relating to Bolington.
- Justify an appropriate audit strategy for the first audit of Bolington.
- Suggest some procedures that Bolington could implement immediately to manage the risks.
- What effect might these risks have on the financial statements?

Student self-testing questions

Questions with answers apparent from the text

a) Define business risk.

b) List some external risks facing companies.

c) List some internal risks facing companies.

d) Why do auditors use a business risk approach?

e) What are the consequences of the approach?

f) What can a company do about risk?

g) The implications of business risk for the audit?

Examination questions

1 You are a manager in Costello, a firm of Chartered Certified Accountants, which has recently adopted a business risk methodology. You have been involved in briefing clients about this 'top-down approach' and promoting the risk management assurance services which Costello offers.

The following information concerns one of your clients, Ferry, a limited liability company:

In July 20x3, Ferry purchased exclusive rights to operate a car and passenger ferry route until December 2x13. This offers an alternative to driving an additional 150 kilometres via the nearest bridge crossing.

There have been several ambitious plans to build another crossing but they have failed through lack of public support and government funds.

Ferry refurbished two 20-year-old roll on, roll off ('Ro-Ro') boats to service the route. The boats do not yet meet the emission standards of Environmental Protection Regulations which come into force in 20x5. Each boat makes three return crossings every day of the year, subject to weather conditions, and has the capacity to carry approximately 250 passengers and 40 vehicles. The ferry service carried just 70 000 vehicles in the year to 31 December 20x7 (20x6: 58, 000; 20x5: 47 000).

Hot and cold refreshments and travel booking facilities are offered on the one hour crossing. These services are provided by independent businesses on a franchise basis.

Ferry currently receives a subsidy from the local transport authority as an incentive to increase market awareness of the ferry service and its efficient and timely operation. The subsidy increases as the number of vehicles carried increases and is based on quarterly returns submitted to the authority.

Ferry employs 20 full-time crew members who are trained in daily operations and customer service, as well as passenger safety in the event of personal accident, collision or breakdown.

The management of Ferry is planning to apply for a recognised Safety Management Certificate (SMC) in 20x7.

This will require a ship audit including the review of safety documents and evidence that activities are performed in accordance with documented procedures. An SMC valid for five years will be issued if no major non-conformities have been found.

Your firm has been asked to provide Ferry with a business risk assessment (BRA) as a management assurance service.

Required:

(a) Identify and explain the business risks facing Ferry which should be assessed.

(b) Describe the processes by which the risks identified in (a) could be managed and maintained at an acceptable level by Ferry.

(ACCA)

2 The principal activity of Bateleur Zoo Gardens (BZG) is the conservation of animals. Approximately 80 per cent of the zoo's income comes from admission fees, money spent in the food and retail outlets and animal sponsorship. The remainder comprises donations and investment income.

Admission fees include day visitor entrance fees ('gate') and annual membership fees. Day tickets may be pre-booked by credit card using a telephone booking 'hotline' and via the zoo's website. Reduced fees are available (e.g. to students, senior citizens and families).

Animal sponsorships, which last for one year, make a significant contribution to the cost of specialist diets, enclosure maintenance and veterinary care. Animal sponsors benefit from the advertisement of their names at the sponsored animal's enclosure.

BZG's management has identified the following applicable risks that require further consideration and are to be actively managed:

(i) Reduction in admission income through failure to invest in new exhibits and breeding programmes to attract visitors.

(ii) Animal sponsorships may not be invoiced due to incomplete data transfer between the sponsoring and invoicing departments.

(iii) Corporate sponsorships may not be charged for at approved rates – either in error or due to arrangements with the companies. In particular, the sponsoring department may not notify the invoicing department of reciprocal arrangements, whereby sponsoring companies provide BZG with advertising (e.g. in company magazines and annual reports).

(iv) Cash received at the entrance gate ticket offices ('kiosks') may not be passed to cashiers in the accounts department (e.g. through theft).

(v) The ticket booking and issuing system may not be available.

(vi) Donations of animals to the collection (e.g. from Customs and Excise seizures and rare breeds enthusiasts) may not be recorded.

Required:

(a) Describe suitable internal controls to manage each of the applicable risks identified.

(b) Explain the financial statement risks arising from the applicable risks.

(c) Comment on the factors to be considered when planning the extent of substantive analytical procedures to be performed on BZG's income.

(ACCA)

15

The audit of assets

INTRODUCTION

A large part of the final audit stage will be taken up with the verification of the assets and liabilities appearing in the balance sheet. There are well-established techniques for verifying specific assets and liabilities. All auditing examinations contain one or more questions on this subject.

The auditor has a duty to verify all the assets appearing on the balance sheet and also a duty to verify that there are no other assets which ought to appear on the balance sheet but don't.

Assets are normally divided into categories like this:

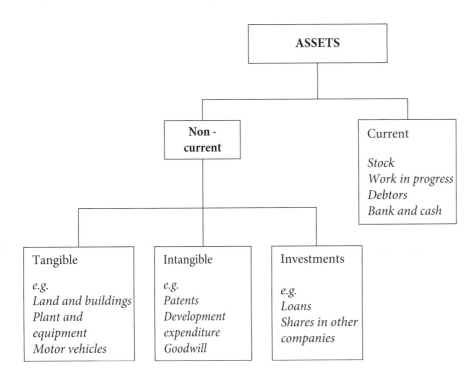

We will look at the audit implications of each category in turn.

This is not an accounting book so it does not include detailed explanations of how these categories of assets have to be disclosed in the financial statements. Students should be aware of the disclosure requirements under the Companies Act and the relevant Financial Reporting Standards. We will refer to them in the text but you should know and understand the key disclosure requirements of each standard. This is a very common area for examination questions.

ASPECTS TO BE VERIFIED

When we are looking to audit assets, whether they be current or non current we have to bear in mind the requirements of the Assertions set out in Chapter 11. In particular we are concerned with the second part of those assertions – *'Assertions about account balances at the period end'*. but, of course, the other assertions, particularly those relating to transactions, also apply.

The Assertions set out the following matters about which the auditor has to gather sufficient reliable evidence so as to verify their truth – or otherwise:

(2) Assertions about account balances at the period end

Existence	• assets, liabilities and equity interests (shareholdings) exist
Rights and obligations	• the company holds or controls the rights to assets, and all liabilities are those of the company
Completeness	• all assets, liabilities and equity interests that should have been recorded have been recorded
Valuation and allocation	• assets, liabilities and equity interests (shareholdings) are included in the financial statements at appropriate amounts and any resulting valuation or allocation adjustments are properly recorded

One mnemonic often used by students in connection with the audit of balance sheet items is:

- **C**ost.
- **A**uthorisation.
- **V**alue.
- **E**xistence.
- **B**eneficial **O**wnership.
- **P**resentation in the Accounts.

CAVEBOP

which does cover all aspects of the assertions and might be easier to remember!

Most examination questions in this area can be answered adequately by running through each of these and devising means of verifying each aspect.

You will also appreciate that the amount of evidence required will depend partly on the risk of a misstatement in the accounts.

Older text books tended to stress *existence, ownership* and *value* only. The addition of *presentation* reflects the relatively greater importance attached now to the 'fair' as well as the 'true' view given by the financial statements and the importance of the appropriate selection and disclosure of accounting policies.

For assets held at the beginning of the year, the acquisition will have been dealt with in a previous year. The presentation will, of course, need to be consistent with the presentation adopted in previous years. Most examination questions state whether or not the assets concerned were purchased in the year under review.

You will appreciate that this distinction does not arise with current assets.

VERIFICATION OF NON-CURRENT ASSETS

Tangible assets

Tangible assets are so called because you can see them and touch them. They primarily consist of such assets as:

- Land and buildings.
- Plant and equipment.
- Furniture and fittings.
- Motor vehicles.

IAS 16 *Property Plant and Equipment* states that assets are:
'held for use in the production or supply of goods and services or for rental to others or administrative use and are expected to be used in more than one period.'

There are four key aspects to consider before we look in detail at audit procedures to verify tangible assets.

- It is permitted to include these assets at valuation rather than original cost. There are extensive disclosure requirements where assets are shown at valuation – we will look at the audit aspects of valuing tangible assets separately.

- Auditors should carefully consider the depreciation policy – the amount to be written off these assets (cost less residual value) should be allocated on a systematic basis over the asset's useful economic life. Auditors should look for consistency in applying depreciation policies and be alert where policies are changed. Rates of depreciation, residual values and economic lives of assets should be reviewed regularly to ensure they are still applicable.

- Auditors should look at the question of *impairment*. Where the value of assets becomes impaired, in other words they are not worth the value at which they are shown in the accounting records, they should be written down to a realistic value. This is particularly true of intangible assets such as brands or goodwill, which we will look at later, but can also apply to tangible assets due to obsolescence or changes in regulations.

- Assets which are leased cause a problem as the auditor has to determine whether assets are financed through operating or finance leases. Finance leases are defined as those which *'transfer substantially all the risks and rewards incidental to ownership of an asset'*. The reason why this is important is that costs incurred under operating leases should be expensed through the profit and loss account whilst assets acquired under finance leases can be capitalised. It is not beyond the realms of possibility that unscrupulous managers will try and capitalise operating lease costs thus increasing asset values and profits incorrectly, so the auditors should activate their professional scepticism whenever they are confronted with leased assets. It is necessary to read the lease agreements carefully to ensure the costs are treated correctly.

Control objectives

The control objectives in relation to tangible fixed assets are:

- To ensure that all tangible fixed assets exist, are owned by the company and are in use.
- To ensure that tangible fixed assets are correctly recorded in the books, adequately secured and properly maintained.
- That acquisitions and disposals are properly authorised.
- That assets are properly depreciated and the depreciation is properly accounted for.

Audit procedures

We will look at the audit procedures applicable to different categories of asset and, at the same time, identify which Assertions these procedures will provide evidence for

Land and buildings

- Physically inspect a sample of land and buildings *(existence)*.
- Inspect all documents of title, lease agreements, invoices, etc. relating to the purchase or disposal of land and buildings. If title deeds or other such documents are held by a third party, for example, a lender as security for a loan, the lender should be asked to certify possession in writing *(ownership, rights and obligations)*.
- Inspect minutes of directors' meetings to ensure all agreements for the purchase or sale of assets are properly authorised and signatures on documents such as title deeds, leases, conveyances, tenancy agreements, etc. are properly minuted and approved *(occurrence, rights and obligations)*.
- Check a sample of entries in the asset register or asset accounts in the nominal ledger and trace back to source documentation *(valuation)*.
- Review depreciation policy and check sample calculations. Consider in relation to expected useful lives of assets *(valuation)*.
- Review assets for any permanent impairment in value *(valuation)*.
- If assets are stated at valuation, if a valuation has been performed in the year, ensure name or qualification of valuer and basis of valuation is appropriate and that proper disclosure is made in the accounts *(valuation)*.
- Ensure asset register reconciles to nominal ledger *(completeness and accuracy)*.
- Ensure fixed assets properly disclosed in financial statements in accordance with IAS 16 *(completeness, valuation and allocation)*.

Land and buildings at cost will be the norm and creates no problems. Land shown at below cost will be unusual and the auditor will need to:

- Examine the reason for the write down.
- Examine the director's minute authorising it.
- Appraise the adequacy of the write down.

Ensure that there is adequate disclosure of the facts in the financial statements.

Buildings can be under construction and can be being constructed by the client. In this case care has to be taken to ensure that only costs, including overheads, which directly relate to the construction of the asset are included. These will include material and labour costs but can also include the costs of borrowing to finance the construction and direct overheads.

Auditors should be aware that:

- Capitalising expenses is a way of 'improving' the profits and asset values.
- The building should not cost more than it can be valued at – excessive costs allocated to the construction of a building should be investigated and the question of 'impairment' considered.

It may be that auditors will have to take specialist advice in this area.

Intangible assets

Intangible assets include:

- Development costs.
- Patents, trade marks, licences, concessions, etc.
- Goodwill – if purchased on an acquisition.

These can be areas of some difficulty for the auditors, the principal one being in the area of valuation. It is, generally, reasonably easy to evidence the fact that intangible assets exist and that the business owns them, it is less easy to decide what they are worth.

Again there are accounting rules, principally set out in IAS 38 *Intangible Assets*, which the student should be familiar with.

There are some key issues which relate to intangible assets generally.

Research and development

You need to know the difference between research and development.

Research is original investigation work often undertaken with a view to developing a commercial project but often only with a view to extending knowledge. This is not an asset and the costs of research should be *written off* in the financial period.

Development is the application of research into a commercial product or service. This is preliminary cost incurred before the product or service goes into commercial production. This may be an *asset* subject to some considerations.

- Is the project technically feasible – i.e. will it be completed and result in a commercial product or service? This may require the auditors consulting an expert to determine the answer.
- Is the ultimate product going to be used or sold? – consult minutes of meetings and discussion papers.
- Can the product be sold – i.e. does the business have the capability to deliver the product to the market place? Again meeting minutes and discussion papers will provide evidence of the company's thinking on this.
- Will the product or service provide an income stream – is there a market for the product, what sort of volumes will be sold and at what price? If it is to be used internally in the organisation what sort of transfer price will be available? Market research reports will give guidance on this.
- Are resources available to complete the project, how much longer will it take and how much more will it cost? – budgets, plans and forecasts will evidence this as well as evidence of costs charged to date.

Whilst there is evidence to be gained from several sources, as suggested above, at the end of the day the auditors are left with having to make a judgement based on the available evidence. An important part of coming to that judgement is the discussion with management. Management needs to demonstrate why it has the confidence in the project and its ultimate benefits, and why therefore the expenditure can properly be capitalised. If necessary they should put it in writing. The auditors may need specialised help in some cases, but the ultimate decision lies with them.

Development costs should be amortised (depreciated) over their expected useful lives which is either the length of time the resulting product or service is in production and being sold or, if this is an inordinately long period, the value should be reviewed annually for impairment.

Trademarks, patents, etc.

These should be capitalised and written off over their expected useful lives. The auditors should consider the value each year – it may be that because of technical changes or changes in rules and regulations the value of a patent or trade mark becomes impaired, in which case it must be written down as the income stream from it will reduce or cease.

The auditor should check that any renewal fees have been paid, and written off, so the patents and trade marks are still current and the auditors should also inspect the agreements to make sure they are still current in the name of the company.

If the company uses a patent agent it may be possible to obtain a third party confirmation from them as to the ownership and currency of the patent.

Goodwill

This is purchased goodwill, i.e. goodwill arising on the acquisition of a business or part of a business. It represents the difference between the price paid and the value of the underlying assets.

This can be capitalised and written off over its useful life – which may, in some circumstances, be quite short.

Auditors must look at the value of goodwill and, assuming they can satisfy themselves over the value it was capitalised at, their main consideration is the expected useful life.

The question is this – if Company A takes over Company B for an amount in excess of the value of the assets of Company B it creates goodwill which the auditors can evidence through the takeover agreement. However, suppose, in the course of its business, Company A assimilates company B to such an extent that Company B's name disappears and all its products and services are marketed under the name of Company A – how then can the balance sheet of Company A continue to carry goodwill as an asset in its balance sheet if the business to which it originally referred has effectively ceased to exist?

The short answer, in reality, is that it cannot justify upholding such goodwill so that it should be written off through the profit and loss account, in much the same way as if the value of the goodwill had become tainted in some way.

It is a matter of judgement. Remember though that it is for management to decide on the value it intends to include in the balance sheet – the auditor has to form a judgement, based on as much evidence as can be found, as to whether that value is true and fair.

Investments

Investments are assets held to generate income or to create a profit from themselves. These can comprise, amongst other things:

• Loans;

- Money market deposits;
- Shares in other companies either quoted or unquoted;
- Properties;
- Gilts (UK Government stock).

Note that for investments in shares, for this purpose we exclude investments in subsidiary companies (holding of more than 50 per cent of the voting shares) or associated companies (holding more than 20 per cent, i.e. having a 'significant' influence).

There is, as might be expected, an accounting standard IAS 39 with which the student should be familiar.

Again the basic audit principles apply regarding evidencing existence and ownership.

- Physical inspection of loan notes, share certificates, title deeds.
- Third party verification from banks, brokers or agents.
- Income streams from dividends, rents, etc.
- Transaction evidence – 'bought' and 'sold' notes.
- Minutes of directors' meetings.

One important point is that ISA 510 *'Audit Evidence – Additional Considerations for Specific Items'* states that where investments are described as 'long term' by the company the auditors must consider whether the company has the capability of holding the investments for the long term.

This is done by discussing the matter with management and obtaining written representations.

The reason for this is obvious – if the company cannot hold the investment for the long term, because, say, it is running out of money and will have to sell them to raise cash, then they are incorrectly disclosed in the accounts.

Valuation can be more difficult. IAS 39 originally requires investments to be stated at cost and them for their value to be re-measured at each balance sheet date to a 'fair value' except for:

- Loans, held to maturity investments and other receivables which should be measured at amortised cost.
- Equity investments whose fair value cannot be measured – this is most likely to apply to investments in unquoted companies.

For quoted investments this is relatively straightforward as a share price can be obtained at the period end from published sources, but the valuation of unquoted investments is more problematic and may require some discussion with the directors. Properties held as investment properties can be valued by a competent valuer.

At each balance sheet date the question of impairment arises and the value must be assessed individually.

CURRENT ASSETS

Introduction

Here we consider some standard verification techniques for current assets including:

- stock and work in progress;

- debtors;
- cash at bank and loans.

The basic asset verification techniques described above (CAVEBOP etc.) apply to current assets as much as to Tangible and Intangible assets.

However, there are some specific techniques which relate to the audit of current assets, particularly stock and work in progress, so it is necessary to describe these particular techniques separately.

The audit of current assets is often the subject of examination questions so students must become familiar with the procedures relevant to each category of asset.

STOCK AND WORK IN PROGRESS

Stock and work in progress is often a key item in the financial statements and its verification is a common examination question.

It cannot be stressed too much that it is the directors' responsibility to ensure that:

- Stock and work in progress are correctly identified.
- Physical quantities are correctly ascertained and recorded and condition assessed.
- Valuation on proper bases is correctly made.
- Proper disclosure is made in the financial statements.

There is an auditing guideline which has a specific relevance to stocks and that is ISA 501 *Audit Evidence – Additional Considerations for Specific Items*.

Students should also be aware of the disclosure requirements of 2 SSAP 9 *Stocks and Long Term Contracts* and, where appropriate, IAS 2 *Inventories*.

Categories of stock

A categorisation, which follows the broad disclosure requirements in the financial statements, is into:

- Finished goods and goods purchased for resale.
- Raw materials and components purchased for incorporation into products for sale and consumable stores (oils, fuels, spare parts etc.).
- Work in progress.
- Payments on account.

Stocks may be:

- verified assessed by periodic physical counts, particularly at the period end;
- recorded on a rolling or continuous inventory system.

Cost and net realisable value

The accounting standards require that stock and work in progress should be valued at the lower of cost and net realisable value.

This means:

- Cost – includes cost of the actual item plus any costs related to bringing it to its present location and condition, so can include import duties, transport costs, handling costs, etc. and net of any rebates or discounts.

- Net realisable value – is the estimated selling price of those goods in the ordinary course of business. This can be calculated after deduction of a proportion to cover selling and distribution costs if this is appropriate. Auditors need to review selling prices of stock items after the year end – the market price may be less than cost.

Note this really only applies to finished goods – it may often be the case that raw materials and consumables have a selling price less than cost but this wouldn't justify writing down stock values.

Valuation

Cost has to be based on:

- For individual items, i.e. 'one-off' items, e.g. a car in a motor dealership – the actual cost for the individual item.
- For interchangeable items – e.g. boxes of welding rods in a store cost calculated on a First In First Out (FIFO) or on a Average Cost basis. The same method must be used for similar items of stock

Production overheads

One of the problems in valuing stock and work in progress is the allocation of overheads as part of the cost. These are overheads incurred in the manufacture of the items – obviously this does not include any element of selling or distribution overhead.

Production overheads can be either fixed or variable. The calculation of the level of overheads to be apportioned should be based on the normal level of activity. Where overheads are allocated using an absorption costing basis, which includes some element of non-production overheads, it is necessary to attempt to exclude these from the valuation.

This might require either recalculating the absorption basis or making an estimate of the non-production overheads and excluding this proportion from the stock valuation.

Stocktaking procedures

In small companies stocktaking may occur on only one day a year, other companies have more regular counts and yet others carry out regular stock checks on a continuous or rolling count basis.

Stocktaking is essentially a part of the internal control system.

A good set of procedures will have the following characteristics:

- Good planning so that the work is carried out carefully and systematically – early issue of stocktaking instructions with consideration of feedback from staff.
- Division of the stocktake into manageable areas for control purposes.
- Identification of stocks and especially of high value items.
- Nomination of people responsible for each aspect of the count. These should, ideally, be persons independent of those normally responsible for the control over stock items. This is based on the internal control principle of segregation of duties – separating those responsible for control of stock from those responsible for counting it.
- Written instructions to counters for counting, weighing, measuring and checking should be issued and all counters must ensure they are familiar with them.
- Controls to ensure all stock is counted and once only.
- Proper control over the issue of blank stock sheets by numbering them and the control over the return of completed and unused stock sheets. This ensures none are mislaid or lost.

- Control of stock movements during the count – no goods in or out.
- Cut-off arrangements – we look at this in more detail later.
- Arrangements for identification of defective, damaged, obsolete, and slow-moving stock.
- Identification of stock on the premises owned by third parties and of client's stock held by outside parties.
- Appropriate treatment for sealed containers, dangerous goods, and goods with special problems.

Stocktaking – the auditor's duties

As mentioned above ISA 501 *Audit Evidence – Additional Considerations for Specific Items* now requires the auditors to attend stock taking.

It says:

'where inventory (stock) is material to the financial statements the auditor should obtain sufficient appropriate audit evidence regarding its existence and condition by attendance at physical inventory counting, unless impractical.'

The purpose of attendance is not only to gather evidence to support the audit opinion but also as part of the auditors' work on the internal controls of the business. In particular:

- the physical count will validate (or otherwise of course) the book stock records;
- it will provide evidence of the operation of internal controls over stocks, including the client's stocktaking procedures;
- it provides substantive evidence for the auditors of a material balance sheet and profit and loss account figure.

The auditors must satisfy themselves as to the validity of the amounts attributed to stock and work in progress in the financial statements. They do this by first considering the client's system of internal control. This applies to stocktaking as it does to all areas of audit enquiry. It is essential for students to understand that stocktaking procedures are part of the system.

The auditor's duties are usually divided into three parts – before, during and after the stocktake.

Before the stocktake – planning

- Review the previous year's working papers and discuss with management any significant changes from the previous year.
- Discuss stocktaking arrangements with management.
- Familiarise themselves with the nature and volume of stocks and especially with high value items.
- Consider the location of stocks (e.g. at branches) and the problems thus caused for the client and the auditors.
- Consider likely points of difficulty, e.g. cut off.
- Consider internal audit involvement and if reliance can be placed upon it.
- Arrange to obtain from third parties confirmation of stock held by them.
- Establish whether expert help may be needed from a third party (e.g. pubs, clubs and restaurants in the licensing trade use specialist valuers, advice may be required with regard to the valuation of specialised stock, e.g. gems, contract work in progress).

- Evaluate the client's stocktaking instructions, especially that they:

  - include stock held in all locations;
  - plan to use staff separate from those concerned with the stock on a day-to-day basis;
  - make arrangements for suspending the delivery of goods into the stores and the taking of goods out of stock – there should be no movement of goods during the count;
  - are discussed with, and adequately communicated to stocktaking staff;
  - include arrangements for marking stock counted so it isn't counted twice;
  - include arrangements for stock takers to count in pairs so counts can be verified as they go around;
  - include arrangements for identifying old, obsolete or damaged stock.

- Ensure that all audit teams have a copy of the client's instructions (and have read and understood them!).
- Review surrounding systems of internal control to identify areas of potential difficulty.
- Plan usage of audit staff as to availability to cover all required locations, etc.

During the stocktake

Remember that the purpose of the attendance is not to take stock or to supervise the stock-take but to *observe* the client's internal control system in action.

The actual work to be done is:

- Observe the stocktake to ascertain that the client's employees are carrying out their instructions.
- Check the count of a selected number of lines. This must be done by selecting some items found to be present in the stores and some items recorded on the stock sheets.
- Note for follow up:

  - Details of items selected by the auditors to compare with final stock sheets.
  - List of items counted by client's staff in the auditor's presence.
  - Details of defective, damaged, obsolete or slow-moving items identified during the count.
  - Instances of stocktaking instructions not being followed.

- Details of items for cut-off purposes. These will consist of recording the details of the last delivery note number for goods inwards and the last goods outward note number.
- Enquire into, observe and discuss with store-keeping staff the procedures for identifying damaged, obsolete and slow-moving stock.
- Form an impression of the magnitude of stock held for comparison with the accounts.
- Record fully the work done and impressions of the stocktake in the working papers.
- If any aspects prove unsatisfactory, inform the management and request a recount.
- High value items should be given special attention.
- Photocopies of rough stock sheets should be taken if possible.
- Details of the sequence of stock sheets should be verified.

After the stocktake

- Check the cut-off with details of the last numbers of goods inward and goods outwards notes during the year and after the year end.

- Test that the final stock sheets have been properly prepared from the count records. In particular the record of stock count sheets issued and returned must be checked.
- Follow up any notes made at the attendance.
- Check final stock sheets for pricing, extensions, additions, summarising, and officials' signatures.
- Inform management of any problems encountered in the stocktake for action in subsequent counts.

If it is not practicable to attend the stocktaking, for example, if the client has stock at remote or overseas locations, the auditors must still attempt to gather evidence concerning the physical existence, ownership and value of stocks.

This can be done by:

- Arranging for the stocktake to be at an earlier date and reconciling the count with the year end stock figure.
- Appointing agents, e.g. for overseas locations.
- Examining continuous stocktake records and carrying out sample testing.

None of these solutions is wholly satisfactory and the auditors must make very extensive enquiries before they give a clean report.

Continuous inventory

Many organisations, and supermarkets are perhaps the most accessible example, cannot close their operations down for stocktaking or find it impracticable to do so.

Instead they practice a continual stocktaking procedure where every item of stock is checked to the book stock records at least once in the year, and probably more than once, in a systematic and orderly manner.

The records of such checking should demonstrate concurrence between the actual stock and the records.

In this case what the auditor has to do is:

- Attend physical inventory counts when they are being carried out by client's staff on more than one occasion.
- Examine the book stock listing at the year end and examine records of counts near the year-end date.
- Examine reconciliations between counts and the book stock records and ensure the client has procedures in place to follow up any discrepancies during counts and adjust book stock records as appropriate.

This last point is probably the most important because, in the absence of an independent physical count at the year end, the auditor has to ensure that the client has sufficient controls in place to maintain the book stock records accurately.

Stocktakes other than at the year end

ISA 501 states that stocktaking carried out before or after the year end may be acceptable for audit purposes provided records of stock movements in the intervening period are such that the movements can be examined and substantiated. The greater the interval the more difficult this will be. Acceptability depends also on the auditors being satisfied that there is a good system of internal control and satisfactory stock records.

Work in progress

All that has been said about stock applies equally to work in progress but this item presents even greater problems of ascertainment and valuation to the directors and to the auditors.

This category relates primarily to *long-term work in progress* i.e. work which will cover more than one, and sometimes several, accounting periods.

With short-term work in progress it is relatively easy to value the work done as the contract may well be completed before the audit is signed off and the auditors can evaluate its outcome, but for longer-term contracts the future may be more uncertain. This requires an exercise of judgement and, sometimes, the involvement or opinion of an expert valuer, such as a Quantity Surveyor.

The auditor's investigations will include:

- Examination of contracts to ensure that salient features such as timescales and penalty clauses are known.

- Enquiry into the costing system from which work in progress is ascertained.

- Enquiry into the reliability of the costing system. In particular a costing system integrated with the financial accounting system will, prima facie, be more reliable because of the discipline of double entry and the inherent checks imposed by external data such as creditors' statements.

- Enquiry into statistical data concerning inputs of materials and outputs of products and expectations, e.g. for given tonnages of materials purchased there should be some identifiable outcome in the contract. Actual progress can be matched with theoretical models.

- Enquiry into the system of inspection and reporting to enable due allowance to be made for scrapping and rectification work.

- Enquiry into the basis on which overheads are included in costs. This should be based on IAS 2/SSAP 9

- Enquiry into the qualifications and experience of any valuers who are certifying valuations of completed work.

- Enquiry into the basis on which any element of profit is dealt with. Profit should be eliminated from work in progress. However, it is legitimate to include an element of profit in long-term contract work in progress in accordance with IAS 2/SSAP 9. The calculation of the amount of profit to be taken should be treated with extreme caution.

- Any losses identified on contracts in progress must be recognised immediately in the valuation. This is to reduce the valuation of work in progress to its estimated realisable value. Auditors have to review not only the costs already included in the calculation of work in progress but also the costs to complete the particular contract. This requires them to form a judgement on the assumptions used by management to calculate such costs.

- Where items such as buildings and plant are constructed internally, it is important for the auditor to make sure that if such items are under construction at the year end they are not included twice, i.e. in fixed assets and work in progress.

Auditors should, where possible, inspect the works in progress in order to familiarise themselves with the scale and nature of the projects, and to provide basic evidence that the project exists.

They may also have to consider the use of experts in connection with the valuation of work in progress and legal advice in connection with any dispute which may be taking place over the contract.

Analytical review

While detailed work on stock and work in progress is imperative in an audit, there are a number of analytical review procedures which the auditors should carry out in order to provide additional, substantive, evidence.

These could include:

- Reconciliation of changes in stocks at successive year ends with records of movements, e.g. purchases and sales.
- Comparison of quantities of each kind of stock held at year end with those held at previous year ends and with purchases and sales.
- Consideration of gross profit ratio with that of previous years, other companies, and budgeted expectations.
- Consideration of rate of stock turn with previous years, etc.
- Comparison of stock figures with budgets for stock, sales and purchases.
- Consideration of standard costing records and the application of variances in the valuation of stock and work in progress.

Valuation of stock and work in progress

Remember that stock and work in progress should be valued in accordance with the provisions of SSAP 9 (or IAS 2) which state that they must be valued at the lower of cost and net realisable value.

Net realisable value is the value the stock would achieve in the open market in its present condition.

The audit tests could include detailed substantive tests such as:

- Ascertain accounting policies adopted for valuing stock and ensure they have been consistently applied.
- Test the stock sheets or continuous stock records with relevant documents such as invoices and costing records to determine if 'cost' has been correctly arrived at.
- Examine and test the inclusion of overheads, as outlined above.
- Test the treatment and examine evidence for items valued at net realisable value.
- Test the arithmetical accuracy of calculations.
- Test the consistency with which the amounts have been computed.
- Consider the calculation of any profits included as part of the valuation of work in progress and the valuation of any losses. This requires the auditor to be familiar with the provisions of the contracts and take a view on management's calculations.
- Consider the adequacy of the description used in the accounts and disclosure of the accounting policies adopted.

CUT-OFF

This subject has been mentioned already and it is extremely important.

Consider a trading account:

	£'000s	£'000s
Sales		1000
Opening Stock	100	
Purchases	750	
	850	
Closing Stock	150	
Cost of sales		700
Gross Profit		300

Two scenarios:

1 Supposing goods valued at £50 000 were:

(a) dispatched and invoiced by the supplier before balance sheet date; and

(b) received after balance sheet date owing to delays in transit,

they would be included in purchases, as a creditor, as a consequence of (a) and they would be excluded from closing stock as a consequence of (b).

In this case either the stock has to be included as stock in transit (and the auditors would have to verify the existence, ownership and value of that stock) or the invoice should be deleted from creditors and purchases and the whole transaction included in the next accounting period. This is a matter for judgement by the auditors.

2 Suppose goods in the stores valued at £50 000 were invoiced as a sale the day before the stock count but not actually despatched to the customer until the day after.

In this case the goods would be included in both stock and debtors (and sales) so the profit would, again, be distorted. Again the auditor has to ensure that only goods actually despatched to customers are included in sales.

Avoiding this possibility is a vital part of the system of internal control as applied to stock and consequently of prime concern to the auditor.

A famous case on the subject of cut-off was *Re, Thomas Gerrard & Son Ltd (1967)*. This was a cotton spinning and manufacturing company. The manager and principal shareholder:

(a) post-dated purchases invoices received before the year end; and

(b) ante-dated sales invoice copies in the new year to dates prior to the year end.

He did this quite openly for five half-year periods for bigger sums each time, thus turning losses into profits and causing the company to pay tax and dividends. The auditors discovered the alterations, asked questions and were put off by answers such as *'these were year end adjustments'* or *'it is more convenient'*.

The judge awarded damages against the auditors on the grounds that once their suspicions were aroused they had a duty to probe the matter to the bottom.

Auditors have a duty to satisfy themselves as to the validity of stock and work in progress and this cannot arise solely out of the assurances from management, however trustworthy in appearance.

Independent stocktakers

In some trades it is found that the stock is counted and valued by an independent firm of stocktakers. Examples include the jewellery, licensed and retail pharmacy trades.

The question arises as to whether this influences the extent of the auditors' examination. The answer is that the auditors have a duty to form an opinion on the amount at which stock is stated.

They cannot simply accept an outside stocktaker's valuation but it is usual to do so if:

- They are satisfied of the stocktaker's independence.
- The stocktaker is suitably qualified.
- The stocktaker has a suitable level of experience in the trade carried on by the company.
- The auditor is satisfied:

  - that the basis of valuation used is appropriate; and
  - proper cut-off procedures were employed.

Remember that the auditors have final responsibility for their audit opinion and cannot blame the stocktaker if things go wrong!

Historical note

There are some lessons for auditors to learn from past cases and these are three of the most famous:

Re, the Kingston Cotton Mill Co. Ltd (1896)

The auditors failed to detect overstatements of the amounts of stock. They accepted a certificate from the manager on the amount of stock after comparing it with the stock journal which contained accounts for each item or class of items purporting to be in stock and a summary. The summary was agreed by the auditors to be in agreement with the detailed accounts. In fact the entries were falsified to show more stock than was actually in existence. The auditors were exonerated on the grounds that it is no part of the auditor's duty to take stock and that they were entitled to rely upon other people for the details of stock in trade.

The judge's remarks contained the famous phrase '*He is a watchdog, not a bloodhound*'. This means that if the auditors discover something which is suspicious they should probe it to the bottom but in the absence of suspicious circumstances they are only bound to be reasonably cautious and careful.

Today the judgment in this case would undoubtedly be against the auditor, but the comfortable words of the judge have been used by auditors as a defence against charges of negligence in relation to frauds – a subject we look at more closely in Chapter 31.

McKesson and Robbins Inc., USA (1939)

In this almost unbelievable (except perhaps in America) case, the directors of the company created fictitious records of trading, sales, purchases, bank accounts, debtors, and stock so that the assets were overstated by over $20m. This extraordinary state of affairs was not detected by the auditors. In particular they did not attend the stocktake. Had they done so they would have rapidly realised that no stock existed!

Allied Crude Vegetable Oil Refining Corporation of New Jersey (1963)

In this scandal, methods were used to fool auditors who were present at the stocktaking.

Three methods, at least, were used:

- the quantity of vegetable oil in a tank was checked and before the quantity was checked in the second tank, the contents of the first tank were pumped through to the second tank.
- Using a dip stick to measure the quantity of oil in a tank. In reality the tank was empty and oil was contained only in a thin drainpipe down which the dipstick was dropped.
- Filling the tanks with mostly water and a small quantity of oil – the oil floated on the top and it looked like a full tank.

The oil 'stocks' were certified by the auditors and were used as collateral for millions of dollars worth of loans which were used fraudulently. The auditors procedures were found to be totally inadequate and they had signed the certificates of value on the basis of very flimsy audit evidence.

DEBTORS

Debtors form a significant item amongst the assets of most companies and its verification is a key part of the audit work.

Debtors generally comprises two main components:

- trade debtors, i.e. sales ledger balances;
- prepayments.

The auditor will be gathering sufficient appropriate evidence to verify the Assertions that:

- The debtors represent bona fide customers *(existence)*.
- The amounts are due to the business *(rights and obligations)*.
- The amounts due are correctly stated at the appropriate value *(valuation and allocation)*.
- All amounts due have been recorded *(completeness)*.

One point to remember is that auditors are only interested in validating the figure for debtors as a *total*, they are not interested in individual debtors accounts except:

- If there is a suspicion of fraud.
- As part of compliance tests of the sales system.

Trade debtors – compliance testing of internal control procedures

As part of their audit of balance sheet items auditors will have regard to the internal controls incorporated into the system in which the debtors are recorded. For example, the figure for trade debtors is largely derived from the sales ledger which is part of the sales system, so controls within the sales system are relevant to the auditor's evidence gathering procedures for trade debtors verification.

The auditor will consider controls designed to ensure that the control objectives for the sales and debtors systems are achieved, i.e.:

- All goods and services despatched are invoiced.
- Invoices are raised for the correct prices.

- All discounts are authorised.
- Goods on credit are only despatched to approved credit-worthy customers.
- All invoices for sales are properly recorded in the books.
- Amounts received from debtors are properly recorded and that the persons responsible for dealing with these are separate from those responsible for processing sales transactions.
- Outstanding balances are reviewed and possible bad debts pursued.
- All credit notes are authorised.
- All balances written off are authorised.

Compliance tests

Determine the system of internal control over sales and debtors. The system for debtors should ensure that:

- Only bona fide sales bring debtors into being.
- All such sales are to approved customers.
- All such sales are recorded.
- Once recorded the debts are only eliminated by receipt of cash or on the authority of a responsible official.
- Debts are collected promptly.
- Balances are regularly reviewed and aged, a proper system for follow-up exists, and, if necessary, adequate provision for bad and doubtful debts is made.

Substantive testing

- Obtain an aged schedule of debtors and agree the total to the control account. Note that with computerised accounting systems the balances will undoubtedly agree.
- Test a sample of balances on ledger accounts to the schedule and vice versa where this has not been produced directly from the sales ledger system.
- Examine the make up of balances. They should be composed of specific items.
- Ensure each account is settled from time to time.
- Enquire into the reason for any credit balances – this may lead to omitted sales.
- Enquire into the reasons for any transfers between accounts or any amounts recorded in the cash book as a receipt for one amount but split into two or more when being recorded in the sales ledger – this could be evidence of fraud (Chapter 20).
- Consider the valuation of debtors. This is dealt with in the next paragraph.

Provision for bad and doubtful debts

The valuation of debtors is really a consideration of the adequacy of the provision for bad and doubtful debts. The auditors should consider the following:

- The adequacy of the system of internal control relating to the approval of credit and following up of poor payers.
- The period of credit allowed and taken.
- Whether balances have been settled after the year end.

- Whether an account is made up of specific items or not, i.e. if the debtor is paying amounts 'on account' this could be indicative of cash flow difficulties and might be the prelude to a bad debt.
- Whether an account is within the maximum credit approved.
- Reports on major debtors from collectors, trade associations, etc.
- Present value and realisability of any security lodged as collateral.
- The state of legal proceedings and the legal status of the debtor, e.g. in liquidation or bankruptcy.

Analytical review

Auditors should carry out analytical review procedures as part of substantive testing. These should include:

- debtor days ratio i.e.;

$$\frac{\text{debtors}}{\text{credit sales}} \times 365$$

- comparisons with budgets or prior years;
- comparison of aged debtor bands with prior years to identify increased debtor ageing.

Note that:

- Debts which are considered irrecoverable should be written off to the profit and loss account.
- Specific provisions for doubtful debts should be set up against debts which are considered doubtful.
- Some companies make round-sum or percentage provisions against doubtful debts. This practice is generally unacceptable as it may be a way of hiding profits with a 'fictitious' provision. Any such provision would have to be justified and be based on statistical evidence which may come from past experience or from data about other similar undertakings which is obtainable from trade associations or which is publicly available.

Debtors circularisation

Good independent audit evidence can be obtained from circularising the debtors (or some of them) for direct confirmation.

The advantages of this technique are:

- Direct external evidence is available for the existence and ownership and value of the amount due.
- It provides confirmation of the effectiveness of the system of internal control. If the sales ledger is recording the debtors correctly it follows that the system that leads up to it, i.e. the sales system, is also functioning properly.
- It assists in the auditor's evaluation of cut-off procedures as it can identify invoices in transit over the year end.
- It provides evidence of items in dispute.

There are two methods:

1 Negative circularisation
The customer is asked to communicate *only* if they *do not* agree the balance. This method has within it a fatal flaw insofar as it is impossible to tell whether the debtor agrees with the balance or has simply thrown the letter away.

2 Positive circularisation

The customer is asked to reply whether they agree the balance or not or is asked to supply the balance themselves. This is the favoured method.
The approach is as follows:

- Obtain the co-operation of the client – only they can ask third parties to divulge information.
- Select a sample. All customers can be circularised but this is unusual.
- Do *not* omit –

  - nil balances;
  - credit balances;
  - accounts written off in the period.

- Give weight to overdue or disputed balances.
- Use stratified samples, e.g. all large balances and only some small ones.
- The letter should be:

  - From the client.
  - It should request a reply *direct to the auditor.*
  - It may contain a stamped, addressed, envelope or a pre-paid reply envelope addressed to the auditor.
  - It must be despatched by the auditor – do not let the client post the letters as this will devalue the independence of the test.

- Receive and evaluate replies.
- Follow up when replies are not received. This is the major problem – it is usual to get less than a 5 per cent response.
- Circularisation is sometimes carried out at dates other than the year end. This can provide evidence about the operation of the sales and debtors system but will not, of course validate the year end figure.

Example of debtors circularisation letter (positive method)

FROM:	TO:
HEDONITE MANUFACTURING LTD	ECSTATIC MINING LTD
CLOGHAMPTON	WIMPTON

Dear Sir,

As part of their normal audit procedures, we have been requested by our auditors Tickitt & Run to ask you to confirm direct to them your indebtedness to us as shown on the enclosed statement as at 31 December 20-7.

If the statement is in agreement with your records, please sign in the space provided below and return this letter directly to our auditors using the pre-paid envelope provided.

If the statement is not in agreement with your records please notify our auditors directly of the amount shown by your records and if possible send them full particulars of the difference.

It will be of assistance to us if you will give this request your early attention.

This is not a request for payment and no remittance should be sent to our auditors.

Yours faithfully,
J. Brown,

Chief Accountant

_____

Name of Debtor   *Ecstatic Mining Ltd*

The balance shown on the statement at 31.12.-7 of £1,432.00 due from us is/is not *(delete as appropriate)* in agreement with our records at 31.12.-7.

If it does not agree the reason for the difference is

_____Signature   _____Date

_____Position

_____Company Stamp

_____

Prepayments

These are amounts paid for in one period which relate to the next period. In many cases these are not material and audit testing will be minimal.

Most prepayments are verified by:

- Reviewing the client's system for ensuring all prepayments are identified and properly calculated.
- Re-performing the calculations.
- Reviewing previous year's working papers for evidence that the same prepayment existed previously.
- Reviewing transactions after the year end.

BANK BALANCES

The auditor will be gathering sufficient appropriate evidence to verify the Assertions that:

- The balances are in the name of the company *(existence)*.
- The balances belong to the business *(rights and obligations)*.
- The balances due are correctly stated at the appropriate value *(valuation and allocation)*.
- All balances due have been recorded *(completeness)*.

These procedures apply whether balances are in hand or overdrawn. Overdrawn balances will be included as creditors (Chapter 16) unless there is a right of set off which the bank will advise.

Verification of bank balances is effected by:

Compliance tests

Appraisal of the internal control system relating to payments and receipts to ensure that:

- all payments are authorised;
- all payments are made in respect of bona fide liabilities;
- all receipts are collected and banked intact;
- all amounts are correctly recorded in the books;
- persons dealing with payments and receipts differ from those who deal with sales and purchases transactions.

Substantive tests

- Examination and investigation of the bank reconciliation, noting particularly:
  - That all uncleared cheques have been cleared after date. These are payments which have been issued by the organisation, and entered in the cash book, but which have not yet been debited to the account by the bank. They should be checked to ensure that they are cleared after the balance sheet date.
  - Lodgements credited after date, but actually paid in before date. These are deposits into the account which have been entered into the cash book as receipts but which had not been credited to the account by the bank at the year end. They should be checked to ensure that the receipts are cleared by the bank and are not subsequently reversed. If the customer has insufficient funds to meet the payment the bank will 'bounce' their cheque. In this case the customers account has to be restored to its debtor status and consideration given by the client to a possible bad or doubtful debt provision.

The auditors should look for evidence that:

- the bank reconciliation is prepared, at least, monthly;
- it is reviewed periodically by a responsible official or checked by Internal Audit.

The auditors obtain the key piece of audit evidence, which can be used to verify Assertions regarding:

- Ownership
- Existence
- Valuation

by direct confirmation from the bank or banks.

The bank must have the permission of the client to do this which is given by asking the client to sign an authority letter to the bank authorising them to release any information the auditors may require directly to them.

The bank letter is usually a standard format and, in addition to requesting confirmation of balances at the balance sheet date, opportunity is usually taken to ask the bank a number of questions at the same time.

These include enquires about:

- Confirmation that all bank accounts with the bank are disclosed, including accounts with nil balances and accounts opened and closed in the period.
- Credit limits and overdraft facilities.
- Existence and terms of loans or other borrowings.
- Knowledge of other bank accounts in other banks.
- Outstanding charges and interest accrued but not applied at the balance sheet date.
- Any outstanding bills of exchange, guarantees, acceptances, etc.
- Foreign currency contracts.
- Asset repurchase or hire purchase/leasing agreements.
- Items held in safe custody or as security for borrowings.

This bank letter plus a validated bank reconciliation will provide the evidence the auditors need.

LOANS

Loans are not usually material assets of companies other than those whose business it is to make loans. We shall consider two types of loans:

1 Loans other than to directors.
   Verification will be:

   - Examine and evaluate internal control. Authority to make loans is particularly important.
   - Obtain a schedule and confirm details with:

     - loan agreements;
     - interest calculations;
     - repayments received.

   - If the loan is material it may be thought necessary to obtain a certificate directly from the borrower.
   - Examine agreements and ensure terms are being adhered to.
   - If a loan is secured, examine the security and consider its value and realisability.
   - If a loan is guaranteed, examine the status of the guarantor.
   - Review the adequacy of any provision for bad debts. For example, a bad debt may occur when a loan to an employee is made and the employee leaves before repayment is complete.

2 Loans to directors and connected persons.
   This subject is the subject of several Companies Act requirements. Section 197, CA 2007 states that a company may not make a loan to a director, or act as guarantor for such a loan, unless the transaction has been approved by the members (i.e. the shareholders). For public companies this also includes what are known as 'quasi loans' – which are situations where, for example, the directors buys goods, the company pays for them and the director reimburses the company, i.e. the company provides credit for the director. This provision can catch use of a company credit card by a director (section 198, CA 2007).

However, there are some exemptions from these provisions, assuming the company doesn't make loans in the ordinary course of business, which would all be exempt anyway if they were made on commercial terms. The following are not prohibited:

- Loans and quasi loans not exceeding £10 000 outstanding at any one time.
- Loans, quasi loans and credit transactions to meet expenditure on company business not exceeding £50 000 outstanding at any time.
- Small credit transactions up to £15 000.
- Money lent to fund a director's defence costs in a legal action in connection with their actions as a director.

Audit procedures

The auditor's duties are as follows:

- Review all transactions involving directors which were outstanding at any time during the year. Materiality does not apply; all loans must be reviewed.
- If approval of shareholders is required ensure the relevant resolution has been approved.
- If felt necessary obtain a certificate of confirmation from the director concerned.
- Ensure that all such loans are subject to board minute.
- Ensure that the law has been complied with.
- Ensure that full disclosure is made as required in the financial statements.
- If the requisite information is not given in the accounts, the auditors are required to give the requisite information in their report.

CASH

In many cases cash will not be a material item in the balance sheet and auditors will, consequently, not carry out any detailed substantive checking work on cash balances at the year end.

However, this does not mean that cash transactions should be ignored completely, even if they are relatively minor, as there is a high inherent risk of fraud in connection with cash.

Auditors should therefore consider the internal control aspects of cash transactions. Internal control objectives in dealing with cash receipts and cash payments, where these are a substantial part of the company's business, are dealt with in Chapter 9.

As far as the balance sheet audit is concerned the auditor should also carry out the following substantive checking work where the amounts are material:

- Review the operation of the cash system. For Petty Cash this should be an imprest system which should be reviewed by a responsible official periodically and the petty cash book initialled as evidence of review. For businesses which deal in substantial cash amounts there needs to be a full internal control review.
- Count the cash, either at the year end if the balance is material or at a random point during the audit as a 'surprise' count.
- If this is to be carried out the auditor must:
  - Ensure they have control of all cash balances simultaneously to ensure funds cannot be 'swopped' from one to another.

- Count the cash in the presence of an independent member of the client's staff to ensure that any shortages cannot be attributed to the auditor.
- List the individual details of notes and coins.
- Ensure any IOUs are recorded and are collectible. Auditors should review the company's policies towards making loans (as evidenced by an IOU).
- Reconcile the count to the petty cash book and investigate any differences.
- Ask the cashier to initial the reconciliation as evidence of agreement.

Summary

- The verification is of assertions about each asset. A useful mnemonic is CAVEBOP.
- Verification methods vary according to the asset but the basic principles are to verify existence and ownership by inspecting the asset, or evidence of it and the relevant title documents.
- Most transactions in assets are evidence in the minutes of directors' meetings and these should be inspected as a matter of course.
- Valuation of both tangible and intangible assets is sometimes complex and auditors may have to exercise a degree of judgement in deciding whether the asset is properly stated in the accounts.
- Auditors should be alert to the possibility of an impairment in the value of assets.
- There are accounting rules on disclosure of non-current assets and you should be familiar with them.
- Stock on a balance sheet is subject to a correct count, a correct assessment of condition, and appropriate valuation.
- Stock can be considered under a number of separate categories.
- ISA 501 makes attendance at stocktaking to observe the incidence of internal control normal audit practice.
- Detailed audit tests must be supplemented by analytical review.
- The valuation of work in progress can be difficult and care has to be taken concerning the inclusion of overheads, the taking of profit or the inclusion of losses.
- Independent stocktakers can be used by clients and within limitations be relied upon by the auditor.
- Cut-off is a key issue in identifying stock values.
- Debtors can be verified directly by circularisation and by reviewing compliance tests of controls.
- A key part of the verification process for bank balances is the bank letter.
- A bank reconciliation is a key procedure. Auditors should check it at the balance sheet date as an evidence-gathering procedure and review other bank reconciliations carried out by the company during the financial period as evidence of internal control procedures operating in the business.
- Loans to directors are subject to company law restrictions which you should know.
- Cash balances should be audited if material, but auditors should be aware of the potential for fraud so might wish to carry out audit work as part of their work on internal control.

Points to note

- All auditing examinations contain questions on asset verification.
- Students fail to answer adequately by making too few points. This chapter will provide enough ideas for students to make sufficient points in their answers.
- Questions on asset verification are sometimes on existence, ownership, value and presentation. Some are specifically on one or two aspects only. It is clearly vital to answer the question asked!

- To answer specific questions, remember the assertions and the mnemonic CAVEBOP and apply them as required.

- Note that many syllabuses require students to have an appreciation of the accounting requirements of the Companies Act 2006 and the Financial Reporting Standards.

- The extent and manner of verification of an asset depends on the degree of risk of misstatement possible with the asset. Inherent risk depends on many factors including the complexity of the assets (e.g. work in progress), the judgement involved (e.g. stock at net realisable value) and the susceptibility to loss or misappropriation (e.g. cash). The extent of reliance on internal control in reducing substantive tests depends on the auditors' perception of control risk.

- Inspection of work in progress by the auditor is desirable in that it gives evidence that work in progress exists and helps with determining the state of completion especially of large contracts.

Case Study

Osocheep Supermarkets Ltd have a main depot and five large supermarkets. Their financial year end is Thursday 31 March 20-X8 and stock is to be evaluated as at the close of business on that date. The next day is an exceptionally busy one with much business in terms of deliveries from supplier, movements of stock, and sales. The sales margins are narrow and it is very important to obtain an accurate figure for stock. Goods in stock in the warehouse are kept on a continuous inventory system (quantities only) on a computer with a printout of the previous day's stock available at noon each day. The stock at branches is not recorded continuously. The bulk of the stock is carried in the back rooms and moved onto the supermarket shelves continuously during the day.

Discussion
  - What are the problems in this case re:
  a) cut-off;
  b) stock identification and quantity determination;
  c) valuation?

Student self-testing questions

Questions with answers apparent from the text

  a) What are the six aspects to be covered in verifying an asset?
  b) List the points that could be covered in verifying an asset.
  c) How is land and buildings verified?
  d) What is the key issue in the valuation of intangible assets?
  e) What is the difference between research and development?
  f) When should purchased goodwill be written off?
  g) What are the directors' responsibilities for stocktaking?

h) List the characteristics of good stocktaking procedures.

i) What are the auditor's duties toward stocktaking:
   a. Before the stocktake?
   b. During the stocktake?
   c. After the stocktake?

j) What is the main audit issue in connection with the valuation of long-term work in progress?

k) Outline the procedures for verifying debtors.

l) What matters should be considered in reviewing the provision for bad and doubtful debts?

m) Outline the procedures for both negative and positive circularisation.

n) What audit evidence accrues from the bank letter.

o) Summarise the contents of the standard bank letter.

p) What are the Companies Act rules on loans to directors and connected persons?

q) What are the auditor's duties on such loans?

Examination questions

I Movit Ltd (Movit) is a company which hires out heavy plant used in the construction industry. All plant is hired out with a driver who is responsible for ensuring that the plant is immobilised and stored securely when left on customers' sites overnight. Movit operates from ten depots throughout England.

The directors of Movit have requested that your firm provides a report on the reliability of the internal control system in respect of the acquisition, custody and recording of its plant. They have provided you with the following information.

All plant is uniquely numbered and logged in a plant register and integrated hire management system which can indicate the location of each item of plant at any point in time. Head office staff are responsible for maintaining the register, reconciling it each month with the nominal ledger and investigating any differences. They also undertake periodic physical checks involving checking items listed in the register to the asset and checking the asset to the register. The results of such checks are reported to the operations manager who authorises any adjustments to the register on a standard form.

The hire management system produces performance measures of usage and downtime for each item of plant. This is used by the operations manager to determine the need for additional new plant or replacement of existing plant. All acquisitions are processed by head office. A capital expenditure form has to be completed and supported by three quotations from suppliers and authorised by the operations and finance directors.

The finance director also undertakes an appraisal exercise to confirm whether it is appropriate to lease or buy the plant and this is evidenced on the capital expenditure form.

New plant is delivered directly to the depot requiring the item. Each depot manager confirms, by entering onto the system via a terminal at the depot, that the items have been received, physically checked and are of the correct specification. Industry regulations require plant to be subjected to regular maintenance checks.

These checks are carried out by engineers who complete a standard checklist evidencing such checks and each depot manager is required to submit a copy of the checklist to head office staff who log the date of each check on the plant register.

Head office staff are responsible for monitoring that timely checks have taken place, investigating any breaches of this policy and reporting their findings to the operations director.

Required:

(a) Identify how Movit's internal control procedures meet the objectives of ensuring that:

(i)   plant acquisitions are required and provide an acceptable rate of return;
(ii) plant is recorded, safeguarded and complies with laws and regulations; and
(iii) plant is appropriately valued.

(b) State the methods that you would use to obtain evidence that procedures established by the management are operating effectively and for each method provide two examples of how you would apply it to Movit.

(ICAEW)

2 Harrier Motors deals in motor vehicles, sells spare parts, provides after-sales servicing and undertakes car body repairs. During the financial year to 30 June 20x7, the company expanded its operations from five to eight sites.

Each site has a car showroom, service workshop and parts storage.

In May 20x7, management appointed an experienced chartered certified accountant to set up an internal audit department.

New cars are imported, on consignment, every three months from one supplier. Harrier pays the purchase price of the cars, plus 3 per cent, three months after taking delivery. Harrier does not return unsold cars, although it has a legal right to do so.

Harrier offers 'trade-ins' (i.e. part-exchange) on all sales of new and used cars. New car sales carry a three-year manufacturer's warranty and used cars carry a six-month guarantee. Many used cars are sold for cash. An extensive range of spare parts is held for which perpetual inventory records are kept. Storekeepers carry out continuous checking.

Mr Joop, the sales executive, selects a car from each consignment to use for all his business and personal travelling until the next consignment is received. Such cars are sold at a discount as ex-demonstration models. Car servicing and body repairs are carried out in workshops by employed and subcontracted service engineers. Most jobs are started and finished in a day and are invoiced immediately on completion.

In May 2003 Harrier purchased a brand name, 'Uni-fit', which is now applied to the parts which it supplies. Management has not amortised this intangible asset as it believes its useful life to be indefinite.

Required:

(a) Using the information provided, identify and explain the audit risks to be addressed when planning the final audit of Harrier Motors for the year ending 30 June 20x7.

(b) Identify and briefly explain the principal matters to be addressed in Harrier Motors' instructions for the conduct of its physical inventory count as at 30 June 20x7.

(c) Describe the audit work to be carried out in respect of the useful life of the 'Uni-fit' brand name as at 30 June 20x7.

(ICAEW)

16

The audit of liabilities

INTRODUCTION

A balance sheet will contain liabilities grouped under various headings including:

- Creditors – due either before or after one year comprising:

    - Trade creditors – e.g. suppliers.
    - Accruals and deferred income.
    - Provisions.
    - Amounts owed to group and related companies.

- Bank loans and overdrafts.

- Debenture loans.

- Share capital and Reserves.

- Corporation Tax and deferred taxation.

In addition the financial statements will contain details of any Contingent Liabilities by way of a note to the accounts.

The auditors task is to gather sufficient, appropriate evidence to validate the Assertions.

- That the liabilities exist *(existence)*.

- That the company is due to pay or discharge these liabilities *(rights and obligations)*.

- That all liabilities which should be included have been included *(completeness)*.

- That all liabilities have been recorded at their full amounts *(valuation)*.

- That liabilities have been properly disclosed in the financial statements *(classification)*.

VERIFICATION PROCEDURES

Amounts falling due within one year – current liabilities

Into this category will fall:

- Trade creditors.

- Accruals.

- Provisions.
- Bank overdrafts and short-term loans (or part of loans due in the next 12 months).
- Amounts due to other group or related companies.

TRADE CREDITORS

Compliance Testing of Internal Control Procedures

As part of their audit of balance sheet items auditors will have regard to the internal controls incorporated into the system in which the liability is recorded. For example, the figure for trade creditors is largely derived from the purchase ledger which is part of the purchases system, so controls within the purchases system are relevant to the auditor's evidence gathering procedures for trade creditors verification.

The auditor will consider controls designed to ensure that:

- Purchased goods and services are properly authorised and documented.
- Purchases of goods and services are only made for the purposes of the business.
- Goods and services received are inspected for quality and condition before being accepted.
- Invoices and similar documents are properly checked before being processed.
- Only valid transactions are entered into the accounting records.

Substantive testing

In addition to testing control procedures the auditors will carry out substantive testing procedures. These include:

- Reconciling the list of trade creditors with the control account – note that in most cases with computerised systems these will automatically agree.
- Reviewing year end cut-off procedures – see Chapter 15.
- Testing individual balances with third party evidence. This could consist of evidence gathered from a creditors circularisation but is more normally carried out by reconciling purchase ledger balances with statements from suppliers.
- In addition a sample of balances should be subject to specific tests such as:

  - Is the balance made up of specific amounts over a reasonable period?
  - Have all the entries making up the balance been authorised?
  - Was the balance paid in full after the year end?

- Carrying out an analytical review of the creditors figure, i.e. look at creditor days, comparison of creditors with previous periods, etc. for reasonableness.

ACCRUALS

Students should understand the definition of an accrual. An accrual is an amount set aside for a specific liability, i.e. where the expenditure has been incurred in the period but for which no invoice has been received.

Commonly these cover such expenses as gas, electricity, rent, telephone, etc. They are often relatively immaterial and analytical procedures will often provide sufficient evidence.

Key audit procedures include:

- Identifying how the client identifies all accruals required to be made – discover and test the procedures.
- Check the schedule of accruals for arithmetical accuracy.
- Check the calculations of accruals.
- Compare with previous periods to ensure consistency.
- If material include reference to accruals in the management letter. We look at this later in Chapter 25.

PROVISIONS

Provisions differ from accruals. FRS 12 defines a provision as a liability which exists but for which the amount or its timing is uncertain. An example of a provision is an amount set aside to meets the costs and any penalties arising from claims against the business. It may not be known when the claims will be made and how much they might amount to, particularly if the company is contesting them.

Auditors should establish procedures to ensure:

- There is a liability of some amount– e.g. legal documents, claim letters, minutes of meetings *(existence)*.
- That the company may be liable and that the liability will not be met by someone else, e.g. an insurer *(rights and obligations)*.
- That management have made as reasonable an estimate in the circumstances, that the assumptions they have used are valid and that the basis on which it has been calculated is on a similar basis to that of previous years, if appropriate *(valuation)*.

The auditors may have to use a certain amount of judgement in order to satisfy themselves as to the value of the liability. They may well, if the provision is material, want to receive specific assurances from management in the Letter of Representation (see Chapter 25), but these will not replace the auditor's own evidence-gathering procedures.

Finally, the auditors must ensure that provisions are properly disclosed in the financial statements, including any explanatory notes *(classification)*.

BANK OVERDRAFTS AND SHORT-TERM LOANS

These will be disclosed separately on the balance sheet even if there are other bank balances in credit unless there is a right of set-off of accounts – which the bank will advise on.

Verification of these overdrawn bank balances is similar to verifying bank balances as detailed above and basically requires the auditors to check the bank reconciliation and obtain independent third party evidence from the bank.

Verification of amounts due on loans will require the auditors to review the loan documentation and confirm any calculations.

It will be necessary to review original documentation and to obtain confirmation that the company has met all its obligations to date and has not defaulted on any loan repayments. If necessary these should be traced through the records.

AMOUNTS DUE TO GROUP AND RELATED COMPANIES

If the auditors are auditors to the other companies in the group the balances can be reconciled with each other. We look at this in more detail in Chapter 29.

Particular attention should be paid to how the balances have arisen to ensure that only bona fide inter-company transactions are included such as head office charges, recharges of costs and expenses, management fees, etc. and that related companies, i.e. those that are not full subsidiaries, in particular are not being used to hide trading losses, etc. (see Chapter 21)

Again assurances from management may be required in respect of transactions with related or associated companies.

LONG-TERM LIABILITIES

These mainly comprise long-term loans and debenture loans.

Audit procedures for long-term loans are the same as for short-term loans, i.e.:

- review the loan documentation;
- confirm the company is not in default; and
- obtain a confirmation from the lender of sums outstanding.

Debenture loans are different insofar as these are, effectively, an issue of loan notes carrying a fixed rate of interest and repayable on a set date. They are part of the company's financing and as such the auditor will have to confirm that the company has the power under its constitution to issue debentures.

If it has then it is only necessary for the auditors to confirm the amounts with:

- the issue documentation; and
- the sums received,

and ensure that they are correctly disclosed in the financial statements.

SHARE CAPITAL AND RESERVES

This is a relatively straightforward procedure but nevertheless should be carried out. The amounts can normally be verified by recourse to:

- Previous period's accounts.
- Minutes of directors' meetings.
- Documentation and sums received in respect of new issues of shares.
- Returns made to the Registrar of Companies.

Note that the Companies Act 2006 abolishes the concept of authorised share capital and shares can be issued by Board resolution, subject to shareholder authorisation where relevant.

There are some transitional provisions restricting the shares which can be issued to an amount no more than the 'old' authorised share capital. As far as auditors are concerned the previous requirement for them to confirm that any issue of shares doesn't exceed the authorised share capital is no longer likely to apply.

Auditors should ensure that Reserves are properly classified and disclosed in the accounts and that the provisions regarding disclosure of, particularly non distributable reserves such as any Share Premium Account, are complied with.

Any movements or transfers to reserves should be evidenced by Board minutes.

INCLUSION OF ALL LIABILITIES

It is not enough for the auditors to be satisfied that all the liabilities recorded in the books are correct and are incorporated in the final accounts. They must also be satisfied that no other liabilities exist which are not, for various reasons, in the books and the accounts.

Examples of such unrecorded liabilities might be:

- Claims by employees for injury.
- Claims by ex employees for unfair dismissal.
- Unfunded pension liabilities. A company may have a liability to pay past or present employees a pension in respect of past service and have no funds separated out for this purpose.
- Liability to 'top-up' pension schemes. When money has been put into separate trusts to pay pensions, inflation has often meant that the amount is insufficient and the company may have to implement clauses in the scheme whereby they have to put in extra money which could run into millions of pounds.
- Bonuses under profit sharing arrangements.
- Returnable packages and containers.
- Value Added Tax and other tax liabilities. The auditors' knowledge of tax may lead them to suspect a liability of which the directors are blissfully ignorant.
- Claims under warranties and guarantees.
- Liabilities on debts which have been factored with recourse. To explain: A owes B £50. B sells (factors) the debt to C for £45. Thus B has no debt any more but £45 in the bank. A fails to pay C. C can claim £50 from B (C has recourse).
- Bills receivable discounted (similar to above).
- Pending law suits.
- Losses on forward contracts. Example: A Ltd makes a contract to sell a million tons of Hedonite, which it does not have, at £50 a ton in six months' time. No entry will appear in the books or accounts, but when the time comes Hedonite has risen on the commodity market to £70 a ton and A Ltd, has to buy in at that price in order to make the sale for which it has contracted, thus making a loss on the transaction of £20 a ton. Auditors will have to ascertain when the loss is incurred and how it should be reported in each financial period, and look at any uncompleted contracts.

It is important that the auditors appreciate that such liabilities exist. It may be in management's interest to understate or omit liabilities for which there are no accounting records and little hard evidence but auditors have a positive obligation to take reasonable steps to unearth them.

How is this to be approached? The actions to take include:

- Direct enquiry of the directors and senior managers.
- Obtaining a Letter of Representation from the Board of Directors – see Chapter 25.

- Examination of post balance sheet events. This will include a review of major transactions in the period from the year end to the date the auditors' report is signed.
- Examination of minutes of director's meetings and senior management meetings where the existence of unrecorded liabilities may be mentioned.
- A review of the working papers and previous years' working papers.
- An awareness of the possibilities at all times when conducting the audit. For example, discovery during the audit that the client deals in 'futures' will alert the auditor to the possibility of outstanding commitments.

CONTINGENT LIABILITIES

This is a very difficult area for both management and auditors as it often demands quite a high degree of judgement and often very little evidence.

A contingent liability is liability arising from a condition which exists at the balance sheet date where the outcome will only be confirmed by the occurrence (or non-occurrence) of some future event which is outside the control of the business. A typical example of this would be the outcome of a court case where the judgement is uncertain.

The first decision to be made is whether any provision needs to be made in the accounts – i.e. is a real liability likely to crystallise even if the precise amount or timing is uncertain? This, in itself, can be a contentious issue.

FRS 12 'Provisions, Contingent Liabilities and Contingent Assets' states that:

- Probable losses should be provided for.
- Possible losses should be disclosed as a note to the financial statements.
- Probable gains should be disclosed as a note to the financial statements.
- Possible gains should be ignored until they crystallise or become probable.

Typical examples of contingent liabilities include:

- Guarantees given to third parties, e.g. in respect of a subsidiary company's overdraft.
- Discounted bills of exchange.
- Forward contracts.
- The outcome of court cases where damages or costs might result.
- Claims under guarantees or warranties.

The amount of any liability, its nature and whether any security has been provided has to be disclosed in the accounts.

Audit evidence

Bank letter – this will provide independent third party evidence in respect of forward currency contracts, discounted bills and guarantees.

Legal matters

This is a specially difficult area in practice because of the inherent uncertainty involved in estimating the outcome of legal actions. There are some audit procedures which will lead to the verification of the existence of, but not necessarily the amount of, liabilities arising out of legal actions.

These include:

- Reviewing the client's system for recording claims and disputes and the procedures for bringing these to the attention of the Board.
- Reviewing the arrangements for instructing solicitors.
- Examining the minutes of the Board or other responsible committees (e.g. Audit Committee) for references to or indications of possible claims.
- Examine invoices from solicitors and the attached Memorandum of Services.
- Obtain a list of matters referred to solicitors from the directors or other responsible official with an estimate of the possible ultimate liabilities.
- Obtain a written assurance from the directors that they are not aware of any matters referred to solicitors other than those disclosed.
- Where possible the auditors should obtain a direct confirmation from the company's legal adviser. The request must be sent by the client requesting the reply or that a copy of the reply be sent direct to the auditor. The letter to the solicitor should include a request for details of cases referred to the solicitor not mentioned in the letter.

Letter to a client's legal adviser to confirm contingent liabilities arising out of pending legal matters

Messrs Scrooge & Co.
New St
Oldcastle   26th September 2008

Dear Sirs,
Joy Manufacturing Ltd

In connection with the preparation and audit of the accounts for the year ending 31 December 20-7 the directors have made estimates of the amounts of the ultimate liabilities (including costs) which might be incurred, and are regarded as material, in relation to the following matters on which you have been consulted. We should be grateful if you would confirm that in your opinion these estimates are reasonable.

Matter	Estimated liability including costs
1. Claim by James Brown for wrongful dismissal	£2 000
2. Claim by Hedonite Manufacturing Ltd for damages in respect of faulty goods	£18 000
3. Action by Difur plc for damages caused by late delivery of equipment – contested	£105 000
4. Action by Joyful Mfg PLC for breach of copyright in our Catalogue	£24 000

> We would also request that you confirm that these are the only legal actions that you are aware of in which our client is a party.
>   Yours faithfully,
>   Tickitt & Run.
>   Chartered Accountants

Note that solicitor's opinion letters often do not satisfactorily resolve the auditor's uncertainties and it may be that the auditor may wish to take independent legal advice.

It should be stressed that the auditors are responsible for their own opinion and it is their judgement which needs to be supported by as much evidence as can be gathered.

ACCOUNTING ESTIMATES

In this chapter we have considered many liabilities which are uncertain as to existence or amount. Liabilities are sometimes certain (e.g. most trade creditors) but some need to be estimated and there are many other areas of accounting where estimates are made such as valuing stock at net realisable value, estimating provisions, etc.

At this point we can summarise the auditing processes attached to accounting for estimates in general taking into account the provisions of the auditing standard ISA 540 'Audit of Accounting Estimates'.

This requires that auditors gather sufficient, appropriate evidence in respect of accounting estimates.

The following remarks can be made:

- Accounting estimates have to be made in all areas where precise means of measurement cannot be applied. We have seen several examples in this book already (losses on work in progress, lawsuits, warranty claims, etc.).

- The responsibility for these estimates lies with the directors or other governing body and may involve special knowledge and judgement. Some are routine, e.g. depreciation, and some are one-off, e.g. the outcome of a lawsuit. Many are capable of reasonable estimation but some might not be. In the latter cases and if the matters are material, the auditor might consider that the uncertainty and/or the lack of objective data is so great that there are implications for the audit report – see Chapter 27.

- Auditors should obtain sufficient appropriate audit evidence on all material accounting estimates. The evidence should give assurance that the estimates are reasonable in the circumstances and, when required, appropriately disclosed.

- Detailed audit procedures include:

  - Review the procedures and methods adopted by management to make accounting estimates. These may include Internal Audit. In some cases a formula will be used (e.g. in estimating warranty claims or in setting depreciation rates). There should be systems for continually reviewing these formulae. The fact that directors do actually consider the formulae or other methods of calculating estimates on a continuing basis is itself reassuring to the auditor!

  - Test these procedures in connection with each estimate.

- Evaluate the data and consider the assumptions on which the estimates have been made. For example, in looking at depreciation, what assumptions on obsolescence have been made?
- Check any calculations or applications of formulae.
- Make an independent estimate on each estimate and compare it with the one made by the directors. Investigate any difference.
- Compare estimates made in previous years with actual outcomes where known to judge the accuracy of previous predictions and to provide experience for current estimates.

- Review subsequent events, i.e. events after the year end date.
- At the final stage of the audit, the auditors should make a review of the estimates (as with all the accounting data in the financial statements) and assess them in the light of:

  - their knowledge of the business;
  - consistency with other evidence obtained during the audit.

- If the auditors consider that a material estimate is unreasonable, they should ask the directors to adjust the financial statements and if this is not done then they should consider there is a misstatement and ponder the implications for the Auditor's Report.

Summary

- The auditor must verify the existence, amount, and adequate disclosure of all liabilities. They must also be satisfied that all liabilities are included.
- Each liability is verified from whatever evidence is available but some general procedures common to most liabilities can be discerned.
- Provisions are a difficult area. The auditor must take special care in considering the adequacy of provisions.
- Share capital is verified like other liabilities but special procedures apply to new issues.
- Contingent liabilities must be considered firstly to see if they are contingent and secondly as to size. Careful disclosure has to be made of such liabilities.
- Pending legal matters can be verified by direct confirmation from the company's legal advisers.
- There are some general points which can be made on the audit of all accounting estimates.

Points to note

- The liabilities section of the balance sheet is subject to numerous Companies Act rules on disclosure. These must be known.
- Be very careful to use the words 'provision' and 'accrual' correctly. They are not synonymous.
- Two important matters in connection with liabilities are contingencies and post balance sheet events.
- The letter of representation may be some form of evidence in this area, especially in the problem of inclusion of all liabilities. This is discussed in Chapter 25.
- Some companies may have enormous potential liabilities arising out of environmental factors. Claims may be made against companies that supplied products, which at the time of supply were considered acceptable, but which are now seen as damaging. Vulnerable companies include tobacco, pharmaceutical and chemical companies. To some extent claims against such companies may be covered by insurance but that may also be a subject for endless litigation.

Case Study

Horsebox, Postillion & Co. are a city firm of Chartered Certified Accountants. The firm's accounts are produced by the administration partner but are subject to audit by Blanket, Mange, another firm of Chartered Certified Accountants. In June 20-6, a partner in Horsebox who was suffering from overwork failed to realise that an error had occurred in the preparation and audit of the Accounts of International Maize Ltd. Stocks of maize in transit had been inadvertently included in the company's stocks in both the producing country and the receiving country. The company had been acquired by Universal Porage Inc. who have now discovered the mistake. They have given notice that they intend to bring an action to recover damages from

Horsebox on the grounds that they relied on the audited accounts for the year ending 30.4.-6 and that they would not have purchased IM had they known of the error.

The stock of IM was overstated by £2.4 million as a consequence of the error. The profit of IM was reported as £4.3 million and UP paid £21 million cash for IM.

Horsebox carry professional indemnity insurance in the sum of £1 million.

The partners of Horsebox dislike each other and rely heavily on Blanket, Mange. No one at Horsebox has informed Blanket, Mange of the pending legal action.

Discussion

- What auditing procedures might allow Blanket, Mange to discover the existence of the action?
- How might the amount of the ultimate award and costs be determined by Blanket, Mange?
- What other hidden liabilities might Horsebox have at their year end – 31.12.-6?

Student self-testing questions

Questions with answers apparent from the text

(a) List the general procedures for verifying liabilities.

(b) List some liabilities that may be omitted.

(c) How can the auditor determine if all liabilities are included?

(d) What is the difference between a provision and an accrual?

(e) What factors about a liability must be verified by an auditor?

(f) How might audit evidence of the truth and fairness of the item 'share capital' be obtained?

(g) How might pending legal matters be dealt with by an auditor?

(h) List audit procedures in connection with accounting estimates.

Examination questions

I   (a) Company A has a number of long- and short-term payables, accruals and provisions in its balance sheet.

Required:

Describe the audit procedures you would apply to each of the three items listed below, including those relating to disclosure.

   (i) A 10-year bank loan with a variable interest rate and an overdraft (a bank account with a debit balance on the bank statement), both from the same bank.

   (ii) Expense accruals.

   (iii) Trade payables and purchase accruals.

(b) Company B has a provision in its balance sheet for claims made by customers for product defects under 1-year company warranties.

Required:

Describe the matters you would consider and the audit evidence you would require for the provision.

(ACCA)

2 Curdco is a company that runs a chain of fast food restaurants. The company has a centralised operating style and managers of individual restaurants have very limited decision-making powers on day-to-day operational matters. The company's centralised administration is responsible for the buying of food, the payment of staff, the maintenance and cleaning of restaurants by staff employed by a national agency, and all other matters relating to the running of the business. The company has good internal controls over purchasing. Inventory counts are conducted at each restaurant at the year-end. Your firm has recently been appointed as auditor to Curdco.

Required:

(a) List the account headings you would expect to find in Curdco's schedule of accounts payable and accrued expenditure.

(b) Describe and give reasons for the audit tests you would carry out to obtain audit evidence for Curdco's accounts payable and accrued expenditure.

(c) Explain the difficulties faced by auditors, and the decisions that auditors have to make, in conducting direct confirmations of accounts payable.

(ACCA)

17

Auditing and computers

INTRODUCTION

Even the smallest organisations have computers now and use computerised accounting packages to maintain their accounts. These are known as computer information systems (CIS).

They have the advantage that:

- they control the information being input into the system – for example:

  - they won't permit single entry;
  - they require a code number to be input thus aiding posting to the correct account.

- they enable managers to produce reports and management information quickly.

However, they can also become a problem both for the auditors and the management if they are not properly controlled.

For example:

- inadequate or malfunctioning computer systems can lead to misleading information being produced;

- computer systems can encourage fraudsters, particularly;

  - if controls around the computer are weak; or
  - management consider that the computer is too complicated for them to understand.

At the planning stage, auditors have to consider how the computerised aspect of the accounting system affects the tracking of information and the flow of documents.

The problem area for the auditor is that transactions can be generated by the computer and the audit trail is lost. The auditor cannot follow the flow of documents which evidence a transaction because there aren't any – all the data is electronic.

Difficulties arise within computerised systems because:

- transactions can be generated by the computer automatically, e.g. direct debits;

- computers perform complex calculations without demonstrating how they were carried out, e.g. interest charges, debt analysis;

- transactions can be exchanged between systems or locations electronically (EDI) without any paper trail, e.g. automatic ordering systems;
- the control principle of segregation of duties can be bypassed because computerised systems use relatively low numbers of staff.

AUDIT RISK AND THE CIS

The evaluation of audit risk for a computer system follows the same basic principles, as set out in Chapter 10, for the system as a whole.

There are several unique aspects of audit risk which have to be considered specifically in connection with computerised systems.

Within a computerised system audit risks can be summarised as:

Risk	Features
inherent risk	• management may feel they have no control over the system and that they are in the hands of IT specialists
	• because many of the operations are automatic incorrect standing data will continue until it is detected, for example an incorrect wage rate or sales price
control risk	• if software has been tampered with or illicit software introduced it is possible to generate fraud within the computer which is hard to detect
	• in a manual system transactions can be viewed by several people in different departments. Computerised environments require fewer staff so the segregation of duties can become blurred
	• it can be difficult to trace the authority for transaction processing through the computer where routines are automated e g. in automatic reordering systems the reorder levels may be authorised once and never be revisited. The computer does not know if an order level has subsequently been amended without authorisation

However, computerised systems also have advantages which the auditor should bear in mind when evaluating audit risk:

- A computer will only do what it is told, consequently processing is uniform and totally accurate. This tends to reduce clerical errors.
- A computer will go on processing as long as it is given information to process.
- With the appropriate software it is possible to generate reports and analysis and provide much more information than is feasible under a purely manual system.
- Auditors can use Computer-Assisted Audit Techniques (CAATs) to interrogate the system and carry out comparative and analytical tests.
- Managers can obtain data and use analytical techniques which may enhance control.

THE CONTROL ENVIRONMENT

The principles of good internal control described in Chapter 9 apply equally in both computerised and manual environments, so the auditor will be looking for many of the same features.

These can be summarised as:

- segregation of duties;
- authorisation levels;
- access to information;
- arithmetical and reconciliation checks.

However, there are certain additional features which the auditor should concentrate on in a computerised environment.

These are:

Controls	Require
strong control environment	• all staff should be aware of the need for internal controls and the procedures to be followed
documented procedures	• staff should be made aware of the control procedures by means of documentation and training
systems documentation	• the suppliers of the software should provide full documentation for the programs in use
control of access	• access to application software, e.g. the programs which control how data is processed, should be restricted
	• access to data should be restricted to the staff that use it in the course of their work and to no-one else.
	• This is done by limiting the menu systems available when a member of staff logs on
password controls	• access to the system should be controlled by passwords and authorised logons. Passwords should be changed regularly and not disclosed or shared
application controls	These consist of controls such as: • batch controls such as prelists and manual totals to compare with computer totals when processing batches of documents • sequential numbering systems • controls over coding as incorrect coding can lead to misstatements in the financial accounts • manual authorisation of input documentation • arithmetical controls such as check digits, gross to net, etc • range checks, i.e. automatic checking that input is within acceptable limits, e.g. hours worked are not more than 50 per week • logging of when and who performed document processing

You need to be aware of controls applicable to computerised systems as questions on this often appear in examinations.

THE AUDIT APPROACH TO COMPUTERISED SYSTEMS

There are two approaches:

- auditing around the computer;
- understanding and interrogating the CIS.

Auditing around the computer

This is an approach often taken where auditors are faced with auditing smaller organisations which use industry standard, 'off the shelf' software packages where systems are likely to be based on a PC or PC network.

The auditor takes the view that the computer simply replaces manual records and that there are few, if any automated routines.

Because it is standard software it is likely to be well tested and error free.

The approach is to:

- examine the controls around data input to ensure that the day-to-day input of transaction information, e.g. invoices, orders, bank transactions, etc, is properly controlled;
- examine the standing or master file data, e.g. wage rates, prices, VAT rate, interest rates, which the computer uses as a basis for making calculations, ensure it is properly authorised and is used currently by the computer;
- examine the output and relate it to the input so that, say, a selection of sales invoices can be traced directly to the customers account in the sales ledger;
- examine the output with external verification, for example, the purchase ledger balances with suppliers' statements.

Understanding and interrogating the CIS

Where computerised systems are more complex, and the computer generates information internally through automated routines, the auditor needs to adopt a different approach.

There are two problems faced by the auditor in this situation:

- in complex systems it may be that even the organisation's own IT staff do not understand all the detail. They may know *what* the system will do but not *how* it does it;
- management may feel that they don't understand the computer system and may actively avoid becoming involved with its day-to-day operations. This can result in a loss of control or dependence on one or two experts.

Auditors will try and adopt an approach whereby they use the computer's ability to process data to interrogate its operations using computer-assisted audit techniques (CAATs).

This is specialist audit software used to interrogate the computer files and to carry out sample audit tests on the contents of the files.

Some software may need the use of specially trained computer auditors to operate it, particularly if it is interrogating live client files.

There are various types of CAAT including:

- audit interrogation software used to request data from client files;
- test data which comprises dummy data run through the client's system to test the operation of the programs;
- embedded audit files set up within the client's system which can be used by the auditor to obtain information on demand or continuously.

Auditors can use interrogation software to examine large volumes of data relatively easily. This is particularly useful in obtaining information from files which can then be examined by audit staff.

There are two main techniques – *exception reporting* and *comparative testing*.

Test	Procedure	Example
Exception reporting	• Report transactions exceeding a set parameter	• All purchases in excess of £5000 • All sales ledger balances over three months old
Comparative testing	• Identical reports at two different dates	• Wages details at two dates in the year
	• Auditors identify and explain differences	• The auditor could use the data as a basis for reviewing the procedures for new staff, staff leaving and changes in wage rates

Test data and embedded programs are generally used to:

- ensure that the client's software has not been tampered with;
- there are no hidden files; and
- that the controls are doing what they are supposed to be doing.

When using test data the auditor feeds dummy data into the client's system and checks that the output is what was expected. The dummy data might include exceptional transactions which the clients system ought to reject or highlight on a report as well as more normal transactions to check the operations of the internal controls within the machine.

Care has to be taken when entering such data into a client's system as it will have to be carefully removed once the tests are complete.

Alternatively the program software can be downloaded from the clients' machine and checked on one of the auditors' machines with dummy data.

Embedded software sits within the clients' systems and monitors it either continuously or when activated. It is looking for irregular entries, abortive logons or signs that the software has been tampered with or that unusual transactions are being processed. Clearly this type of software can only be introduced with the permission of the client, and one problem with it is that, quite often, it has to be embedded at the design stage of the system, it has to be written into the program software in some way so that it is monitoring the actual processing on a real-time basis.

In both cases they are techniques which should be handled with care and usually requires the use of experts to operate them. For this reason they can be expensive and are often only used on larger audits.

Summary

- Auditors can use two approaches to auditing computerised systems, auditing around the computer or using computer-assisted audit techniques.
- Auditing in a computerised system environment requires the auditor to evaluate the internal controls which relate to the computer system.
- CAATs may require specialists to operate them in order to obtain information from client files and to maintain the audit trail.

Points to note

- Auditing with computers should be approached with caution, particularly if it is proposed to interfere in any way with the client's accounting system.
- This method of auditing is becoming more prevalent as the use of computers gradually supersedes written records. Many companies now scan in documents and send all paper records to deep storage.
- This method of auditing requires skills which perhaps one day all auditors will have to acquire.

Case Study

Bing Properties Plc is a large property developer in the north of England. It has two divisions, industrial and domestic. The industrial division builds factories and offices for various clients and also contracts on major construction projects such as schools and hospitals as one of several contractors.

Its domestic division builds houses. Bing has a substantial land bank acquired over many years but also specialises in converting 'brownfield' sites, former factory sites, into housing developments.

It has recently purchased a new computer system. All incoming documents, letters, invoices advice notes, etc. are be sent to the central processing office where they are scanned into the computer. They are then sent to a warehouse for storage. As they are scanned in they are identified by type by the operator and the computer then allocates the document a unique number which is used to track its progress through the system. Staff are able to call up images of the documents on screen.

A purchase invoice, for example, from a supplier is batched with several others and then the batch is scanned in to the computer. The suppliers name is read electronically and the operator enters the invoice details such as amount, VAT, etc. and a nominal code. The transactions are then processed by the computer.

If the invoice is queried its image can be held in a special file in the computer. Copies can be printed as required.

Sales invoices and requests for payment are generated on screen and only printed to be sent to the customer. There are no copies, but an image of the invoice can be created on screen as required.

Only cash and bank transactions are dealt with in a conventional way.

Discussion
- What approach could be taken by the auditors?
- How will this type of system affect conventional audit approaches?

Student self-testing questions

Questions with answers apparent from the text

a) What approaches to a computer audit can auditors take?

b) What types of CAATs are there?

c) How does the use of embedded software provide good audit evidence?

d) What internal controls would you expect to find in a computer environment?

e) What is test data?

18

Audit working papers

INTRODUCTION

An audit has been defined as a process by which the auditor amasses paper; the more paper they have collected the better the audit they have done! This view is by no means a totally frivolous one, for audits generally do involve the collection of papers in such large numbers that an orderly file structure is invariably required.

Note that working papers may, in part, be held in computer form.

There is an ISA 230 *'Audit Documentation (Revised)'*. The ISA states:

The auditor should prepare on a timely basis audit documentation that provides

(a) *a sufficient and appropriate record of the basis for the auditor's report;*

(b) *evidence that the audit was performed in accordance with ISAs and applicable legal and regulatory requirements.*

It goes on to say that they should be sufficiently detailed to enable an experienced auditor, having no previous connection with the audit, to understand:

- the nature, timing and extent of the procedures carried out;
- the results of the audit procedures and the evidence obtained; and
- significant matters arising during the audit and decisions reached.

What this means, in effect is that:

- auditors should prepare working papers that are sufficiently complete and detailed to provide an overall understanding of the audit;
- auditors should document in their working papers matters which are important in supporting their audit opinion;
- working papers should record the auditors' planning, the nature, timing and extent of the audit procedures performed, and the conclusions drawn from the audit evidence obtained;
- auditors should record in their working papers their reasoning on all significant matters which require the exercise of judgement and their conclusions thereon.

PURPOSES

Audit working papers are produced and collected for several reasons. These include:

- To evidence the planning of the audit and the design of audit procedures.
- To control the current year's work. A record of work done is essential:
  - to record the detailed testing, including compliance and substantive testing and analytical review;
  - to record the conclusions drawn from the audit tests performed;
  - to record evidence of review at each stage of the audit testing;
  - enabling the audit team to be accountable for its work.
- To assist the members of the audit team responsible for supervision to direct and supervise the audit work and to evidence the fact of their reviews.
- Enabling evidence to be available in the final overall review stage of an audit so that it can be considered whether the Financial Statements show a true and fair view and comply with statutory requirements.
- To enable an experienced auditor to conduct quality control reviews and inspections (Chapter 7) or external inspections as required by any legal or regulatory requirements.
- To form a basis for the plan of the audit of the following year. Clearly a starting point for a year's audit is a review of the previous year's work. However, a slavish following of the previous year's work must be avoided and new initiatives taken.

However, auditors should beware of formulaic auditing, where they simply re-perform the same tests each year. Rigidly following the same audit procedures year after year can lead to:

- Client staff getting to know the procedures.
- Client staff designing frauds which the procedures will not uncover.

EVIDENCE OF WORK CARRIED OUT

Audit staff need to provide evidence that they have carried out the audit tests prescribed in the audit programme, that they have drawn a valid conclusion from each test and that the work carried out has been reviewed at a more senior level.

Each audit working paper should contain:

- The name of the client, the accounting period and the assertion, transactions or balance being tested.
- Objective of the test to be carried out.
- Details of the work done, i.e. details of the sample transactions tested or the substantive tests undertaken.
- The outcome of the tests.
- The conclusions that can be drawn.
- The initials or name of the person carrying out the test and the reviewer.
- Date of test and date of review.

NATURE AND CONTENT OF WORKING PAPERS

The form and content of working papers are affected by:

- The nature, size and complexity of the business.
- The nature and complexity of the internal controls.
- The need for direction, supervision and review of work performed by audit staff.
- Specific audit methodology and technology used in the course of the audit.
- The form of the audit report – see Chapter 27.

Auditors will use standardised forms and checklists to improve the efficiency of the audit and will also incorporate schedules and analyses prepared by the business, providing these have been properly prepared.

The extent of working papers is a matter of judgement. A useful way of deciding what is needed is to consider what information would be needed to provide another auditor who had no experience of the client with an understanding of the work performed and the basis of the decisions reached.

In the case of significant matters that may require the exercise of judgement, the working papers should contain:

- Details of the matter and all information available.
- The management's conclusions on the matter.
- The auditors' conclusions on the matter.

This is because:

- the auditor's judgement may be questioned later by someone with the benefit of hindsight;
- it will be important to be able to tell what facts were known at the time when the auditor reached their opinion;
- it may be necessary to demonstrate that, based on the then known facts, the conclusions were reasonable.

For example, the matter in doubt may be the question of whether or not to include in the accounts a provision for an amount expected to be paid under a guarantee given by the client company to a bank which has lent money to a related company in financial difficulty, or to include it by way of a note as a contingent liability.

The working papers should contain:

- All the facts with copies or extracts from relevant documents (the related company's financial statements, the document containing the guarantee given to the bank, budgets and forecasts for the related company, etc).
- The management's conclusions. Perhaps the related company will survive and meet its commitments so that no payment will be required of the client company. The reasons for this conclusion should be summarised.
- The auditor's conclusions. Perhaps that a payment of £x will be required. Again reasoning should be spelt out in detail so if the audit partner has to make a final decision they will be in possession of all the facts.

DEPARTURE FROM BASIC PRINCIPLES

Recording is particularly important if the auditors are departing, for some reason, from basic principles or essential procedures. If they do this they must record how, in their view, the alternative course they have adopted, and the evidence they have gathered, supports the audit objective.

CONTENT OF WORKING PAPERS

The auditors' working papers will consist of:

- Details of the audit engagement – i.e. a copy of the engagement letter and any relevant instructions.
- Information and documents which are of continuing importance to each annual audit, for example the information obtained in understanding the business and its internal control. Such as:

  - the organisational structure;
  - extracts from important legal documents;
  - background information about the industry, etc.;
  - details of the management and senior staff;
  - extracts from company manuals if relevant.

- Evidence of the planning process. (Chapter 10)
- Details of the client's systems and records with the auditor's evaluation of them, i.e. flow charts, ICQs, ICEQs, etc.
- Evidence of the evaluation of the efficiency of internal audit, if applicable.
- Analyses of transactions and balances.
- Analyses of significant ratios and trends.
- Identified and assessed risks of material misstatements at both the financial statements and assertion level.
- Details of the nature, timing and extent of audit work carried out, notes of queries raised with action taken thereon and the conclusion drawn by the audit staff concerned.
- Copies of communications with third parties, e.g. banks, legal advisors and other auditors (in the context of a group audit).
- Copies of letters or notes in respect of audit matters discussed with management and their responses.
- Conclusions reached by the auditor in respect of significant audit matters including any exceptional or unusual items.
- Copies of the financial statements and auditors report.

SAMPLE WORKING PAPERS

Working papers can be in any form desired by the auditor but a usual division is between a Permanent File and the Current File.

The Permanent File

The Permanent File usually contains documents and matters of continuing importance
which will be required for more than one audit.

A sample index for a permanent file is shown below.

		FILE INDEX – PERMANENT FILE
Section	**Title**	**Contains**
1	Constitution	• Memorandum and articles – *Note that the Companies Act 2006 changed the requirements around the company's Memorandum and Articles of Association and these are no longer as significant as they once were, however auditors should ensure they fully understand the legal position of the company and its rules* • Partnership agreements • Trust Deeds
2	Background and Organisation	• History of the business • Activities • Ownership • Registered office • Management structure – *organisation chart* • Industry – *background, client's relative importance and position, economic factors, seasonality* • Premises and equipment – *locations, capital expenditure details, etc., owned or leased, age* • Products • Main suppliers • Main customers distribution, pricing, exports, etc. • Staff – *numbers, departments/functions, method of remuneration (monthly/ weekly), contracts, union agreements, pension liabilities*
3	Systems	• Processing method – computerised/manual • Records and location • Flowcharts and notes, ICQs, ICEQs, etc. • Nominal ledger code lists • Copies of relevant sections of company accounts manuals • Statistical analysis – five year summary/benchmark data
4	Legal documents and minutes	• Leases • Title deeds • Royalty agreements • Ongoing minutes – directors meetings/AGM • Stock Exchange undertakings • Funding documents
5	Group	Structure and details

Section	Title	FILE INDEX – PERMANENT FILE
		Contains
6	Other advisors	Lawyers Bankers Other lenders Stockbrokers Insurers
7	Administration	Copy Engagement Letter Authority letters from client Time budget, costings Staff budgets
8	Audit testing	Rotation of visits Rotational audit testing Examination of title documents Review of other auditors Management letters
9	General	Any other relevant information

The Current File

The current file will contain matters pertinent to the current year's audit. A copy of a current file index is shown below.

Section	Title	FILE INDEX – CURRENT FILE
		Contains
1	Financial statements	• Copy of draft accounts • Copy of final accounts
2	Reports	• Reports to client • Comments from client • Letter of representation • Points for next year • Management letters • Final journal entries • Companies Act Disclosure Checklist • Partner review • Audit completion checklist
3	Job planning	• Planning programme • Budget and fee estimate • Time and costs • Briefing notes for staff
4	Systems audit	• Audit programme • Working papers • Queries and explanations • Letter of weakness and non-reported weaknesses

		FILE INDEX – CURRENT FILE
Section	**Title**	**Contains**
5	Accounts schedules	• Schedules for Balance Sheet items • Copy of accounts • Key schedules for P& L items • Supporting schedules and evidence of audit work • Management account information • Third party confirmations including bank letter • Disclosure Checklists • Queries and replies
6	Minutes	Minutes of directors and other relevant committee meetings
7	Analytical review and statistics	Final overview and analytical review of statistical information
8	General	Any other relevant information

Throughout the Current File, reference should be made as to how each item is used as audit evidence. Conversely, for each type of transaction and balance, the nature of the audit evidence supporting it should be demonstrated. This evidence may be from internal control reliance, substantive testing or from analytical review or from a combination of these sources.

Remember – a procedure not documented is a procedure not carried out!

The audit programme

An audit programme is simply a list of the work the auditors do on the audit.

The tests are designed to check the internal control procedures or to substantiate balances or transactions rather than the authenticity of individual entries. The results of tests, particularly if based on statistical sampling, would need some evaluation and the audit programme should provide space for this.

The advantage of using audit programmes are:

• They provide a clear set of instructions on the work to be carried out.
• They provide a clear record of the work carried out and by whom.
• Work can be reviewed by supervisors, managers, etc.
• Work will not be duplicated.
• No important work will be overlooked.
• Evidence of work done is available.

The disadvantages of audit programmes are:

• Work may become mechanical.
• Parts may be executed without regard to the whole scheme.
• Programmes are rigidly adhered to although client personnel and systems may have changed.
• Initiative may be stifled.
• When an auditor's suspicions are aroused they should probe the matter fully. A fixed audit programme and limited time tends to inhibit such probing.
• If work is performed to a predetermined plan, client staff may become aware of the fact and fraud is facilitated.

Example of an audit programme

This is a systems-based approach to the audit of a sales and debtors system and here is an example of an audit programme using that approach.

Note how it is set out.

- The control objectives are identified for the sales and debtors system.
- Tests are then devised to check that control procedures exist to ensure those control objectives are achieved and the risk of a material error or misstatement is minimised.
- Substantive testing is them carried out on parts of the system in order to provide sufficient, appropriate evidence.

Audit working papers will be prepared for each test carried out showing the control objective, the nature of the test, the work done and a conclusion. These will also carry the initials of the person carrying out the work and the reviewer. Clearly more than one objective can be tested using the same sample data.

Example of an audit programme

Audit area:	Sales & debtors	Prepared by: JT
Client	Bodgitt Ltd	Date: 5 /4/20x8
Period	31 March 20x8	Reviewed by: AM
		Date: 29/4/20x8

Control objectives

- Sales are made to approved, credit worthy customers in accordance with company objectives.
- Customer orders are authorised, controlled and recorded.
- Uncompleted orders are controlled and recorded so as to be filled at the earliest opportunity.
- Goods delivered are controlled and recorded to ensure that invoices are issued for all sales.
- Goods returned and claims by customers are controlled to ensure that claims are valid and credit notes are approved and issued as appropriate.
- Invoices and credit notes are authorised and checked before being entered in the debtors ledger.
- Procedures are in place to ensure that overdue debts are pursued and appropriate provisions made in respect of debts where recovery is doubtful.

Tests of controls	Initial & date
Test new customer procedure to ensure credit checks and references completed	
Test allocation of credit limits	
Check sample of customer orders to ensure approved by sales department	
Check sample of delivery notes to ensure goods signed for by customer on receipt	
Check sample of sales invoices for authorisation by sales department	
Check sample of sales invoices for matching against sales order and delivery note	
Check sample of sales invoices for evidence of arithmetic checks	
Check batching procedure for posting sales invoices to sales ledger	
Confirm all order forms, sales invoices and credit notes numerically sequenced	
Review selection of customer claims and check authorisation of credit note or refund	
Check selection of credit notes with copy goods returned note	

Check credit notes authorised by sales manager or equivalent

Check statements sent to customers monthly

Confirm aged debtors printout produced monthly and confirm evidence of review by sales manager

Substantive procedures

Check sample of sales invoices for:

    arithmetical check

    match to sales order

    match to delivery note

Vouch sample of sales invoices to customer account in sales ledger

Check numerical sequence of:

    customer order forms

    sales invoices

    credit notes

Ensure all sequence numbers accounted for and cancelled documents retained on file

Test batch processing procedures and ensure cash totals agree

Check sample of authorised credit notes against customer claims

Review period end aged debtor analysis for possible doubtful debts

Review subsequent payment or clearance

Check client's provision for doubtful debts

Notes

- Note the header describing the client, the accounting period and the area being audited.
- Note also the initials of the person carrying out the work, the initials of the person reviewing the work and the relevant dates.
- Each of the tests of control and the substantive tests will be evidenced by working paper on the current audit file.

Other working papers

Other audit working papers may include:

- Manuals

  Most audit firms of any size have printed audit manuals which complement internal instruction given to staff. They contain general instructions on the firm's method of auditing in each area and on the audit firm's procedures generally.

- Time sheets

  These are not strictly a part of the audit working papers but are of great importance in controlling the work of audit staff and making a proper charge to the client.

- Review Checklists (if kept separate)

  These, again, are usually incorporated in the working files. They are papers which are concerned with a review of the work done by audit staff and acceptance of the work by supervisors, managers, partners, and reviewing committees. In most cases evidence of review will be entered on the working paper but such sheets can be used to evidence final review prior to signing the Auditor's Report (see Chapter 26).

STANDARDISATION OF WORKING PAPERS

Most firms adopt a system of standard working papers which can be used on all audits.
    This has many advantages including:

- efficiency;
- staff become familiar with them;
- matters are not overlooked;
- they help to instruct staff;
- work can be delegated to lower level staff;
- work can more easily be controlled and reviewed.

    The disadvantages are:

- work becomes mechanical;
- work also becomes standard;
- client staff may become familiar with the method;
- initiative may be stifled;
- the exercise of necessary professional judgement may be reduced.

FINALISATION

Once the audit is complete and the audit report signed the auditor should complete the file in a timely manner, ensuring it is complete. The audit documentation within that file should not then be altered, removed or amended until the time comes to destroy the file.
    If, in exceptional circumstances the auditor has to carry out new or additional procedures after the audit report has been signed then:

- the circumstances of this have to be documented;
- the work done and the conclusions reached; and
- who carried out the work and when,

have to be included in the file.
    These circumstances might arise if matters come to light which the auditors were unaware of at the time of the audit and which might have affected their auditors report had they been aware of them at the time.

OWNERSHIP OF BOOKS AND PAPERS

The ownership of the working papers of an accountant hinges on whether the accountant is acting as an agent for the client. The leading case is *Chantrey Martin & Co v Martin (1953)*.
    The general rules are:

- Where the relationship is that of client and professional, then all documents are the property of the accountant. The only exceptions are original documents, e.g. bank statements, invoices, etc., which remain the property of the client.

- Where the relationship is that of principal and agent a relationship which will exist in situations where the accountant, say, is dealing with the HM Revenue & Customs to settle tax liabilities, or acting in connection with a takeover or sale of a business. In these cases the papers may technically be the property of the client.

The ownership of working papers may not seem important, but it may be relevant in situations such as changes in professional appointments, legal proceedings for the recovery of documents, negligence actions, etc.

ACCOUNTANT'S LIEN

Accountants are considered to have a particular lien, i.e. the right to retain physical possession, over any books of account, files and papers which their clients have delivered to them and also over any documents which have come into their possession in the course of their ordinary professional work.

A particular lien gives the possessor the right to retain goods until a debt arising in connection with those goods, i.e. any outstanding fees, is paid.

The leading case is *Woodworth v Conroy (1976)*.

RETENTION OF WORKING PAPERS

Auditors should retain their working papers for at least *five years* after the signing of the auditor's report.

Other retention periods are dependent on a number of factors including:

- Prospectus requirements are for accounts for the preceding six years.

- Tax assessments can be made up to six years after the end of the chargeable period but in fraud cases, can be made at any time.

- Actions based on contract or tort (e.g. professional negligence) must be brought within six years.

In most cases detailed Current File information may probably be safely disposed of after six years, but auditors would be wise to retain information about any non-routine or contentious issues on which they had to make a decision.

Permanent File data is what it says it is, i.e. permanent and should probably only be destroyed six years after losing the client – it should be retained for that length of time to ensure the period for bringing any legal actions is safely past.

Summary

- Working paper collection is an essential part of an audit.
- The reasons for collecting working papers include:
  - The reporting partner needs be satisfied that all audit work has been properly performed. This is done by reviewing the working papers.
  - Working papers provide for future reference, details of work performed, problems encountered, and conclusions drawn.
- The preparation of working papers encourages the audit staff to adopt a methodical approach.
- Audit working papers will typically contain:
  - Information and documents of continuing importance to the audit.
  - Audit planning information.
  - The auditor's assessment of the client's accounting system and if appropriate, a review and assessment of internal controls.
  - Details of all audit work undertaken, problems and errors met and of all conclusions drawn.
  - Evidence that all audit work by the staff has been reviewed by more senior staff and/or a partner.
  - Records of relevant balances and other financial information including summaries and analyses of all items in the Accounts.
  - A summary of significant points affecting the Accounts and the auditor's report, and how they were dealt with.
- The working papers detail what evidence has been obtained for each class of transaction and balance.
- Working papers are often divided into Permanent and Current files.
- Working papers will also include:
  - Internal control questionnaires.
  - Internal control evaluation forms.
  - Flow charts.
  - Audit programmes.

Points to note

- Accounts are subject to much regulation (by the Companies Act or other Acts and by Accounting Standards). Audits are regulated by the professional bodies acting as supervisory bodies. It is essential that auditors perform all the tests and reviews that are necessary to ensure that financial statements comply with the regulations, that the audit is comprehensive and that nothing has been overlooked. All actions must be fully recorded. One way of ensuring that all is done is to have checklists which must be completed, signed and reviewed by staff, managers and partners.
- Working papers can be stored in a choice of media – paper, film, electronic or other.

- Auditors use many schedules, analyses and other documentation prepared by the client. It is essential that there is adequate audit evidence that such information is properly prepared. This is especially true of computer printouts.
- ISA 230 requires that auditors should adopt appropriate procedures for maintaining the confidentiality and safe custody of their working papers.

Case Study

Charlatan Furniture Ltd are a large company engaged in the manufacture and import of self-assembly furniture kits. Their system for the placing of purchase orders is:

(a) Requisitions are drawn up by production control, by marketing and by stores accounting who keep stores records on a micro-computer. Requisitions are not pre-numbered.

(b) All requisitions must be cost allocation coded and be signed as approved by a departmental manager. Certain codes (e.g. capital expenditure) are excluded from this process.

(c) Requisitions are passed to the purchasing department. They approve requisitions and complete purchase orders. Orders are placed with approved suppliers. There is an ongoing programme to find the optimal suppliers.

(d) The orders are in triplicate – 1 retained, 2 to requisitioner and 3 to the supplier.

Orders are pre-numbered and are valued. Cost codes and total purchases for that cost code are entered on the order together with budgeted allowance for that code.

(e) The orders are checked and signed by the purchasing manager.

Discussion
- What information would you expect to see on the permanent file in respect of this company?
- Draft and document an audit programme for the audit of the above system.
- What information would you keep on the current file?

Student self-testing questions

Questions with answers apparent from the text

a) What are the objectives of working papers?

b) List the contents of a permanent file.

c) List the content of a current file.

d) Who owns an accountant's working papers?

e) What is a lien and why might it be important to an accountant?

f) How long should auditors retain their working papers?

g) In the case of significant matters that require the exercise of judgement, what should working papers do?

h) List the advantages and disadvantages of standardising working papers.

Exercises

1 Rapidrise Ltd are a firm of plumbers' and electricians' merchants which has expanded very rapidly to a turnover of some £3 million in five years. There are three founder director/shareholders and some 20 staff + six clerical staff including Ted who is a part qualified accountant. The system for ordering and paying for incoming goods is:

Each morning Ted visits the warehouse and the foreman and his deputy tell him precisely what to order in order to replace existing stocks and to obtain new lines. New lines are usually suggested by the directors. Ted telephones through the orders to the regular suppliers. Some suppliers require a written order and for them he writes out an order from a duplicate pad which is not sequentially numbered.

On arrival of the goods, the goods are checked by the foreman or his deputy and the delivery note marked 'OK' and passed to Ted. Ted places the delivery notes in a file.

When the invoices arrive they are placed in a box. Approximately once a week, Jean, a clerk, compares the invoices with the delivery notes, settles queries and staples the invoices to the matching delivery notes. She then enters the details of the invoices (supplier, net, gross, VAT) into a micro-computer floppy disc used only for this purpose.

At the end of each month the file is printed out and a listing obtained of the outstanding invoices in supplier name order. When the monthly statements are received, Jean compares them with the printout and settles any queries over the phone with the supplier or with the foreman.

She then passes the statements to Ted who decides which items are to be paid (the company has cash flow difficulties caused by its rapid expansion). He marks the items to be paid and gives the lot back to Jean. Jean makes out cheques for these items and sends them to Ted. He signs the cheques (only his signature is required) and Jean hands them to Mary who sends out the post.

Jean enters the cheques in the invoice disc. The computer system also:

- prints out lists of invoices (and credit notes);
- prints out lists of cheques drawn;
- updates the cash book disc which is used by Ted to control the bank overdraft;
- matches cheques with items and eliminates them where possible.

Jean journalises entries to match and eliminate invoices where several are settled with one cheque.

Jean has no other duties apart from some typing and the keeping of the petty cash.

There are no stock control systems and the warehouse is open during the day to all staff and to customers. Good security operates at night and at weekends.

Required:

(a) Flow chart this system.
(b) Identify and list the weaknesses in this system.
(c) List the possible consequences of these weaknesses. These should include possible frauds as well as errors.
(d) Suggest a better system.

2 Alset Ltd have 12 electrical appliance shops in the Midlands. The company maintains a warehouse in Bilston and supplies goods to the branches using two lorries. There is a central accounts department at the warehouse with five staff under the chief accountant Louise.

Supplies are ordered for the central warehouse from specific suppliers (these are changed as necessary and a director Toby is in charge of an effective system for selecting suppliers). A stock control system is used in the central warehouse which works well.

The 12 shops are in the charge of individual managers who have autonomy over most aspects of the shop including hiring staff. They are expected to indent for supplies from the central warehouse but are permitted to buy some supplies elsewhere if the central warehouse does not stock items and there is customer demand. Prices for items supplied from head office are fixed by head office as there is central advertising with prices given.

The accounting system is:

- Shop managers send in a weekly form of requisition for supplies to the central warehouse.
- The supplies are invoiced to the shops at cost and the invoices form input for the warehouse stock control system.
- Supplies bought for individual shops are paid for by head office when the invoices and delivery notes are sent to head office with a covering letter from each manager stating why they were purchased.
- Sales are made in the shops for cash or cheque (no credit cards). These are recorded on till rolls and the managers count the takings daily each morning and bank the proceeds. They agree the till rolls and retain the bank paying in counterfoils and the till rolls. Petty cash and wages are taken out of takings before banking. Each manager maintains his own wages records but payments to the Inland Revenue are made centrally. A weekly return is sent to head office showing takings and payments made from takings.
- Overheads of the branches such as rent, rates and electricity are paid for centrally.
- Stock is counted half yearly by the managers and accounts prepared for each shop based on the data at head office. Action is taken if the profit margins are less than expected.
- Some sales are made on hire purchase (HP). The managers fill in the HP forms and keep the recording in the branches. They collect the instalments which are normally paid in cash. Full details are sent to head office on the weekly return. Some HP customers pay direct to head office bank account by standing order.
- Each shop manager is remunerated up to 50 per cent by a commission on the net profit of the shop he/she manages.

Required:

(a) List the weaknesses in this system indicating the possible frauds and errors that could occur.
(b) Prepare a flow chart/flow charts of a system which would prevent/detect errors and frauds.
(c) Devise auditing tests for the existing system indicating whether these are compliance tests, substantive tests or analytical review.
(d) Devise auditing tests on the system you have designed for (b).

19

Internal audit

INTRODUCTION

The role and function of the internal auditor is defined by The Institute of Internal Auditing (IIA):

> *Internal auditing is an independent, objective assurance and consulting activity designed to add value and improve an organisation's operations. It helps an organisation accomplish its objectives by bringing a systematic, disciplined approach to evaluate and improve the effectiveness of risk management, control and governance processes.*

They are different from external auditors because they do not focus solely on financial statements or financial risks, much of their work is looking at operational or strategic risks. As can be seen from the IIA's definition internal audit sees itself very much as part of the management function, particularly as part of the quality system.

It does *not* see itself as a corporate police force constantly checking on people's work with a view to finding fault and attaching blame. Internal auditing is intended to be proactive not reactive, their intention is to add value to the organisation, not to be simply an overhead cost.

ROLE OF INTERNAL AUDIT

Internal auditors look at how organisations are managing their risks. They provide the Audit Committee (if there is one – see Chapter 2) and the board of directors with information about whether risks have been identified, and how well they are being managed.

The responsibility to manage risk always resides with management. Internal Audit's role is:

- to identify potential problem areas; and
- recommend ways of improving risk management and internal control systems.

  Their role will include:

- Examination and evaluation of information – both financial and non-financial. This can result in what amounts to a continuous audit of the organisation's operations as the internal auditors review all aspects of its activities on a rolling basis and is similar in many ways to the work of external auditors.

- To give an opinion on whether internal controls – such as policies and procedures put in place to manage business risks – are actually working as intended.

  These will include:

  - A review of the policy making/procedural process.
  - Assessment of the adequacy of guidance given to managers and staff.
  - Organisational, personnel and supervisory arrangements within the organisation.
  - Procedure for accounting for and safeguarding from loss assets, business interests and income streams.
  - Controls to ensure the appropriateness, timeliness, reliability and integrity of information.

- Review of the economy, efficiency and effectiveness of operations. This is sometimes known as 'value for money' auditing.

- Review of compliance with applicable laws and regulations. Internal audit can have specific responsibilities, for example, in the area of money laundering or insider trading.

- Review of and advice in connection with the development of information systems. Note that, as auditors, they should *not* get involved in systems design – they cannot audit independently a system they helped design!

DIFFERENCES BETWEEN INTERNAL AND EXTERNAL AUDIT

The best way to highlight this is by means of a table which will contrast the respective roles.

	Internal audit	External audit
Objectives	• To evaluate the organisation's risk management processes and systems of control and to make recommendations for the achievements of organisational objectives	• To provide an opinion on whether the financial statements show a true and fair view, and whether proper accounting records have been maintained
Responsibility	• To management • Part of quality system and corporate procedures on an ongoing basis	• To shareholders • Report on financial accounts on an annual basis
Scope	• All aspects of the organisation's activities, including operational considerations and compliance issues	• Financial records and processes, risk management processes
Approach	• Risk based • Evaluate internal control systems • Test systems • Evaluate operational efficiencies	• Risk based • Test basis on which financial accounts produced and reliability of systems • Verification of assets and liabilities
Legal status	• Report to management • No specific legal requirement but Stock Exchange Listing Agreement requires internal audit	• Report to shareholders • Companies Act 2006

PUBLIC SECTOR

It is not within the scope of this book to cover the role of internal audit in the public sector.

However, within that sector, encompassing all aspects such as local and national government, the NHS and bodies such as Housing associations, internal audit plays a much more significant role than in private sector organisations.

This is due to two factors:

- Accountability – most public sector organisations are funded primarily through taxpayers money – and so it has to be properly accounted for as they are accountable to the public for how the money has been spent.
- Regularity – this is a term used in the public sector and it means use of funds for the purpose for which they were intended, i.e. capital funds cannot be used for revenue, grants for specific activities must be spent on those activities.

To a large extent these are not issues which affect private organisations who raise their income from selling goods and services in the marketplace and are accountable, primarily, only to their shareholders.

The accountancy body responsible for training accountants with a specific role in the public sector, the Chartered Institute of Public Finance and Accountancy (CIPFA) has issued several bulletins on the role of internal auditing in the public sector and students who are interested in this should study CIPFA's pronouncements.

EXTERNAL AUDITORS AND INTERNAL AUDIT

ISA 610 *'Considering the Work of Internal Audit'* requires that external auditors obtain a thorough understanding of the internal audit function so as to assist in the planning of the audit work and determine the degree of reliance on internal audit.

There are some specific problems the auditor has to deal with:

- How closely do the objectives of internal and external audit coincide? Are the internal auditors mostly looking at, for example, efficiency gains, or are they properly evaluating internal controls?
- What is the scope of the internal auditors' work – are they constrained by management in any way, or told to concentrate only on specific aspects of the organisation's activities?
- How independent is the internal audit function:
  - Can it decide its own pattern of work?
  - Does it have unrestricted access to management at the highest level, i.e. the CEO or the Audit Committee?
  - Does the head of internal audit have a senior management or board level position, independent of the Financial Director?
  - Is it free of any operational responsibilities?
  - Can it communicate freely with the external auditors?
- How competent is the internal audit function? Does the department contain sufficient numbers of trained, competent professional accountants to carry out the role effectively. Is it well enough resourced? Do they have professional qualifications and training programmes both for trainees and for continuing professional development?

The external auditors have to consider these factors and evaluate how much reliance can be placed on the work carried out in the period by the internal auditors.

This is particularly important if the auditors are adopting a risk-based audit strategy, as a strong, independent internal audit function is a significant part of the overall internal control environment.

If the external auditors decide to place a reliance on the work of internal audit they must consider the timing of the work, the approach to sampling, etc., materiality levels and how it is to be documented. This should be discussed with the internal auditors prior to the work being carried out. In particular external auditors should review:

- the materiality of the areas or items tested;
- the level of audit risk inherent in those areas;
- the level of judgement required;
- how good the corroboratory evidence for the work done by the internal auditors is;
- whether the internal auditors have the skills needed to carry out the work effectively, especially any specialist skills.

The auditors must build this into their planning documentation, together with the rationale for using the work of the internal auditors.

Once the work is done it should be reviewed by the external auditors to:

- Consider whether the work has been properly supervised and reviewed when completed.
- Consider how the work compares with work carried out by the auditor's own staff in a similar area.
- Ensure any issues coming to light have been properly resolved.
- Read reports prepared by internal audit and management's responses.
- Ensure working papers are up to an acceptable standard.

OUTSOURCING INTERNAL AUDIT SERVICES

Internal audit may be provided by in-house staff, or an outsourced team. Either way, it should be independent from the management structure, and report directly to the Audit Committee or the Chief Executive *not* the Financial Director or CFO, to maintain the independence of the internal audit function.

If it is provided by an outsourced team this can be drawn from the external audit firm, however this has to be handled with care.

There are both advantages and disadvantages to this.

The advantages to the organisation are:

- The auditors are independent from the organisation.
- There is a wide range of best practice expertise available.
- There are no staff administration or training costs.
- The facility can be 'right sourced', i.e. only used when needed.
- The resource can be used flexibly as required.
- Professional firms are responsible for the level of service and its ethical standards – it can be sued for any failures.

- External audit firms tend to have a higher level of training, numbers of professional staff and technical resources.
- Specialised skills, e.g. computer auditors may be available.

There are, however, a number of significant disadvantages:

- Costs may be high.
- There is likely to be a lack of commitment to the goals and objectives of the organisation.
- Consistency of staff is not always available.
- Professional firms cannot be ordered about in the same way as your own staff.
- There is loss of control over quality of staff provided.
- You pay for what you have contracted for and anything else is extra.

If the outsourced team is drawn from a firm other than the external audit firm there is the issue of client confidentiality.

The internal audit firm will have to obtain their client's permission to reveal the information gleaned during its audits. If it cannot make full disclosure the external auditors could be faced with a limitation of scope qualification in their auditors report.

If both teams are from the same firm this should not be a particular problem, but the client should understand that the internal audit team will be disclosing its findings to the external audit team. If the client attempts to limit this the audit firm should consider its position regarding the trustworthiness of their client.

Summary

- Internal auditors see themselves as part of the management function and try to operate more as consultants than corporate police officers.
- The aim of internal audit is to add value to the company's operations and to safeguard its assets.
- Internal auditors are part of the management of the business, external auditors are statutorily appointed.
- The internal audit function should be independent of the finance function and should be adequately resourced.
- Internal auditors carry out work in much the same way as external auditors but the scope of what they do is much wider.
- If external audit wish to use internal audit they should consider the independence and competence of the internal audit function.
- ISA 610 sets out the process whereby external auditors can consider using the work of internal auditors.
- Internal audit can be outsourced to external audit providers.

Points to note

- The nature of internal audit has changed over the years and it is now much more proactive in company processes and procedures.
- The Institute of Internal Auditors sets out competencies and standards for internal auditors.

Case Study

Shark Estate Agents Ltd is a company offering estate agency services to the public through a network of branches in the Midlands. The company has some 270 staff in all.

The board consists of six people, a part-time chairman, a chief executive, two other full time executives and two representatives of the owners. The company is jointly owned by an American bank and a city property group. The company have an internal audit department consisting of Legge who is a young chartered certified accountant and Foot who is an accounting technician. They also have a secretary, Mavis. They report their activities monthly in detail to the board and to the audit committees of the American bank and the city property group.

Discussion
- What work would the internal audit department do?
- In what ways may the external auditors place reliance on their work?
- Draw up a checklist which the external auditor could use to assess the internal auditors as potentially being capable of producing work on which the external auditors may rely.

Student self-testing questions

Questions with answers apparent from the text

a) Why might an external audit rely on the work of an internal auditor?

b) In what way may they co-operate?

c) How may the external auditor assess the internal auditor and his work?

d) What factors influence the extent of reliance in a particular area?

e) How might the co-operation be planned and controlled?

f) What implications has all this for the external auditors' working papers?

Examination questions

1 Internal auditors often assist management in performing internal review assignments covering, for example, human resources, procurement (purchasing), marketing and treasury activities. Such reviews involve:

(i)   the identification of risks;

(ii) the identification of control systems and procedures implemented to manage those risks;

(iii) tests of controls to ensure that internal controls are operating effectively;

(iv) an evaluation of the overall effectiveness of the design and operation of controls in managing the risks identified.

You are the internal auditor for a private company, Cleanco. Cleanco provides cleaning services to shops and offices and has a reputation for high-quality work. You have been asked to review the human resources, procurement and marketing functions within the company.

Cleanco employs about 500 cleaning staff, all of whom are on the payroll, and most of whom work part-time. Cleanco does not employ subcontractors. Cleanco has a high turnover of staff.

The company buys its computers, office stationery and furniture, cleaning materials, equipment and work clothes for staff, from a variety of different suppliers. It processes its payroll in-house.

The company has recently decided to outsource its marketing to a large, aggressive, third party company that will advertise Cleanco's services by means of direct mail, sometimes by offering discounts; this company has been criticised in the past for breaching advertising regulations. There is growing price competition in Cleanco's market.

Cleanco is struggling to maintain its profitability and would like to expand its client base.

Cleanco has three main functions:

(i)   human resources;

(ii) procurement;

(iii) marketing.

Required:

For each of the three main functions at Cleanco describe the:

(a) risks that you expect the company to face;

(b) controls you expect to be in place to manage the risks you have identified in (a), above;

(c) tests of control you should perform to check that the controls you have identified in (b) above are operating properly.

You may present your answer in tabular format, if you wish.

(ICAEW)

2 Reports produced by internal auditors are different from audit reports produced by external auditors performing audits under International Standards on Auditing. The reports are produced for different purposes, and are directed at different users. They differ substantially in both form and content.

Internal audit reports often comprise the following:

(i)   A cover page;
(ii) Executive summary;
(iii) The main report contents;
(iv) Appendices.

Required:

(a) List and briefly describe the general categories of information that you would expect to find in an internal audit report under each of the four headings above.

(b) List the main contents of most external audit reports (see Chapter 27).
NB: You are not required to reproduce a full external audit report.

(c) Explain why the contents of external audit reports prepared under International Standards on Auditing and internal audit reports are different.

(d) Some reports produced by internal auditors are similar to the report to management (management letter) on internal controls and other matters that are produced by external auditors during the course of the audit. The steps taken by internal and external auditors in drafting, issuing and following up such reports are also similar.

Required:

Describe the common characteristics of the steps taken by internal and external auditors in producing reports to management. *(Note students may wish to read Chapter 28 before attempting this part of the question.)*

(ACCA)

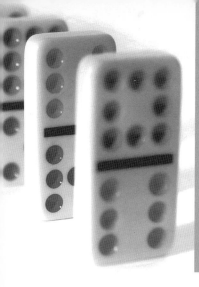

20

Errors, frauds and unlawful acts

INTRODUCTION

There is a difference, known as the 'Perception Gap' between the public and the auditing profession in relation to an auditor's duty regarding errors and fraud.

The auditors see their duty as:

the independent examination of, and expression of opinion on, the financial statements of an enterprise by an appointed auditor in pursuance of that appointment and in compliance with any relevant statutory obligation.

The emphasis is on the financial statements. However, the public, including much of the business community, tend to see an auditor's duties primarily in terms of the detection, and possibly prevention, of fraud and error. This section explores the relationship which an auditor has with the prevention, discovery and reporting of fraud and error.

There is an ISA 240 *The Auditor's duty to Consider Fraud in an Audit of Financial Statements.* Also relevant are ISA 315 *Understanding the Entity and its Environment and Assessing the Risks of a Material Misstatement* and ISA 330 *The Auditors' Procedures in Response to Assessed Risks.*

ERRORS

Errors can be described as 'unintentional mistakes'. Errors can occur at any stage in business transaction processing and can take many forms, mathematical or clerical, or in the application of accounting principles; there can be mistakes of commission (doing something wrongly), mistakes of omission (leaving something out) or errors in the interpretation of facts.

Auditors are primarily interested in the prevention, detection and disclosure and correction of errors for the following reasons:

- The existence of errors may indicate to an auditor that the accounting records of the client are unreliable and thus are not satisfactory as a basis from which to prepare financial statements. The existence of a material number of errors may lead the auditor to conclude that proper accounting records, as required by section 386, CA 2006, have not been kept. This is a ground for qualification of the auditor's report under section 498 (Chapter 27). For example, the financial position of the company may be unable to be disclosed with reasonable accuracy (s 386(2)(b)) or all sums of money received are not entered in the accounting records (s 386(3)(a)).

- If the auditors wish to place reliance on internal controls, they should ascertain and evaluate those controls and perform compliance tests on their operation. If compliance tests indicate a material number of errors then the auditors may be unable to place reliance on internal control to the extent that they would want to.
- If errors are of sufficient magnitude they may be sufficient to affect the truth and fairness of the view given by the financial statements.
- The effect of the total number of errors may not be material enough to affect the true and fair view, in which case the auditors are not concerned with them directly. However, if they show a pattern or some fault in the system they should include the details in the Letter of Weakness (Chapter 28). Note that the auditors will have to have good evidence that the effect of the errors is not material before they decide to ignore them.

For audit purposes errors can arise in three ways:

- A mistake in gathering or processing data from which the financial statements are prepared.
- An incorrect accounting estimate arising from a oversight or misinterpretation of facts.
- A mistake in the application of accounting principles relating to measurement, recognition, classification, presentation or disclosure of transactions and balances,

When all the audit testing work is completed the auditor must assess the total level of errors and misstatements detected and form a judgement as to the adequacy of the accounting records and the truth and fairness, or otherwise, of the financial statements. Large, material errors would have to be corrected, and the system errors highlighted by the checking work would provide good points for the letter of weakness.

The auditor is left with the decision as to whether, taking into account:

- the level of errors and misstatements detected; and
- the level of audit work carried out,

the audit report can be signed without any form of qualification as to the quality of the accounting records.

FRAUD AND OTHER IRREGULARITIES

Fraud is now defined specifically in the Fraud Act 2006. This says:

(1) *A person is guilty of fraud if he is in breach of any of the sections listed in subsection (2) (which provide for different ways of committing the offence).*

(2) *The sections are—*

    (a) section 2 (fraud by false representation),

    (b) section 3 (fraud by failing to disclose information), and

    (c) section 4 (fraud by abuse of position).

Fraud by false representation is fraud which involves the use of deception to obtain an unjust or illegal financial advantage. An example of this would be, say, a department store manager diverting cash takings into his own pocket and then falsifying sales and stock records to cover up the theft.

Fraud by failing to disclose information and fraud by abuse of position cover circumstances where individuals fail to disclose relevant information with the intention to commit a fraud or abuse a position of trust which enables them to commit a fraud. An example of this kind of fraud might be the action of the directors of a company in falsifying financial information given to a bank in order to raise additional finance by hiding the fact that the company is not a going concern, thus keeping their jobs and salaries.

There is a difference between fraud and error insofar as fraud is a deliberate act and may well require specific procedures in order to detect it. Errors should be picked up either by the internal control procedures or the auditor's own procedures.

The auditors are primarily concerned about two types of fraud:

- Misappropriation of assets and consequent misstatements arising from that, i.e. a cover up involving the alteration of the accounting records to disguise the theft.
- Misstatements arising from fraudulent financial reporting.

Characteristics of fraud

Misappropriation of assets is what most people immediately think of when fraud is mentioned. This can often be frauds committed by employees for relatively minor amounts which may not, in themselves, be material and which may not be detected by routine audit checking work. However, it also encompasses management fraud where managers are in a position to disguise misappropriations in ways that are difficult to detect.

This includes:

- Embezzling receipts, e.g. misappropriating sales revenues or diverting receipts in respect of written-off accounts to personal bank accounts.
- Stealing physical assets or intellectual property, e.g. stock theft, theft of scrap for resale, colluding with a competitor to disclose trade secrets in return for payment.
- Causing the business to pay for goods not received, e.g. payments to fictitious suppliers, kickbacks paid to purchasing managers in return for inflating prices, payment of fictitious employees.
- Using the business's assets for personal use, e.g. as collateral for a loan.

Fraudulent reporting frequently involves the *management override* of controls that otherwise might appear to be operating correctly.

Examples of this are:

- Recording fictitious journal entries, especially close to the end of the accounting period, to manipulate operating results or other figures.
- Inappropriately adjusting assumptions and changing judgements used to estimate account balances.
- Omitting, advancing or delaying recognition in the financial statements of events or transactions which have occurred during the financial period.
- Concealing or not disclosing facts that would affect the amounts recorded in the financial statements.
- Engaging in complex transactions which are structured to misrepresent the financial position or financial performance of the business.
- Altering records and term related to significant or unusual transactions.

Auditors should be aware that recent research indicates that fraudsters who commit the largest frauds are most likely to be:

- men;
- in their mid thirties to mid fifties;
- in a relatively senior position in the organisation;
- who have worked for the organisation for a number of years;
- who commit fraud over a period of years;
- who commit multiple fraudulent transactions.

These are quite often likely to be the very people the auditors come to for explanations, information and assurances. As fraudsters frequently tell lies auditors must remain sceptical and evaluate everything they are told carefully in the light of their knowledge of the business and corroboratory evidence.

Materiality of fraud and error

A true and fair view may be given by financial statements of Huge PLC with or without disclosure of a minor petty cash theft. On the other hand, a theft by an employee of £50 000 from Small Ltd, would have to be disclosed if the profits were reported as £45 000. The latter is material to the accounts and the former is not.

Materiality is discussed in Chapter 10 and should be fully understood.

If the auditors know or suspect that an error or irregularity has occurred or exists, then they cannot apply materiality consideration until they have sufficient evidence of the extent of the error or irregularity. Consequently, investigations may need to be made (by the auditor or by the client) into *all* errors and irregularities so that the auditor can have evidence of the materiality of the matter concerned.

Responsibilities for prevention and detection of fraud and error

Primary responsibility for the prevention and detection of fraud and error rests with *management*.

This responsibility arises out of a contractual duty of care by directors and managers and also because directors and other managers act in a stewardship capacity with regard to the property entrusted to them by the shareholders or other owners. How they exercise this duty of care is a matter for them, but in most cases their duty may be discharged by instituting and maintaining a strong system of internal control.

There are many ways the directors can discharge their duty toward prevention and detection of fraud and error. These include:

- complying with the Combined Code on Corporate Governance;
- developing a Code of Conduct, monitoring compliance and taking action against breaches;
- emphasising a strong commitment to fraud prevention. This involves establishing a culture of honesty and ethical behaviour within the organisation with clearly communicated policies on the corporate attitude to fraud and fraudsters;
- establishing a strong control environment, monitoring its effectiveness and taking corrective action;

- establishing an Internal Audit function;
- establishing a compliance function, that is a separate department of the enterprise specifically charged with ensuring compliance with regulations of all sorts;
- having an Audit Committee.

The auditor is not required to assist the directors in this task but guidelines suggest that an auditor should remind directors of their responsibilities of this kind, in the Engagement Letter or other communication, and of the need to have a system of internal control as a deterrent to errors and irregularities.

The Engagement Letter (Chapter 10) should educate the client in the true nature of an audit and outline the auditors' duties towards irregularity and fraud.

The letter should say that the auditors will endeavour to plan the audit so that they have a reasonable expectation of detecting material misstatements in the financial statements resulting from irregularities or fraud, but that the examination should not be relied upon to disclose all irregularities and frauds which may exist. Some clients may desire a special examination for irregularities and fraud outside the audit.

As we have seen, it is the responsibility of the auditors to obtain sufficient relevant reliable audit evidence to support their opinion that the systems are functioning properly.

ISA 240 requires them to adopt an attitude of *professional scepticism*, recognising the possibility that a material misstatement due to fraud could exist, notwithstanding the fact that in previous years the client may have been considered honest and trustworthy.

The auditor's responsibility is to properly plan, perform, and evaluate their audit work so as to have a reasonable expectation of detecting material misstatements in the financial statements, whether they are caused by fraud, other irregularities or errors.

THE AUDIT APPROACH

Before preparing the audit plan, the auditors should appraise the risk of misstatements due to errors and fraud. Factors to take into account would include the situation facing the client (e.g. financial difficulties) or known problems with internal controls. The whole approach to the audit may be affected by the risks involved.

In detail, the matters to be considered might involve:

- In the case of a new client the auditor must gain an understanding of the client and its environment, including its internal control, sufficient to identify and assess the risks of a material misstatement due to fraud or error. This, of course, could still mean the auditor has been misled by unscrupulous management but evidence of this preliminary review will help to justify the auditors' approach.
- The auditor should assess the risks of a material misstatement due to fraud or error by considering:
  - the nature of the business, its services and its products which may be susceptible to misappropriation. Organisations which involve cash takings (e.g. retailers) and easily portable and valuable assets (e.g. jewellers) are particularly at risk as also are organisations where assets are held in a fiduciary capacity (e.g. solicitors who hold clients' monies before handling them on to the appropriate persons). Also vulnerable are areas where payment is made on the basis of an opinion, i.e. the value of work certified in the construction industry or the value of extras to contract. This may involve corrupt practices such as bribery of a quantity surveyor. Evidence of cash

payments of an unusual size may be indicative of corrupt practices however they are described in the accounts.
- circumstances which may induce management to overstate profits (or understate losses) e.g. to retain the confidence of investors, bankers or creditors, to meet profit forecasts, to increase profit-related remuneration or to stave off the threat of insolvency proceedings, or where management have shares or share options.
- the known strength, quality and effectiveness of management.
- the internal control environment including the degree of management involvement and supervision and the degree of segregation of duties, and where there is excessive authority vested in a senior manager.
- The ability of the management to override otherwise effective controls.

- The existence and effectiveness of internal audit.

This risk assessment is an ongoing, dynamic process and the risk assessment for each client must be kept under continual review.

At the transaction level matters to consider include:

- The susceptibility of an area to irregularity, e.g. cash sales, portable and valuable stock, exclusion of liabilities, cash payments.

- The presence of unusual transactions.

- The existence of related party transactions.

- The materiality of transactions and the areas considered most vulnerable.

- The complexity of transactions e.g. financial futures, hedging operations etc.

The information on the matters outlined above will come from both from prior experience and the auditors' review of the business and control environment as part of the audit planning process: see Chapter 10.

AUDIT TESTS AND FRAUD

The first point to bear in mind was established as long ago as 1896 by the judge in the Kingston Cotton Mill case who said that an auditor *'is a watchdog not a bloodhound'*.

Tests designed specifically and uniquely to detect and establish the extent of fraud will be performed only when the auditor's suspicions are aroused.

However, ISA 240 does require the auditor to undertake specific procedures with regard to fraud. These can be summarised as:

- Perform procedures which can identify the risks of a material misstatement due to fraud – this is part of the planning process – see Chapter 10 – and the auditor should consider fraud as part of the evaluation of the integrity of the management and the inherent risks surrounding the client's business.

- Identify and assess the risks of fraud at both the individual transaction level and at the level of the financial statements as a whole. This involves making an assessment of the efficiency or otherwise of the internal control procedures relevant to those assessed risks.

- Decide on audit responses to the assessed risks including the assignment of experienced personnel and the development of a level of unpredictability in the audit testing.

- Design and perform procedures to address the risk of management override of controls.

- Consider whether any misstatements or apparent errors detected may be indicative of fraud.
- Ensure that all staff engaged on the assignment adopt the right degree of professional scepticism when evaluating their audit tests and dealing with management responses, despite any previous experience of the integrity of staff and management.
- Ensure that members of the audit team discuss the susceptibility of the client's financial statements to material misstatements due to fraud. This discussion should include the engagement partner and key members of the audit team but need not involve everyone. It is at the discretion of the audit partner how much of that discussion is disclosed to more junior members of the audit team.

Limitations on audit procedures

Auditors should recognise that there are limitations on the ability of an audit to detect fraud in particular because:

- The primary objective of the auditor is to form an opinion on the financial statements not detect fraud.
- Auditing is based on testing samples of transactions and evaluating controls. Inherent in this approach is the possibility that not all errors or misstatements, whether due to fraud or not, will be detected even if the audit is properly planned and carried out.
- Management, particularly senior management, have the capacity to hide fraud from the auditors and deliberately manipulate the accounting records.
- Where the misrepresentation involves the exercise of judgement, for example accounting estimates, it is difficult to decide whether these were caused by fraud or error.
- Fraud may involve sophisticated and carefully organised schemes designed to conceal it including collusion, forgery, deliberate non-recording of transactions or intentional misrepresentations made to the auditor.

Action to be taken on discovery by an auditor of potential errors or fraud

The following sequence of actions may be appropriate:

- Consider materiality. If the matter is material in the context of the accounts then take no further action apart from informing management, unless the management are themselves involved.
- If the matter may be material, perform appropriate additional tests.
- If it appears that irregularities or errors have occurred, and may be material, then consider the effects on the financial statements and ensure that these have been prepared with such adjustments and amendments (and disclosures) as may be required.
- If further investigations are required and the accounts cannot be delayed, then the auditors' report may have to be qualified for uncertainty (see Chapter 27).
- Where errors or irregularities have occurred ensure top management are aware of such events. If top management is involved, reports may have to be made to non-executive directors or regulators.
- Any weakness in the system of accounting and internal control which may give or have given rise to error or irregularity should be fully discussed with, and reported to, management.

Reporting

To members (shareholders)

Errors and irregularities need not be reported to members as such. But if financial statements or any part of them do not or may not give a true and fair view or conform to statute or if proper accounting records have not been kept, then the auditors have their statutory duties under Section 386.

To top management

In the event of the auditors suspecting that lower level management may be involved in or condoning irregularities, then a report to the main board or the Audit Committee may be necessary. In companies with non-executive directors the auditors may well have a mechanism for reporting executive management irregularities by reporting to them in the first instance.

To management

All actual or potential irregularities discovered should be in the Management Letter, with recommendations for changes.

To third parties

This is a very difficult area and the auditors have to proceed with caution, primarily because of the duty of client confidentiality they have. In cases involving specific breaches of the law, i.e. money laundering, the auditors have a statutory duty to report to the relevant authority but in other cases their duty may not be so clear cut.

Some audits under statutes or regulations other than the Companies Act give auditors more extensive duties towards internal control and irregularities. For example, the Financial Services and Markets Act 2000 requires the auditors of banks, building societies, insurance companies and similar bodies to report irregularities and breaches of regulations to the Financial Services Authority, particularly where the auditor's report may be being qualified or where solvency of the organisation might be an issue.

Guidance on this matter is now given to auditors in the ISA 250 *The Auditors' Right and Duty to Report to Regulators in the Financial Sector*, which is, in general, outside the scope of this book. This is a very sensitive matter but it does allow the auditor to report serious breach of statutory requirements to the regulatory body in order to protect the investing public, providing the auditor has gathered sufficient evidence and considers that any supposed breach of the regulations is reportable to the regulator.

The auditors should:

- Take legal advice or advice from their professional body.
- Disclose to third parties (e.g. the regulatory authorities) only matters where they have a clear public duty to disclose (e.g. if a serious crime is contemplated).
- Consider resignation. ISA 240 considers resignation only if the circumstances are exceptional and make it impossible for the auditor to continue. Examples of this might be if the business fails to take the remedial action the auditor considers necessary in the case of a serious incidence of fraud or where the trust in the organisation's management has been seriously undermined. Legal advice should be taken before this step is contemplated.

If the auditors do resign they must notify the Registrar of Companies accordingly and have to notify members (and creditors in the case of an unquoted company) of any circumstances surrounding their leaving office which the auditors feel should be brought to their attention by depositing a statement at the Registered Office. This will require very careful wording which should only be contemplated with legal advice.

UNLAWFUL ACTS OF CLIENTS AND THEIR STAFF

Introduction

This subject is a fascinating one for students who may see themselves in the role of detective. However, the reality of discovering or being involved in crimes committed by a client or members of the client's staff is usually very unpleasant or a cause for anguished inner conflict.

In practice, auditors must always act scrupulously and correctly and in accordance with the law. They should:

- Take legal advice if necessary.
- Read the guidance provided by their professional body and by the Auditing Standards.

Current guidance is contained in:

- APB Ethical Standards or the ethical standards of the RSB of which the individual auditor is a member (see Chapter 6).
- *APB Practice Note 12 – Money Laundering - interim guidance for auditors in the United Kingdom – revised*
- *APB Bulletin 2005/1 Audit risk and fraud – supplementary guidance for auditors of charities.*
- *Statement 1.306 Professional Conduct in Relation to Defaults or Unlawful Acts* (this is ICAEW guidance for members in practice).
- *ISA 240 The Auditors' Responsibility to Consider Fraud in an Audit of Financial Statements.*
- *ISA 250 Consideration of Law and Regulations in an Audit of Financial Statements (Section A and Section B) The Auditor's Right and Duty to Report to Regulators in the Financial Sector.*

The auditor's legal position

Auditors must not themselves commit a criminal offence and they would do so if they:

- Advised a client to commit a criminal offence.
- Aided or conspired with a client in devising or executing a crime.
- Agreed with a client to conceal or destroy evidence or mislead the police with untrue statements.
- Knew a client has committed an arrestable offence and acted with intent to impede their arrest and prosecution. Note that 'impede' does not include refusing to answer questions or refusing to produce documents without the client's consent, unless legally obliged to do so. This is because of the accountant's duty of confidentiality to their client.
- Knew the client has committed an offence and agreed to accept consideration (e.g. an excessive audit fee) for withholding information.
- Knew that the client had committed treason or terrorist offences and failed to report the offence to the proper authority.
- Had committed various activities in connection with money laundering (see Chapter 6). Note that, in this case, there is a legal requirement to disclose illegal acts to the authorities.

Discovery of unlawful acts

If auditors discover an unlawful act, or if they are asked by the police or a regulatory authority to disclose information about a client 'to help with enquiries', they are in a difficult position.

Under normal circumstances they ought to first discuss any disclosure of information with the client – as they are bound by a duty of confidentiality.

However, discussing possible disclosure with the client may not be appropriate and, indeed, it may well be an criminal offence to do so – particularly in respect of the 'tipping off' rules under the Money Laundering Regulations (See Chapter 6).

Consequently, the auditors must investigate the circumstances under which the disclosure is required and may make disclosures *without* consulting the client if it is justified:

(a) *by the law or legal process to the proper authorities*

Proper authorities are defined in the courts as those third parties who have a proper interest in receiving such information. Proper authorities include, but are not limited to;

- the police;
- recognised professional bodies;
- the Serious Fraud Office; and
- HM Revenue & Customs.

(b) *in the public interest*

'Public interest' includes matters of public concern, not public curiosity. Public concern may extend to the concerns of clients, government, financial institutions, employers, employees, investors, the business and financial community and others who rely upon the objectivity and integrity of the accounting profession to support the propriety and functioning of commerce.

Examples of situations which may be regarded as being in the public interest include:

- a criminal offence;
- a failure or likely failure to adhere to legal obligations;
- miscarriage of justice;
- health and safety matters which endanger or are likely to endanger members of the public; and
- damage or possible damage to the environment.

Disclosure depends on several issues including

- the gravity of the issue;
- the extent to which members of the public could be affected; and
- the intention of the client to remedy the situation.

(c) *to protect the auditor's own interests*

In general, auditors should only disclose information which is adequate, relevant and necessary in order to protect their own interests – for example, to enable them to defend themselves in disciplinary proceedings.

Disclosure rules

When disclosing confidential information to the proper authorities, either proactively or due to a request, auditors should consider the following:

- the employing organisation's internal policies and procedures;
- the identity of the authority, agency or regulator and under what legal authority the disclosure is required or permitted;
- who can be informed of the disclosure or request for disclosure; and
- what documentation should be kept in relation to the disclosure.

Auditors should keep detailed contemporaneous notes of meetings and telephone conversations relating to situations where they disclose confidential information to a third party, as well as a record of:

- any consent given;
- discussions held or decisions taken concerning the disclosure of confidential information;
- a schedule summarising disclosures and to whom they were made;
- copies of relevant documentation; and
- details of any legal or other advice obtained.

AUDIT ISSUES ARISING FROM NON-COMPLIANCE

Auditors should plan and perform their audit procedures, and evaluate and report on the results, recognising that non-compliance by the entity with law or regulations may materially affect the financial statements.

Some clients, in heavily regulated sectors such as banking, insurance or waste disposal, together with their auditors, should be particularly aware of the effect of non-compliance on both the organisation being audited and of possible disclosures in the financial statements. Auditors also should recognise, however, that all businesses are now regulated generally in such areas as planning, health and safety, racial and sexual discrimination and many others and consider the effect of non-compliance on their client.

The effect of non-compliance can be fines, penalties or civil claims from third parties which will result in actual or contingent liabilities to be included in the financial statements. In addition, in very serious cases, directors may be held personally liable in criminal proceedings and face imprisonment.

Penalties may be material in amount and auditors need to gather sufficient appropriate evidence to evaluate the effect of such issues on the financial statements. Auditors will also have to consider the possibility of entities having to pay compensation, which may be wholly or partly insured, and the effect of this on the financial statements and the ability of the entity to continue trading in its present form.

The effect of non-compliance can be extremely serious and include the loss of licences or authorisations to continue in business. This may have implications for the financial statements in many ways, including the assumption of the going concern basis. For example, if a business running online gambling websites has its licence to operate withdrawn the very future of the business could be in jeopardy.

Directors' responsibilities

Under the general provisions of good corporate governance, and the specific provisions of the Combined Code (Chapter 2), it is the responsibility of directors to take steps:

- to ensure that their entity complies with laws and regulations;

- to establish arrangements for preventing and detecting any non-compliance; and

- to prepare financial statements which comply with all laws and regulations.

Directors may fulfil their responsibilities by:

- Adopting the principles of good corporate governance (Chapter 2), including the involvement of non-executive directors.

- Instituting and operating appropriate systems of internal control, including an independent, properly resourced internal audit function which has compliance as one of its remits.

- Maintaining an up-to-date register of relevant laws and regulations and monitoring any changes to these.

- Developing an internal, business code of conduct to inform employees, ensure employees are properly trained and that sanctions exist against breaches of the code.

- Engaging legal advisers to assist in this area.

- Maintaining a register of complaints and breaches.

Role of the auditors

Auditors plan their work with a reasonable expectation of detecting material misstatements in the financial statements that may arise through non-compliance.

It is not the auditors' role, generally, to search for breaches of laws and regulations, however it is part of the auditors' role to include, in their audit work, consideration of the company's policies and procedures for *monitoring* possible non-compliances with applicable laws and regulations, particularly where a risk based auditory strategy has been adopted.

The auditors cannot be expected to detect non-compliance hidden by collusive behaviour, forgery, override of controls or intentional misrepresentations by management. However, their audit procedures should be designed taking that possibility into account and should incorporate procedures to gather as much sufficient appropriate evidence as they can without relying too heavily on management or staff representations.

The auditors should obtain sufficient, appropriate audit evidence about compliance with those laws and regulations which relate directly to the preparation of, or the inclusion or disclosure of, specific items in the financial statements. Examples are the Companies Act, other statutes and compliance with financial and accounting rules.

The auditors should perform procedures to help identify possible or actual instances of non-compliance with those laws and regulations which provide a legal framework within which the entity conducts its business and which are central to the entity's ability to conduct its business and hence to its financial statements. This is part of the consideration of going concern issues (Chapter 24).

Procedures may include:

- obtaining a general understanding of the rules;

- inspection of licences;

- obtaining confirmation from the regulatory authority that the entity is still entitled to carry on its business and has not committed any fundamental breach of regulations;

- enquiry of the directors on any non-compliance; and

- obtaining written assurance from the directors that they have given the auditors all information on non-compliance.

Audit staff should be alert for instances of actual or possible breaches which might affect the financial statements.

When actual or possible breaches are encountered the auditors should gather all possible information and evidence, evaluate it and fully document their evidence, reasoning, findings and conclusions.

The matters should be discussed with management, if appropriate, depending on:

- The nature of the non-compliance or illegal act.
- The nature and extent of managements' involvement in it.

After due consideration and taking legal advice the acts or omissions may be reported to relevant third parties.

One problem area is where illegal acts or non-compliances are discovered to involve the directors of a subsidiary company who are not directors of any holding company. Auditors should be aware of their duty of confidentiality to their client, i.e. the subsidiary, and should obtain permission from that client to disclose the facts of the case to the holding company. In practice this should not be a difficulty as, ultimately, the auditors will report to the holding company as shareholders, however, care must be taken in the interim not to breach client confidentiality.

Remember that auditors are appointed specifically to each company in a group as they will be signing an auditors' report in respect of each company – so the subsidiary company is just as much a client as the holding company which owns it.

However, if the board of directors of the subsidiary includes holding company directors who have not been informed of the illegal acts, they are entitled to know about them in their capacity as directors of the subsidiary – so the auditors could make their disclosure to the holding company board via that route.

The auditors, on discovering an unlawful act, should consider:

- That they must do nothing to assist in the offence or to prevent its disclosure.
- That they must bring all offences of employees to the notice of the client.
- Consider the effect on the Auditors' Report – if the offence has a material effect on the accounts which has not been properly disclosed, so that the non-disclosure means that the accounts do not show a true and fair view, they must insist on disclosure or qualify their report.
- If the auditor is prevented by the client from discovering the full effect of the non-compliance or offence, so they are unable to judge its materiality, they should express a qualified opinion on the basis of a limitation of scope of the audit.

Should the auditors resign?

If the organisation does not intend to take any form of remedial action once the offence has come to light, or the offence involves the most senior management of the company the auditor should consider resignation. This last point is important in that, if senior management are involved, the reliability of any management representations given by them to the auditors must be called into question and the auditors' position may well become untenable.

However, resignation is seen as a last resort. ISA 240 considers that, if possible, it is preferable for the auditors to remain in post and continue to fulfil their duties as auditors. Auditors are acting on behalf of the shareholders and it is their interests and the interests of other creditors which have to be considered.

If the directors refuse to release accounts, or the auditors are not given an opportunity to communicate their concerns to members they should consider resigning.

Remember that, if auditors resign, they must make a Statement of Circumstances, detailing the circumstances surrounding the resignation.

They must also inform any incoming auditors, under the ethical code, of any professional reason why they may not take up the new appointment – and instances of illegal acts by directors just may be considered to be relevant. Remember that any disclosure of information to incoming auditors requires the permission of the client so, if this is not forthcoming, the outgoing auditors should inform the proposed new auditors of that fact. The incoming auditors should then decline to act.

The auditors should take legal advice and, probably, consult their professional body before acting.

In a liquidation the auditors can disclose any matter they wish to the liquidator who in fact becomes their client. Note that the ethical codes of the professional bodies prohibit an auditor from being appointed liquidator of the same company they have previously audited.

Summary

- There is a difference in perception of the auditor's duties on errors and fraud between auditors and the public.
- An auditors' primary duty is to give their opinion on the truth and fairness etc. of financial statements, detection of frauds is secondary.
- Discovery of some errors and frauds may be a by-product of the audit.
- Discovery of the existence of and disclosure of errors and fraud may be essential to the true and fair view.
- Errors are unintentional misstatements in, or omissions of amounts or disclosures from, an entity's accounting records or financial statements. Fraud involves the use of deception to obtain an unjust or illegal financial advantage, intentional misstatements in or omissions of, amounts or disclosures from an entity's accounting records or financial statements as defined in the Fraud Act 2006.
- Materiality is an important concept in this area and the auditor must have evidence that a matter is not material before disregarding it for accounts reporting purposes.
- Audit planning must take into account the risks of a material misstatement due to errors or irregularities.
- Auditors may uncover criminal offences committed by a client or an employee of the client. This puts them in a difficult position. The auditor should act carefully and correctly and take legal advice.
- Auditors must not themselves commit criminal offences and should know the circumstances in which a criminal offence may be committed by not doing something.
- The auditor should not jeopardise a professional relationship by disclosing offences except in specified circumstances.
- The auditor should investigate the circumstances under which the information is required. They will not usually disclose confidential information to the police or other authority unless:
  - The client authorises disclosure.
  - The disclosure is compelled by process of law, e.g. a court order.
  - Disclosure is required in the auditors' own interest, e.g. in defending themselves against civil or criminal actions.
  - The circumstances are such that the auditors have a public duty to disclose.
  - Disclosure is required in the circumstances envisaged by advice given on money laundering and disclosure to regulators in the financial sector.
- Auditors have a responsibility to give an opinion on company accounts which they should not avoid by resignation.
- Directors have a responsibility to manage the company in a proper way and they should comply with the principles of corporate governance.
- Auditors must be aware, in their audit planning and procedures, of the possible impact of non-compliance with law and regulations on the financial statements.
- Firms of accountants must have procedures in place to recognise and report suspicions of money laundering activities.

Points to note

- Irregularities in the form of falsifying financial statements are a special risk in companies with going concern problems. The auditor must always be aware of temptations of management to dress or falsify their financial statements to present an untrue but desirable view of the results and position.

- Auditors have the right to require from management any information and explanations they may need. It is reasonable for auditors to ask management if any irregularities have occurred and, if any are discovered, for the full facts.

- If the auditors feel that they have not been given all the information and explanations that they need then the scope of the audit has been restricted and they could consider qualifying the report. In extreme cases they should resign and invoke the Companies Act rules.

- The auditor' duty when they discover an unlawful act or when they are made aware of an unlawful act while conducting the audit is not always clear.

- Regulatory authorities have mechanisms to detect non-compliance and it is not the role of the auditor to act on their behalf unless statutorily bound to do so, e.g. in connection with money laundering.

Case Study

Megachem plc is a multinational agri-business dealing in the import and export of agricultural produce, the manufacture and sale of fertilisers and pesticides and the sale of agricultural machinery worldwide.

During the audit, the auditors discover:

(a) several delivery notes for 'agricultural machinery' recording deliveries of crates of what are described as 'machinery parts' to several countries in the world where there are local conflicts. These delivery notes had been kept in a separate file in the CEO's office and marked 'confidential' and the auditors had been given it by the CEO's secretary, by accident, when requesting information about another, unrelated issue. No other documentation appears to exist in respect of the client's names recorded on the delivery notes and they do not appear in the sales ledger.

(b) The company recorded the receipt of substantial bank transfers from accounts in Switzerland and Panama. These were recorded as 'consultancy fees' but there are no other records relating to these transactions and the actual client's name is not recorded.

(c) The firm appears to be employing consultants in various countries in the Balkans and the Far East as 'commissions' are being paid to them but it is unclear precisely what services these individuals provide. When asked the Financial Director refused to divulge any information citing confidentiality.

(d) In addition to the sums received from Switzerland the company are making material payments to a numbered Swiss bank account. The Financial Director has told the auditors that these are commissions to government officials in various countries who obtain business for the company.

(e) Visits to one of the manufacturing plants reveal that workers appear to be handling what look like dangerous chemicals without proper protective gear. The factory manager says that the gear is provided but the workers refuse to wear it on the grounds that it makes them hot and impedes movement.

(f) There is an article on an environmental news website that a pipe at one of the company's plants is discharging chemicals into the adjacent river. The company says the effluent is treated and that they have a licence to do this but can't show it to the auditors as they claim they have lost it.

Discussion

Discuss the implications of these discoveries for:

1 the auditors;
2 the company;
3 the financial statements.

Student self-testing questions

Questions with answers apparent from the text

a) Define errors and frauds.

b) What are the auditors duties towards errors?

c) What is the relevance of materiality to these matters?

d) Who is responsible for internal control in a company?

e) What should auditors do if he discovers an irregularity in the form of (i) a material error or (ii) fraud?

f) To whom should auditors report such irregularities?

g) What options do auditors have if they detect a fraud by management?

h) When can an auditor disclose unlawful acts to the police?

i) How does the auditors' professional duty of confidence affect disclosures to third parties?

j) What should auditors do if they discover an unlawful act?

k) What are the circumstances in which an auditor can make disclosures without permission from their client?

l) What are the responsibilities of directors in connection with illegal acts?

Examination questions

1 The audit of Binkle Ltd for the year ended 31 December 20x7 was completed on 2 February 20x8. Materiality was judged to be £150 000. As all tests yielded satisfactory results, the auditors, Tickitt & Run, issued a clean opinion. In accordance with the quality control procedures operating in the firm, a partner reviewed the file in March

and concluded that the audit complied with all auditing standards and that sufficient, appropriate and reliable audit evidence was on file to support the opinion issued.

On 14 May 20x8 the firm received an e-mail from Nicholas Tasker, the Managing Director of Binkle Ltd, informing them that he had just received a postcard from the company's Financial Controller showing a nice picture of the beach in Burovia where he had absconded with the Marketing Assistant and £2.4m of the company's cash.

Preliminary investigations carried out by the Managing Director indicated that the sum had been misappropriated over a period of five years. The Managing Director concluded his e-mail by asking, rather pointedly, how was it possible for Tickitt & Run to miss such a large fraud for such a long period of time and how they could justify the clean audit opinion issued a few months previously? He hinted darkly at possible legal action.

Required:

Prepare a draft memorandum addressing the concerns of the Managing Director of Binkle Ltd with specific reference to:

(a) the respective responsibilities of the auditor and the directors with regard to the company's financial statements; and

(b) the auditor's responsibilities in relation to fraud.

21
Related parties

INTRODUCTION

ISA 550 *Related Parties* defines a parties as being related if one has the ability to control or significantly influence the actions of the other or both are under common control.

These are related parties as defined in FRS 8 *Related Party Disclosures.*:

- Parties that control or are controlled by the reporting entity.
- Parties under common control, e.g. subsidiaries of a common holding company.
- Joint ventures.
- Associates of the reporting entity).
- Key management personnel (including directors and senior managers of the reporting entity).
- Close family members of those directors and managers.
- Pension schemes for the benefit of the employees of the reporting entity.

However, ISA 550 goes on to say that the definition of a related party may not be self-evident and parties may be related or connected in ways different from those outlined above. Auditors need to take steps to ensure that all related parties have been identified.

Transactions between related parties may not be at arm's length and disclosure of the existence of such transactions gives important information to users of the financial statements.

DISCLOSURE

Students should be familiar with the accounting requirements dealing with related party transactions.

FRS 8 indicates that disclosure may be required where related parties are concerned in the following types of transactions of arrangements:

- Purchases and sales of goods.
- Purchases and sales of property and assets.
- Agency arrangements.

- Leasing arrangements.
- Research and development transfers.
- Licence agreements.
- Finance.
- Guarantees or indemnities.
- Management contracts.

Clearly inter-group transactions eliminated on consolidation do not have to be disclosed.

Note that it is common for groups to use 'captive' subsidiaries, joint venture or consortium arrangements or partnerships as part of their normal trading and transactions between the parties may or may not be at arm's length for bona fide reasons. Note also, however, that in the giant Enron collapse in the USA, huge operating losses were hidden in what were effectively related parties. Disclosure of these losses would have changed the face of the whole Enron situation.

It is therefore of interest to the readers of the accounts that the nature and extent of related party transactions are disclosed in order to paint a complete picture of the nature and scale of the entity's operations.

Disclosure will include:

- The nature of the relationships between the parties.
- The types of transactions.
- Elements of the transactions necessary for an understanding of the situation, including volumes, pricing policies and amounts outstanding.

THE AUDITORS' DUTIES RE RELATED PARTIES

The auditors are required to perform audit procedures designed to provide sufficient, appropriate evidence regarding the identification and disclosure by management of related parties and the effect of related party transactions that are material to the financial statements.

The auditors should:

- Plan and perform the audit with the objective of obtaining sufficient, appropriate audit evidence regarding the adequacy of disclosure of related party transactions and the nature and extent of the transactions.
- When planning the audit, assess the risk that material *undisclosed* related party transactions may exist.
- Review for completeness information provided by the directors identifying material transactions with those parties that have been related parties for any part of the financial period.
- Be alert for evidence of material related party transactions that are not included in the information provided by the directors.
- Obtain sufficient, appropriate audit evidence that material identified related party transactions are properly recorded and disclosed in the financial statements.
- Obtain sufficient, appropriate audit evidence that disclosures in the financial statements relating to control of the entity are properly stated.

- Obtain written representations from the directors concerning the completeness of information provided regarding the related party and control disclosures in the financial statements.
- Consider the implications for their report if:
    - they are unable to obtain sufficient, appropriate audit evidence concerning related parties and transactions with such parties; or
    - the disclosure of related party transactions or the controlling party of the entity in the financial statements is not adequate.

AUDIT PROCEDURES

The auditors should review information supplied identifying the names of known related parties and carry out the following procedures:

- Review previous year's working papers to identify known related parties.
- Review the entity's procedures for identifying related parties.
- Enquire if directors and senior managers have relationships or connections with other entities.
- Obtain details of principal shareholders from share registers.
- Review minutes of directors, managers and shareholders meetings.
- Review register of directors' interests in statutory records and the Annual Return.
- Review tax returns and information supplied to regulatory agencies.

The auditors then need to review the nature and extent of related party transactions based on information supplied and be alert for other material related party transactions.

The auditors will consider the adequacy of internal controls over the authorisation and recording of related party transactions.

Auditors need to be alert to transactions which appear unusual in the circumstances, and which might indicate a related party, in particular by:

- reviewing large or unusual transactions especially around the period end;
- reviewing loans received and made;
- reviewing third party confirmations such as the bank letter for indications of guarantees;
- reviewing sales of assets;
- reviewing investment transactions, e.g. an investment in a joint venture;
- reviewing details of and transactions with pension and other trusts;
- reviewing returns to tax authorities, Companies House, the Stock Exchange, regulatory agencies and others;
- reviewing correspondence with lawyers.

During the course of the audit, staff should be constantly alert to matters which may reveal an undisclosed related party. Such instances may include:

- abnormal terms of trade, e.g. unusual prices, payment periods or discounts;
- unexpected contract terms;
- transactions lacking commercial logic;

- transactions where substance differs from form;
- transactions processed in an unusual manner;
- high volumes of business with certain customers or suppliers as opposed to others;
- unrecorded transactions such as receipt or provision of management services at no charge.

This may require a degree of substantive testing of transactions and balances.

The auditors must obtain evidence that the recording and disclosure in financial statements is appropriate. They may need to enquire more closely into disclosed transactions, and obtain additional third party confirmations.

The auditors should obtain written assurances from management, in the Letter of Representation (Chapter 25) that:

- all related parties and transactions involving them have been notified to the auditors;
- proper disclosure has been made in the accounts.

CONTROL OF THE ENTITY

The auditors need to obtain sufficient, appropriate evidence concerning disclosures in the financial statements about control of the entity. In most cases this will not be a problem, but where an entity is controlled from overseas or by a consortium care will be needed. If the ultimate controlling party is not known then that fact should be disclosed.

QUALIFIED AUDIT REPORTS

In a few cases the auditors may conclude that they have been able to gather insufficient evidence on this subject. This is a limitation of scope and may require a qualified opinion or, in extreme cases, a disclaimer of opinion.

If the auditors conclude that the disclosure is not adequate then they may issue a qualified opinion or an adverse opinion. They may also consider giving, in their report, the information which should have been given in the financial statements.

Summary

- A true and fair view often requires the disclosure of related party transactions and of controlling parties.
- ISA 550 sets out the auditors duties and FRS 8 deals with disclosures.
- The auditors need to plan for procedures to deal with related party transactions disclosed to them and also to identify related party transactions which have remained unidentified. This can be difficult but the auditors need to demonstrate they have tried.
- The auditors need to assess the risk of inadequate disclosure and act accordingly.
- The directors are primarily responsible for the disclosure of related party and ownership matters and the auditors should obtain written representations from them.

Points to note

- Related parties can be of many kinds – owners, directors, 'shadow' directors, key management and their families.
- Auditors need to be alert to the fact that using related parties has been a common feature of financial scandals over many years and be alert for unusual or out of pattern transactions.
- Some persons and entities are not considered to be related parties for these purposes. For example, regulatory bodies, banks, major customers or suppliers, despite the fact that they may have considerable influence over the conduct of the company's affairs.
- Pension funds and pension fund trustees are related parties.

Case Study

Convoluted Ltd is a company dealing in rare metals internationally. It has 40 employees (25 in the UK). It is owned by Joe King Ltd, a company registered in the Cayman Islands and is known to deal with several other UK and overseas companies also owned by that company. The company has four directors who are all UK residents and who do not own any shares in the company.

The company has a pension scheme with employee and employer trustees and is heavily indebted to its bankers.

The auditors are Tickitt & Run, who are newly appointed.

Discussion

(a) List some possible related parties of this company.

(b) From the auditors' point of view what risks are there that all the requirements of FRS 8 may not be met?

(c) Set out a section in the overall audit plan covering the requirements of ISA 550.

(d) List some possible substantive tests on the subject of related party transactions and ultimate control.

Student self-testing questions

Questions with answers apparent from the text

a) Why are related party transactions and ultimate ownership important to the true and fair view?

b) List the requirements of ISA 550.

c) What are the risks that auditors face in this area?

d) How might an auditor seek confirmation of directors' representations and assess their completeness?

e) What matters might give concern to the auditors in preparing the auditors' report?

Examination question

I Tickitt & Run have recently been appointed auditors to Massive Holdings PLC, a group of ten companies based in the North of England. Massive has subsidiary companies, all of which are wholly owned, which trade in various activities from machinery importers to car dealerships.

One of the auditors, whilst looking for biscuits one night whilst the auditors were working overtime stumbles accidentally across the minutes of a directors meeting which is not in the minute book.

One of the minutes refers to a partnership called Dragon which Massive appears to have lent money to, although there is no record of this in the books. In turn Dragon appears to have granted Massive a very lucrative machinery importing contract on which Massive has reported a substantial profit. The other partners in Dragon appear to be the directors of Massive.

Massive has transferred shares into a company called Bluebottle Ltd. Bluebottle appears to be a joint venture between Massive and a company called Dragon 2, about which nothing is known, for a time share development in Spain.

The wife of the CEO is reported to own 15 per cent of one of the company's major suppliers of office equipment.

Massive appears to have made a loss on a contract to supply agricultural machinery to a company based in Africa which hasn't paid. The loss appears to have been covered by a transaction with a partnership called Massive 1. The auditors have checked the transaction in the books of Massive and to all intents and purposes the African contract made a profit and the debt was cleared by discounted bills of exchange. It is unclear how this transaction has been funded by Massive 1 but there is reference to a loan from an unknown bank to Massive 1 secured by Massive itself. This does not appear in the books of Massive.

Required:

i) Explain what actions the auditors should take in respect of these revelations.

ii) How are they likely to affect the future conduct of the audit?

22

Service organisations

INTRODUCTION

Many businesses use outside specialist organisations to perform functions which would otherwise be performed in house. This process is known as 'outsourcing'.

Functions outsourced can include:

- Information processing and maintenance of financial records.
- Internal audit.
- Debt management and collection.
- Facilities management.
- Maintenance of safe custody of assets, such as investments.
- Initiation or execution of transactions on behalf of the client business.

The use of service organisations can create problems for auditors and this chapter considers the issues.

There is an ISA 402 *Audit Considerations Relating to Entities Using Service Organisations.*

WHY DO FIRMS OUTSOURCE?

Advantages of outsourcing are:

- The problems of employing personnel (e.g. employment legislation, health and safety, etc.) are passed on to others.
- It can be cheaper, if not, firms may well consider that they can use internal resources for more productive activities.
- It creates a certain level of independence from the commissioning organisation, which can be beneficial, particularly in the case of outsourcing internal audit (see Chapter 19).
- Expertise is often not available in house.

- Service organisations can keep up to date on equipment and expertise more easily than the user enterprise in a fast-moving world.
- It reduces the time management have to spend on housekeeping functions.

    Disadvantages are:

- Cost.
- The service level the client wants has to be specified from the outset – if the client wants additional services or enhanced productivity this will have to be paid for or might not be possible.
- The client has to be sure that the quality of service is appropriate.
- The client has to be sure that the standards of the service organisation's internal controls are compatible with its own.
- The client has to be sure that issues such as confidentiality of data are properly understood and dealt with.

AUDIT PLANNING ISSUES

ISA 402 says:

'The auditor should consider how the entity's use of a service organisation affects the entity's internal control so as to identify and assess the risk of material misstatement and to design and perform further audit procedures.'

The auditor should, as always, obtain a thorough knowledge of the client's business in accordance with ISA 315 – see Chapter 10.

The auditor, in planning the audit, should determine which activities are undertaken by service organisations which are relevant to the audit.

Likely areas for concern include:

- Maintenance of accounting records.
- Internal audit provision.
- Other finance functions, e.g. tax, payroll, debtor management, credit control.
- Management of assets.
- Undertaking or making arrangements for transactions as agent for the business.

The latter item may include, for example, firms selling on the Internet which outsource the collection of sales proceeds to service organisations which deal with credit card processing.

Some outsourced functions will have little relevance to the audit – for example, office cleaning.

Once the auditors have determined which outsourced functions are pertinent to the audit, they need to assess the possible impact on the audit. Possible areas of concern include:

- risk of misstatement in the financial statements;
- whether or not proper accounting records have been kept;
- the independence, or otherwise, of the outsourcing organisation from the client.

Having assessed the risks, the auditors can plan their actions in relation to each relevant outsourced function.

Contractual terms and obligations

The auditor should obtain and document an understanding of the contracted terms which apply to relevant activities and the way the user (ie. the client) monitors those activities so as to ensure that it meets its fiduciary and other legal responsibilities.

Relevant points here include:

- Right of access, by the user and/or the auditor to records held by the outsourcing company.
- Whether the terms take proper account of statutory or regulatory body requirements. Of particular importance is the Companies Act requirement for proper accounting records.
- Performance standards.
- The extent of reliance on controls operated by the service organisation.
- Any indemnity offered to the user.

The first point is especially important as lack of access to records may mean that the auditors have to consider qualifying their report on the grounds of limitation of scope (see Chapter 27). The problem is that the systems of the outsourcer belong to them, and they may process information for more than just the one client, so there is a major confidentiality issue.

Auditors need some form of access or assurances from the service organisation.

Inherent risk

The auditors should determine the effect of relevant activities on their assessment of inherent risk.

The first issue is the competence, integrity and going concern status of the outsourcing company.

Items include:

- The reputation of the service organisation for competence and integrity.
- The existence of external supervision, e.g. of investment management by regulatory authorities.
- The extent to which indemnities offered by the outsourcer can be honoured.

The latter matter may be important, for example, if the accounting records were lost and the outsourcer could not honour its indemnity due to insolvency. This may then even affect the going concern status of the client.

Control risk

Issues here include:

- The extent of controls operated by user personnel in the providing company.
- The extent of undertakings by the outsourcing company on controls.
- User experience of errors and omissions.
- The degree of monitoring by the user.
- The extent of information on controls provided by the outsourcer.
- The quality assurance in the outsource, e.g. ISO 9000 or internal audit.

As always the auditors have to gather sufficient, appropriate evidence to ensure that the information obtained from the outsourcer is reliable. They have to assess the risks involved in respect of the impact of the use of an outsourcing organisation on the reliability of their audit opinion.

If the outsourcing company is considered to represent a low risk to the audit opinion the procedures will be little different from what they might be if the audit work was being conducted in house. Risks may even be reduced if the outsourcing company can demonstrate a high level of internal control as part of its own procedures.

ACCOUNTING RECORDS

When any or all of the accounting records are outsourced, the auditor faces special problems.

These include:

- Whether the requirements of s 386, Companies Act 2006 have been met.
- Whether the requirements of any relevant regulatory bodies have been met.
- Whether all the information and explanations required by the auditor have been made available.
- Whether all information required in respect of internal controls of the processing organisation is available.
- Whether the records generally accord with relevant law and regulations.

AUDIT EVIDENCE

Various approaches are available to satisfy the auditors' needs and these include:

- Inspecting records and documents held by the client as a basis of procedures in respect of reports produced by the service organisation.
- Obtaining an undertaking by the service organisation so as to form an opinion as to whether its control systems do provide assurance as to the reliability of financial information.
- Obtaining representations to confirm balances and transactions from the service organisation.
- Analytical review of such records as are held by the audit client, and of returns and reports received by the client from the service organisation ie. comparing inputs from the client with outputs from the service organisation.
- Inspecting records and documents held by the service organisation.
- Reviewing information from the outsourcer and its auditors on the design and operation of internal controls operated by the outsourcer.
- Requesting the service organisation's auditors or the user's internal audit function perform specified procedures.

The latter approach is perhaps very powerful but its application depends on the service agreement between the service organisation and the client.

REPORTS BY SERVICE ORGANISATION'S AUDITORS

One possible piece of audit evidence is a report issued by the service organisation's auditors.

These may be issued to user auditors and might cover such matters as:

- a description of the service organisation's accounting and internal control systems, prepared by the management of the service organisation; and
- an opinion by the service organisation auditor that:
  - the description is accurate;
  - the systems' controls are in operation;
  - the accounting and internal control systems are suitably designed to achieve their stated objectives; and
  - the accounting and internal control systems are operating effectively based on the results from tests of controls. In addition to the opinion on operating effectiveness the service organisation auditor would identify the tests of control performed and related results.

The user auditors then have to assess the report for sufficiency and reliability. They might do this by:

- Assessing the standing and reputation of the service organisation's auditor.
- Assessing the scope of the work performed.
- Assessing the timing of the work performed.
- Assess whether the report is sufficient and appropriate for its intended use.

A critical aspect of the report is the period covered. The user auditor must be content that the accounting records and the concomitant controls and systems were adequate for the *whole period* covered by the financial statements.

Summary

- Outsourcing is a common way of dealing with many necessary functions.
- This can present problems for an auditor, especially if accounting functions are outsourced.
- Auditors need to obtain knowledge of all functions outsourced by the client.
- The auditors need to assess the risk of a material misstatement arising from the use of an outsourcing organisation.
- The user auditor needs evidence that proper books of account have been kept and that the records form a reliable basis for the preparation of the financial statements.
- Various approaches are possible in assessing the records including the records and controls operated by the user, assessing the competence, integrity and going concern status of the outsourcer, assessing the reports by the outsourcer and its auditor, inspecting the records at the outsourcer.

Points to note

- The user's auditors should be wary of accepting the certificates of the outsourcing company or its auditor without considerable enquiry.
- Ultimately the auditors need to be satisfied that the outsourced records meet statutory and other requirements, form a reliable basis for the preparation of the financial statements and are adequately controlled.
- Enquiry should be made of the standing and competence of the outsourcer and its auditors that the certificates cover all the relevant times and records and that testing was adequate.

Case Study 1

Cuthbert Ltd outsources most of its accounting function to Speedy Accounting Services Ltd. They have found the relationship with Speedy very effective. However, recently it has come to Cuthbert's attention that the statements of account sent by Cuthbert's main supplier have not been successfully reconciled for six months. The accountant of Cuthbert has also heard a rumour that Speedy are in financial difficulties having lost clients recently. Speedy have sent a report by Bludger & Co, their auditors, on the suitability of design and operating effectiveness of the system by which Cuthbert's records are maintained.

Tickitt & Run, the auditors of Cuthbert, are engaged on the audit of Cuthbert for the year ended 31 December 20x7.

Discussion
- Why might Cuthbert Ltd outsource its accounting function?
- What risks do Cuthbert Ltd run as a result of the outsourcing and how might these risks impinge on the financial statements?
- What risks do Tickitt & Run face in the conduct of the audit?
- Draw up a checklist of matters that might concern Tickitt & Run on the issue.

Case Study 2

Hippay PLC, a listed company, have outsourced all their employee (including directors) remuneration to a service organisation. Hippay write bespoke and general application software for environmental recording and employ 97 people.

Discussion

- Discuss the business risks attached to this company both in general and in respect of the outsourcing.
- Discuss the problems occasioned to the auditors by the outsourcing and how they might be overcome.

Student self-testing questions

Questions with answers apparent from the text

a) Which ISA relates to service organisations?

b) Why do firms outsource?

c) What clauses in an outsourcing contract may be relevant to the auditor?

d) List risks which arise to a firm as a result of outsourcing.

e) What special risks arise from outsourcing accounting records?

f) List actions that auditors can take to amass audit evidence in the presence of an outsourced function.

g) What might be covered in a report to users by an outsourcer's auditor?

h) What actions should the client's auditors take in respect of such a report?

Examination question

I You are the auditor of Petite Ltd, a small company. In order to reduce the company's administrative costs the financial director proposes transferring all the sales and purchase ledger processing to a computer bureau.

   Batches of invoices will be sent weekly to the bureau who will process them and send them back together with a printed transaction report.

   The bureau will also produce a monthly list of balances and an aged debtors listing.

   The sales and purchase ledger programmes are the property of the bureau and Petite's auditors may not access them in any way.

Required:

(a) What problems might this present to the auditor?

(b) How may the auditor overcome the problems you have listed in (a) above?

23

Evaluation and review

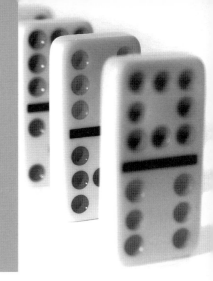

OPENING BALANCES AND COMPARATIVES

Introduction

This section is concerned with the financial statements of the business for the year prior to the one for which the financial statements are being audited.

There are two ISAs involved – ISA 510 *Initial engagements – Opening Balances and Continuing Engagements – Opening Balances* and ISA 710 *Comparatives*.

The techniques involved are similar and we will deal with both together.

Companies Act requirements

The Companies Act states that corresponding amounts are required to be disclosed in respect of every item in a company's balance sheet and profit and loss account for the financial year immediately preceding that to which the balance sheet and profit and loss account relates.

Corresponding amounts for the previous year are commonly known as the comparative figures and current practice is to print one narrative and two sets of figures as:

	20 × 8	20 × 7
	£'000s	£'000s
Fixed assets	£6420	£6180

Where the corresponding amount is not comparable (= able to be compared) with the amount shown in the previous years' accounts then:

- the previous year's figure should be adjusted; and
- particulars of the adjustment, and the reasons for it, shown in the notes.

Students should be aware of the reporting requirements of UK GAAP in respect of:

- acquisitions;
- discontinued operations;
- prior period adjustments; and
- comparative figures.

THE AUDITORS' INTEREST

The auditors are interested in the preceding year's figures because:

- These figures form the opening position from which the present year's figures are derived.

  For example, the opening stock is a component of the cost of sales figure. Thus the auditors must be assured that the opening figures have been properly brought forward.

- Accounting policies must be applied consistently from year to year.

- Corresponding amounts must be shown and the auditors must seek evidence that they are properly shown.

The auditors are not required to express any opinion on the corresponding figures, as such, but they are responsible for seeing that they:

- are the amounts which appeared in the preceding period's accounts; or

- have been restated to achieve consistency or comparability; or

- have been restated due to a change in accounting policy or a correction of a fundamental error.

Audit procedures

Both ISA 510 and ISA 710 require that the auditors obtain sufficient appropriate evidence as to the opening figure brought forward into the current period and that the comparative figures from the previous accounting period are properly stated.

If the auditors were also the auditors of the preceding financial statements (a continuing auditor) and issued an unqualified report then they should:

- Consider whether the audit of the current period has revealed any matters casting doubt on the previous year's figures.

- Satisfy themselves that the balances have been properly brought forward and incorporated in the books.

- Satisfy themselves that the preceding period's figures have been properly and consistently classified and disclosed as comparative figures.

- Satisfy themselves that consistent accounting policies have been applied.

When the preceding period's financial statements were audited by another firm (known as 'predecessor auditors') the auditors will have to perform additional work.
This might involve:

- Consultations with the client's management.

- Reviewing the client's records, working papers and accounting and control procedures for the preceding period, particularly as they affect the opening position.

- Considering whether work on the present year's financial statements also provides evidence regarding opening balances.

- If the above are insufficient then the auditors may have to perform some substantive tests on the opening balances.

- Consulting with the previous auditors and reviewing or obtaining assurances on working papers and relevant management letters.

- It may be that the incoming auditor will obtain details of the closing position from the predecessor auditor.
- The auditors should carry out substantive testing in respect of these balances, if necessary, on a sample basis.

Normally, the actions outlined will enable the auditor to give an unqualified report at least in respect of use of the previous year's figures. If, however, some material matter cannot be adequately evidenced they will have to consider the implications for their Auditors' Report (see Chapter 27).

This may result in an 'except for' qualification on the grounds of a limitation of scope, i.e. that they were unable to assemble sufficient appropriate evidence to validate the comparative figures and the opening position. Here is an example of an 'except for' qualification. The key points are in bold for clarity.

Example

Extract from the Auditors Report to the shareholders for the year ended 31 December 20X2.

*We did not observe the counting of the physical inventory stated at £XXX as at 31 December 20X1 since that date was prior to our appointment as auditors. **We were unable to satisfy ourselves as to the inventory quantities by other audit procedures.***

*   ***In our opinion, except for the effects of such adjustments, if any, as might have been determined to be necessary had we been able to observe the counting of physical inventory and satisfy ourselves as to the opening balance of inventory,** the financial statements give a true and fair . . . etc.*

This is likely to be quite rare, however, care has to be taken that last minute audit adjustments from the preceding year have been incorporated into the current year's figures.

SUBSEQUENT EVENTS REVIEW

Introduction

ISA 560 *Subsequent Events* states:

When the auditor becomes aware of events which materially affect the financial statements the auditor should consider whether such events are properly accounted for and adequately disclosed in the financial statements.

Systems-based auditing

If they are using a systems-based audit strategy, during the course of their checking work, the auditors will have spent most of their time looking at events and transactions that occurred in the financial year being audited.

Only a limited amount of their work will have involved them in looking beyond the year end. For example:

- reviewing payments of debtors balances after the year end;
- tracing uncleared cheques and uncredited lodgements from the bank reconciliation;
- carrying out audit work on the client's cut-off procedures.

Risk-based auditing

If the auditors are using a risk-based auditing strategy their work will not have encompassed the same level of detailed checking work but, on the assumption that they will have carried out some level of substantive testing on the balance sheet, they may well have carried out some, if not all, of the above procedures.

The consideration of business risks will not have stopped at the year end, however, and events since the balance sheet date will have a direct bearing on the auditors' view of the financial statements.

They will be interested in:

- Events since the balance sheet date in any particular high-risk areas they have identified.
- Material transactions since the balance sheet date in key business risk areas or areas where fraud or manipulation of financial accounting is considered feasible or possible.
- Results since the balance sheet date, provided by management information, to assist a general overview and analytical review of the financial statements.

Post balance sheet events

The auditors should consider the effect of subsequent events on the financial statements and on the Auditors' Report.

During the period between the end of the financial period and the date the Auditor's Report is signed there may be events which shed new light on the financial statements. These are known as post balance sheet events.

Examples of these sorts of events are:

- Notification of insolvency of a customer after the year end resulting in adjustment of the bad debt provision.
- Adjustments to stock or work in progress valuations, for example, where finished goods stock has proved to be unsaleable or where a dispute has arisen in respect of work done on a contract and the amounts receivable look in doubt.
- Significant changes to borrowings from banks or other lenders which shed new light on the financial structure of the business, for example, where the company's bankers refuse to renew overdraft facilities or provide a loan which the company needed in order to continue its operations at their current level.
- An issue of new shares.
- A change in the way the business is carried on, for example, a clothing retailer decides to close all its high street shops and concentrate on selling over the Internet.

Some of these events will mean that the accounts will have to be amended to take account of them; others may simply require a mentioning in a note to the accounts or in the Directors Report.

ADJUSTING AND NON-ADJUSTING EVENTS

From the list above, events such as:

- the insolvency of a significant debtor;
- material writing down the values of stock and work in progress; or
- major problems with financing the business.

would be likely to mean that the accounts would be adjusted because they cast new light on something which *already existed* at the balance sheet date. These are *adjusting events*.

However, again from the list above, events such as:

- an issue of shares after the balance sheet date; or
- a change in the way business was conducted after the year end

would only require including in a note to the accounts or the Directors' Report – these are *non-adjusting events*.

This is because, whilst these events are informative and add to the general financial picture of the company, they don't relate to something which actually existed at the balance sheet date or which happened within the financial period.

Obviously these are only examples and there are many types of events which could happen about which a decision would have to be made.

If after discussion with the auditors, the directors of the business decide not to amend the accounts when the auditors think they should, the auditors will have to consider the effect of this on their audit report and we will look at this later in the chapter.

Audit tests for a subsequent events review

ISA 560 states that the auditors:

should perform audit procedures designed to obtain sufficient appropriate audit evidence that all events up to the date of the auditors' report that may require adjustment of, or disclosure in, the financial statements have been identified.

In order to satisfy themselves that all events after the year end have been appropriately dealt with and disclosed in the Financial Statements the auditors should carry out certain audit tests.

These will include:

- Reviewing management's procedures for identifying subsequent events which might affect the financial statements in any way.
- Reading minutes of board meetings, shareholders or other committee meetings since the balance sheet date and enquiring about matters discussed at meetings where the minutes are not yet available.
- Reviewing management accounts, cash flow forecasts or other information since the balance sheet date.
- Enquiries to legal advisors about outstanding legal matters.
- Enquiries of management about:
  - matters which have already been dealt with but on the basis of preliminary or inconclusive information;
  - whether any new borrowing or guarantee commitments have been entered into;
  - details of any proposed or actual major additions to assets;
  - whether any mergers or acquisitions are planned or any new issues of shares;
  - whether any assets have been appropriated (e.g. nationalised) or destroyed;
  - any developments in areas of risk or where contingent liabilities have been identified;
  - whether any unusual accounting amendments have been made or are planned to be made, e.g. reversals of transactions recorded during the financial year;
  - whether there are any events which would call into question the appropriateness of the accounting policies used or accounting bases adopted, in particular that of going concern (see Chapter 24).

- Reviewing transactions since the year end for large or unusual items such as sales of assets, issues of credit notes, exceptional discounts allowed or received, commissions paid, etc.

Note that there is no obligation on auditors to apply procedures to discover relevant subsequent events from the date of signing their report to the date of laying the financial statements before the company, e.g. at an AGM.

However, if the auditors become aware of such events they should discuss the matter with the directors, consider the implications for their report and take such actions as may seem necessary depending on the significance to the company, and thus to the financial statements, of the events.

Summary

- Preceding financial statements have a bearing on the current year's statements because:

  - they are the opening figures to the current year's financial statements;
  - consistency of accounting policies is required;
  - they are comparative figures.

- The Companies Acts have requirements for comparative figures to be shown.

- The auditors have a duty towards these figures.

- Problems arise if the previous year's audit was performed by another firm or if the previous year's audit report was qualified.

- Post balance sheet events, events occurring in the period between the end of the financial year and the date the Auditors' Report is signed, have an effect on the financial statements.

- Authority for the treatment of post balance sheet events is found in ISA 560.

- Auditors should apply procedures to discover the existence of relevant subsequent events which occur from the date of the financial statements to the date of signing the auditors' report.

- Some events may require the amounts to be adjusted if they relate to events or conditions which existed at the balance sheet date. Other events may be of interest but don't cause any adjustment of the accounts.

Points to note

- The auditor, as ever, needs to be aware of the requirements of the relevant reporting standards as to the disclosure in the accounts of comparative figures, and ensure they are correctly disclosed.

- The comparative figures in respect of the profit and loss account should include in the continuing category only the results of those operations included in the current period's continuing operations. The auditor should verify that correct comparatives of continuing, discontinued and acquisition operations are shown.

- To some extent the auditing standards are not specific but use terms like '*the auditors should consider the implications for their report*'. In essence the auditor will normally check only that the comparatives agree with previous year's accounts and consistent policies have been applied. The auditors must also bear in mind disclosures, acquisitions, prior year adjustments, etc.

- Problems arise when there are report qualifications in the previous year's audit report when the previous year's accounts were audited by predecessor auditors or were not audited, when the auditor comes across material misstatements in the previous year's accounts or if the opening balances cannot be substantiated.

- Apart from reviewing the period from the balance sheet date to when the auditors' report is signed for significant events auditors should be aware of attempts to 'window dress' the accounts. This is in connection with the auditors' responsibilities under ISA 240 *The Auditors' Responsibility to Consider Fraud in an Audit of Financial Statements.*

Case Study 1

Tickitt & Run have been appointed auditors of Spottypants PLC manufacturers of underwear in succession to Limp, Lettice & Co. They are currently reviewing the final accounts (The Audit is on the year ending 31 December 20x8) and discover the following:

(a) An examination of the stock sheets at 31 December 20x7 reveals that stock has been valued at prime cost £585 000 instead of £679 000 the full direct cost. Limp, Lettice & Co had not picked this up.

(b) A freehold property had been purchased on 23 February 20x7 for £800 000 (inc. land £200 000).
No depreciation had been charged in 20-x7. The building is old and the management estimated its useful economic life at 25 years.

(c) The auditors' report on the 20x7 accounts was qualified. Limp Lettice & Co had discovered that there was a cut-off uncertainty on creditors in the amount of £130 500. Limp Lettice cannot provide full details and it looks as though this will never now be resolved.

(d) In view of the errors found in the 20x7 accounts Tickitt & Run are unhappy about all the figures in the 20x8 balance sheet.

Discussion

(a) What work should Tickitt & Run do on the figures in the 20x7 balance sheet?

(b) How should the items (a), (b), (c), be treated in the accounts for 20x8 with their corresponding figures?

(c) Draft a paragraph for inclusion in the Auditor's Report on the 20x8 accounts. Assume no problems arose other than those stated.

Case Study 2

Tickitt & Run are conducting the final audit of Woodhood PLC who are importers and dealers in timber and manufacturers of packing materials. The accounts show results which are comparable to those of the previous year. The auditors are puzzled by this as they know that the company are having difficulties and that creditors are pressing and the bank is making difficulties over the overdraft. The auditors are suspicious of the accounts and resolve to be especially vigilant in the audit of post balance sheet events. The company's year end is 31 March 20x7 and they are doing the audit in mid June. Two specific items have come to their attention:

(a) In the sales office the auditors found some promotional literature offering special very low prices for obsolete stock in July.

(b) In conversation with the purchasing manager the auditors discovered that the company had signed a barter deal with an exporter in China for the exchange of specialised wood products for some woodworking machinery of Westwood that is surplus to requirements. The contract was signed in February for completion in the winter of 20x7/8.

Discussion

- List the procedures that the auditors should adopt re post balance sheet events.
- What particular further facts should they elicit re (a) and (b)?
- What might be the significance of these items for the accounts?

Case Study 3

The auditor of Smokestack Manufacturing PLC is reviewing the financial statements of the company for the year ending 31 December 20x7. The following matters have come to light:

(a) The company have given warranties on a new product that has had many sales in the year. Some of the products are faulty but the company have made no provision for them in the financial statements.

(b) The company have an old factory site in Ruritania which has become polluted with heavy metals. There is no legal obligation to clear up the site (which they are trying to sell) but they have a prominent note in the annual report as to their commitment to environmental matters.

(c) New legislation requires that the company fit smoke filters to their factory in Rotherham by 31 December 20x7. They have not done so.

Discussion

- What should the auditor do about these matters?

Student self-testing questions

Questions with answers apparent from the text

a) What is the auditor's interest in comparative figures?

b) What aspects of the comparative figures is the auditor responsible for?

c) What should the auditors do re previous accounts if they audited them and gave a clean report?

d) What additional work should be performed if the previous accounts were audited by another firm?

e) What paragraphs would appear in an auditor's report if there was an uncertainty in the opening balances on fixed assets?

f) What is the definition of an adjusting event?

g) After the year end, but before the Auditors' Report is signed, there is a big fire at Megablast plc and their biggest factory burns down throwing the future of the company into doubt. How should this be treated (i) in the accounts and (ii) by the auditors?

h) List general and specific procedures to be adopted to identify relevant subsequent events.

i) Summarise an auditor's duties in respect of events occurring between the date of the auditors' report and the laying of the financial statements before the company.

Examination questions

1 An unqualified audit report normally states that the financial statements to which the report refers give a true and fair view of the state of the company's affairs at the balance sheet date and of its profits for the year ended on that date.

Bearing in mind the above statement the directors of Midland Builders Ltd have drawn up accounts for the year ended 30 April 20x7 which do not reflect certain events which have occurred since the year end. They justify their action on the grounds that the books and records correctly reflect what was known at the year end. The following are the events which are not reflected in the draft financial statements (in all cases the figures are material).

(i) At a meeting in May 20x7 the local planning authority rejected the company's plans to develop one of its freehold sites. The site was included in the company's assets at its cost of £500 000 but it is likely that the site will have to be sold and will realise no more than £350 000 because of its reduced development potential.

(ii) Following the completion of a long-term contract in June 20x7 it has been possible to calculate the final profit on the contract. It appears that the profit accrued at 30 April 20x7 was underestimated by £220 000. This arose from a material error at 30 April 20x7 in estimating the amount of work still to be completed.

(iii) A public company in which Midland Builders Ltd held shares as a long-term trade investment announced in June 20x7 that it was going into liquidation. The investment is shown in the balance sheet at its historical cost of £140 000 and a note of its stock market value at 30 April 20x7 of £146 000 is included in the notes to the accounts. It now appears likely that the investment will prove worthless.

Required:

(a) Discuss generally the effect which facts and events relating to a period but becoming known or occurring after the end of an accounting period can have on the financial statements for the period in question. Comment on the directors' view that the books and records reflect what was known at the year end and that no further adjustments are required.

(b) List FOUR detailed procedures which an auditor should adopt in order to detect post balance sheet events.

(c) In respect of each of the three events described above, list the detailed work which the auditor should undertake and comment on the acceptability of the company's decision not to adjust its financial statements.

(i) Refusal of planning permission.
(ii) Completion of long-term contract.
(iii) Liquidation of trade investment.
(ACCA)

2 You are completing the audit of Chocs Ltd (Chocs) for the year ended 31 August 2007. The principal activity is the manufacture of confectionery which it sells under its own brand name and that of a national supermarket chain Terose. On 13 November 2007, the directors of Chocs were informed by Terose that following a strategic review of its

supply base, it was giving notice that it would not be renewing its contract with Chocs when the current contract expires in May 2008. It also notified the company that, with immediate effect, it would reduce its demand for products to the minimum stipulated in the contract.

Although sales to Terose represent 40 per cent of revenue, the directors are convinced that the company will be able to continue to trade as they have always had a contingency plan in the event of losing the contract. This plan entails Chocs scaling down its operations and focusing on its own brand goods which have a higher margin. In addition, they plan to focus on their export range which has already exceeded sales targets following its successful launch. The property, plant and equipment dedicated to producing goods for Terose will be sold. The freehold property was purchased many years ago and has recently been valued at an amount substantially greater than its current carrying amount.

The directors have prepared forecasts which indicate a loss for the year ending 31 August 2008 and a return to profitability for years ending 31 August 2009 onwards.

Required:

(a) State the auditor's responsibilities in relation to subsequent events. Your answer should distinguish between responsibilities up to the date of the auditor's report and responsibilities after the date of the auditor's report.

(b) Explain the possible effect of the loss of the contract with Terose on the financial statements of Chocs for the year ended 31 August 2007 and the audit report thereon.

(c) From the information provided above, identify the specific matters you should consider when reviewing the assumptions underlying the income and expenditure included in the profit forecast.

(ICAEW)

24

Going concern

INTRODUCTION

ISA 570 *Going Concern* states:

> *The auditor's responsibility is to consider the appropriateness of management's use of the going concern assumption in the preparation of the financial statements and consider whether there are material uncertainties about the entities ability to continue as a going concern that need to be disclosed in the financial statements.*

One of the fundamental accounting concepts is that the accounts of the company are assumed to be prepared on a going concern basis – but what does this mean?

The assumption is that the business will carry on its activities in the same way for the foreseeable future. In other words that:

- the management will be able to influence the way the business is run;
- that its products or services will continue to be bought by its customers;
- that suppliers will continue to supply it; and
- that it will have the cash to fund its operations.

The last point is probably the most important of all. Most businesses fail because they run out of cash and are unable to pay their bills.

The 'foreseeable future' is a vague definition but is usually taken to mean something between three and five years ahead.

INDICATORS OF PROBLEMS

Auditors should be alert to indicators which might show actual or potential going concern problems.

Financial indicators

- net liability or net current liability position on the balance sheet;
- necessary borrowing facilities not having been agreed;
- fixed term borrowing nearing maturity without any realistic prospects of its renewal or reliance on short-term borrowings to finance long-term assets;

- major restructuring of debt or refinancing of debt repayments so the business can continue;
- indications of withdrawal of support by bankers or lenders;
- failure to comply with loan conditions or banking covenants;
- substantial operating losses or deterioration in the value of assets used to generate cash flows, including events since the balance sheet date;
- negative cash flows from current activities with little prospect of improvement;
- inability to pay creditors on their due dates, reduction in normal terms of trade by suppliers or change from credit to cash on delivery for supplies;
- inability to finance new products or product development.

Operating indicators

- loss of key management without replacement;
- labour difficulties or shortage of key supplies;
- loss of a major market or key supplier;
- fundamental changes in the market or in technology to which the company cannot respond;
- excessive dependence on a few products in a depressed market.

Other indicators

- changes in legislation which might adversely affect the business;
- major legal claims against the company which cannot be met,

Any or all of these might mean than the company will no longer be able to carry on for the foreseeable future.

Again, it is the responsibility of the management to come to this decision and draft the financial statements accordingly.

CONSEQUENCES OF GOING CONCERN

The adoption of the going concern basis in financial statements means amongst other things:

- Assets are expected to be used for many years into the future and depreciated accordingly. Abandonment of the going concern basis would mean that the enterprise might have to immediately sell its assets which may fetch only a small fraction of their book value.
- Liabilities are recognised and measured on the basis that they will be discharged in the normal course of business. The balance sheet shows creditors due after 12 months and creditors due in less than 12 months. Abandonment of the going concern basis would make them all payable immediately.

If financial statements are drawn up without the going concern basis then:

- All assets would be valued at net realisable values. Most would have much lower values than going concern values.

- All liabilities would be shown at the amount due. In addition to liabilities already identified additional ones might have to be provided for as a result of the possible closure of all or part of the operation of the business such as:

  - Redundancy pay;
  - Closure costs;
  - Losses on sales of assets;
  - Penalties and guarantees under contracts;
  - Claims from customers.

DIRECTORS' DUTIES

The directors should consider carefully whether the going concern basis is appropriate.

This does mean that they have to make a judgement about future events which are inherently uncertain, the question that arises is 'how far into the future do they need to look?'.

The answer to that depends on a number of factors. Firstly, they should consider the inherent risk in the business such as:

- The nature of the business. The future of a civil engineering contractor is inherently more uncertain than that of a food retailer.
- The riskiness of the company or its industry. A one-customer firm is more at risk than a firm with many customers; a highly geared company is more at risk than an all-equity one when interest rates are rising.
- External influences, for example, a change in legislation might increase costs to such an extent that the business becomes unviable.

Secondly, they should review their operations and consider the validity of the assumptions which underlie:

- forecast financial statements;
- budgets and strategic plans;
- cash flow forecasts.

Thirdly, they need to review the financing of the business, both currently and for the foreseeable future to ensure:

- That sufficient finance is available to continue current operations in the same way for the foreseeable future without the need for major refinancing.
- That finance is available for future plans or developments.

THE AUDITORS' PROCEDURES

The auditors, when forming an opinion as to whether financial statements give a true and fair view, should consider the entity's ability to continue as a going concern, and any relevant disclosures in the financial statements. The auditors should review the management's processes for establishing whether or not the entity is a going concern, over the same period the management have used, which has to be for more than *12 months* after the balance sheet date.

The auditors have to gather sufficient, appropriate evidence to satisfy themselves that the going concern basis is appropriate. This must be done in respect of all audits, no matter how viable the company appears to be. The auditors must be able to demonstrate that they have considered it.

This is particularly the case where a risk-based audit strategy is being adopted.

It is difficult to be comprehensive and auditors should adopt suitable procedures for each individual client in order to obtain the evidence they need but some possible procedures are:

- Assess the adequacy of the means by which the directors have satisfied themselves that the adoption of the going concern basis is appropriate.

- Examine all appropriate evidence, e.g. budgets, forecasts, minutes of meetings, etc.

- Assess the adequacy of the length of time into the future that the directors have looked. This may depend on the nature of the business, e.g. a company engaged in long-term contracting may require an assessment over a longer period than, say, a caravan manufacturer.

- Assess the systems or other means by which the directors have identified warnings of future risks and uncertainties.

- Examine budgets and other future plans and assess the reliability of such budgets by reference to past performance.

- Examine management accounts and other reports of recent activities.

- Consider the sensitivity of budgets and cash flow forecasts to variable factors both within the control of the directors (e.g. capital expenditure) and outside their control (e.g. interest rates or debt collection).

- Review any obligations, undertakings or guarantees arranged with other entities for the giving or receiving of support. Other entities may mean lenders, suppliers, customers or other companies in the same group. A UK company may be viable in itself but may have given guarantees to other members of the group and when, say, the holding company in Australia fails, the company goes down with it.

- Verify the existence, adequacy and terms of borrowing facilities and supplier credit and consider their adequacy.

- Consider the value of assets given as security for borrowings.

- Review correspondence with bankers either existing or proposed, particularly where facilities are coming up for renewal.

- Appraise the key assumptions underlying the budgets, forecasts and other information used by the directors.

- Assess the directors' plans for resolving any matters giving rise to concern (if any) about the appropriateness of the going concern basis. Such plans should be realistic, capable of resolving the doubts, and the directors should have firm intentions to put them into effect.

Finally the auditors should review all the information they have and all the audit evidence available and consider whether they can accept the going concern basis.

They should always have all their evidence and conclusions documented.

IF EVENTS ARE IDENTIFIED

If events are identified which cast doubt on the appropriateness of the going concern basis the onus is on the management to demonstrate to the auditors that they have identified the problem and have plans to deal with it.

The auditors must:

- Review the plans and consider their adequacy. If the auditors consider the plans inadequate and that the company is likely to fail they must consider an adverse opinion in their auditors report (see Chapter 27) if the directors will not amend the financial statements to reflect the loss of the going concern assumption.
- Consider if a material uncertainty exists (see Chapter 27) which might need to be brought to the attention of the shareholders.
- Seek written representations from management as to its plans and the expected outcome. This may not be sufficient, appropriate evidence of anything but the auditors need it. This must come from the top level of the company's management.
- If auditors are dealing with an actual or potentially insolvent subsidiary company they should look to the holding company for guarantees of continuing financial support – particularly where there is considerable inter-company indebtedness.

Clearly the auditors will need to carry out audit procedures in respect of these plans. They should consider:

- how realistic they are;
- the reactions of lenders or bankers;
- the effect on customers and suppliers;
- the effect on key members of staff;
- the consequences of any breaches of the terms of any lending and whether this will render any plans invalid.

EFFECT ON AUDIT REPORTS

We will look at this in more detail in Chapter 27 but for the moment the auditors have three scenarios:

- The going concern basis is valid but a material uncertainty exists – the auditor has to consider how well this is explained in the financial statements – this is an Emphasis of Matter.
- The auditors disagree with the directors approach to the financial statements or the disclosures in the accounts – this is an Adverse Opinion.
- The auditors have not been able to gather sufficient appropriate evidence in respect of the disclosures made in the accounts for some reason – this is a Limitation of Scope,

Look at Chapter 27 for the appropriate form of words.

Of course the auditors may agree with everything the directors have done and the financial statements may disclose everything properly, in which case the auditors will not need to modify their report at all.

One thing to bear in mind is that any qualification of a set of financial statements in respect of going concern is a very serious step. Indeed it may precipitate the very thing the company does not wish to happen if, as a result of the qualification, creditors or lenders take fright and financial support is withdrawn.

Summary

- Going concern is a major issue.
- ISA 570 is relevant to this subject.
- The definition of going concern is the assumption that the business will carry on its activities in the same way for the foreseeable future.
- Abandonment of the going concern basis means that assets will be valued at net realisable values and some additional liabilities might become payable, including redundancy pay and other costs arising from any closure.
- The directors have a duty to consider the going concern basis very carefully and make suitable enquiries.
- The auditors have a duty also to consider the going concern basis and review and seek audit evidence on the directors' own considerations and opinions.
- A major issue in many going concern basis doubts is borrowing facilities. If in doubt the auditors need to confirm these directly with the bank and form an opinion on the bank's attitude toward supporting the company.
- The time period which has to be reviewed for going concern basis is relevant. The length of the period clearly relates to the circumstances of the entity and the consequent risks. Directors should pay attention to a period of at least one year from the date of approval of the financial statements.
- There are numerous situations where going concern basis is an issue. Some of these are financial, some operational, and some external to the entity.
- The auditors will make no mention of going concern basis in their report if the company is clearly a going concern.
- If it clearly is not then an adverse opinion is called for if the financial statements are prepared on a going concern basis.
- If the financial statements are not prepared on a going concern basis, there are adequate explanations of the circumstances and the auditor concurs then an unqualified opinion is appropriate.
- The grey area is when there are doubts about going concern but the auditor still considers that the going concern basis gives a true and fair view. In such cases the notes to the accounts should give adequate explanations of the situation and the directors' assumptions. If they do so the auditors should include an explanatory paragraph in the opinion but not qualify their report. If the notes are inadequate then the auditor should qualify for disagreement.
- The going concern basis is one of the issues requiring mention in the Directors' Report on compliance with the Combined Code on Corporate Governance.

Points to note

- The going concern principle can be considered in relation to the enterprise as a whole or a part only. For example, if a branch were not a going concern, realisable value of assets would need to be substituted for book values and new liabilities may appear in respect of the branch.
- The probability that a going concern qualification of an auditor's report may bring about a receivership or liquidation is a very real problem to auditors who have doubts about a

client's future. The auditors must maintain their objectivity and should give their opinion without fear of the consequences to the client.

- The Combined Code on Corporate Governance requires the directors of listed companies to make a statement on going concern in the annual report and accounts. The auditor is required to review the statement.

Case Study

Pingo Manufacturing Ltd imports electronic components and assembles them in a factory to make consumer gadgets which appeal to a younger market. They have traded have traded successfully for many years because of favourable market conditions and extended their factory in 20x6 with the aid of a very large bank loan because they anticipated a further increase in sales as they brought some new products to the market.

The company has always been short of working capital as it paid for the components before they were delivered, in order to help the cash flow of their overseas suppliers, some of which were in developing countries. They also have a substantial overdraft which frequently exceeds the facility.

Sadly the expected increase in turnover never occurred because the market suddenly declined due to a credit squeeze and the fashion for buying fairly pointless gadgets came to a sudden slowdown.

The directors think they have enough core business selling television monitors and closed circuit TV cameras to see them through until the market turns up again, although they may have to reduce the scale of their operations.

Discussion

- What evidence would the directors have to produce to justify their opinion that the company is a going concern and how might the auditors validate the evidence?

Student self-testing questions

Questions with answers apparent from the text

a) Define the going concern basis.

b) List the consequences of the going concern basis.

c) List the directors' duties in respect of going concern basis.

d) List the auditors' procedures.

e) List the possible auditors' reports.

f) State the Combined Code requirements on going concern basis.

Examination question

1 You are planning the external audit of Steady Eddy Ltd (Steady Eddy) whose principal activity is the provision of road haulage services. You have been provided with the following information in respect of the year ended 31 May 20x7.

The company made a loss for the year to 31 May 20x7. This is mainly due to the loss of a major customer to a competitor and exceptional costs incurred in relocating to new premises. In previous years the company has been profitable but has recently experienced reduced margins due to the high cost of fuel.

Despite its poor trading results, the company has managed to stay within its overdraft limit of £500 000. This was achieved by the managing director temporarily lending the company £200 000 and delaying payments to creditors. The overdraft facility is to be reviewed by the bank in September 20x7 after the audited financial statements are available.

The company has a loan instalment falling due in October 20x7 which it plans to repay with the proceeds from the recently vacated premises which are currently for sale.

The company has fallen behind with its payments to HM Revenue & Customs, but the directors have successfully negotiated a scheme for settling the arrears over a period of four months. A condition of this concession granted by HM Revenue & Customs is that the company pays all its future monthly tax liabilities on the due dates.

The finance director is optimistic about the future and his profit forecasts indicate a return to profitability for the year ending 31 May 20x8. The company has recently negotiated a substantial contract with a national supermarket chain, which will generate at least £2 million in annual revenue for the next three years. In order to service the contract, the company will need to enlarge its fleet of refrigerated trailers and the finance director is negotiating with leasing companies to fund the acquisitions.

Required:

(a) Explain what is meant by the going concern concept and why the auditor should consider whether a company is a going concern.

(b) Explain the circumstances particular to Steady Eddy which may indicate that it is not a going concern.

(c) Identify the matters to which you would direct your attention during the subsequent events review, in the audit of Steady Eddy.

(ICAEW)

25

Management representations

INTRODUCTION

ISA 580 states:

> The auditor should obtain audit evidence the management acknowledges its responsibility for the fair presentation of the financial statements in accordance with the . . . financial reporting framework . . . .
>
> The auditor should obtain written representations from management on matters material to the financial statements when other sufficient appropriate evidence cannot reasonably be expected to exist.

In Chapter 11 we looked at the ways in which the auditors gather evidence to come to a conclusion on the truth and fairness of the financial statements prepared by the directors.

Wherever possible the auditors should:

- generate their own evidence through compliance and substantive testing, attending stock-takes, physically verifying assets, etc.;
- obtain third party evidence, e.g. debtors circularisation, bank confirmation letters;
- ask questions and raise points with management and staff on which they will receive verbal assurances and responses.

The Letter of Representation is a letter, written by the directors to the auditors which confirms, in writing, statements which the directors have made during the course of the audit about key aspects of the accounts.

CONTENTS OF A LETTER

The contents of the Letter of Representation *should not* include routine matters, for example, confirmation that all fixed assets exist and are the property of the company or that stock is valued at the lower of cost and net realisable value.

The letter *should* include matters which:

- are material to the financial statements; and
- for which the auditors cannot obtain independent corroborative evidence and thus have to rely on the directors as the primary source.

The letter will contain assurances from the directors such as:

- Acknowledgement of their responsibility for presentation of the financial statements.
- Acknowledgement of their responsibility for maintaining a system of internal control.
- Confirmation that the accounts are free from material errors or misstatements.
- Confirmation that there have been no material irregularities by management or staff.

The letter will also include reference to specific matters on which the auditors require confirmation of items included in the financial statements such as:

- Any subsequent events and their effect on the business.
- The basis of valuation of assets where reference is made in the financial statements to asset values.
- The basis of any provisions or estimates where corroboratory evidence is minimal and the directors are expressing an opinion or 'best guess'.
- Confirmations of compliance with regulatory authorities and of the terms of any contracts.

During the course of the audit there may be certain items for which the auditor is unable to find sufficient, appropriate evidence and so require specific written assurances from the management.

Examples of these are:

- A provision has been made for a future loss on a major contract based on the opinion of the directors and for which there is no supporting documentation.
- The directors state that a legal claim against the company has been settled and they anticipate no further claims for the issue involved.
- The directors consider the value of goodwill to be partially impaired and are writing down its value.

RELIANCE ON LETTER OF REPRESENTATION

In these circumstances there may be limited evidence to substantiate the figures shown in the financial statements. Consequently the auditors are reliant on the word of the directors as a form of evidence.

The auditors will request that the management provide them with a Letter of Representation to provide assurance as to the information given to them.

A written assurance is more reliable than a verbal assurance but it is important to realise that this is additional supporting evidence and is *not* a substitute for audit testing.

If a risk-based audit strategy is adopted this letter may assume a significance out of proportion to its value as evidence and it is important that auditors do not use it as a substitute for proper risk evaluation and audit testing.

EXAMPLE OF A MANAGEMENT REPRESENTATION LETTER

This is an example of a Letter of Representation. It is indicative only and every letter should be written to reflect the circumstances of a particular client and a particular audit.

WIBBLE plc
GRUB STREET
BIGTOWN
BG3 4 TT

Messrs Tickitt & Run
Addit Road
Bigtown
BG1 5ER

6 April 20x8

Dear Sirs

This letter is provided in connection with your audit of the financial statements of Wibble plc for the year ended 31 December 20x7 for the purposes of expressing an opinion as to whether the financial statements give a true and fair view of the financial position of Wibble plc as of 31 December 20x7 and of the results of its operations and its cash flows for the year then ended in accordance with the Companies Act 2006 and UK GAAP.

We confirm to the best of our knowledge and belief, and after having made enquiries of other directors and officials of the company, the following representations made to you in connection with your audit of the financial statements for the year ended 31 December 20x7.

1 We acknowledge, as directors, our responsibilities under the Companies Act 2006 for preparing the financial statements which show a true and fair view and for making accurate representations to you. We confirm that all the accounting records have been made available to you and all transactions made by the company have been recorded in those records. All other information and any related records, including minutes of directors' and management meetings, have been made available to you.

2 There have been no irregularities involving management or employees who have a significant role in internal control or that would have a material effect on the financial statements.

3 The financial statements are free of material misstatements including omissions.

4 The company has complied with all aspects of contractual agreements that could have a material effect on the financial statements in the event of non-compliance. There has been no non-compliance with requirements of regulatory authorities that could have a material effect on the financial statements in the event of non-compliance.

5 We have no plans or intentions that may materially affect the carrying value or classification of assets and liabilities recorded in the financial statements.

6 We have no plans to abandon lines of product or other plans or intentions that would result in any excess or obsolete inventory.

7 The company has a satisfactory title to all its assets and there are no liens or encumbrances on the company's assets except as disclosed in Note XX to the financial statements.

8 We have recorded or disclosed as appropriate all liabilities both actual and contingent.

9 Other than those disclosed in Note XX to the financial statements there have been no events since the balance sheet date which require adjustments of or disclosure in the financial statements.

10 In respect of specific matters:

- The legal claim against us by Hugo Faster plc has been settled out of court by a payment of £250 000. No further claims have been received.
- We confirm that the factory premises at Smalltown were properly valued by Messrs G Estimate & Co Chartered Surveyors and Valuers who are qualified to undertake this work. Their valuation of those premises on an open market existing use basis was £1.75 million which has been properly reflected in the accounts.
- The loan and overdraft facilities were renewed by the bank on 2 February 20x8 with no adjustments to the terms and conditions of the loans.
- The fire at the offices in Grub Street is not expected to cause any detriment to the trading capability of the business.

Signed on behalf of Wibble plc

_____   _____

Managing director   Financial director

Minuted by the board at their meeting on 6 June 20x8.

The letter should be:

- signed by the chief executive and/or financial director;
- approved and minuted at a board meeting at which, ideally, the auditor would be present.

In certain circumstances auditors might want separate written representations from particular directors or managers in respect of specific issues. For example, they may require confirmation that the minutes of meetings are complete from the person responsible for them.

REFUSAL TO CO-OPERATE

If there is a refusal by management to cooperate then the auditors should consider if they have obtained all the information and explanations they require in respect of all audit issues. If they have sufficient, appropriate evidence they may be able to dispense with a letter. However, they should consider the effect of the management's refusal to supply such a letter in their estimate of audit risk and on their future relationship with the client.

If they do not have sufficient, appropriate evidence and require the letter to support their audit opinion they may have to consider a qualification of the auditors' report on the grounds of limitation of scope.

Summary

- A letter of representation is a letter from the management to the auditor confirming, in writing, opinions conveyed to the auditor orally.
- It is obtained on the occasion of each audit.
- ISA 580 governs this subject.
- The letter should contain only matters which are material and for which the auditor cannot obtain corroborating evidence.
- The principal items will be matters of which management alone have knowledge and matters of judgement and opinion.
- The letter should also contain the directors' acknowledgement for their responsibilities under the Companies Act 2006 for preparing financial statements which give a true and fair view.
- Ideally the representation letter should be dated the same day as the directors formally approve the accounts.

Points to note

- The letter of representation is a form of audit evidence but not, of course, the only form or even a very reliable form. Thus, the auditor cannot rely on the letter of representation to save carrying out audit work.
- The letter is used only on the restricted number of matters discussed in this chapter.
- It is advisable for the auditors to ascertain that the persons responsible for the letter should fully understand what it is that they are being asked to confirm and why.

Case Study

Tickitt & Run are auditors of the Zombrit Group PLC. The accounts for the year ending 31.12..20x7 are being subjected to the final review. The following matters have been noted by the audit manager:

a. The company has engaged in a number of long-term contracts in the Far East. During the last few years a minority of these have sustained losses. Work in progress at 31.12.20x7 includes a substantial amount of these contracts. Some are valued at cost and some include attributable profit.
    One contract has been valued with a provision for ultimate loss.
b. The group has set up a subsidiary in Africa to manufacture motor parts for sale in that country. The group have lent this subsidiary material amounts but so far production difficulties, political problems and difficulties in finding adequate markets have plagued the project. All assets acquired by the subsidiary have been valued at cost.
c. The group have a property in Milton Keynes which they used as the regional headquarters.

This office has been closed and the staff transferred, with considerable opposition, to London. The property has been let to another company on a two year lease and has been treated in the accounts as an investment property.

d. The company have a project to manufacture and sell a range of video conferencing equipment as a package. Production should commence in 20-7. All expenditure so far has been treated as development costs as although prototype packs have been assembled they are not yet in production.

Discussion

- Identify the matters connected with these items which the auditor may include in a letter of representation.

Student self-testing questions

Questions with answers apparent from the text

a) Why should a letter of representation be obtained?

b) What kind of matter should be included in a letter of representation?

c) What should the auditor do if the client refuses to give one?

Examination questions

(a) Explain the purpose of a management representation letter.

(b) You are the manager in charge of the audit of Crighton-Ward, a public limited liability company which manufactures specialist cars and other motor vehicles for use in films. Audited turnover is $140 million with profit before tax of $7·5 million.

  All audit work up to, but not including, the obtaining of management representations has been completed. A review of the audit file has disclosed the following outstanding points:

Lion's Roar

  The company is facing a potential legal claim from the Lion's Roar company in respect of a defective vehicle that was supplied for one of their films. Lion's Roar maintains that the vehicle was not built strongly enough whilst the directors of Crighton-Ward argue that the specification was not sufficiently detailed. Dropping a vehicle 50 metres into a river and expecting it to continue to remain in working condition would be unusual, but this is what Lion's Roar expected. Solicitors are unable to determine liability at the present time. A claim for $4 million being the cost of a replacement vehicle and lost production time has been received by Crighton-Ward from Lion's Roar. The director's opinion is that the claim is not justified.

Depreciation

  Depreciation of specialist production equipment has been included in the financial statements at the amount of 10 per cent per annum based on reducing balance. However, the treatment is consistent with prior accounting periods (which received an unmodified auditor's report) and other companies in the same industry and sales of old equipment show negligible profit or loss on sale. The audit senior, who is new to the audit, feels that depreciation is being undercharged in the financial statements.

Required:

For each of the above matters:

    (i) discuss whether or not a paragraph is required in the representation letter; and

    (ii) *if appropriate*, draft the paragraph for inclusion in the representation letter.

(c) A suggested format for the letter of representation has been sent by the auditors to the directors of Crighton-Ward.

     The directors have stated that they will not sign the letter of representation this year on the grounds that they believe the additional evidence that it provides is not required by the auditor.

Required:

Discuss the actions the auditor may take as a result of the decision made by the directors not to sign the letter of representation.

(ACCA)

26

The final review stage of the audit

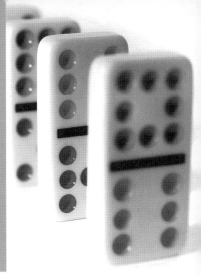

INTRODUCTION

At the end of the detailed work of the audit, auditors should make an overall review of the financial statements before preparing their report. The review should be sufficiently detailed to enable the auditors, using the conclusions drawn from the audit evidence obtained during the course of their audit work, to develop a reasonable basis for their audit opinion on the financial statements.

The auditors need to determine if the financial statements, as a whole, tell a consistent and logical story about the financial results of the organisation for the reporting period.

The final review assists in this determination. The review of the financial statements should be carried out by a suitably experienced manager. The ultimate review should be carried out by the audit partner who has responsibility for the audit opinion.

FINAL ACCOUNTS

The auditors need to ensure that:

- The financial statements use acceptable accounting policies, which have been applied consistently and are appropriate to the business.
- The results of operations (profit and loss account), state of affairs (balance sheet) and all other information included in the financial statements are compatible with each other and with the auditors' knowledge of the enterprise and the evidence gathered during the course of the audit work.
- There is adequate disclosure of all appropriate matters and the information contained in the financial statements is suitably classified and presented— for example, short-term loans should not be included in long-term finance liabilities.
- There is compliance with statutory requirements, for example, the Companies Act 2006.
- There is compliance with other relevant regulations, for example, the Combined Code.
- There is compliance with accounting standards, for example, IAS 1 *Presentation of Financial Statements*.

Most auditors will use checklists to:

- facilitate the review – to ensure nothing is missed inadvertently;
- evidence the fact a final review has been carried out.

PROCEDURES

The following set of procedures should be adopted for the final review:

Accounting policies

Review all accounting policies and, in particular, consider if they:

- are in accordance with Generally Accepted Accounting Principles (GAAP) and comply with the fundamental accounting concepts – going concern, accruals, consistency and prudence;
- conform to the substance over form convention – management may well have an interest in using accounting rules to help them disclose, or not disclose, information in as favourable a light as possible. Auditors need to balance the need to tell the true story ('true and fair') to the shareholders against the need to overrule an accounting standard so the substance of transactions are disclosed and not merely their form (see Chapter 2);
- are acceptable to the particular circumstances;
- are commonly adopted in the particular industry;
- are consistently applied over the years;
- are consistently applied throughout the enterprise;
- comply with all relevant accounting standards.

The results for the period

- Consider whether the accounts are consistent with the auditor's knowledge of the underlying circumstances of the business and the information, explanations and conclusions reached on the audit.
- Review the information in the accounts to determine if there are any abnormalities or inconsistencies. Background knowledge of the company is clearly essential for this.
- Carry out an analytical review of the financial statements including comparisons with previous periods, etc. For example, gross profit ratios or liquidity ratios should be consistent with previous financial periods. Suitable benchmark data could also be used if possible.
- Consider whether:
  - individual amounts shown in the accounts are compatible with each other and with comparative figures;
  - they are consistent with previously reported management information, e.g. accounts, budgets, etc.

Audit evidence

- Review the audit planning to ensure that it was properly carried out and that audit procedures were designed to produce sufficient, appropriate evidence to support the audit opinion.

- Review all audit working papers to ensure that:

    - all audit procedures set out in the audit programme were carried out as required;
    - the results of those audit procedures were reviewed and the conclusions reached based on the audit checking work done are valid.

- Review any points arising from the audit work and confirm whether or not they have been settled satisfactorily with management.

- Consider whether or not the going concern basis is appropriate based on the evidence gathered.

- Consider whether all necessary representations required from management have been received and properly minuted (see Chapter 25) and whether they comprise sufficient, appropriate audit evidence to support the audit opinion where no corroborative evidence is available.

- Ensure all representations and evidence required from third parties, e.g. bank letters, solicitors' letters, etc. have been received and are appropriate.

- Review the outcome of the subsequent events review and ensure all outstanding issues have been cleared.

- Decide if the amount of audit work carried out and the evidence gathered as a result of that work is sufficient to support the audit opinion.

- Consider whether a second partner or 'hot' review is required before signing the auditors' report.

Presentation and disclosure

- Consider if any conclusion that a reader might draw from a reading of the accounts would be justified and is consistent with the circumstances of the enterprise.

- Consider if the review has indicated that there are new factors which might alter the policies used or the presentation of the accounts, and special attention needs to be paid to any going concern issues.

- Consider if all matters of importance have been disclosed by way of note if not by inclusion in the financial statements.

- Consider the form of the auditors' report and whether any qualification is required.

Summary

- The final review is the last chance the auditors have to consider any issues arising from the audit before their report is signed.
- The review should be carried out and evidenced on the file.
- The final review should be carried out by the audit partner responsible for signing the auditors' report.
- The final review may reveal:

  - That all is well.
  - That further audit evidence may be required in some areas.
  - That amendment to the accounts may be desirable. The client should be requested to make any such amendment.
  - That a qualified audit report may be required.

- The overall review of the financial statements is concerned with:

  - Accounting policies.
  - That the results, etc. are compatible with each other and with the auditor's knowledge of the enterprise.
  - Disclosure and compliance with statutory and other regulations.
  - What type of opinion, if any, can be given.

Points to note

- The final review is particularly important as the shareholders are not the only users of the financial statements and consideration has to be given to overall disclosure.
- The detail is still important but emphasis must be on the view given by the accounts which must be true in detail and fair in totality.

Case Study

Angela Goodbody is a partner in Tickitt & Run and has come to the audit of E-musica Ltd to carry out a hot review of the audit which is in progress for the year ended 31 March 20x8.

E-musica have their own record label for dance and rap music, they sell musical equipment, and control three recording studios.

She has noted comments on the audit file to the effect that:

(a) Stock of CDs is valued at the lower of cost and net realisable value. Cost includes production overheads based on a global labour hour rate based on output in 20-7. Unsold stocks of CDs from before 31 March 20x6 are written down to £1.

(b) Advances to bands are written off as they are paid.

(c) Equipment is written off on the straight line basis over ten years.

(d) The freehold property is amortised over 30 years.

She has also noted that:

(a) The directors' report is optimistic about the current year and future year's success in selling dance and rap music despite the revival in live artistes in which E-musica have no representation. They do not consider themselves a niche label, insisting that dance music is still mainstream.

(b) Stock appears simply as Stocks £120 000.

(c) The company rents out a leasehold property it owns but has no use for. The notes to the accounts say 'gross rental income £4900.'

(d) No mention is made of the entry into liquidation on 13.3 x8 of a wholesale music distributor who owed E-musica £142 000 on 13.3.x8 and £71 000 on 31.12.x7. Angela knows of the liquidation as her boss is the liquidator.

(e) No mention is made of an action against a group for breach of copyright. The action was commenced on 31.3.x7 and already uncharged legal fees of about £10 000 have been incurred.

(f) The list of directors shows 14 names and the remuneration breakdown only 13.

(g) The directors' report shows that Joe Gigli, a director, has 1000 shares in the company. She happened to note that the dividend paid to him indicated a shareholding substantially greater than that.

Discussion
– What should Angela do about these matters?

Student self-testing questions

Questions with answers apparent from the text

a) What actions may be required as a result of a final review?

b) Distinguish analytical review from overall review of financial statements.

c) Why is it necessary to carry out a final review?

d) At what other stages of the audit are analytical procedures performed?

e) Distinguish between a hot review and a cold review.

f) Who would carry out a hot review and when?

g) List the necessary procedures which would take place at a final review.

Examination questions

Your firm is the external auditor of Octavia Ltd (Octavia). The team conducting the audit for the year ended 31 December 20x7 has recently returned to the office following completion of the audit fieldwork. You are conducting your final review procedures. The audit file contains the following relevant information:

(i) Historically, Octavia's core business has been the manufacture of cast iron railings for supply to the construction industry. Over recent years Octavia has also developed a growing customer base for the manufacture of specialist cast metal products, an area where the company has established a recognised niche market.

In its core business, Octavia has seen its revenues decline by 30 per cent and its gross profit margins worsen over the last five years. These effects have been caused by increasing competition from overseas competitors who have lower operating costs. This has resulted in trading losses for Octavia in recent years, including the year ended 31 December 20x7.

Octavia underwent a major factory reorganisation during the year to enable it to diversify its activities away from its core business and concentrate on its specialist cast metal business. This reorganisation, which was completed in November 2007, was partly funded by a large bank loan. The profit and cash-flow forecasts prepared by the company to support the application for bank finance indicated a return to profitability for the year ending 31 December 2008.

(ii) During the year one of Octavia's major customers went into liquidation. Octavia has presented a claim to the customer's liquidator both for recovery of the outstanding debt, and for the return of product which was supplied to the customer on a sale or return basis. Octavia has negotiated a sale of the returned product to another of its customers, dependent upon the successful recovery from the liquidator of the product in question. Initial indications from the liquidator are that 50 per cent of the outstanding debt is likely to be recovered by Octavia. The liquidator is also pursuing the recovery of the sale or return product on Octavia's behalf.

Octavia has included the receipt of this proportion of the debt, and the sale of the returned product to its alternative customer, within its cash-flow forecast.

(iii) Shortly before 31 December 2007 the company's solicitors notified the company of an action being brought by a former employee who suffered a serious injury from an accident which occurred whilst operating heavy machinery in Octavia's factory. The former employee claims that the company did not have the necessary health and safety procedures in place to ensure that such an accident could not occur. The former employee is pressing for at least £750 000 in damages, an amount which is material to the financial statements of the company.

The directors of Octavia are adamant that the accident occurred due to the employee's own negligence, and they maintain that their health and safety procedures are of an excellent standard. Octavia has to date had an exemplary accident record and previous health and safety inspections have raised no material issues. Octavia's solicitors have told the directors that the case is unlikely to come to court for at least 18 months. The company's insurance policy provides an element of cover for such situations. For these reasons the directors have not provided for the claim in the financial statements. However, a reference to the action has been made in the notes to the financial statements.
Required:

(a) Briefly set out the reasons why work performed by audit staff during an audit is reviewed by other more senior staff or the engagement partner.

(b) Identify the matters to which you would direct your attention during the subsequent events review, in the audit of Octavia.

(c) Comment on the treatment in the financial statements of the matter referred to in (iii) above and indicate, with reasons, what kind of audit report modification, if any, may be appropriate.

(ICAEW)

27

Auditors' reports to shareholders

INTRODUCTION

ISA 700 'The Auditor's Report on Financial Statements' states:

> *The auditor's report should contain a clear written expression of opinion on the financial statements taken as a whole.*

The auditors' primary task is to report to the shareholders on the truth and fairness of the financial statements prepared by the directors.

Having gathered all the necessary audit evidence and reviewed events since the balance sheet date the auditors are now in a position to come to an opinion on the Financial Statements.

The audit opinion can either be:

- an unqualified opinion;
- a qualified or modified opinion.

If the auditors' opinion is that the accounts *do not* give a true and fair, or that something has prevented them from forming an opinion on all or part of the financial statements, the client will receive a *modified* audit report.

There are a number of different types of modified audit report that we will look at later, but first we will look in more detail at the contents of an unqualified auditors' report.

The student, and indeed the practising auditor, should be familiar with:

- the form and content of an unqualified report;
- when a modified audit report is appropriate and what form the wording would take.

CONTENTS OF AN AUDITORS' REPORT

The auditors' report to the shareholders is a detailed document which should leave the reader in no doubt as to the way in which the audit has been carried out and the reasoning behind the opinion that has been reached.

Note that the company's Annual Report often contains, in addition to the financial statements and the Auditor's Report, some additional statements such as:

- a Chairman's Statement;
- a five-year review;
- a trading review of the year.

The auditors *don't* have to report on these and will specifically exclude them from their report. Auditors do, however, have to ensure that, where figures or similar references are quoted in these parts of an Annual Report they are consistent with the financial statements.

The table below sets out what an unqualified report contains together with the form of words.

The wording has been based on a suggested report issued by the Auditing Practices Board.

Remember that, for examination purposes, students are unlikely to have to remember the precise form of words, but they should be familiar with what is included in an auditor's report.

Contents of the auditor's report	Sample wording
A clear heading including the word 'independent'	*'Independent auditors' report'*
It should be addressed to the shareholders	*'to the shareholders of XYZ Ltd'*
It should set out what is comprised in the financial statements, i.e. what has been audited	*'We have audited the financial statements of . . . for the year ended . . . which comprise the profit and loss account, the balance sheet the cash flow statement and the statement of recognised gains and losses and the related notes'*
It explains the basis on which the accounts have been prepared	*'The accounts have been prepared under the accounting policies set out therein. (Note: For small companies this section would also include reference to the Financial Reporting Standard for Smaller Entities (FRSSE))'*
The responsibilities of the directors should be set out	*'The directors' responsibilities for preparing the Annual Report and the financial statements in accordance with applicable law and United Kingdom Accounting Standards are set out in the Statement of Directors' Responsibilities*
It sets out the responsibilities of the auditors	*'Our responsibility is to audit the financial statements in accordance with relevant legal and regulatory requirements and International Standards on Auditing*
	(Note: The auditors might include a disclaimer here to the effect that they are only reporting to the shareholders and accept no responsibility towards any third party. See Chapter 31 Auditors' Liability)
It explains what the primary purpose of their report is	*'We report to you as to whether the financial statements give a true and fair view and are properly prepared in accordance with the Companies Act 2006'*

Contents of the auditor's report	Sample wording
And what the secondary purpose of their report is	'We also report to you if, in our opinion, the Directors Report is not consistent with the financial statements, if the company has not kept proper accounting records, if we have not received all the information and explanations we require for our audit or if information specified by law regarding directors' remuneration and other transactions is not disclosed'
It comments on the parts of the financial statements not covered by the audit	'We read other information contained in the annual report and consider whether it is consistent with the audited financial statements.' (Followed by a statement of what the 'other information' is – see above)
	We consider the implications for our report if we become aware of any apparent misstatement or material inconsistencies with the financial statements
A clear statement of where the auditor's responsibility ends	Our responsibilities do not extend to any other information'
It sets out the basis of the audit opinion, i.e. how was the work carried out in order to provide evidence for the opinion	We conducted our audit in accordance with International Standards on Auditing issued by the Auditing Practices Board
	An audit includes examination, on a test basis, of evidence relevant to the amounts and disclosures in the financial statements
	It also includes an assessment of the significant estimates and judgements made by the directors in the preparation of the financial statements and of whether the accounting policies are appropriate to the company's circumstances, are consistently applied and adequately disclosed
It includes a statement about the level of evidence required, i.e. enough to give 'reasonable assurance'	We planned and performed our audit so as to obtain all the information and explanations which we considered necessary in order to provide us with sufficient appropriate evidence to give reasonable assurance that the financial statements are free from material misstatement, whether caused by fraud or other irregularity or error. In forming our opinion we also evaluated the overall adequacy of the presentation of information in the financial statements
It gives the auditors opinion (in this case an unqualified one)	'In our opinion • the financial statements give a true and fair view, in accordance with United Kingdom Generally Accepted Accounting Practice, of the state of the company's affairs as at . . . and of its profit (or loss) for the year then ended, and • the financial statements [and that part of the Directors' Remuneration Report to be audited*] have been properly prepared in accordance with the Companies Act 2006'

Contents of the auditor's report	Sample wording
It makes reference to the Director's Report	*The information given in the Directors' Report is consistent with the Financial Statements*
It needs a name and a date	*ABC & Co* *Registered Auditors* *1 May 200X*

Note – applies only to listed companies – see below.

WHEN IS AN UNQUALIFIED REPORT APPROPRIATE?

As you have seen from the sample wording above an unqualified report says:
  In our opinion

- *the financial statements give a true and fair view, in accordance with United Kingdom Generally Accepted Accounting Practice, of the state of the company's affairs as at . . . and of its profit (or loss) for the year then ended, and*
- *the financial statements have been properly prepared in accordance with the Companies Act 2006*

  What this means is that:

- the auditors agree that proper accounting records have been kept and proper returns have been made from any branches they haven't visited;
- the financial statements agree with the underlying accounting records and returns;
- all information and explanations they needed have been received from the staff and the directors and managers;
- the auditors have had unrestricted access to the books and records;
- details of all transactions involving the directors have been correctly disclosed;
- there are no material errors or misstatements in the accounts.

  In other words the audit has been completed satisfactorily and the auditors have been able to gather all the evidence they need to support their unqualified opinion.
  If however, there is:

- a difference of opinion between the directors and the auditors about something in the financial statements; or
- the auditors have had problems gathering the evidence they need,

the auditors may have to issue a qualified audit report.

QUALIFIED AUDIT REPORTS

Under ISA 700 '*The Auditor's Report on Financial Statements*' the auditors report is considered to be modified in the following situations . . .

- a qualified opinion;
- a disclaimer of opinion;
- an adverse opinion.

We will look at each of these in turn.

For simplicity, and because students will not be asked to write an Auditors' Report, we have confined the examples to the significant areas where auditors might issue a modified report, including going concern issues. We have included some sample wording to illustrate how a modified Audit Report might be drafted.

Firstly, it is important that you understand that auditors do not have the power to insist that the financial statements are amended for any errors or omissions that have been found during the course of the audit.

The financial statements are the responsibility of the directors and the auditors have no authority to overrule them when it comes to the content.

What the auditors can do is use their Auditors' Report to tell the shareholders of the company what they have discovered and to express their opinion on the truth and fairness of the financial statements.

EFFECT OF A QUALIFIED AUDIT REPORT

Auditors' generally feel that modifying their report is a last resort.

In practice they will discuss these issues with the client's management at some length in order to avoid having to issue a modified report. In most cases the directors are prepared to adjust the financial statements for any material errors and omissions which the auditors have brought to their attention, as they are keen for the accounts to be accurate.

They will also be aware that a modified report can have serious consequences for the company:

- it could affect the shareholders confidence in the company and its management;
- it could discourage potential investors;
- it could affect the willingness of lenders to continue offering a facility to the company;
- it could affect the company's creditworthiness with its suppliers.

However, if the auditors feel that a modified opinion is appropriate they must be able to justify the basis for the qualification and fully explain this in the audit report.

ISSUING MODIFIED AUDIT REPORTS

Where the auditors have serious doubts about the truth and fairness of the financial statements or have been prevented from carrying out their work to its full extent they must consider issuing a modified audit report.

The auditors must use their professional judgement to decide how serious the issues involved are. This will then influence precisely which form of qualification will be included in the audit report.

What they have to decide is how seriously the issue, or issues, affect the truth and fairness of the financial statements. If the issue is so significant that the accounts presented by the directors clearly do not show a true and fair view then the issue is said to be 'pervasive'.

If, however, the issue is not detrimental to the accounts as a whole, but affects only part of them it is said to be '*material but not pervasive*'. Clearly any issue which has such an effect on the accounts will be material, but in this case only part of the accounts are affected and the rest will be 'true and fair'.

The three situations which give rise to the types of qualification above are:

Qualified 'except for' opinion

The issue is material but not to the extent that the financial statements no longer give a true and fair view. In this case the issue is not so pervasive or material so as to require the auditors to disclaim an opinion or to gave an adverse opinion but does require the auditor to draw the attention of readers of the accounts to the issue which they have been unable to resolve.

Note that a minor limitation of scope can result in an 'except for' opinion. This form of words is used in most cases except where the auditors consider that the financial statements are fundamentally flawed or where they cannot evidence their report to a significant extent.

The auditors may have more than one issue which, individually, might result in an 'except for' qualification. If this is the case they must consider whether, collectively, the issues become pervasive enough for the auditors either to decline to express an opinion or to issue an adverse opinion.

Disclaimer of opinion

The auditors' work has been limited either by the management or by lack of opportunity so they were not able to gather all the evidence they require. This is known as a *limitation of scope.*

In order to issue a disclaimer the auditors must have been unable to gather sufficient, appropriate evidence in order to support their opinion, either of the financial statements as a whole or of such a material or fundamental part of the financial statements, that to issue any other opinion would be unsupportable.

Adverse opinion

The issue is so material, involving significant uncertainties or lack of disclosure that it affects the truth and fairness of the financial statements as a whole.

Note that the auditors must make all reasonable efforts to find the evidence they need before issuing a modified report. This will include discussing the situation with directors and staff and seeking all alternative means to gather evidence suitable for their purposes. A modified audit report is very much a last resort.

Here is a table summarising the options:

Audit Issue	Pervasive	Material but not pervasive
Disagreement	Adverse opinion	Except for
Limitation of scope	Disclaimer of opinion	Except for

This table gives some examples of situations where each type of report might be issued:

Wording of report	Example of situation where it might apply
'Except for' – issues are material but not pervasive	• Inadequate provision for doubtful debts • Disagreement over the value of some part of stocks, e.g. obsolete stocks still valued at cost instead of scrap value • Non-disclosure in the accounts of going concern problems
'Except for' – limitation of scope	• Limited evidence available for cash purchases • Some cash sales records lost due to accidental flooding • Cash flow statements only prepared for nine months after the year end so full consideration of going concern issues not possible
Disclaimer of opinion – limitation of scope	• Appointed as auditors after year end and unable to attend stocktaking where stock is material item • Directors deny access to information regarding significant claims against the company • No cash flow forecasts or cash budgets prepared so the going concern situation cannot be considered
Adverse opinion	• Failure to comply with Companies Act 2006, accounting standards or UK GAAP without an acceptable reason • Significant uncertainties regarding the existence, ownership valuation or recording of assets and liabilities to a material extent, e.g. failure to provide for material losses on long-term contracts • Significant concern about the company's ability to continue as a going concern and the accounts have been prepared on a going concern basis

WORDING MODIFIED AUDITORS' REPORTS

The wording of auditors' reports must be as clear and precise as possible ensuring that the reader is in no doubt as to why a qualification has been necessary.

Whatever the basis of their qualification the auditors should always:

• explain the facts of the disagreement;
• detail the implications to the financial statements;
• where possible quantify the financial effect.

ISA 700, and the bulletins issued by the APB, offer a range of alternative reports, but for simplicity we have only included one example of each type of qualification so you can see how auditors express these qualifications formally.

In each of the reports below we have and extracted the wording from some sample auditors report to illustrate the different forms of qualification. Key words and phrases have been **made bold** to make them clearer.

'EXCEPT FOR' QUALIFICATIONS

If the issue is material but not pervasive the auditors will use an 'except for' qualification.

Basically, the auditors are saying that the financial statements give a true and fair view, *except* for the matters in dispute.

Here are four examples of wording of Auditors' Reports in the following situations.

A 'Except for' report arising from a disagreement which is material but not pervasive.

B 'Except for' report arising from a limitation of scope which is material but not pervasive.

C Adverse opinion – a fundamental disagreement which is pervasive.

D Disagreement – limitation of scope which is pervasive.

A) 'Except for' report material but not pervasive – disagreement

Example of an 'except for' qualification caused by a disagreement which is material but not pervasive.

Independent auditors report to the members of XYZ Limited

(Extract)

Basis of audit opinion

We planned and performed our audit so as to obtain all the information and explanations which we considered necessary in order to provide us with sufficient evidence to give reasonable assurance that the financial statements are free from material misstatement, whether caused by fraud or other irregularity or error. In forming our opinion we also evaluated the overall adequacy of the presentation of information in the financial statements.

Included in debtors is an amount of £1 million due from a company which has ceased trading. In our opinion the company is unlikely to receive any payment and full provision should have been made for this debt, reducing the profit before taxation and net assets by that amount.

Qualified opinion arising from disagreement about accounting treatment.

Except for the absence of this provision in our opinion:

- the financial statements give a true and fair view, in accordance with United Kingdom Generally Accepted Accounting Practice, of the state of the company's affairs as at ... and of its profit (or loss) for the year then ended; and

- the financial statements have been properly prepared in accordance with the Companies Act 2006;

- the information given in the Directors' Report is consistent with the Financial Statements.

Registered Auditors

Date   Address

B) 'Except for' report arising from a limitation of scope which is material but not pervasive

Example of an 'except for' qualification caused by limitation of scope:

Independent auditors report to the members of XYZ Limited

(Extract)

Basis of audit opinion

We conducted our audit in accordance with International Standards on Auditing issued by the Auditing Practices Board, **except the scope of our audit work was limited, as explained below.**

An audit includes examination on a test basis of evidence relevant to the amounts and disclosures in the financial statements.

It also includes an assessment of the significant estimates and judgements made by the directors in the preparation of the financial statements and of whether the accounting policies are appropriate to the company's circumstances, consistently applied and adequately disclosed.

We planned (**delete the words 'and performed'**) our audit so as to obtain all the information and explanations which we considered necessary in order to provide us with sufficient evidence to give reasonable assurance that the financial statements are free from material misstatement, whether caused by fraud or other irregularity or error.

However, the evidence available to us was limited because £x of the company's purchases of string were paid for in cash without adequate documentation. There was no system of control over these payments on which we could rely for the purposes of our audit. There were no audit procedures we could adopt to confirm that these purchases were properly recorded.

In forming our opinion we also evaluated the overall adequacy of the presentation of information in the financial statements.

Qualified opinion arising from limitation in audit scope

Except for the financial effects of any adjustments as might have been necessary had we been able to obtain sufficient evidence concerning these purchases in our opinion:

- the financial statements give a true and fair view, in accordance with United Kingdom Generally Accepted Accounting Practice, of the state of the company's affairs as at . . . and of its profit (or loss) for the year then ended; and

- the financial statements have been properly prepared in accordance with the Companies Act 2006.

- The information given in the Directors' Report is consistent with the Financial Statements.

Registered Auditors

Date   Address

C) Adverse opinion arising from a fundamental disagreement which is pervasive

If the auditors feel that the items they are in dispute with the directors about are so serious that they mean that the financial statements are misleading they must issue an adverse opinion.

This says that that 'the financial statements *do not* give a true and fair view'.

Here is an example of an adverse opinion:

Independent auditors report to the members of XYZ Limited

(Extract)

Basis of audit opinion:

We planned and performed our audit so as to obtain all the information and explanations which we considered necessary in order to provide us with sufficient evidence to give reasonable assurance that the financial statements are free from material misstatement, whether caused by fraud or other irregularity or error. In forming our opinion we also evaluated the overall adequacy of the presentation of information in the financial statements.

As explained in Note 13 no provision has been made for losses expected to arise on certain long-term contracts currently in progress. In our opinion provision should be made for foreseeable losses on individual contracts as required by Statement of Standard Accounting Practice No 9. If a provision for such losses had been made the effect would have been to reduce the profit before taxation and the net assets by £10 million.

Should the losses on these contracts materialise there is significant doubt as to whether the company will be able to continue as a going concern in the foreseeable future. This issue has not been addressed by the directors and the financial statements have been prepared on a going concern basis which may not be appropriate.

Adverse opinion

In view of the failure to provide for losses referred to above and to consider the effects of those losses on the future position of the company, in our opinion the financial statements **do not** give a true and fair view, in accordance with United Kingdom Generally Accepted Accounting Practice, of the state of affairs as at and of its profit (loss) for the year then ended.

In all other respects, in our opinion the financial statements have been properly prepared in accordance with the Companies Act 2006.

Registered Auditors

Date

Address

As you can see in this case, although the auditors only had an issue with one aspect of the accounts, the effect of that was so significant that failure to mention it would completely mislead anyone reading the financial statements.

D) Disclaimer of opinion arising from limitation of scope which is pervasive

If the scope of their work has been so limited that the auditors have been unable to carry out sufficient audit testing to the extent that they are unable to form a view on the financial statements they must issue a disclaimer of opinion.

This basically says: 'we can't express an opinion because the scope of our work has been so restricted'.

Here is an example of a disclaimer:

Independent auditors report to the members of XYZ Limited

(Extract)

Basis of audit opinion

We conducted our audit in accordance with International Standards on Auditing issued by the Auditing Practices Board, **except the scope of our audit work was limited, as explained below.**

An audit includes examination on a test basis of evidence relevant to the amounts and disclosures in the financial statements.

It also includes an assessment of the significant estimates and judgements made by the directors in the preparation of the financial statements and of whether the accounting policies are appropriate to the company's circumstances, consistently applied and adequately disclosed.

We planned (**delete the words 'and performed'**) our audit so as to obtain all the information and explanations which we considered necessary in order to provide us with sufficient evidence to give reasonable assurance that the financial statements are free from material misstatement, whether caused by fraud or other irregularity or error.

However, the evidence available to us was limited because we were not able to observe all physical stock and confirm trade debtors due to limitations placed on our work by the company. As a result of this and in the absence of any satisfactory alternative procedures we have been unable to perform our necessary audit procedures on both physical stock and trade debtors. Because of the significance of these items we have been unable to form a view on the financial statements.

In forming our opinion we also evaluated the overall adequacy of the presentation of information in the financial statements.

Opinion: disclaimer on view given by financial statements

Because of the possible effect of the limitation in evidence available to us we are unable to form an opinion as to whether:

- the financial statements give a true and fair view, in accordance with United Kingdom Generally Accepted Accounting Practice, of the state of the company's affairs as at . . . and of its profit (or loss) for the year then ended; and

- the financial statements have been properly prepared in accordance with the Companies Act 2006;

- the information given in the Directors' Report is consistent with the Financial Statements.

> In respect alone of the limitation of our work referred to above:
>
> - we have not obtained all the information and explanations that we considered necessary for the purpose of our audit; and
> - we were unable to determine whether proper accounting records were maintained.
>
> Registered Auditors
>
> Date   Address

In this case the auditors have an issue with two aspects of the accounts which, together, were so significant, or pervasive, that they affected the audit opinion on the accounts as a whole.

LISTED COMPANIES – SPECIAL PROVISIONS

There are particular situations which apply only to companies listed on the London Stock Exchange.

- The auditors are required to comment on the disclosures made in the Directors' Remuneration Report. They will include in their Auditors' Report a reference to this, so that the second paragraph of their opinion is modified to read:

> 'The financial statements and the part of the Directors' Remuneration Report to be audited have been properly prepared in accordance with the Companies Act 2006.'

- All companies whose shares are listed are required to comply with the Combined Code on Corporate Governance (see Chapter 2), or explain in the financial statements why they haven't complied. This is part of the Listing Rules.

  If, in the opinion of the auditors, the company hasn't complied, and furthermore has not given any reason for the non-compliance in the financial statements, the auditors will comment on the non-compliance and non-disclosure in their Auditors' Report. Note that in these cases the auditors only report negatively; that is they only comment is some provision has **not** been complied with. If they make no comment then the reader should assume all is well.

Example

Assuming only that the Listing Rules have not been complied with, the auditor will add, immediately after the opinion section.

Other matter

The Listing Rules of the London Stock Exchange require us to report any instances when the company has not complied with certain of the disclosure requirements set out in the

Rules. In this connection we report that in our opinion, the company has not complied with the requirements of paragraph 12.43A(c)(ix)(b)(ii) of those Rules because the Board's Report on Directors' Remuneration does not disclose the right of Jane Doe to receive a commission based on the Toytown contract achieving its target profits in 20X9.

- As part of the Listing Rules the directors are also required to review the internal control environment and include a statement on their review as part of the accounts.

  If the review reveals some non-compliance, again, the auditors do not qualify their report but include a statement after the opinion section.

Other matter

We have reviewed the board's description of its process for reviewing the effectiveness of internal control set out on page x of the Annual Report. In our opinion the board's comments concerning their review of typhoon risk management do not appropriately reflect our understanding of the process undertaken by the board because only 50 per cent of the Pacific locations were included.

EMPHASIS OF MATTER

There is another situation which the auditors may have to consider and that is where they wish to draw the attention of the shareholders to a significant item in the accounts.

The reason for this is that there may be some situations which arise where the outcome is far from clear but where the company has taken all steps it reasonably can to provide for any costs, if appropriate, and to draw the attention of readers of the accounts to it, usually in a note to the accounts.

The auditors are therefore *not* qualifying their report but *are* drawing attention to the disclosure.

An example of this kind of situation might be the outcome of legal proceedings where there are claims and counter claims on both sides and the question of liability cannot easily be settled.

Here is an example of emphasis of matter wording based on that type of situation:

Independent auditors report to the members of XYZ Limited

(Extract)
   (Usual paragraphs from an unmodified report – see above)

Opinion

In our opinion

- the financial statements give a true and fair view, in accordance with United Kingdom Generally Accepted Accounting Practice, of the state of the company's affairs as at . . . and of its profit (or loss) for the year then ended; and

> - the financial statements have been properly prepared in accordance with the Companies Act 2006.
>
> **Without qualifying our opinion we draw attention to Note X to the financial statements.** The company is defendant in legal proceedings alleging infringement of certain patent rights and claiming royalties and punitive damages. The company has filed a counter claim and preliminary hearings on both actions are in progress. The ultimate outcome of the matter cannot presently be determined and no provision for any liability that may result has been made in the financial statements.
>
> Registered Auditors
>
> Date   Address

AUDIT REPORTING – SPECIAL CIRCUMSTANCES

There are three sets of circumstances relating to audit reports which we cover in other chapters:

- Auditing of opening balances and comparatives – see Chapter 23.
- Groups of companies – see Chapter 29.
- Assurance or non-audit assignments – see Chapter 32.

AUDITORS' LIABILITY IN RESPECT OF AUDIT REPORTS

The Companies Act 2006 brought in a new offence which affects auditors signing audit reports.

Under Section 507 it is an offence:

- knowingly or recklessly to cause an audit report made under s 495 to include '*any matter that is misleading, false or deceptive in any material particular*';
- knowingly or recklessly cause a report to omit a statement that is required under certain sections of the Act. These are:
  - s 498(2)(b) – statement that company's accounts do not agree with accounting records and returns;
  - s 498(3) – statement that necessary information and explanations not obtained; or
  - s 498(5) – statement that directors wrongly took advantage of exemption from the obligation to prepare group accounts.

We look at this in more detail in Chapter 31 – Auditors' Liability – but auditors need to be aware that signing the Auditors' Report is the culmination of a proper process which must have been performed in a competent, professional manner in accordance with the relevant ISAs. The implications of any shortcuts or risks which have been taken must be properly considered before the audit report is finalised and signed.

The offence is punishable by a fine – and no doubt disciplinary proceedings will follow.

THIRD PARTIES – DISCLAIMERS OF LIABILITY

The format of auditors' reports discussed here do not contain any disclaimers as to liability to third parties, i.e. parties other than the shareholders, collectively, who might read and rely on the audited accounts for their own purposes, e.g. to decide whether or not to invest in the company.

Since the Caparo judgment (see Chapter 31), banks and other lenders have sought ways to establish that a direct relationship exists between themselves and their customers' auditors so as to entitle them to place reliance on audit reports on financial statements prepared for statutory purposes.

Following the decision in *Royal Bank of Scotland v Bannerman Johnstone Maclay* (Scottish Court of Session, 2002), The Institute of Chartered Accountants in England & Wales (ICAEW) issued a technical release (Audit 01/03) which recommended that its members incorporate a disclaimer to third parties in their standard audit reports.

The Association of Chartered Certified Accountants (ACCA) however took a different view. They felt that a disclaimer was not a proportionate response to the Bannerman decision as, essentially, there was nothing new within it which distinguished it from the law as established by Caparo.

They argued that, since Caparo, it has always been the case that professional advisers can assume a duty of care exists provided that proximity to a third party is established. Bannerman highlighted that proximity can exist even where the adviser has no actual knowledge (as opposed to constructive knowledge) that the third party intends to rely on the advice (although this aspect was not fully argued through by the court).

The argument is that the incorporation of a disclaimer such as:

'This report, including the opinion, has been prepared for and only for the company's members as a body in accordance with sections 495–497 of the Companies Act 2006 and for no other purpose. We do not, in giving this opinion, accept or assume responsibility for any other purpose or to any other person to whom this report is shown or in to whose hands it may come save where expressly agreed by our prior consent in writing.'

as a standard feature of the audit report could have the effect of devaluing that report and could also cause problems for third parties and regulators; and the inclusion of such blanket disclaimers and limitations on an audit report would not help encourage trust between the audit profession and investors.

The reason why auditors are being found negligent is primarily a failure to carry out their audit work in compliance with the ISAs. If the work was carried out with reasonable skill and care to a good professional standard the question of negligence could not arise.

The APB, in their bulletin 2006/6, which gives pro forma audit report wording, does not suggest any wording for a disclaimer of liability to third parties.

It may be appropriate for auditors to issue specific disclaimers where they are aware of a third party's interest in the accounts. For example, they may be made aware that a lender may rely on the audited accounts when considering an application for borrowings by the company. In this case it may be appropriate for there to be a specific disclaimer in the report to shareholders for this purpose and for the auditor to undertake a separate assurance assignment on behalf of the bank evidenced by a separate letter of engagement.

Summary

- Auditors should summarise their findings and discuss them with management to identify any alterations to the accounts.
- If all is well the auditors can sign an unmodified report.
- If the scope of their audit has been limited auditors must either issue an 'except for' opinion or a disclaimer of opinion depending on how limited their work has been and how material that limitation is to the accounts.
- If they disagree with the accounting treatment or disclosures they can issue either an 'except for' opinion or an adverse opinion if the disagreement is material and so pervasive that it casts doubt on the integrity of the financial statements as a whole.
- If there is doubt about a significant event the auditors might want to draw the shareholders attention to it by including a emphasis of matter paragraph in their report.

Points to note

- Students must understand the terminology used in these reports and when each type of report is appropriate. It is a common examination failing to advise use of the wrong type of report in the wrong situation or to adopt the wrong form of wording.
- Whilst students are unlikely to have to write an auditors report from scratch they may be asked to criticise a badly written one, which obviously requires a sound knowledge of what a properly written auditors report should contain.

Case Study

Tickitt & Run have just completed the audit of Gofaster Motors Ltd for the year ended 31 December 20x7. They asked one of the audit staff to draft the audit report and he produced this:

'Report of the auditors to Gofaster Motors Ltd
  Basis of opinion
  We conducted our audit in accordance with Auditing Standards. An audit includes examination, on a test basis, of evidence relevant to the amounts and disclosures in the financial statements. It also includes an assessment of all the estimates and judgements made by the directors in the preparation of the financial statements, and of whether the accounting policies are appropriate to the company's circumstances, consistently applied and adequately disclosed.
  We planned and performed our audit so as to obtain as much information and explanation as possible given the time available for the audit. We confirm that the financial statements are free from material misstatement, whether caused by fraud or other irregularity or error. The directors however are wholly responsible for the accuracy of the financial statements and no liability for errors can be accepted by the auditor. In forming our opinion we also evaluated the overall adequacy of the presentation of information in the company's annual report.'

Discussion
- Identify and explain the errors in the above extract.

    (ACCA)

Student self-testing questions

Based on answers apparent from the text

a) List the main contents of an auditors' report.

b) Why are there paragraphs concerning directors in the auditors' report?

c) What does 'pervasive' mean?

d) Define 'material'.

e) If auditor scope is restricted partially what form of report might be made?

f) Under what circumstances would the auditor state that the financial statements do not present a true and fair view?

g) What is an emphasis of matter?

Examination questions

1 Described below are situations which have arisen in three external audit clients of your firm. The year end in each case is 31 March 20x7.

Maris Ltd

A fire in the accounts office in April 20x7 destroyed the company's records of the physical inventory count undertaken at the year end. This was the only record of the inventory as the company does not maintain continuous inventory records. There were no reasonable alternative audit procedures that could be undertaken to verify the amount of inventory at the year end. The company has included an estimated inventory figure of £1.2 million in the financial statements for the year ended 31 March 20x7.

The total assets of Maris Ltd at 31 March 20x are £5.9 million and the profit before tax for the year ended 31 March 2007 is £1.5 million.

Piper plc

The company builds and operates cable networks and during the year ended 31 March 20x the company incurred costs of £3.2 million in respect of repairs and maintenance to its networks. These costs have been capitalised and included in non-current assets. The directors refuse to make any adjustments in respect of this matter.

The total assets of Piper plc at 31 March 20x7 are £1250 million and the profit before tax for the year ended 31 March 20x7 is £152.6 million.

Tima Ltd

The directors have included a note to the financial statements for the year ended 31 March 20x7 explaining the status of litigation against the company for an alleged breach of environmental regulations. The note specifies that, in the opinion of the company's legal advisers, the future settlement of this litigation could possibly result in significant additional liabilities but it is not possible to quantify the effects, if any, of the resolution of this matter.

Required:

(a) In each of the circumstances outlined above, reach a conclusion on whether or not you would modify each audit report. Give reasons for your conclusions and outline the potential effect, if any, on each audit report.

(b) Explain the concept of reasonable assurance in the context of an external audit.

(ICAEW)

2 (a) Explain why quality control may be difficult to implement in a smaller audit firm and illustrate how such difficulties may be overcome.

(b) Kite Associates is an association of small accounting practices. One of the benefits of membership is improved quality control through a peer review system. Whilst reviewing a sample of auditor's reports issued by Rook & Co, a firm only recently admitted to Kite Associates, you come across the following qualified opinion on the financial statements of Lammergeier Group:

'Qualified opinion arising from disagreement about accounting treatment relating to the non-adoption of IAS 7.

The management has not prepared a group cash flow statement and its associated notes. In the opinion of the management it is not practical to prepare a group cash flow statement due to the complexity involved. In our opinion the reasons for the departure from IAS 7 are sound and acceptable and adequate disclosure has been made concerning the departure from IAS 7. The departure in our opinion does not impact on the truth and fairness of the financial statements.

In our opinion, except for the non-preparation of the group cash flow statement and associated notes, the financial statements give a true and fair view of the financial position of the Company as at 31 December 20x7 and of the profit of the group for the year then ended, and have been properly prepared in accordance with . . .'

Your review of the prior year auditor's report has revealed that the 20x6 year-end audit opinion was identical.

Required:

Critically appraise the appropriateness of the audit opinion given by Rook & Co on the financial statements of Lammergeier Group for the years ended 31 December 20x7 and 20x6.

(ACCA)

28

Auditors' reports to directors and management

INTRODUCTION

ISA 260 *'Communication of Audit Matters with Those Charged With Governance'* sets out recommendations as to which matters and in what form the auditors should communicate audit matters to persons who it describes as 'those charged with governance'.

THOSE CHARGED WITH GOVERNANCE

Who are 'those charged with governance'? For this purpose they can be defined as the governing body of the entity – in most cases the board of directors.

ISA 260 requires disclosure to *all* members of that board so it would include non executive directors. The reason for this is connected to Corporate Governance (Chapter 2) and is designed to ensure that the non-executive directors particularly are kept fully informed of audit findings and audit issues. In this way the executive directors cannot hide significant matters from the non-executives.

How the auditor communicates these issues is left open.

The auditors must consider whether the two way communications during the course of the audit between themselves and the management have been adequate for an effective audit.

FORMAL AND INFORMAL COMMUNICATION

Auditors communicate in two formal ways, in addition to the numerous meetings and discussions which naturally occur as part of the audit process. The two formal documents are:

- the Letter of Engagement; and
- the Management Letter or Letter of Weakness.

(Remember that the Auditors' Report is not a communication to management – it is a report to the shareholders.)

ISA 260 makes a number of points. It requires the auditors to report to 'those charged with governance' the general approach and overall scope of the audit, including details of any limitations and the form of the reports they expect to make. This will normally be communicated in the Letter of Engagement which we dealt with in Chapter 8.

In addition the auditors must inform the directors of:

- The selection of, or any changes in, any significant accounting policies and practices that have or could have a material effect on the entity's financial statements.
- The potential effect on the financial statements of any material risks and exposures such as pending litigation that are required to be disclosed in the financial statements.
- Material uncertainties related to events and conditions that may cast doubt on the company's ability to continue as a going concern.

These relevant matters should be communicated to the management of the enterprise promptly enough to enable them to take appropriate action.

During the course of the audit and, as it nears a conclusion, the communication with management will intensify. Auditors will want to inform management of the detailed findings of their audit work, in particular:

a) those which relate to the financial statements and the Auditors' Report, such as:

- expected modifications to the Auditor's Report (see Chapter 27);
- any audit adjustments that have or could have a material effect on the financial statements;
- unadjusted misstatements in the financial statements which were determined by the management to be immaterial, both individually and in aggregate;
- notes of any disagreements with management about matters which could be significant to the financial statements or the Auditors' Report, including whether or not the matter has been resolved.

b) those matters which relate to the accounting systems and the systems of internal controls; in particular:

- any material weaknesses in accounting and internal controls;
- their views on the qualitative aspects of the entity's accounting policies and financial reporting, matters specifically required by other auditing standards to be communicated.

These last two matters are dealt with through the formal reporting mechanism of the Management Letter.

THE MANAGEMENT LETTER

These letters are variously known as a:

- management letter;
- letter of weakness;
- internal control memorandum;
- letter of recommendation; or
- constructive service letter,

but their object is the same – to inform the company of problem areas within the internal control environment, including specific control procedure problems.

We will call it a Management Letter as this is a frequently used term.

During their audit work the auditors may well uncover weaknesses in the accounting systems, incidences of poor accounting practice or other matters which should be reported to the client. They do this by reporting separately to the directors, or any other governing body including the Audit Committee, or to senior management as appropriate.

The object of this letter is to assist the directors and managers in improving the accounting systems and the internal control environment and to highlight any instances which may be of relevance to future audits.

It is not a substitute for a qualified audit report – it is an ancillary document designed to benefit the client by recommending suitable improvements. This will also, hopefully, have the added benefit of making the auditors' life easier in future years!

Purposes

The purposes of the Management Letter are:

- to enable the auditors to give their comments on the accounting records, systems and controls;
- to enable the auditors to bring to the attention of management areas of systems weakness that might lead to material errors or misstatements;
- to enable the auditor to communicate matters that may have an impact on future audits;
- to enable the management to put right matters that may otherwise have led to an audit report qualification;
- to enable the auditor to point out areas where management could be more efficient or more effective or where economies could be made or resources used more effectively.

Note that in some audit engagements there is a specific requirement to make a management report on internal control and the control environment. These include audits of local authorities, stock exchange firms, housing associations and organisations in the financial services sector. The detail is outside the scope of this book but the principles shown here apply to such letters or reports.

Remember that what is being reported on, generally, doesn't affect the audit opinion; in most cases the auditors are simply suggesting systems improvements or pointing out weaknesses in the system, which may exist but which haven't prevented them giving an unqualified report.

If the auditors have had to qualify their report, particularly on the grounds of limitation of scope, the matters which forced them to do so would clearly have to be included in the Management Letter as they would be of great significance.

Timing

If it is to be effective the management should receive the Management Letter as soon after the completion of the audit work as possible. As the Management Letter is a natural by-product of the audit its production should be incorporated in the audit plan.

It should be sent as soon as possible after the end of the audit procedures from which the report arises.

Where the audit is spread over several visits then it may be appropriate to send a report after each visit. Frequently two reports are sent – one after the interim and one after the final.

Where procedures need to be improved before the year end (e.g. on stock control or identification of doubtful debts or undisclosed liabilities) then the report must be sent as soon as the weaknesses are identified by the auditor.

Procedures

There is a procedure for agreeing and sending Management Letters. What the auditors should never do is send a letter to the board or to the Audit Committee which they haven't discussed beforehand with the appropriate directors or senior managers.

The procedure is:

- As weaknesses or breakdowns are identified they should be discussed in detail with the operating staff involved and/or with more senior management. It is vital that the auditors have their facts right!
- The letter should then be written, and discussed informally with the board or the Audit Committee prior to being formally submitted.
- The letter should then be sent.
- An acknowledgement should be obtained from management stating what they propose to do about the weaknesses.
- The weaknesses should be followed up on the next visit.

It is usual to address the letter to the board or the Audit Committee who may then choose to send it down the line for action. Alternatively, with the agreement of the board, it may be sent to the management of the appropriate section, branch, division, region, etc.

In some cases separate letters are prepared for the board and for line management. This situation might arise where the auditors have a point to make, which is not material or unduly significant in the context of the company as a whole, but is relevant to one particular department or division. The auditors might consider making a separate report to the senior management of that department or division without including the points in the main letter addressed to the main board.

Care must be taken with this however for two reasons:

- The directors are entitled to know of any points the auditors make to their line managers, however limited they may be, and might not take kindly to not being informed.
- The matter may not be significant to the organisation as a whole, as far as the auditors are aware, but may have greater significance to management in the context of operational issues with which the auditor has no concern or is unaware.

It is therefore wise for the auditors to inform the directors of these points on an advisory basis.

Contents

The Management Letter will include:

- A statement that the accounting and internal control systems were audited only to the extent that was necessary to provide evidence for audit purposes and not necessarily for management purposes or to provide any assurance for management.
- A statement that only the weaknesses that have come to the auditor's attention are reported and there may be others.
- A list of any weaknesses in the structure of accounting systems or internal control procedures which have been uncovered during the audit and details of any controls which are ill-designed, inadequate or not functioning fully.

- A list of deficiencies in operation of the records or controls. In principle good records and controls may have been designed but they may be being bypassed or not always carried out by staff.

- Unsuitable accounting policies and practices – if material this would have to be discussed in the context of the Auditors' Report but that would not prevent it also being included also in the Management Letter.

- Details of any non-compliance with accounting standards or legislation, which should have already been discussed with management in the context of the Auditors' Report.

- Explanations of the risks arising from each weakness. The company should be advised of the implications of any weaknesses in the system and the possible consequences which may flow from not dealing with it.

- Comments on inefficiencies or waste in the systems which the auditors feel it appropriate to make.

- Recommendations for improvement. In some cases the required changes may be complex and the auditors should not delay their report if suggestions cannot be made quickly. Also improvements, such as improvements to the computer system, may require research and, in such cases, the auditors would not be able to recommend specific action.

Format

There is no set format or layout for these letters. Sometimes they are prepared as a letter, others prepare them as a table in a columnar format showing:

- the weakness;
- the implications for the company; and
- the corrective action needed.

  Whatever format is chosen the report should be clear, constructive and concise.
  The Management Letter format includes, as a minimum:

- an opening paragraph explaining the purpose of the report;
- a statement that it is for the use of the organisation and possibly its holding company if it is a member of a group;
- a note that it contains only those matters which came to the auditors' attention and cannot be a comprehensive list of all weaknesses which may exist in the systems;
- if required the report may be tiered by having major weaknesses separated from minor weaknesses;
- a request that the management should reply to each point made.

RESPONSE BY MANAGEMENT

It is essential that the auditors should obtain a response from the client on each point in the Management Letter. The auditors should expect an acknowledgement of receipt, a note of the actions to be taken and, in some important cases, the directors' discussions should be recorded in their minutes.

THE REPORT AND THIRD PARTIES

The auditors should not disclose the report to any third party without permission from the client, unless there is a legal responsibility to disclose as in the case of Money Laundering or Insider Dealing or the auditors can claim a public interest defence. In these cases the auditors should seek legal advice before any such disclosure is made.

It may be that the client discloses the report to others (e.g. the bank, regulatory bodies). The auditors should include a disclaimer paragraph stating that the report has been produced for the private use of their client only and/or requesting that it not be shown to third parties without permission from the auditors.

As the report may be critical of individuals, care should be taken that all its contents are factually accurate and that there are no gratuitously derogatory remarks.

EXAMPLE OF A MANAGEMENT LETTER

Note: There are other layouts but this is a common one. This example is of a report sent to the company with a covering letter addressed to the directors, others may include material issues in the body of the letter.

Example

Private and Confidential

The Directors
Bodgitt Ltd
Upper Street
Downtown
DT1 2OK

20 June 20x8

Dear Sirs

Matters arising from the Audit for the year ended 31 March 20x8

In common with our normal practice we enclose details of matters which have arisen during the course of our audit for the year ended 31 March 20x8 which we feel are significant enough to bring to your attention.

Our responsibilities as auditors are set out in the Companies Act 2006 and require us to form an opinion on the truth and fairness of the financial statements presented to us by the directors. In addition we are required to form an opinion as to whether proper accounting records have been maintained for the accounting period.

This report has been prepared exclusively for the sole use of the directors of Bodgitt Ltd. None of its content may be disclosed to third parties without our written consent and we accept no liabilities to third parties in connection with this letter.

The matters recorded in this letter are those which have come to our attention during the course of the audit. They are not intended to be a comprehensive statement of all weaknesses which exist or all improvements which could be made to the financial systems.

We should be pleased to discuss these matters further with you at a suitable time. In any event we should be grateful if you would kindly acknowledge receipt of this letter and comment on the points contained within it.

Yours faithfully
Tickitt & Run
Chartered Accountants

MATTERS ARISING FROM THE AUDIT FOR THE YEAR ENDED 31 MARCH 20X8

The following points arose from the audit for the year ended 31 March 20X8.

Note that this is not a comprehensive statement of all weaknesses which may exist or of all improvements which could be made. We set out below those matters which we consider to be of fundamental importance.

Weakness	Implication	Recommendation
Internal control – general points		
Budgeting		
At the moment we understand that you prepare an annual budget prior to the commencement of the financial year and submit it to the bank to support the application for the renewal of your overdraft	As the budget does not appear to be used other than to support the finance application an opportunity is being lost to improve management's control of the business	A budgetary control system be introduced comprising a monthly budget and management accounts and an explanation of significant variances
Budgeting is a useful management tool and it would greatly assist the management of your business if the budget was used to monitor the progress of the business	It is preferable for management to respond positively at the time problems or opportunities appear rather than have to rely on historical data which may be several months old by the time management see it	This should be produced in a timely manner each month and presented to the board for discussion
Management reporting		
We note that you have no system of monthly management reporting. It would assist the management of your business if you were to receive accurate monthly management accounts	The company is losing the opportunity to act quickly when comparison of actual results against forecast indicates a problem might be developing	Any estimates or assumptions which have been used in the production of monthly management accounts should be disclosed to the board
These could be compared with the monthly budgets to monitor the performance of the business	Similarly if management reporting indicates a potential benefit or opportunity the quicker this can be exploited the better the opportunity for management to maximise profits and cash flow	The monthly accounts should include, amongst other things i) the contribution made by different product lines and ii) a cash flow statement
	It is important that managers monitor cash flows to avoid any cash shortages developing which may hinder the operations of the business	
Internal control – accounting system		
The computer software currently being used is obsolete. You are using Version 3. The latest issue is Version 8	Use of outdated software is a missed opportunity to enhance the speed, accuracy and flexibility of financial reporting	The computer software should be upgraded to Version 8
		The cost of doing this will be likely to be outweighed by increased efficiencies in the system and the

Weakness	Implication	Recommendation
Whilst it continues to support the basic accounting system, that is the day books and ledger, it has no facility for stock control nor has it any facility for recording costing information	The additional features provided by the upgraded software will improve mangers' control of business activities and provide the information on which they could base business decisions	abolition of some of the current paper-based systems For example, improved stock control might serve to reduce current stock holding levels and free up cash for use in the business
Internal control – detail points *(Important points arising from the audit of the internal controls should be included here. We have shown a few as examples)*		
Payroll		
There is no evidence of review of the payroll	The payroll may contain unauthorised or fictitious employees or payments at incorrect or unauthorised rates	The payroll should be reviewed and signed by the production manager each week
There is no independent evidence of authorisation of recruitment of new staff	Fictitious employees might be introduced to the payroll	New starter forms should be authorised by the production manager
At present the starters form is signed by the wages clerk	Employees might not receive all the documentation they are entitled to under the legislation which would cause the company to be in breach of legal requirements	
Debtors		
An aged debtor analysis is only produced quarterly Slow-paying customers are often not identified until well after their terms of trade have expired	Poor credit control means that slow-paying customers are not identified quickly and steps taken to collect sums due. This means that the working capital requirement is greater than it otherwise could be. As this is presently financed by overdraft facilities the company is currently incurring excess interest cost because of slow-paying debtors	Aged debtor reports should be prepared monthly The acquisition of new computer software should enable this to be done automatically All customer should be reminded of the terms of trade and credit control procedures introduced to collect overdue debts

This is a final report but reports could be prepared after the interim audit as well if sufficient credible audit points are unearthed during the checking work.

Note that auditors should resist the temptation to include all weaknesses discovered however minor. Only weaknesses which may lead to material errors or misstatements or areas where significant improvements may be made for the benefit of the client should be included as inclusion of trivial or insignificant points devalues the authority of the letter.

Summary

- The auditors are required to communicate details of the scope and function of their audit and the findings from their audit work to those charged with governance.
- They communicate the scope, etc. of the audit formally using the Letter of Engagement. There are informal communications during the course of the audit. Reports of findings pertinent to weaknesses in financial systems are communicated formally by means of the Management Letter.
- The Management Letter has several purposes which include constructive advice to the client on economies or more efficient use of resources, comments on accounting, records, systems and controls with weaknesses and recommendations for improvement.
- Management Letters can be sent after the interim or final audit or both.
- The contents should include an explanation as to the purpose of letter, a third party disclaimer and details of the weaknesses and recommendations for improvement.
- Management should make a formal response to each of the points contained in the letter.

Points to note

- Clearly distinguish the Auditors' Report and a report to management.
- The audit plan should include the preparation of the Management Letter and a review of actions taken (if any) on previous letters.
- In some cases the weaknesses are not material enough to merit a full scale letter so the auditors should choose not to send a report and communicate any minor weaknesses informally.
- A notable misapprehension is that the Letter of Weakness can absolve the auditor from blame and hence a legal responsibility to pay for any losses which flow from weakness in internal control. If a weakness is discovered by the auditors and they are unable to satisfy themselves that, to a material extent:
  - losses have not occurred;
  - the records can be relied upon,

then they must qualify their report.

Case Study

Dunbar Manufacturing PLC is a multi-product manufacturing company with four factories around the country. The auditors, Tickitt & Run, have completed the interim audit for the year ending 31.12.x7 in September 20x7 and are considering their report to management.

The matters they have discovered include:

(a) Each factory has a separate bank account. Sometimes the individual accounts are overdrawn but the bank have agreed to set-off for interest calculation. At times there is a net credit balance.

(b) The factory at Tipton shares the policy of straight line depreciation for its plant but unlike the others does not keep a plant register.

(c) The factory in Oldham buys large quantities of scrap copper from scrap merchants, paying by cash. Each purchase is approved in writing by the plant works manager but there is no regular check of the cash balance kept to make these purchases.

(d) The stock of finished goods at Wigan is valued at total absorption cost using budgeted direct wages for overheads purposes. The other factories use a more sophisticated system of departmental overhead recovery based on machine hours.

(e) In all the factories some of the manual workers, classed as casual employees, are paid in cash. Their wages packets are simply given to the foremen to hand out with no formalities.

(f) The factories each use a computerised sales ledger system with complex analytical facilities. One facility, to analyse sales on a month to month and year by year basis for each customer, is not used.

Discussion

- How should these matters be treated in reports to management?
- Draft such reports.

Student self-testing questions

Questions with answers apparent from the text

(a) How do auditors communicate with management?

(b) When should these management letters be sent?

(c) Apart from weaknesses in systems what other matters need to be communicated to management?

(d) List the contents of a management letter.

Examination questions

Stopwatch PLC is an independent television production company. It specialises in the production of 30-minute long children's programmes in series of 10 to 15 episodes each.

Stopwatch PLC's main customers are the major television networks within the UK. The company's creative team present an idea for a television programme to the network and, if successful, the programme is then commissioned. A production budget, including an agreed profit margin for Stopwatch PLC, is agreed with the network before production commences. Stopwatch PLC's production team is then responsible for making the programme within these agreed budget limits. If the production goes over budget, Stopwatch PLC is responsible for meeting the additional cost of completing the programme concerned.

The following significant points have been identified during your audit of the company:

1 Production budgets

On 6 out of the 22 commissions received by Stopwatch PLC during the year, the company has not adhered to its own internal control procedures which call for the weekly comparison of budget to actual spend. As a result large overruns against budget in time and cost have occurred on these productions.

2 Freelance staff

The company employs a large number of writers, directors, and presenters in the making of its programmes. Under Inland Revenue guidelines, depending upon the length of their individual contract and the nature of their role, some must be paid after deduction of income tax and National Insurance whereas others are treated as freelance and can be paid without such deductions being made. Any such sums deducted must be paid over to the Inland Revenue monthly.

Due to staff changes within the company's human resources department during the year, a number of individuals for whom income tax and National Insurance should have been deducted, were found to have been treated as freelance and paid without the appropriate deductions being made.

3 Audio-visual equipment

On four separate occasions during the year, equipment was found to have been ordered for the company by individual production staff without proper authorisation and in contravention of company policy which calls for three quotes for all capital expenditure.

Required:

(a) Set out, in a manner suitable for inclusion in a report to management, the possible consequences arising from the weaknesses identified above, and your recommendations to remedy these weaknesses.

(b) Outline the points to be included in the covering letter accompanying the above report to management and explain why they should be included.

(ICAEW)

29

Group accounts

INTRODUCTION

Larger companies are generally arranged in groups comprising a holding company which owns, either wholly or partly, other companies called subsidiaries. In addition there may also be associates, where the holding company does not have overall control but can exercise a significant influence over its affairs, together with other related parties such as partnerships and joint ventures.

It is worth pointing out at this stage that the issues surrounding related parties have assumed particular significance following the Enron affair, when related parties were used to conceal the extent of losses which would otherwise have had a detrimental effect on the reported results of Enron itself. Auditors should pay particular attention to these.

Most listed companies are groups but many private companies are also groups. UK company legislation (and most other legal regimes) requires a financial statement to be prepared for the group as a whole as well as for the individual companies comprising the group.

Accounting for groups in the UK is governed by:

- The Companies Act 2006.
- FRS 2 *Accounting for Subsidiary Undertakings.*
- FRS 6 *Acquisitions and Mergers.*
- FRS 9 *Associates and Joint Ventures.*

  Internationally there is:

- IAS 24 *Related Party Disclosures.*
- IAS 27 *Consolidated and Separate Financial Statements.*
- IAS 28 *Investments in Associates.*
- IAS 31 *Investments in Joint Ventures,*

The Companies Act and the Financial Reporting Standards have numerous and detailed requirements on the presentation of a holding company's own balance sheet. Students should make themselves aware of the various disclosure requirements as it is outside the scope of this book to detail them except where they are relevant to specific audit considerations.

This chapter covers:

- the audit of holding companies;
- the audit of groups; and
- the special considerations pertaining when the group auditor is not the auditor of all of the subsidiaries.

AUDIT CONSIDERATIONS

The key thing for the student to understand, and from which all the procedures logically follow, is that the auditors who sign the group audit report are responsible for all matters arising from the audit, even in respect of subsidiaries not audited by them.

The audit of group accounts creates specific planning problems, in particular:

- Reviewing the respective size and location of all the operating units of the group.
- If not all the subsidiaries are to be audited by the lead audit firm there are issues of:
  - Quality control of audit work.
  - The risk of material misstatements in work audited by other auditors.
  - Arrangements for review of work completed.
  - Timing and co-ordination of audit work.
  - Standardisation of audit working papers.
  - Standardisation of information to be sent to group auditors.
- The main or group auditor should audit a significant proportion of the group financial statements. The reason for this is that the group auditor cannot reasonably be expected to understand the business of their client if they do not carry out a significant part of the audit.
- The group auditor should have knowledge of all group activities, including those not audited by them, in order to be able to evaluate the risks of a material misstatement arising in a subsidiary.

At the planning stage of the audit the holding company auditor will have to consider, in addition to the normal planning considerations for the holding company itself as highlighted in Chapter 10, the managements' arrangements for preparing the consolidated accounts including:

- Collection of data from subsidiary companies.
- Group accounting instructions to ensure consistency of presentation.
- Group accounting timetable.
- Translation of financial information supplied by overseas subsidiaries.
- Additional information requests from overseas subsidiaries where local accounting regimes are not as comprehensive as those of the holding company's country.
- Liaison with other audit firms – particularly overseas firms.
- Staffing and budget issues.

All of these arrangements should be reviewed by the holding company auditor and incorporated in their planning.

In addition the auditor's own planning will need to incorporate the issues mentioned below:

- audit staffing and the mix of experienced staff required to ensure that the audit strategy adopted can be carried out satisfactorily.
- liaison with other auditors of subsidiaries and associates.
- anticipation of problem areas.

RELIANCE ON OTHER AUDITORS

The main considerations are set out in ISA 600 *'Using the Work of Another Auditor'*.

In addition to the considerations as to the acceptance of the role of principal auditors (i.e. the auditors who will sign the auditors report on the consolidated group accounts) that:

- the firm is competent to carry out the work;
- it has sufficient knowledge of the business of the group and its components;
- it audits a sufficient proportion of the group to enable the risk of a material misstatement to be properly assessed; and
- the additional procedures required result in the principal auditor having a significant participation in each audit.

The principal auditor has to assess the competence of any other auditors, who are responsible for the audits of subsidiary companies, in the context of the specific audit assignment.

This is done by ensuring the subsidiary company auditor is properly qualified and by enquiry with the audit firm and other professional sources.

Professional competence is not usually an issue. The chief considerations are often:

- size;
- availability of suitably competent staff; and
- timing of audit work.

The holding company auditor has to be sure the subsidiary auditors have the resources to carry out the work.

The holding company auditor also has to ensure:

- that there are no independence issues either at subsidiary or group level (e.g. that no one in the subsidiary audit firm holds shares in the group), and obtain a written confirmation that this is so.
- that the subsidiary auditors are aware of any specific group issues such as identification of inter-group balances and transactions and related parties, etc.

In addition they should advise the other auditors as to what use will be made of their audit work, i.e. for the purposes of the group audit only and not for any other purpose. Note that subsidiary company auditors are required by ISA 600 to co-operate with the holding company auditors.

During the course of the group audit, before the reports are signed, the holding company auditors should carry out procedures designed to obtain sufficient, appropriate evidence that the work of the other auditor is adequate.

In most cases the holding company auditors will use a Consolidation Questionnaire which will include requests for information which may not be available from the published accounts. Such information will include:

- Information required for the consolidation, e.g. inter-group balances, etc.
- Information relevant to the group financial statements but not for the subsidiary's own.
- Any audit issues which are required to be drawn to the attention of the group auditors.

AUDITING INVESTMENTS IN SUBSIDIARIES AND OTHER UNDERTAKINGS

The auditors have to consider three aspects of the audit of investments in subsidiaries and related organisations in the books of the holding company:

- Obtaining evidence of the existence and ownership of the investment as stated on the balance sheet of the holding company's own accounts. The audit procedures here will be similar to those carried out in relation to the audit of investments as described in Chapter 15.
- Ensuring that the client has accounted for the investments correctly. This is not particularly difficult in the case of 100 per cent owned subsidiaries, but can present problems where the subsidiary is not wholly owned. The extent of the shareholding can be determined by reference to the share register of the subsidiary and, from that, the relevant accounting policy can be determined through legal and regulatory requirements.
- The nature of the relationship with partnerships, joint ventures and related parties. The question of any 'significant' or 'controlling' influence needs to be established. This can be evidenced by such factors as the composition of the controlling boards of the organisation, funding arrangements, contractual arrangements, the existence of guarantees and support arrangements, etc.

The student should be familiar with the various financial accounting requirements for dealing with these issues.

AUDITING THE CONSOLIDATION

There are several key issues relating to the preparation of consolidated accounts which the auditors must address specifically, in addition to their work on the holding company's own financial statements.
These include:

- *Co-terminous accounting periods* – all accounts consolidated should be made up to the same accounting reference date. IAS 27 deals with this issue where periods are not co-terminous. Any difference in year ends should not exceed three months.
- *Accounting policies* – these should, as far as possible, be consistent across the group. Where it is not possible, say in the case of overseas subsidiaries which adopt a different accounting regime, consolidation adjustments may be required in order to effect the required consistency of presentation. If this is not possible departures from group accounting policies have to be disclosed, where these are material, giving reasons for the inconsistency and an explanation of the sums involved.
- *Consolidation adjustments* – auditors should verify all consolidation adjustments, whether arising from acquisitions or as a result of inter-group trading. This includes adjustments arising from issues such as inconsistent accounting policies, elimination of

unrealised inter-group profits, elimination of inter-group balances, etc. This is an area which should be reviewed by an experienced member of the audit team to ensure that the consolidation is not being used to distort the presentation of the financial accounts.

- *Loss-making subsidiaries* – directors need to consider the value of any investment in a loss-making subsidiary both in the balance sheet of the parent company and in the consolidation. This may require a write down in the carrying value of the investment in the holding company balance sheet and any goodwill arising on consolidation. In addition the holding company will be undoubtedly guaranteeing the financial position of the subsidiary by means of a support letter. We will look at these in more detail later.

- *Acquisitions and disposals of interests in subsidiary or related companies or parties* – there are accounting rules and requirements which arise when the composition of the group changes and auditors must be aware of the nature of the change and the effect on both the group and the holding company's financial position. This will include the effect of any changes on such matters as going concern considerations (Chapter 24).

- *Any restrictions on paying dividends* – auditors have to ensure the parent company has sufficient distributable reserves to pay any distribution. Consideration has to be given to the availability of profits from subsidiary companies, especially where these are overseas companies.

- *Subsequent events* – as detailed in Chapter 23 auditors have to consider events between the balance sheet date and the date on which the financial statements are signed. This applies to the group as a whole and appropriate disclosures may have to be made where subsidiaries have been acquired or disposed of in that period.

MODIFIED AUDITORS' REPORTS

The holding company auditor has to consider any significant findings of the subsidiary auditors in the context of the group as a whole. Items may be material at a subsidiary company level but not at the group level.

An audit qualification, for example, at the subsidiary company level need only be repeated at group level if the point in issue is material in the context of the consolidated accounts. For example, depending on the materiality of the issue involved, a disclaimer of opinion in the subsidiary's auditors' report (*'these accounts do not present etc.'*) may only result in an 'except for' qualification in the group report, as issues in the subsidiary may not be sufficient to invalidate the accounts of the entire group. This, of course, as with so many things in auditing, is a matter of professional judgement.

If the issue is material at both the subsidiary and the group level the holding company auditors should modify their report accordingly. If the subsidiary is not audited by the group auditors it is not necessary to state this in the holding company auditors' report when reporting the modification.

FOREIGN SUBSIDIARIES

Auditors need to be aware of the problems of auditing subsidiaries based in other countries.
The key issues are:

- The auditors need to consider whether there will be any difference in scope between the local audit and what the equivalent audit in the UK would comprise. If the local auditor does not carry out sufficient work additional testing work should be requested.

- Where international accounting standards have not been adopted in the country the holding company directors should request additional work be carried out by the local directors to bring them in line with the IASs or the local auditors should be employed to do so.

- If the parent company auditors have significant doubts about the standard and quality of either the financial information produced by the subsidiary or the audit of that information, or indeed both, and the subsidiary is material to the group accounts they may have to consider issuing a modified opinion.

- As stated above accounting policies may differ from country to country and the holding company auditors should be aware of the impact of any differences.

- There may well be language problems both in the presentation of the accounts and in liaising with the local auditors.

- The effect of foreign currency translations have to be considered and the impact on the group results considered, particularly where the local currency is devaluing year on year against the parent country currency. For example, if the local currency exchange rate weakens substantially, an asset may appear to be declining in value when, in reality, its value has been maintained or has increased in local currency terms.

JOINT AUDITS

In some circumstances, the most common being where the auditors of a newly acquired subsidiary are required to work alongside the parent company auditors, two firms will act jointly as auditors, i.e. the auditors report will be signed jointly. Note this is not the same situation as a parent company auditor liaising with the local auditor of a subsidiary – they are not joint auditors.

This requires both firms to agree on:

- The audit approach to be adopted.
- Timing and staffing.
- Division of work.
- Sharing of audit working papers and who keeps what.

Where two firms are to act jointly issues of client and industry experience are as relevant as the size of each firm and the availability of staff. Geographical and language factors, in the case of overseas audits, are also relevant.

There needs to be a genuine spirit of co-operation between the two firms so that:

- All discussions are documented and shared with all audit staff.
- There is free exchange of information both during and after the audit.
- Both firms need to agree the audit opinion and the content of any Management Letter (Chapter 25).

There are both advantages and disadvantages to joint audits, particularly when the client company is a very large one with a wide geographical spread.

Advantages include:

- Wide geographical coverage.
- Close co-operation between the firms.

- Wider range of expertise.
- Added assurance to client as report is signed by both firms.

  However, there are disadvantages, principally:

- Joint liability means taking responsibility for the work of the other firm.
- It is likely to cost more.
- It requires a high standard of supervision and control to ensure that nothing 'falls through the cracks'.

SUPPORT LETTERS TO SUBSIDIARIES

As stated above, it happens from time to time that a subsidiary makes losses and loses value. Perhaps, for operational reasons the group deliberately runs a subsidiary at a loss or it may simply be as a result of poor trading.

Consequently it may be that the subsidiary, taken on its own, ceases to be a going concern. If this were the case the group accounts would have to recognise this, however, the group will not allow its subsidiary to go under and so undertakes to continue to support it.

This means that the subsidiary is therefore a going concern and no audit reporting problem arises. However, the auditors need to evidence this and so they require what is known as a 'support' or 'comfort' letter from the holding company directors.

This commonly states:

- That the holding company will continue to support its subsidiary financially so that external creditors will be able to be paid in full.
- The holding company will not demand repayment of any inter-company loans or balances until all other creditors have been paid in full.

Summary

- Holding (parent) companies have, as their principal asset, investments in and loan and current accounts with subsidiaries and related undertakings.
- The group auditor is responsible for the opinion on the group accounts. They have to consider the effect of any modified reports in subsidiary companies.
- Where not all the group is audited by one firm arrangements must be made for the holding company auditors to review the work of the auditors of the subsidiaries to ensure that the standard of audit work is satisfactory.
- There are particular problems associated with auditing overseas subsidiaries, including consideration of local accounting and auditing standards and foreign currency issues.
- Where a subsidiary makes losses the auditors have to consider the carrying value of the investment.
- They will require a support letter where subsidiaries are not a going concern.
- Joint auditors present logistical problems centred around planning and sharing information.
- The subsequent events review must include the group as a whole.

Points to note

- The accounting rules relating to groups are complex but students of auditing need to know them.
- Be careful to distinguish auditing questions on holding companies as companies in their own right from those on groups and those on different auditors of subsidiaries.
- The relationship between group (primary) and subsidiary (secondary) auditors is a popular exam topic.

Case Study

Bangi Chemicals Ltd make chemicals for the defence industry. They had no subsidiary companies but in mid 20x7, they acquired 60 per cent of the share capital of an American company for £6m paid partly in cash and partly in shares in Bangi. The net assets of the American company, Chemola Inc., were about £4.8m at the time of purchase. Since then the company has made a loss of £1.5m, but is expected to break even next year and make a large profit after that. The auditors of Chemola are based in the USA and it is proposed that they will continue to carry out the audit as Tickitt & Run have no representation in the USA.

Discussion
a. Draw up a list of audit procedures that Tickitt & Run, the auditors of Bangi, should carry out in connection with Chemola. The audit of Chemola is carried out by an American firm. Tickitt & Run is engaged on the audit of Bargi's 20x7 accounts.
b. How should the matters connected with Chemola appear in Bangi's own accounts? Bangi advanced £1.2m as a temporary loan to Chemola to cover a cash flow shortage and, in addition, has a trading balance of Dr £600 000 at 31.12. x7.

c. What matters should Tickitt & Run consider when reviewing the group accounts?

d. What actions should they take with regard to the audit by the American firm of the accounts of Chemola?

e. Identify the risks and the risk areas that Tickitt & Run should worry about.

Student self-testing questions

Questions with answers apparent from the text

a) What considerations as to the value of investments on a holding company balance sheet are relevant to the audit?

b) List the auditor's duties re group accounts.

c) How should a principal auditor evaluate the work of a secondary auditor?

d) Why is it difficult to form an opinion when consolidated accounts include associated companies?

Examination questions

(a) Explain the role of 'support letters' (also called 'comfort letters') as evidence in the audit of financial statements.

(b) You are an audit manager in Moltisant, a firm of Chartered Certified Accountants, and currently assigned to the audit of Capri Group. The consolidated financial statements of Capri Group are prepared in accordance with the accounting standards and interpretations issued by the International Accounting Standards Board (IASB).

The draft financial statements for the year ended 30 June 20x7 show profit before taxation of $6·2 million (20x6 – $5·5 million) and total assets $32·5 million (20x6 – $29·8 million).

One of the Group's principal subsidiaries, Capri (Overseas), is audited by another firm, Marcel. You have just received Marcel's draft auditor's report as follows:

'Basis of audit opinion (extract)

'As set out in notes 4 and 5, expenditure on finance leases has not been reflected in the balance sheet but included in operating expenses and no provision has been made for deferred taxation. This is in accordance with local taxation regulations.

Opinion

In our opinion the financial statements give a true and fair view of the financial position of the company as of 30 June 20x7 and of the results of its operations and its cash flows for the year then ended in accordance with . . .'

The draft financial statements of Capri (Overseas) for the year ended 30 June 20x7 show profit before taxation of $1·9 million (20x6 – $1·7 million) and total assets $6·5 million (20x6 – $6·6 million). The relevant notes (in full) are as follows:

(1) Leased assets

During the year the company has incurred expenditure on leasing agreements that give rights approximating to ownership of fixed assets with a fair value of $790 000. All lease payments are charged to the income statement as incurred.

(2) Taxation

This includes current taxes on profit and other taxes such as taxes on capital. No provision is required to be made for deferred taxation and it is impracticable to quantify the financial effect of unrecognised deferred tax liabilities.

Required:

Comment on the matters you should consider before expressing an opinion on the consolidated financial statements of the Capri Group.

(ACCA)

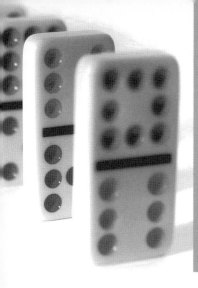

30

Small company audits

INTRODUCTION

Most companies trading in the UK are private companies and a significant proportion of them are classified as small companies.

However, for the auditor the audit of small companies can bring with it some particular problems.

SMALL COMPANY AUDIT EXEMPTION

Under s 477, Companies Act 2006 a small company is exempt from the requirement to have its accounts audited and consequently does not need an auditor.

This is subject to certain conditions:

- Turnover not more than £5.6 million.
- Balance Sheet total not more than £2.8 million.
- It employs less than 50 people.
- It is not a public company or a banking or insurance company.
- It is not authorised person or an appointed representative under the Financial Services & Markets Act 2000.

However, members of the company holding not less than 10 per cent of the share capital can require an audit and an auditor.

Small companies are permitted to file, at Companies House, abbreviated financial statements. Students should be aware of the form and content of such accounts.

The auditors' report need not be filed but the auditors have some duties where abbreviated accounts are filed. They have to attach a special report stating that in their opinion:

- The company is entitled to deliver abbreviated accounts.
- The abbreviated accounts to be delivered are properly prepared.

If the auditors' report is qualified then the special report must include the full auditors' report together with any further information necessary to understand the qualification.

Dormant companies do not need an auditor as they have had no significant accounting transactions in the relevant period.

ADVANTAGES AND DISADVANTAGES OF AN AUDIT

Advantages

Small companies don't have to have an audit but many of them do because:

- The provider of finance, e.g. the bank requires audited accounts. If they were to ask for their own independent audits this might increase costs to the company.
- Audits can help protect creditors which is important because of limited liability. Again if no statutory audit is performed major suppliers might ask for their own independent audit.
- An audit helps establish the credibility of the company at a time when fraudsters are committing so-called 'long firm' frauds – i.e. building up trust over a period of time and then disappearing with a substantial amount of money or goods having created a false picture of the activities of the company.
- There may be shareholders who are not involved in the business and their interests need to be protected by an independent audit.
- It provides reassurance for directors that the figures they are using are reliable and reinforces financial discipline.

Disadvantages

- There is an argument that an audit is only for compliance and doesn't assist management in running the business – it is simply 'red tape'.
- The costs of the audit represent a non-productive expense and the money could be better used elsewhere.
- Banks and other lenders, including suppliers, can make their own conditions for lending and don't really need historical audited accounts. For example:
  - banks will lend on security and personal guarantees;
  - they will monitor performance of the accounts;
  - they may require regular monthly management information;
  - suppliers will deal on a pro-forma basis (i.e. cash before supply) until a depth of trust has been established.
- Historical accounts, taking advantage of limited disclosure requirements, are of little value as they can be up to nine months old when they become publicly available.

ETHICAL STANDARDS

The Auditing Practices Board have issued a set of ethical standards applicable to the audit of smaller companies, '*Provisions Available for Small Entities*'.

In it they point out a number of dangers the auditor faces when dealing with such clients.

These are:

- The auditor is not required to carry out an external independent quality control review of the kind detailed in Chapter 7.
- The firm must be aware of the 'self review' threat where the audit firm is carrying out accountancy services in addition to carrying out an audit. The danger is obviously that the auditor is auditing their own work and there is no objective overview of the figures.
- There is the danger that, in the absence of capable management, the audit firm will make what are, effectively, management decisions. This is known as the 'management threat'. The ethical rules state that audit firms should attempt to avoid any situation where it has to become involved in the decision-making process, but the APB recognise that this may not always be possible. This standard creates an exemption from the ethical requirement providing the firm explains to the management the need for it to retain its objectivity and independence.
- The APB Ethical Standards require that the audit firm should not act as an advocate for its client in any tribunal or court – this is the 'advocacy' threat. The danger is for example, where the audit firm provides, say, tax services, that it will be drawn into an appeals procedure which will result in the firm appearing in the tribunal on behalf of the client. This will, again, reduce independence and objectivity.

Again the standard creates an exemption from this requirement for the small client providing the ethical position is discussed with the them.

There are provisions in the APB Ethical Standards regarding an audit partner leaving an audit firm and joining a client where at any time in the previous two years they have been a lead audit partner, an independent review partner or in the chain of command of the firm. It states that in these situations the firm should resign as auditors and not accept reappointment for a two-year period.

This provision is relaxed in the case of smaller entities providing the audit team can demonstrate that the employment of the former partner does not present any threat to the integrity, independence and objectivity of the audit team.

If the auditors take advantage of any of these exemptions they must disclose the fact in their Auditors' Report.

THE AUDIT OF SMALL BUSINESSES

There is an APB Practice Note (No 13) 'The Audit of Small Businesses', which is now quite old, but of more relevance is International Auditing Practice Statement (IAPS) 2 *Special Considerations in the Audit of Small Entities*.

Key points are shown below.

Independence issues

- Small businesses present problems because of their intrinsic characteristics, in particular the nature of the professional relationship between the auditors and the directors of a small businesses. Auditors are often seen as business advisors and tend to become involved with their clients at a much deeper level than would the auditors of a larger business (see above regarding the management threat').
- Auditors of small businesses often prepare the accounts and usually perform other tasks for the business (balancing the books, tax matters, advice, etc.) and this close

acquaintance with the business can constitute good audit evidence. However, there is always the danger that the auditors are auditing their own work - the 'self review' threat.

- Smallness and uncomplicated activities, and the close personal relationship with auditors, make a thorough knowledge of the business much easier but can make it difficult for the auditors to raise contentious issues with the management.

- Auditors of small businesses must always stay objective and should not take over the role of management. There is a danger that advice can evolve into active management, albeit unofficially and the auditors must not find themselves involved in company activities.

Internal control

- Internal control, or more likely the lack of it, is the biggest problem the auditors face.

- Small businesses tend to have:

  - a concentration of ownership and management;
  - few sources of income and uncomplicated activities;
  - relatively uncomplicated record keeping and limited management information.

- Segregation of duties is often a major problem as there are usually limited numbers of staff.

- Bookkeeping might be fairly informal without much in the way of systems. Whilst some level of basic controls might be instituted, e.g. pre-printed, consecutively numbered sales invoices, wages preparation done independently, etc. the auditor is generally not able to rely on them for audit purposes to any significant extent.

- Owner-managers generally have unlimited opportunities for overriding what controls there are.

Failure to separate corporate and private activities

- One of the biggest problems facing the auditors is the lack of distinction owner/managers often have between assets and income which belong to the company and assets and income which belong to them as individuals. Similarly costs may be charged to the company which are, in fact personal expenditure.

- As a result errors may be overlooked, assets may be misappropriated and fraudulent transactions take place and the auditors can be put under pressure to 'turn a blind eye'. This can become difficult for the auditors if they have developed a good personal relationship with their client.

- Conversely, owner-managers can exercise much personal control over transactions so auditors should neither assume that management is dishonest nor assume unquestioned honesty.

- Problems arise when businesses are expanding rapidly. Owner-managers give their time to the expansion of the business and do not worry about bookkeeping procedures. They may also lose some of the day-to-day contact with aspects of the business which creates opportunities for fraud and error.

Going concern and uncertainty

- Small businesses have more going concern uncertainty than larger businesses as they are often vulnerable to cash flow problems, limited numbers of key customers, vulnerability to bad debts, competition, etc.

- Lack of proper management information and limited financial expertise can compound these problems. This is where the auditors can be drawn in to acting as quasi financial directors if they are not careful. Clients request advice in preparation of budgets and cash flows, the audit firm prepares them and then discusses them with the directors. Great care must be take to ensure that any decisions taken are taken solely by the owner-managers and not by any member of the accounting firm who may later act as auditor.

- Occasionally the uncertainty surrounding small businesses can be so pervasive that the business is unauditable. In such cases it may be better to decline to accept or to resign the post of auditor. There is no point in disclaiming an opinion as this really negates the purpose of carrying out any audit work and incurs costs the client will be reluctant to pay!

- Completeness is a major problem for small business audits due to the lack of internal controls and the possible danger of owner-managers manipulating the business for their own purposes. It is not always possible for auditors to ensure that all the business transacted is reflected in the records.

SPECIFIC AUDIT CONSIDERATIONS

As always, the first duty is for the auditors to consider the suitability of the firm to accept the assignment. This will involve not only the usual procedures centred around finding out about the suitability of the client (Chapter 8) but also consideration of the level of costs which the client might incur and the relative size of the client and the audit firm.

It may be that the auditors are familiar with the client's business and management due to the close nature of the relationship, but the important thing to remember is that the appointment would be that of *auditor* which carries with it specific ethical considerations, particularly those of independence and integrity.

Specific audit considerations and procedures include:

- Agree an engagement letter. This is essential as it will set out for the benefit of both the auditors and the client the precise nature of the relationship between them. Whilst the relationship may be somewhat less formal than with a larger client it will remove any misunderstandings as to the role the auditors will play.

- Where there is to be a significant level of accountancy work it may not be possible to accept the appointment as auditor.

- Plan the work to be done, including the materiality level.

- With small company clients the emphasis is likely to be on a high level of substantive checking work because of the inadequacies of the internal control environment.

- In particular key balance sheet items such as stock (inventories) and sales debtors will be significant. Other audit areas to consider include verification that all income has been received and that costs are all bona fide business expenses and do not include any element of private expenses.

- The important consideration for the auditor is that, if internal controls are weak, no amount of substantive testing will give the auditors the assurance they need. The particular problem is likely to be completeness – especially if the business deals a lot in cash.

- If the auditors cannot gather sufficient appropriate audit evidence they should decline to express an opinion.

- Included in the checking work should be an in-depth analytical review of the financial statements. It is not easy to determine the depth of this but it will include comparing ratios against previous years, budgets and industry averages. Other matters may include inspecting an aged list of debtors for anomalies, and reviewing items that required particular management judgement. Problems may arise if the amount of management information is limited or rather simplistic and, of course, if internal controls are weak the underlying information may not be totally reliable.

- The auditor may be faced with some problems concerning comparability if the business is expanding.

- Obtain management representations (Chapter 25). Whilst these are not a substitute for audit evidence they may be supportive where other audit evidence exists. Representation letters may be relied on to a greater extent than in the audit of larger businesses and should be used to focus management's attention on particular issues, supported by analytical review and substantive procedures.

- Consider subsequent events, i.e. events after the performance of the audit up to the date the financial statements are approved. Particular attention needs to be paid to going concern issues (see Chapter 24).

- The audit report should contain either a disclaimer or an 'except for' opinion on the grounds of limitation of scope if the records or explanations are not considered adequate (see Chapter 27).

Summary

- Most small companies need not have an auditor.
- An important issue is whether a small company's financial statements should be audited – there are advantages and disadvantages.
- Small and medium-sized companies may file abbreviated accounts.
- Dormant companies do not need an auditor.
- Audit issues centre around the degree of control the owner-manager may have and the lack of proper internal controls.
- Auditors need to ensure they maintain their independence, particularly where they are advising their client or assisting in the raising of finance.
- Auditors cannot rely on management representations – they must still gather evidence to support their opinion.
- Going concern and completeness are key audit issues.

Points to note

- The arguments for and against an audit are good exam subjects.
- The whole issue of excessive laws, rules, regulation and bureaucracy as they affect small and medium-sized businesses is always a current issue, despite extensive deregulation. Changes need to be monitored.
- Audits of all companies and enterprises are governed by the same audit principles and need for evidence irrespective of size.
- Small companies are often owned and run by entrepreneurs who are not interested in obeying bureaucratic rules and see the company as an extension of themselves.
- This can make life difficult for the auditor. As a result audit risk can be higher in small companies. The need for evidence is still paramount but the type of evidence available may be different from that available in larger enterprises.

Case Study

Winfred Metal Reclamation Ltd, a small company, buys scrap metal residues from local companies and treats the residues to recover the metal which is then sold to other local companies.

The company is 75 per cent owned equally by Joe Winfred and his brother Eric, with their mother owning the remaining 25 per cent. The directors are Joe and Fred. The bank has advanced the company £0.5m for a new smelter.

Some purchases are made from itinerant scrap merchants. No evidence is available for the purchase of this scrap which totalled £160 000 in the year ending 30 November 20x7. However, there is no evidence that it is incorrect and Joe is willing to give a letter of representation containing the usual assurances re completeness and validity. The auditors find all other matters to be satisfactory and records are reasonable.

Office staff consists of Mary and Susan, who deal with all accounting matters including wages between them. There is no formal split of responsibilities, they just do what needs doing when it needs doing. Mary is living with Fred.

Some figures in the year ending 30.11.x7 are:

	£
Purchases	3 176 000
Net Profit	124 000
Balance sheet total	981 000
Employees	9

Discussion

(a) Is it possible for this company to dispense with an audit? Is this a good idea?

(b) Can the company file abbreviated accounts? What should the auditor do if they do?

(c) Draft the audit report on the alternative basis of an unqualified report, a report qualified on purchases, a report qualified on accounting records, a disclaimer.

(d) What would you do if you were the auditor?

Student self-testing questions

Questions with answers apparent from the text

a) How are auditors appointed if a company elects not to appoint them annually?

b) What companies are exempt from audit?

c) Rehearse the arguments for and against small company audits.

d) What companies can file abbreviated accounts?

e) What are the key audit considerations when auditing small businesses?

f) What are the implications for auditor's independence and objectivity in connection with small company audits?

Examination question

International Standards on Auditing (ISAs) apply equally to the audit of all entities, whatever their size. However, the manner in which ISAs are applied differs from entity to entity and depends on the use of the auditor's judgement. The characteristics of smaller entities may include:

(a) Common ownership and management.

(b) A control framework that is different to the control framework for larger entities.

(c) The use of standardised computer packages.

(d) Reliance on the auditor for accounting expertise.

(e) A lack of sufficient appropriate audit evidence to support financial statement assertions relating to income from cash transactions.

These characteristics have an effect on the way the audits of smaller entities are approached, how audit risk is assessed, how the audit is conducted, the auditor's report and the relationship between auditor and client.

Required:

Describe the nature and effect of each of the five characteristics listed in (a)–(e) above on the audit of smaller entities and on the relationship between auditor and client.

(ACCA)

31

Auditors' liability

INTRODUCTION

You will already have appreciated that the law has relevance for auditors, in particular the Companies Act and its effect on auditors which has been detailed in Chapters 2 and 3.

However, other branches of the law also affect auditors and this chapter considers some of them.

Auditors perform audits and sign audit reports which, as we know, contain the auditors' opinion on the truth and fairness, etc. of financial statements. Auditors are reputed to be independent, competent and honest so if the auditors say financial statements show a true and fair view, readers of the financial statements will have faith in them because they have faith in the auditors.

Because their work is relied upon by others, auditors clearly have a responsibility to do their work honestly and carefully. The judge in the *London & General Bank* case (1895) summed it up when he said, about an auditor:

He must be honest – that is, he must not certify what he does not believe to be true, and he must take reasonable care and skill before he believes that what he certifies is true.

This set a standard for the performance level of audit work – auditors are not meant to be all seeing and all knowing, they must simply exercise 'reasonable care and skill' in carrying out their work. This is known as their 'duty of care' to the people to rely on the accounts.

However, what 'reasonable care and skill' actually means depends on the circumstances of each case and it is very difficult to generalise. What is clear is that:

- Auditors may fail to exercise sufficient care and skill in carrying out their audit work.

- As a consequence, fraud or a material error may go undiscovered at the time of the audit, or they may fail to discover that the accounts do not show a true and fair view because they contain a material misstatement.

- Because of that somebody who relies on the work of the auditor may lose money.

- This loss of money flows from the failure of the auditors to do their job properly.

If those who have lost money are to somehow claim it back two questions need to be addressed. It is these questions which have been left to the courts to decide in a series of landmark cases which have, so far, set the boundary on the auditor's liability to third parties and to their clients.

The questions are:

- To whom does the auditor owe a duty of care – to the shareholders or to the world at large?
- What constitutes negligence – how badly do auditors have to have performed their work to be guilty of negligence?

We will return to these questions later.

CRIMINAL LAW

Auditors are subject to a code of ethics and are generally held to be honest and trustworthy individuals. However, there are cases where professionally qualified individuals either become embroiled in, or worse, actually institute criminal acts so it is worthwhile having a working knowledge of the main aspects of the criminal law as it affects auditors and accountants.

There are some specific offences which are criminal offences under various statutes. It is not necessary to detail all of the legislation but the nature of the offences are listed here.

Companies Act offences

- It is an offence(under the Companies Act 2006) to:
  - accept an appointment as an auditor when disqualified to do so or to continue as an auditor after becoming ineligible;
  - conspire with others to carry on a company with intent to defraud;
  - knowingly or recklessly to cause an audit report to include *'any matter that is misleading, false or deceptive in any material particular'*;
  - knowingly or recklessly cause an audit report to omit a statement that is required under certain sections of the Act. These are:
    - s 498(2)(b) – statement that company's accounts do not agree with accounting records and returns;
    - s 498 (3) – statement that necessary information and explanations not obtained or;
    - s 498(5) – statement that directors wrongly took advantage of exemption from obligation to prepare group accounts.

The last two offences, concerning 'knowingly or recklessly' issuing a false audit report, are new under CA 2006 (s 507). They can be committed by a director, member, employee or agent of an audit firm if such person is an accountant who would be eligible to be the auditor of the company and, on conviction, offences are punishable by a fine.

This provision applies for audit reports issued in respect of accounting periods beginning after 6 April 2008.

The audit profession were concerned that negligence or honest mistakes could come to be penalised as a criminal offence. The problem lies in the definition of 'recklessly'. The government said:

> *the auditor would have to know that failure to act carried unreasonable risks and consciously decide to go ahead despite that. The real point is that it is a long way above*

negligence. One cannot be reckless inadvertently, a degree of consciousness has to be shown.

This opens up several issues.

If negligence is proved because the auditor failed to carry out proper professional procedures, i.e. decided at the planning stage of the audit deliberately not to carry them out, this can almost certainly be negligent but is it reckless?

Courts may chose to look at the situation in this way:

- If the decision was taken as the result of a faulty risk assessment, and the auditors honestly believed the procedures weren't necessary, they may be guilty of negligent auditing, assuming they weren't being deliberately misled by the directors, perhaps because they failed to carry out proper procedures under the ISAs.
- However, if they decided not to carry out audit procedures simply to save money by reducing audit time, perhaps based on some very superficial reasoning about the trustworthiness of their client, they may not only be negligent but also reckless.

Clearly it will require some prosecutions before the attitude of the courts becomes clear. Consequently audit documentation will become even more significant, in terms of justifying decisions taken at the audit planning stage.

Fraud

It is an offence under the Fraud Act 2006 to commit fraud by:

- making a false representation (i.e. written or verbal statement) dishonestly, knowing it was false or misleading, with the intention of making a gain, causing a loss to another or exposing them to the risk of a loss.
- Failing to disclose information when under a legal duty to do so, dishonestly intending to make a gain or cause a loss.
- Abuse of position when in a position where there is a duty to safeguard, and not to act against, the financial interests of another person, dishonestly with an intent to make a gain or cause a loss. The abuse may arise from an omission as well as a deliberate act.

To be found guilty of fraud in any of the three ways, the behaviour in question must be dishonest and there must be an intention either to gain from the dishonest actions or to cause loss or a risk of loss to another. Unlike previous deception offences, there is no need to prove that actual loss or gain occurred, provided the *intention* is there.

The Act creates a new offence of fraudulent trading applicable to non-corporate traders. This parallels the current corporate offence under S993(1)-(3) Companies Act 2006.

Other offences

- It is an offence to steal another's property – simple theft.
- Insider trading – It is an offence to buy or sell a security by someone who has access to material, non-public information about that security. It is illegal when the material information is still non-public. Trading whilst having special knowledge is unfair to other investors who don't have access to such knowledge. Illegal insider trading therefore includes tipping others by someone (e.g. an auditor) who has any sort of non-public information. Directors are not the only ones who have the potential to be convicted of insider trading, people such as brokers, reporting accountants and even family members can be guilty.

- There are numerous offences connected with money laundering which we dealt with in Chapter 6.
- There are various offences in connection with financial services and investment relating to providing false information or creating a false market – principal legislation is the Financial Services & Markets Act 2000.

CIVIL LIABILITY UNDER THE COMMON LAW

The most complex area for auditors is the civil law and this brings us back to the earlier questions relating to duty of care and negligence.

Duty of care

'Duty of care' is the obligation to exercise a level of care, as is reasonable in all the circumstances, in carrying out professional work so as, in the case of an audit for example, to minimise the risk of material errors or misstatements being included in the financial statements. This would require auditors to exercise the level of skill care and competence expected of a suitably qualified professional in the circumstances.

Note that this duty of care does not require any form of superhuman effort, nor does it require any particular foresight other than a reasonable consideration of the possible consequences of actions carried out.

The duty of care is, therefore, based upon the relationship of the parties, the negligent act or omission and the reasonable probability of foreseeing any loss.

Only a negligent act will be regarded as having breached a duty of care.

Negligence

What is negligence? One definition is:

an act or omission which occurs because the person concerned (e.g. an auditor) failed to exercise that degree of reasonable skill and care which is reasonably to be expected in the circumstances of the case.

For an allegation of negligence to succeed the claimant must prove:

- The defendant had a duty of care to the claimant.
- There was a breach of the duty of care.
- The claimant suffered actionable harm or damage.
- The damage was caused by the breach.

There are two situations under civil law where auditors can be sued for negligence.

- Under contract law where a contractual relationship exists.
- To a third party where a duty of care exists but is not contractual.

One of the key issues we will be looking at in this chapter is quite how far that duty extends. Clearly auditors owe a duty of care to the shareholders, but what about other readers of the accounts such as lenders, suppliers or investors?

LIABILITY UNDER CONTRACT LAW

We have established (Chapter 8) that the Letter of Engagement, duly signed by the auditors and the client, represents the basis of a contract between them. Because there is a contract the auditors' can be sued for a breach of it if they:

- don't provide an audit report; or
- provide a negligently prepared audit report.

The reason for this is that the existence of the contract creates a duty of care between the auditors and the shareholders to whom they report. Although the Letter of Engagement is signed by the directors they are signing it on behalf of the company, which is owned by the shareholders, so the duty of care is owed to the company, not to the directors. If the auditors fail to carry out their duties they can be liable.

As we have already seen the auditors are only bound to exercise 'reasonable skill and care' in carrying out their activities. Quite what this means has often been left to the courts to decide.

This has been reflected in the ethical codes of various accounting bodies. For example the ACCA requires their members to carry out their work with:

due skill, care diligence and expedition with proper regard to the technical and professional standards expected of them as members.

The ICAEW expects their members to display what they call 'professional competence' and their ethical rules state:

The principle of professional competence and due care imposes the following obligations on professional accountants:

(a) *To maintain professional knowledge and skill at the level required to ensure that clients or employers receive competent professional service; and*

(b) *To act diligently in accordance with applicable technical and professional standards when providing professional services.*

The courts have given guidance as to what they consider is 'reasonable skill and care'.

Re London & General Bank (No 2) (1895)

We have already noted, above, part of the wording of the judgement in the London & General Bank case but here is another point the judge made:

[The auditor's] business is to ascertain and state the true financial position of the company at the time of the audit and his duty is confined to that. But then comes the question: How is he to ascertain such position? The answer is by examining the books of the company.

But he does not discharge his duty by doing this without enquiry and without taking the trouble to see that the books and records of the company show the company's true position. He must take reasonable care to ascertain that they do. Unless he does this his duty will be worse than an idle farce.'

Re Kingston Cotton Mill (1896)

It is the duty of an auditor to bring to bear on the work he has to perform that skill, care, and caution which a reasonably competent, careful, and cautious auditor would use.

An auditor is not bound to be a detective, or, as was said, to approach his work with suspicion, or with a foregone conclusion that there is something wrong. He is a watchdog, but not a bloodhound.

Auditors must not be made liable for not tracking out ingenious and carefully laid schemes of fraud, when there is nothing to arouse their suspicion . . . So to hold would make the position of an auditor intolerable.

This judgement set the tone for the audit profession for a century – auditors were to be passive checkers rather than be proactive in searching out errors, misstatements and frauds.

However, this statement may no longer have the force it once did in the light of ISA 240 *The Auditors' Responsibility to Consider Fraud in an Audit of Financial Statements*. Auditors have now to recognise at least the possibility that fraud may exist and, consequently, adopt an attitude of 'professional scepticism' in their approach to audit work. They have to recognise that schemes of fraud may involve complex misrepresentations and carry out their work accordingly.

This ISA may well be interpreted by the courts as placing on auditors a rather greater element of awareness, if not actual sleuthing, than the previous decisions admitted. Auditors still do not have to actively seek out fraud, but they have to be alert watchdogs!

Re Thomas Gerrard & Son (1968)

For many years the managing director of the company falsified the inventory figures in the accounts in order to conceal losses and to enable dividends to be paid. To do this he included non-existent stock and he also altered invoices, which were discovered by the auditors but not followed up or investigated.

The auditors relied on stock certificates given to them by the managing director, a person who they trusted. They contended that it was not part of the auditor's role to take stock, merely to verify the figures, and that they were entitled to rely on the assurances given by a responsible official of the company. This was supported by the decision in the *Kingston Cotton Mill* case where the judge stated that an auditor: '*is justified in believing tried servants of the company in whom confidence is placed by the company*'.

However, in this case the court held that the discovery of the altered invoices had put the auditors on enquiry and they should have investigated the matter.

They were no longer able to trust the assurances given to them and should have made enquiries, if necessary from suppliers, to verify the assurances given. Once the auditors' suspicions were aroused they had to investigate the matter fully. If they had done so the fraud would have been revealed. They were thus guilty of negligent auditing.

This is particularly relevant where auditors are obtaining information from officials of the company without a concomitant amount of corroborative checking work. If they have reason to doubt or are suspicious of any transactions they must follow it up. This is supported by the content of ISA 240 which requires auditors to follow up on queries and anomalies.

LIABILITY IN TORT

This is the most contentious area of auditors' liability and has given the courts, and the audit profession, no end of trouble over the years.

The problem is this:

Auditors can be liable to a third party – i.e. someone they are not contracted to if:

- they owe a duty of care;
- they have breached that duty by being negligent; and
- the third party has suffered a loss as a result.

The purpose of the court case is to establish whether or not a duty of care was owed – if the auditors did not owe a duty of care they cannot breach it and so cannot be liable for damages for negligence.

A review of the key cases in this area will give some guidance on how the legal arguments have progressed and of the present position.

Candler v Crane Christmas & Co. (1951)

In *Candler v Crane Christmas* (1951), Candler sued the accountants (Crane Christmas) of a company as he had relied on the accounts they had prepared for the purposes of making a decision to invest money in that company. The accounts turned out to have been negligently prepared.

The courts ruled that, although the accountants had acted negligently, they did not have a contract with Candler and therefore did not owe him a duty of care. This ruling was taken by the accountancy profession as meaning that no duty of care was owed to third parties.

Hedley Byrne v Heller and Partners (1964)

This was a case concerning banks but it sent shockwaves through the auditing profession. The plaintiff (Hedley Byrne) lost money when a bank reference was negligently produced – the bank indicated that their client was a good credit risk when this was not the case.

The court ruled that, in principle, although there was no contract between Hedley Byrne and the bank, it was liable to pay damages because of its negligence. In fact it did not actually have to pay as the letter contained a general disclaimer of liability.

The key point was, however, that the judgement held that if a third party could show that it relied on the work of another, e.g. an auditor, which turned out to be wrong it could claim damages. However, the judgement was restricted to parties where the identity was known, unknown parties still couldn't claim.

JEB Fasteners v Marks Bloom (1980)

The audited accounts of the company did not show a true and fair view of the state of affairs and the auditors were held to be negligent in stating that they did. At the time it was accepted that the auditors were aware of the plaintiffs' interest in the company but not that they were contemplating a takeover bid.

The courts held in favour of the auditors as the plaintiffs had not suffered a loss and would have bought the share capital at the agreed price whatever the accounts had said.

The duty of care issue was therefore irrelevant and was not considered by the court.

What makes this case important however is that the courts stated that a duty of care *will* exist where the auditors:

- knew or *reasonably should have foreseen*, at the time that the accounts were audited, that a person might rely on those accounts for a particular purpose; and
- that, in all the circumstances, it would be reasonable for such reliance to be placed on those accounts for that particular purpose.

This case raised the possibility that an auditor might owe a duty of care to a third party who reads the accounts and then makes an investment or some other decision after relying on those accounts.

Effectively, after this decision, the auditor might owe a duty of care to an unknown person.

Caparo Industries v Dickman and Touche Ross & Co (1990)

Caparo had alleged that it had based its decision to make a successful take over bid of Fidelity PLC on the strength of the latter's 1984 accounts which were audited by Touche Ross. Before the takeover bid Caparo had been a minority shareholder in Fidelity PLC.

The accounts significantly overstated the true position of Fidelity and so, subsequent to the eventual takeover, Caparo sued the auditors. The plaintiff argued that a duty of care was owed to them by the auditors. The Court of Appeal originally found for Caparo in 1989, however, on appeal the House of Lords overturned the decision and found in favour of Dickman (the Touche Ross partner).

The judgement against Caparo was clear that, in the circumstances of this case, the auditor did not owe a duty of care to *potential* investors.

It held that the auditor's duty of care was owed to the shareholders as a body and not to individual shareholders for purposes such as to assist them in making investment decisions.

In his judgement, Lord Bridge referred to the salient features of earlier cases, stating that, for a duty of care to arise in respect of the advice or information given, the person who it is alleged owes that duty of care must be fully aware:

- of the identity of any third party who purports to rely on the adviser's advice;

- of the nature of the transaction contemplated by the third party;

- that the advice or information given would be passed to the third party, directly or indirectly; and

- that it was very likely that the third party intended to rely on that advice or information in deciding whether or not to engage in the transaction.

In these circumstances, the judge considered that, subject to the effect of any disclaimer of responsibility, the person giving advice or information would be expected to be aware that the third party would rely on the advice or information given in deciding whether or not to engage in the transaction being contemplated.

This would create a duty of care and the auditors would be liable for any negligent misstatements.

This is the current situation as far as UK civil law is concerned, however, there is another decision which is relevant to a full appreciation of the legal position.

Royal Bank of Scotland v Bannerman Johnstone Maclay (Scottish Court of Session) (2002)

The defendants were auditors of a company which, in 1998, went into receivership with debts of around £13 million owing to Royal Bank of Scotland (RBS). RBS claimed that, due to a fraud, the accounts of previous years had misstated the true financial position of the company and the defendants had been negligent in not detecting it. RBS was the company's main banker/lender and, over a period of time, had also exercised options to subscribe for a majority of the company's shares. A requirement of the lending agreement was that monthly management accounts and audited accounts were to be sent to the bank as soon as was practicable.

The court held in favour of RBS on the basis that, broadly following the guidelines set by Lord Bridge in Caparo, the auditors knew the identity of the third party, the use to which the information would be put and that the bank intended to rely on it for the known purpose.

The court dismissed the defence's arguments that, for a duty of care to exist, there must be an express assumption of responsibility to the third party by the auditor.

Significantly the judge commented that, having become aware of the details of the requirements of the lending agreement, the auditors could have disclaimed responsibility to the bank.

Although, at the time of writing, this case is being appealed, and the original decision is not binding on other national courts, it does raise new questions about the duty of care to third parties.

Other cases

It is useful to examine the circumstances of other cases so students can understand the limitations of these decisions which are the cornerstone of the audit profession's understanding of its legal position.

ADT Ltd v BDO Binder Hamlyn (1995)

Assurances had been given to ADT by the auditors of Britannia Security Group ('Britannia'), BDO Binder Hamlyn (BBH). ADT asked them if they stood by their audit opinion and they replied that they did. This created a relationship between ADT and BBH who knew that ADT were looking to buy Britannia. After ADT had bought Britannia they discovered that its assets were overstated by £65m.

The court held that by confirming its audit opinion to ADT, BBH had created a contractual relationship and were liable for damages and costs totalling £105m.

Peach Publishing Co v Slater & Co (1997)

In this case the auditor gave an oral assurance as to the reliability of some unaudited management accounts which the purchaser relied on when buying a business. The judge said that an accountant does not automatically assume liability and that, in any case, the purchaser should have made his own checks rather than try and obtain some form of warranty where none was intended.

This case does, however, highlight the dangers of third parties trying to obtain some form of assurance from the auditors and care has to be taken in statements made to them, especially where there may be a possibility of that third party placing a reliance on the assurance given.

The general principle of liability to a third party, where the auditors' know that the audit is going to be relied on as some form of assurance, is reflected internationally.

International decisions

In the USA the decision in *Ultramares v Touche (1931)* was that the auditors could be liable if they *knew* that the audit was for the primary benefit of the plaintiff, e.g. that the audited accounts were to be relied by the plaintiff (a bank) who was to lend money to the client but not in general circumstances. As the judge put it that would expose the auditors to:

liability in an indeterminate amount for an indeterminate time to an indeterminate class.

This decision has been followed in another leading case *Credit Alliance v Arthur Andersen & Co (1985)* and was strengthened by the ruling that the auditors had to have performed some form of linking act such as sending a copy of the accounts to the plaintiff.

The Australian case *of Mutual Life v Citizens Assurance Co Ltd v Evatt (1971)*, involving negligent financial advice given by an insurance agent and the Canadian case of *Haig v Bamford (1976)* both held that:

- no duty of care is owed to a stranger;
- the liability to third parties cannot arise in the absence of knowledge that the third party is going to rely on the information given; and
- the person giving the advice must be doing so in their professional capacity and not as a citizen.

Clearly, therefore, the consensus is that auditors might be liable to third parties where they are aware of the third party and they could reasonably foresee that the third party might rely on the information contained in the audited accounts. Accordingly it is becoming the practice to include a disclaimer of such responsibilities in audit reports (see Chapter 27).

MINIMISING RISK TO AUDIT FIRMS

Auditors and accountants can minimise their potential liability for professional negligence in several ways:

- by not being negligent, i.e. by having a functioning quality control system (Chapter 7);
- ensuring that the audit procedures in accordance with IAS 315 '*Obtaining an Understanding of the Entity and Assessing the risks of Material Misstatement*' are carried out properly;
- carrying out audit work in accordance with the International Standards on Auditing;
- agreeing the duties and responsibilities in an Engagement Letter. This should specify the specific tasks to be undertaken and exclude specifically those that are not to be undertaken. It should also define the responsibilities to be undertaken by the client and specify any limitations on the work to be carried out.
- defining in their audit report the precise work undertaken, the work not undertaken, and any limitations to the work. This is so that any third party will have knowledge of the responsibility accepted by the auditor for the work done;
- stating in the Engagement Letter the purpose for which the report has been prepared and that the client may not use it for any other purpose;
- stating in any report the purpose of the report and that it may not be relied on for any other purpose;
- by identifying the authorised recipients of reports in the Engagement Letter and in the report;
- by limiting or excluding liability by a term in the Engagement Letter or, to third parties, by a disclaimer in the report;
- by obtaining an indemnity from the client or third party;
- by defining the scope of professional competence to include only matters within the accountants' competence.

Finally the RSB's require that all auditors must carry Professional Indemnity Insurance (PII) – just in case!

LIMITED LIABILITY PARTNERSHIPS (LLPs)

The key features of an LLP include:

- It is a corporate body, i.e. a separate legal entity distinct from its members. The LLP can own and hold property, employ people and enter into contractual obligations. Debts incurred are the debts of the LLP not of the individual partners.
- An LLP does not have any restrictions on its activities.
- An LLP has members but does not have directors or shareholders, nor does it have share capital. Two of the members are classed as 'designated members' and are responsible for

corporate legal matters such as signing the accounts, appointing auditors, filing returns, etc. at Companies House.

- The members of an LLP have limited liability. The LLP is liable for all its debts to the full extent of its assets. Individual members are only liable to the extent of their investment in the LLP. Individual members can be made liable for negligent advice, but any claim against them will not affect other members. This is the major change from the old partnership structure where liability was 'joint and several', i.e. the liabilities of one partner affected all the others.

- An LLP has complete flexibility as to the internal structure which it wishes to adopt: there are no requirements for board or general meetings or decision-making by resolution. An LLP does not have a memorandum or articles of association.

- As the members have limited liability, the protection of those dealing with an LLP requires that the LLP maintains accounting records, prepares and delivers audited annual accounts to the Registrar of Companies, and submits an Annual Return in a similar manner to companies. However, the exemptions available to companies, for example, with respect to the delivery of abbreviated accounts and exemption from audit, also apply to LLPs.

Broadly therefore, the partners of an auditing firm are afforded the protection of a corporate structure with its limited liability, but the price they have to pay is the loss of financial anonymity. They must prepare and publish accounts which will reveal such previously closely guarded secrets as the profits shared between the partners.

Where big audit firms audit huge clients, operating across boundaries, the potential for a disastrous claim against the firm is increased. The destruction of Arthur Andersen, post-Enron, showed how vulnerable even a mega-firm could be to catastrophic loss of clients following adverse publicity. The adoption of the LLP structure is a way for partners to preserve their personal assets at the expense of some disclosure and regulation.

LIMITING AUDITORS' LIABILITY

Until recently auditors were not able to limit their exposure to claims for negligence. As we have seen they can adopt a form of corporate structure – the Limited Liability Partnership – and they have to have in place Professional Indemnity Insurance, but these are defensive measures designed to avoid the audit firm being wiped out by claims.

Under ss 534–538, CA 2006 shareholders of both public and private companies can, by ordinary resolution, agree to limit the liability of their auditors in respect of any negligence, breach of duty, default or breach of trust occurring during the course of an audit. This is called a Liability Limitation Agreement (LLA).

There are, however, some provisos in the legislation:

- No agreement can reduce the auditors' liability to less than what is considered to be 'fair and reasonable' in the circumstances, taking into account the auditors' responsibilities, their contractual obligations and the professional standards expected of them.

- Shareholder approval can be gained either before or after the company enters into an LLA and private companies can agree to waive the requirement for approval.

- Any LLA made with the auditors has to be disclosed in the accounts or the Directors' Report.

- The LLA is only operative for one financial year and should be renewed annually.

- The shareholders have the right, by means of an ordinary resolution, to terminate the LLA in respect of any act or omission subsequent to the date set by that resolution – i.e. the LLA can be terminated by the shareholders.

- The limit on auditor's liability need not be a sum of money or some sort of formula (e.g. a multiple of the audit fee) but could be, for example, a percentage of any loss suffered by the company, taking into account the level of the auditors' responsibility for such loss.

- When considering what is 'fair and reasonable' no account should be taken of events arising after the loss or damage has occurred, or any matters affecting the possibility of recovering the loss from any body or individual considered liable in respect of it.

This last point was to alleviate the concern that the auditors may be the only people with any money after the loss or damage has occurred, because of their liability insurance, and the risk that the courts may find it expedient to make the auditors liable for all of the compensation when, for example, the directors might be equally culpable.

Mid-tier audit firms have expressed concerns that these LLAs would limit competition in the audit market.

The establishment of these LLAs is by no means certain, particularly in larger, listed, companies. Institutional shareholders have expressed reservations about them on principle and may oppose resolutions to introduce them. However, if the audit profession stands firm and insists on them, shareholders may have little choice but to accept them.

THE FUTURE

The worries are that:

- increased caution by auditors will increase audit costs as they undertake more work in order to reduce risks;
- the threat of criminal proceedings may make auditors even more risk averse than they are at present so that they will be more inclined to qualify audit reports.

These worries may be unfounded. Auditors who carry out their work properly should not be guilty of negligence and cannot therefore be guilty of an offence under the Act. In fact, if the government's view is sustained that 'recklessly' is some way beyond 'negligently', it requires auditors to have been incredibly lax in carrying out their audit – in which case some might say they deserve to be prosecuted!

Alternatively, it requires them to deliberately issue a false report which would probably be likely only where additional criminal circumstances were present, such as corruption, blackmail or threatening behaviour.

However, this may not stop some firms of auditors using these provisions as an excuse to increase audit fees and to increase the level of written representations from directors and senior managers as some form of protection!

Summary

- The criminal law makes possible prosecutions against auditors who act dishonestly or recklessly or connive at dishonesty.
- Auditors can also be found guilty of offences in connection with Money Laundering and Insider Trading.
- Civil liability can arise under Common Law where the auditor is sued to recover losses caused by their negligence in breach of contract.
- In certain circumstances, civil liability can arise to third parties. This can arise where third parties use audited information and suffer loss as a consequence because that information was negligently prepared. As the law presently stands the auditor has to be aware of the possibility.
- The Caparo decision is still the leading precedent in the UK although non-binding decisions such as Bannerman may well have a bearing on the future trend of court decisions.

Points to note

- Liability can only arise if:
  - The auditor can be shown to be negligent.
  - Loss has been suffered.
  - The negligence is the direct cause of the loss.
  - The auditor has legal liability in the circumstances.
- The tests of liability in court are proximity, foreseeability and reasonableness.
- The section on minimising auditors liabilities is very important. All auditors have to have insurance cover under Professional Indemnity policies.
- Cases of professional negligence concerning auditors very rarely come before the courts as such cases are mostly settled out of court to avoid incurring huge legal fees, if for no other reason. The authors take the view that if more cases were allowed to come to the courts the issues of:
  - what is negligence?
  - to whom does the auditor have a legal responsibility?

  would become clearer.
- However, in individual cases, a court hearing would involve enormous costs in terms of legal fees, partner time and adverse publicity.
- Auditors are required to perform their work with reasonable skill and care. It now seems well established that this means that the auditor must apply the standards of a reasonable, competent, professional auditor. The professional auditor applies all the auditing standards and guidelines.
- Because auditors are required to carry Professional Indemnity Insurance there is a tendency to sue the auditor knowing that they will not have to pay but the insurer will.
- The effect of this is that the insurer will insist on reasonable skill and care on the part of the insured. In addition, the professional bodies act as regulators of the conduct of their members.

Case Study 1

Tickitt & Run are the auditors to AHM Publishing Co. Ltd, publishers of textbooks. They carried out the audit for the December 20x6 and signed an unqualified audit report. Shortly after the AGM which was on 23.6.x7 negotiations began for the sale of the company to Amalgamated Publishers PLC who acquired the company in November 20x7.

The audit of AHM's 20x7 accounts by Puce, Watermelon in March 20x8 revealed that a printing bill for two of AHM's best selling titles dated 30.11.x6 had been disputed and thus not entered in the books. The matter was resolved in August 20-7 when AHM paid the £288 000 owing. The bill was not accrued in the 20x6 accounts.

Amalgamated paid £1m for AHM whose reported profits net of management remuneration were: 20x3 £216 000, 20x4 £213 000, 20x5 £217 000.

Amalgamated sued Tickitt & Run for damages.

Discussion

- Discuss in detail all the issues raised by this case.
- How might Tickitt & Run defend themselves against this action?

Case Study 2

Tickitt & Run, the auditors to Daffodil Ltd, gave an unqualified report on 14 December 20-7 on the accounts for the year ending 30 June 20-7. These accounts were seen by The Wednesfield Bank PLC in September 20-8 and the bank lent £250 000 to Daffodil on short-term overdraft on 19 September 20-8. In March 20-9 the company went into liquidation still owing the bank £200 000. The company was hopelessly insolvent and the bank recovered nothing. It turned out that the accounts of June 20-7 were defective in that several substantial creditors were omitted from the accounts. Had these creditors been included it would have been apparent that Daffodil was not a going concern in June 20-7.

Discussion

- Can the bank recover from Tickitt & Run?

Student self-testing questions

Questions with answers apparent from the text

- How can an auditor be criminally liable under the Companies Act?
- How can an auditor be liable under the law of Tort?
- What conditions must be satisfied for an auditor to have to pay damages for a tort? How can an audit firm minimise its potential for paying damages?
- Summarise the Caparo case.

32

Non-audit assurance services

REVIEW ENGAGEMENTS

Introduction

Accountants in practice perform many different assignments for their clients. This book is about auditing assignments but frequently accountants are also asked to carry out work which is non-audit but which includes many of the aspects of audit work, for example, planning, gathering of evidence and risk evaluations.

For example, accountants are often asked to carry out reviews of financial information, such as interim accounts or management accounts prepared in support of a finance application, or are asked to perform investigations based on their client's instructions and to report on the results. Accountants often prepare accounts or management information – perhaps for smaller clients – and do not wish to give any form of assurance or opinion on those figures.

These types of assignment are governed by International Standards on Review Engagements (ISREs) produced by the International Auditing and Assurance Standards Board (IAASB).

They fall into two basic types:

- Those in which the accountants carry out some form of work and simply report to their client factually without giving any form of assurance or opinion.
- Direct reporting engagements where accountants carry out work, which falls short of an audit, on which they will give some form of limited assurance or opinion.

The first type of assignments on which no assurance is given comprise:

- Attest functions – witnessing something.
- Compilation assignments – assembling financial statements from information supplied.
- Agreed upon procedures assignments – work performed on a basis agreed with the client,

and we will deal with these first. We will deal with direct reporting engagements later in the chapter.

Attest functions

To attest to something is to bear witness or affirm it.

Example

A trade association may require that all its members must annually review the procedures they perform in order to secure compliance with the quality control requirements of the association. The directors of A Ltd duly performed the review but the association need confirmation that the review has been performed.

To that end Tickitt & Run, Chartered Accountants, are engaged to assure the society that the review has been performed. Tickitt might do this by:

- Enquiry of the directors so as they can understand the processes carried out by the company in carrying out its review to ascertain if it complies with the requirements for the review set out by the association.

- Reviewing documentation prepared by or for the directors to support their statement and assessing whether or not it provides sound support for that statement.

- Reporting to the association that the review has been carried out.

The accountants may well say that the review by the board was conducted in accordance with the association's recommendations but will not say anything about the internal processes adopted by the company to secure compliance with the association's quality control requirements. Their work and their report is simply to *attest* to the fact that the Board carried out a review.

Compilation assignments

Accountants are often called upon to compile or prepare financial accounts or other statements from client records. This is most common for sole traders, small partnerships and unincorporated bodies, e.g. charities.

The following procedures should be adopted:

- Agree an Engagement Letter with the client making it clear that the engagement is not an audit and that management is responsible for the accuracy and completeness of the compiled financial statements.

- Plan the work so that it is properly carried out and documented.

- Gain an understanding of the business – this need not necessarily be as extensive as would be required for an audit.

- Prepare the financial statements using generally accepted accounting principles. The financial statements should also comply with Accounting Standards. Ideally the financial statements should include a statement of any significant accounting policies.

- It is usual to perform limited audit-type procedures including analytical review and enquiry of management. The accountants should then ascertain that the financial statements are in accordance with their understanding of the business.

- Request a Letter of Representation from the management (Chapter 25). This will cover:

  - estimates made by the management;
  - an assurance that all necessary information has been given to the accountants; and
  - that the information is complete and reliable.

  Any relevant explanations given orally will also be included.
- Ensure that the accountants receive some written acknowledgement from the client that the clients are solely responsible for the presentation and content of the financial statements and that they have provided all the information and explanations necessary to the accountants.

The compilation report which the accountants attach to the accounts will be something like:

On the basis of information supplied by management we have compiled, in accordance with the International Standard on Related Services (or other national standard as appropriate), applicable to compilation engagements, the financial statements of Tinyco as at 31 December 20X7.

Management is responsible for these financial statements. We have not audited or reviewed these financial statements and accordingly express no opinion thereon.

It should then be signed and dated.

In the event of the accountants finding that the financial statements contain a material misstatement or are otherwise misleading, they should discuss the matter and recommend amendment. If the management refuse to alter the accounts the accountants should either resign or include an explanatory paragraph in their report.

Agreed-upon procedures engagements

An agreed-upon procedures engagement is one in which the party engaging the professional accountant, or the intended user, determine the procedures to be performed and the professional accountant provides a report of factual findings as a result of undertaking those procedures.

It is not an assurance engagement and no opinion will be expressed.

You will note that, in normal reporting engagements, the accountants decide upon their own procedures and their engagement is about reporting the results of carrying out those procedures, not about what to do or how to do it, i.e. ends not means. In agreed-upon procedures engagements the procedures are determined by the client or the end user of the report (who may not necessarily be the same) and the accountants merely carry them out as instructed and report.

The underlying authority for such assignments is the International Standard on Related Services (ISRS) 4400 '*Engagements to Perform Agreed-upon Procedures Regarding Financial Information*'.

The process is as follows:

1 The auditor will agree the terms of the assignment in an Engagement Letter to include:

- The nature of the engagement including the fact that the procedures performed will not constitute an audit or a review and that accordingly no assurance will be expressed.
- The stated purpose for the engagement.
- Identification of the financial information to which the agreed-upon procedures will be applied.
- The nature, timing and extent of the specific procedures to be applied.
- The anticipated form of the report of factual findings.
- Limitations on distribution of the report of factual findings. When such limitation would be in conflict with any legal requirements the accountants should not accept the engagement. It would include a statement that the distribution of the report of factual findings would be restricted to the specified parties who have agreed to the procedures to be performed.

2 The accountants should plan the work so that an effective engagement will be performed.

3 The accountants should document matters which are important in providing evidence to support the report of factual findings, and evidence that the engagement was carried out in accordance with the ISRS and the terms of the engagement.

4 The accountants should carry out the procedures agreed upon and use the evidence obtained as the basis for the report of factual findings.

The procedures applied in an engagement to perform agreed-upon procedures may include the following:

- Inquiry and analysis.
- Re-computation, comparison and other clerical accuracy checks.
- Observation.
- Inspection.
- Obtaining confirmations.

5 The final report will be a simple recitation of the work carried out and will not give any form of assurance at all,

Example

Example of a Report of Factual Findings in Connection With Accounts Payable.

REPORT OF FACTUAL FINDINGS

To (those who engaged the accountant)

We have performed the procedures agreed with you and enumerated below with respect to the accounts payable of Megablast Ltd as at 31.12 20x7, set forth in the accompanying schedules (not shown in this example). Our engagement was undertaken in accordance with the International Standard on Related Services (or refer to relevant national standards or practices) applicable to agreed-upon procedures engagements. The procedures were performed solely to assist you in evaluating the validity of the accounts payable and are summarised as follows:

1 We obtained and checked the addition of the trial balance of accounts payable as at 31.12.20x7, prepared by Megablast Ltd, and we compared the total to the balance in the related general ledger account.

2 We compared the attached list (not shown in this example) of major suppliers and the amounts owing at 31.12.20x7 to the related names and amounts in the trial balance.

3 We obtained suppliers' statements or requested suppliers to confirm balances owing at 31.12.20x7.

4 We compared such statements or confirmations to the amounts referred to in 2. For amounts which did not agree, we obtained reconciliations from Megablast Ltd. For reconciliations obtained, we identified and listed outstanding invoices, credit notes and outstanding cheques, each of which was greater than £XXX. We located and examined such invoices and credit notes subsequently received and cheques subsequently paid and we ascertained that they should in fact have been listed as outstanding on the reconciliations.

We report our findings below:

(a) With respect to item 1 we found the addition to be correct and the total amount to be in agreement.

(b) With respect to item 2 we found the amounts compared to be in agreement.

(c) With respect to item 3 we found there were suppliers' statements for all such suppliers.

(d) With respect to item 4 we found the amounts agreed, or with respect to amounts which did not agree, we found ABC Company had prepared reconciliations and that the credit notes, invoices and outstanding checks over £XXX were appropriately listed as reconciling items with the following exceptions:

(Detail the exceptions)

Because the above procedures do not constitute either an audit or a review made in accordance with International Standards on Auditing or International Standards on Review Engagements (or relevant national standards or practices), we do not express any assurance on the accounts payable as of 31.12.20x7.

Had we performed additional procedures or had we performed an audit or review of the financial statements in accordance with International Standards on Auditing or International Standards on Review Engagements (or relevant national standards or practices), other matters might have come to our attention that would have been reported to you.

Our report is solely for the purpose set forth in the first paragraph of this report and for your information and is not to be used for any other purpose or to be distributed to any other parties. This report relates only to the accounts and items specified above and does not extend to any financial statements of ABC Company, taken as a whole.

Tickitt & Run

Date

Address

It may be that the accountants are asked to give some level of assurance. In that case the assignment becomes an assurance assignment. It is important that the accountants carry out sufficient work to support their report. Indeed it may be that the assignment ceases to be an agreed upon procedures assignment and takes on some of the characteristics, if not all of them, of the next type of engagement.

Direct reporting engagements

Direct reporting engagements are those where accountants are required to give a special report on some aspects of a client's affairs.

This is not easy to define, because of the varied nature of such assignments, but a special report arises:

- at the request of their client;
- in accordance with instructions received and any relevant statutory or contractual obligations;
- where accountants carry out an independent examination of financial or other information prepared by their client for use by a third party;
- when they report their findings and conclusions *by expressing an opinion*, on the information.

Special reports do not include:

- reports on audited financial statements;
- prospectuses or profit forecasts,

which are dealt with separately

- comfort letters associated with published documents, circulars or, valuations; and
- the preparation of financial statements or information on which no opinion is expressed.

An example of a direct reporting engagement is a due diligence review into a target company on behalf of a possible acquirer (see below).

The approach to a direct reporting engagement is:

- Carry out the work in accordance with the ethical code.
- Agree a precise Letter of Engagement. It is important to ensure that all parties (the audit firm, the persons requiring the special report, the person or enterprise who is responsible for the information being reported on) understand their responsibilities, the relationship between them and what is to be done.
- Plan, control and record the work done.
- Obtain evidence – from documents and records, enquiries of management and others, including analytical review and enquiry of third parties.
- Draw conclusions.
- Report.
- Sign and date.

Due diligence

Due diligence covers a wide range of matters, some of which may not require a professional opinion. In that case they may or may not be assurance assignments.

Due diligence is work, commissioned by a client, involving agreed inquiries into aspects of the accounts, organisation or activities of another organisation, usually one the client is attempting to acquire or invest heavily in. The assignment is evidenced by the usual Letter of Engagement which will set out the work to be done and when by.

The term 'due diligence' is most frequently associated with takeovers and mergers because when a company is taken over or two entities are merged all parties to the transaction need to be assured that what is purported to be actually is.

For example, Huge PLC takes over Medium PLC and needs to be assured that the assets of Medium are as stated. An accounting firm will be engaged to investigate and report on this aspect of the purported information. Note that, particularly in connection with acquisitions, due diligence can be carried out not only by accountants but also by actuaries, surveyors, lawyers and other professionals and sometimes by the staff of the taking-over company. Usually the takeover or merger is not completed until the due diligence is completed.

Where the accountants are asked to express an opinion, view or assurance, such an assignment should be classed as a direct reporting assignment where objectivity is required.

Each report is different and is tailored to the assignment as set out in the Letter of Engagement. The accountants must be sure that they have dealt with all the items included in the Engagement Letter.

If they are asked to express an opinion they must have gathered sufficient, appropriate evidence to support it.

Reports usually contain a restriction on the purpose for which the report can be used and the persons to whom it can be circulated.

Due diligence reports are too varied to provide an example, however the report should, broadly, contain the following parts:

- Title – 'Accountant's report to . . . on . . .'.
- Addressee.
- A description of the subject matter of the engagement and time period.

- Responsibilities of all parties.
- Restricted nature of the report – who the report may or may not be shown to.
- Identification of standards used in the engagement, e.g. the International Standards on Assurance Engagements.
- The criteria against which the subject matter was evaluated.
- The conclusion and any reservations or qualifications to the conclusion. This will include the form of assurance appropriate to the assignment (see below).
- The date.
- The name, description and address of the reporting accountant.

Engagements to review financial statements

This is a form of engagement which is something less than an audit, but on which auditors are required to give some form of assurance.

The reporting standard here is International Standards on Review Engagements 2400, 'Review of Interim Financial Information Performed by the Independent Auditor of the Entity'.

This provides guidance for performing review engagements particularly where:

- the review is performed by the entity's auditor; and
- interim financial information is prepared in accordance with an applicable financial reporting framework,

but can also be in connection with small companies where the accountants do not or cannot perform a full audit, which would involve compliance with all of the various ISAs, etc. and the issuing of an audit report which:

- seeks to give a positive opinion on the financial statements, i.e. includes a conclusion as to whether or the accounts represent (or do not represent) a true and fair view; or
- which results in the auditors failing to express an opinion because of the lack of sufficient appropriate evidence.

The form of assurance that the auditors will give under the provisions of ISRE 2400 is called *negative assurance.*

NEGATIVE ASSURANCE

What this means is that the auditors will carry out a limited amount of testing work which will provide sufficient appropriate evidence to give an opinion that there is *no reason to believe that the financial statements are not true and fair.*

Note the difference in the approach to the wording of the auditors reports from the opinion paragraph in Chapter 27.

The differences between an audit and this type of review engagement can be summarised thus:

Audit	Review
High assurance	Moderate assurance
Positive opinion	Negative opinion
Tests of compliance and substantive tests of detail	Analytical procedures and enquiry of management
Obtain and document evidence for all financial assertions	No evidence required
Report to members	Report to the Board

The ISRE requires the auditor to:

- Comply with ethical requirements relevant to an audit of annual financial statements, i.e. gaining an understanding of the client and its activities and ensuring the firm is independent and able to conduct the review etc. as described in earlier chapters of this book.

- Formalise the terms of the engagement with the client in an Engagement Letter which should include provisions concerning:

  - the objective of the review;
  - management's responsibility for the relevant financial statements;
  - the scope of the review;
  - the auditors' access to information;
  - the form of report to be issued;
  - the fact that the review cannot be relied on to detect fraud or error;
  - the fact that an audit is *not* being performed.

- Plan and perform the review with an attitude of professional scepticism recognising that circumstances may exist that cause the financial information to be misstated.

Specific review procedures include:

- Gaining an understanding of the entity and its environment, including its internal control, as it relates to the preparation of financial information, sufficient to plan and conduct the engagement so as to be able to:

  - identify the types of potential material misstatement and consider the likelihood of their occurrence; and
  - plan the audit work so that it will provide the auditor with a basis for reporting whether anything has come to their attention that causes them to believe that the financial information contains material misstatements.

- Make inquiries primarily of persons responsible for financial and accounting matters. In particular enquire about major matters affecting the company in the year (e.g. new finance, acquisitions, major capital expenditure) and any problems concerning impairment of assets, provisions required, specific disclosures, contingencies, commitments, post balance sheet events, related party transactions, etc.

- Carry out analytical review procedures which will include comparing ratios against previous years, budgets and industry averages. As well as the generally accepted ratios (GP%, Liquidity Ratio, Stock turn etc). These may include such procedures as inspecting an aged list of debtors for anomalies, and reviewing items that require particular management judgement.

- Read the minutes of directors', shareholders and management meetings and review correspondence with lenders, legal advisors, etc.

- Obtain evidence that the financial information agrees or reconciles with the underlying accounting records. This will include control account and bank reconciliations, etc.

- Inquire whether management has identified all events up to the date of the review report that may require adjustment to or disclosure in the financial information.

- Inquire whether management has changed its assessment of the entity's ability to continue as a going concern.

- Evaluate, individually and in total, whether uncorrected misstatements that have come to the auditor's attention are material to the interim financial information.

- Obtain written representations from management on significant issues.

- Read any other information that accompanies the financial statements to consider whether any such information is materially inconsistent with them.
- Issue a written report in accordance with the ISRE.
- Prepare review documentation that is sufficient and appropriate to provide a basis for the accountants' conclusion and to provide evidence that the review was performed in accordance with the ISRE and any applicable legal and regulatory requirements.

Despite the number of points above, careful reading reveals that, in fact, the accountants work is very much less than that which would be performed in a full audit. It basically consists of analytical review and enquiry together with a review of the client's accounting efficiency and a reading of minutes and letters which might give an indication of unrecorded liabilities or significant issues affecting the accounts.

Because of this, as you will see, the wording of this type of report is significantly different to the wording of a Companies Act type audit report as detailed in Chapter 27. The ISRE refers to 'moderate assurance' as a way to describe the opinion paragraph which will give the opinion in the form of negative assurance we saw earlier.

Example

Review report to …

We have reviewed the accompanying Balance Sheet of AB Limited at 31 December 20X7, and the related statements of income and cash flows for the year then ended. These financial statements are the responsibility of the company's management. Our responsibility is to issue a report on these financial statements based on our review.

We conducted our review in accordance with the International Standard on Review Engagements 2400 (or other national standard) applicable to review engagements. This standard requires that we plan and perform the review to obtain moderate assurance as to whether the financial statements are free of material misstatement.

A review is limited primarily to enquiries of company personnel and analytical procedures applied to financial data and thus provides less assurance than an audit.

We have not performed an audit and, accordingly, we do not express an audit opinion.

Based on our review, nothing has come to our attention that causes us to believe that the accompanying financial statements do not give a true and fair view in accordance with International Accounting Standards.

Tickitt & Run
High Street
Anytown

10 March 20X8

Note the wording of the last paragraph which states the negative view that there is *no reason* to believe that the financial statements do *not* give a true and fair view and accord with International Accounting Standards.

Report qualification

If the accountants are not happy with the accounts they are reviewing, and the management refuse to alter them, it is, of course, possible for them to give a qualified report. The first two paragraphs would be the same and a third and fourth might be amended to:

'*Management has informed us that no provision has been made for a possible bad debt. We consider that a provision of £x should be made and net income and shareholders' equity reduced by that amount.*

'*Based on our review, except for the effects of the overstatement of debtors described in the previous paragraph, nothing has come to our attention that causes us to believe that the accompanying financial statements do not give a true and fair view in accordance with International Accounting Standards.*'

In practice, it is unlikely that the directors would issue or publish a review report with a qualification and normally the suggestions of the reviewer would be taken up in the financial statements.

Interim financial information

Most listed companies issue interim accounts, at half yearly or quarterly intervals depending on the relevant Stock Exchange listing agreement.

There is generally no requirement that these be audited, however, it may be that management request a review of these accounts.

The work to be performed would be similar to that detailed above, as this is a review assignment, but the report will be slightly different.

There is an auditing standard – ISA 34 – but this has not, at the time of writing, been adopted in the UK by the APB.

We will look at the guidance given, as to the form of report, in ISRE 2410 '*Review of Interim Financial Information Performed by the Independent Auditor of the Entity*' (UK and Ireland) which has been adopted.

Example

Report on Review of Interim Financial Information

(Appropriate addressee)

Introduction
We have reviewed the accompanying balance sheet of Megablast plc as at March 31, 20X7 and the related statements of income, changes in equity and cash flows for the three-month period then ended, and a summary of significant accounting policies and other explanatory notes.

Management is responsible for the preparation and fair presentation of this interim financial information in accordance with [indicate applicable financial reporting framework, e.g. UK GAAP]. Our responsibility is to express a conclusion on this interim financial information based on our review.

Scope of review
We conducted our review in accordance with International Standard on Review Engagements 2410, 'Review of Interim Financial Information Performed by the Independent Auditor of the Entity.'

A review of interim financial information consists of making inquiries, primarily of persons responsible for financial and accounting matters, and applying analytical and other review procedures. A review is substantially less in scope than an audit conducted in accordance with International Standards on Auditing and consequently does not enable us to obtain assurance that we would become aware of all significant matters that might be identified in an audit.

Accordingly, we do not express an audit opinion.

Conclusion

Based on our review, nothing has come to our attention that causes us to believe that the accompanying interim financial information does not give a true and fair view of (or 'does not present fairly, in all material respects') the financial position of the entity as at March 31, 20X7, and of its financial performance and its cash flows for the three month period then ended in accordance with [applicable financial reporting framework].

AUDITOR
Date
Address

If the auditors feel that their work has been restricted in any way they can qualify the report for limitation of scope, or if the accounts don't comply with the appropriate reporting framework they can qualify on those grounds also.

This is the form of wording for such a qualification – the first part of the report is unchanged. The key wording in the text has been set in **bold** type for clarity.

Example

Example (extract)
Basis for Qualified Conclusion

As a result of a fire in a branch office on (date) that destroyed its sales records, we were unable to complete our review of debtors totalling £_____ included in the interim financial information. The company is in the process of reconstructing these records and is uncertain as to whether these records will support the amount shown above and the related allowance for uncollectible accounts.

Had we been able to complete our review of accounts receivable, matters might have come to our attention indicating that adjustments might be necessary to the interim financial information.

Qualified Conclusion

Except for the adjustments to the interim financial information that we might have become aware of had it not been for the situation described above, based on our review, nothing has come to our attention that causes us to believe that the accompanying interim financial information does not give a true and fair view of (or 'does not present fairly, in all material respects') the financial position of the entity as at March 31,20X7, and of its financial performance and its cash flows for the three-month period then ended in accordance with [applicable financial reporting framework].

AUDITOR
Date
Address

Clearly if the auditors feel that the interim accounts don't present a true and fair view they can issue an adverse report.

If, for any reason, the accountants cannot complete the review they should explain to management, in writing, why this is so. They would have to decide whether or not it is appropriate to issue a report.

If there is a material uncertainty in the financial statements, providing this is adequately disclosed in the accounts the auditors should include an emphasis of matter paragraph in much the same way as they would in a statutory auditors report (Chapter 27).

PROSPECTIVE FINANCIAL INFORMATION

Prospective financial information is information based on assumptions about events which may, or may not, happen in the future and how the organisation will perform in the light of those events.

It is, naturally, highly subjective as it takes the form of budgets, profit projections and assumptions about performance of various parts of the organisation.

Students should be aware of the following definitions.

Prospective financial information – means financial information based on assumptions about events that may occur in the future and possible actions by an entity. It is highly subjective in nature and its preparation requires the exercise of considerable judgement. Prospective financial information can be in the form of a forecast, a projection or a combination of both, for example, a one-year forecast plus a five-year projection.

A forecast – means prospective financial information prepared on the basis of assumptions as to future events which management *expects* to take place and the actions management *expects* to take as of the date the information is prepared (best-estimate assumptions).

A projection – means prospective financial information prepared on the basis of:

- Hypothetical assumptions about future events and management actions which are not necessarily expected to take place but may do in certain circumstances (i.e. if *this* happens then we will do *that*). This is common when all or part of an entity is in a start-up phase or is considering a major change in the nature of its operations; or

- A mixture of best-estimate and hypothetical assumptions. Such information illustrates the possible consequences as of the date the information is prepared if the events and actions were to occur (a 'what-if' scenario).

Prospective financial information can include financial statements, or one or more elements of financial statements, and may be prepared:

(a) As an internal management tool, for example, to assist in evaluating a possible capital investment; or

(b) For distribution to third parties in, for example:

   - A prospectus to provide potential investors with information about future expectations.
   - An annual report to provide information to shareholders, regulatory bodies and other interested parties.
   - A document for the information of lenders which may include, for example, cash flow forecasts.

The International Standard on Assurance Engagements (ISAE) 3400 '*The Examination of Prospective Financial Information*' sets out the approach. It applies to assumptions and forecasts in their entirety and does not apply, for example, to general narrative comments made by directors about future performance in the annual accounts.

Management is responsible for the preparation and presentation of the prospective financial information, including the identification and disclosure of the assumptions on which it is based. The accountants may be asked to examine and report on the prospective financial information to enhance its credibility whether it is intended for use by third parties or for internal purposes.

Letter of engagement

Before accepting an engagement to examine prospective financial information, the accountants would consider, amongst other things:

- the intended use of the information;
- whether the information will be for general or limited distribution;
- the nature of the assumptions, that is, whether they are best-estimate or hypothetical assumptions;
- the elements to be included in the information; and
- the period covered by the information.

The accountants should not accept, or should withdraw from, an engagement when the assumptions are clearly unrealistic or when the accountants believe that the prospective financial information will be inappropriate for its intended use.

The accountants and the client should agree on the terms of the engagement. It is in the interests of both the organisation and the accountants that the accountants send an Engagement Letter to help in avoiding misunderstandings regarding the engagement.

The Engagement Letter should address the issue of who the recipient of the information is likely to be and will set out management's responsibilities for the assumptions and for providing the auditor with all relevant information and source data used in developing the assumptions.

Knowledge of the business

The accountants should obtain a sufficient level of knowledge of the business to be able to evaluate whether all significant assumptions required for the preparation of the prospective financial information have been identified. The accountants would also need to become familiar with the organisation's process for preparing prospective financial information, for example, by considering the following:

- The internal controls over the system used to prepare prospective financial information and the expertise and experience of those persons preparing the prospective financial information.
- The nature of the documentation prepared by the entity supporting management's assumptions.
- The extent to which statistical, mathematical and computer-assisted techniques are used.
- The methods used to develop and apply assumptions.
- The accuracy of any prospective financial information prepared in prior periods and the reasons for significant variances.

The accountants should consider the extent to which reliance on the entity's historical financial information is justified.

Period covered

The accountants should consider the period of time covered by the prospective financial information. Since assumptions become more speculative as the length of the period covered increases, the ability of management to make best-estimate assumptions decreases as the period lengthens.

The period should not extend beyond the time for which management has a reasonable basis for the assumptions. This might be as long as five years or more in the case of, say a construction company engaged in long-term projects, or as short as, say, two years in the case of an Internet retailer. Each case is different.

Audit approach

In an engagement to examine prospective financial information, the accountants should obtain sufficient, appropriate evidence as to whether:

- management's best-estimate assumptions on which the prospective financial information is based are not unreasonable and, in the case of hypothetical assumptions, such assumptions are consistent with the purpose of the information;
- the prospective financial information is properly prepared on the basis of the assumptions;
- the prospective financial information is properly presented and all material assumptions are adequately disclosed, including a clear indication as to whether they are best-estimate assumptions or hypothetical assumptions; and
- the prospective financial information is prepared on a consistent basis with historical financial statements, using appropriate accounting principles.

When determining the nature, timing and extent of examination procedures, the accountants' considerations should include:

- the likelihood of material misstatement;
- the knowledge obtained during any previous engagements;
- management's competence regarding the preparation of prospective financial information;
- the extent to which the prospective financial information is affected by the management's judgment; and
- the adequacy and reliability of the underlying data.

Specifically the accountants should:

- Assess the source and reliability of the evidence supporting management's best-estimate assumptions. Sufficient, appropriate evidence supporting such assumptions would be obtained from internal and external sources including consideration of the assumptions in the light of historical information and an evaluation of whether they are based on plans that are within the entity's capacity.
- Consider whether, when hypothetical assumptions are used, all significant implications of such assumptions have been taken into consideration. For example, if sales are assumed to grow beyond the company's current plant capacity, the prospective financial information will need to include the necessary investment in the additional plant capacity or the costs of alternative means of meeting the anticipated sales, such as subcontracting production.
- The accountants would need to be satisfied that hypothetical assumptions used are consistent with the purpose of the prospective financial information and that there is no reason to believe they are clearly unrealistic.
- Make arithmetical checks and review the statements for internal consistency.

- Review areas that are particularly sensitive to variation and which will have a material effect on the results shown in the prospective financial information.
- Obtain written representations from management regarding the intended use of the prospective financial information, the completeness of significant management assumptions and management's acceptance of its responsibility for the prospective financial information.

Disclosure

The accountants should assess the presentation and disclosure of the prospective financial information, in addition to the specific requirements of any relevant statutes, regulations or professional standards.

They will need to consider whether:

- The presentation of prospective financial information is informative and not misleading.
- The accounting policies are clearly disclosed in the notes to the prospective financial information.
- The assumptions are adequately disclosed in the notes to the prospective financial information. It needs to be clear whether assumptions represent management's best-estimates or are hypothetical and, when assumptions are made in areas that are material and are subject to a high degree of uncertainty, this uncertainty and the resulting sensitivity of results needs to be adequately disclosed.
- The date as of which the prospective financial information was prepared is disclosed. Management needs to confirm that the assumptions are appropriate as of this date, even though the underlying information may have been accumulated over a period of time.
- The basis of establishing points in a range is clearly indicated and the range is not selected in a biased or misleading manner when results shown in the prospective financial information are expressed in terms of a range.
- Any change in accounting policy since the most recent historical financial statements is disclosed, along with the reason for the change and its effect on the prospective financial information.

Reporting

The report by the accountants on an examination of prospective financial information should contain the following:

(a) title;

(b) addressee;

(c) identification of the prospective financial information;

(d) a reference to the ISAE or relevant national standards or practices applicable to the examination of prospective financial information;

(e) a statement that management is responsible for the prospective financial information including the assumptions on which it is based;

(f) when applicable, a reference to the purpose and/or restricted distribution of the prospective financial information;

(g) a statement of *negative assurance* as to whether the assumptions provide a reasonable basis for the prospective financial information;

(h) an opinion as to whether the prospective financial information is properly prepared on the basis of the assumptions and is presented in accordance with the relevant financial reporting framework;

(i) appropriate caveats concerning the achievability of the results indicated by the prospective financial information;

(j) date of the report which should be the date procedures have been completed;

(k) accountant's address; and

(l) signature.

Here is an example of an extract from an unmodified report on a *forecast*. We have set key words in **bold**:

> 'We have examined the forecast in accordance with the International Standard on Assurance Engagements applicable to the examination of prospective financial information. Management is responsible for the forecast including the assumptions set out in Note X on which it is based.
>
> Based on our examination of the evidence supporting the assumptions, **nothing has come to our attention which causes us to believe that these assumptions do not provide a reasonable basis for the forecast**.
>
> Further, in our opinion the forecast is properly prepared on the basis of the assumptions and is presented in accordance with . . . (relevant financial reporting framework). Actual results are likely to be different from the forecast since anticipated events frequently do not occur as expected and the variation may be material.'

Here is an example of an extract from an unmodified report on a *projection*. Students should note the differences in wording between this report and the one above, which are significant.

> 'We have examined the projection in accordance with the International Standard on Assurance Engagements applicable to the examination of prospective financial information. Management is responsible for the projection including the assumptions set out in Note X on which it is based.
>
> This projection has been prepared for (describe purpose ie. the purpose for which the entity exists). As the entity is in a start-up phase the projection has been prepared using a set of assumptions that include hypothetical assumptions about future events and management's actions that are not necessarily expected to occur. Consequently, readers are cautioned that this projection may not be appropriate for purposes other than that described above.
>
> Based on our examination of the evidence supporting the assumptions, **nothing has come to our attention which causes us to believe that these assumptions do not provide a reasonable basis for the projection, assuming** that (here the accountants would state or refer to the hypothetical assumptions).
>
> Further, in our opinion the projection is properly prepared on the basis of the assumptions and is presented in accordance with . . . (relevant financial reporting framework).
>
> Even if the events anticipated under the hypothetical assumptions described above occur, actual results are still likely to be different from the projection since other anticipated events frequently do not occur as expected and the variation may be material.'

If the accountants believe that:

- the presentation and disclosure of the prospective financial information is not adequate; or
- the assumptions don't provide a reasonable basis for the prospective financial information; or
- they have been limited in some way in the scope of their procedures,

then they should express a qualified or adverse opinion in the report on the prospective financial information, or withdraw from the engagement as appropriate.

Summary

- Accountants are often called upon to prepare (compile) financial statements without necessarily being asked to audit them, to perform attest functions, to review financial statements and to perform agreed upon procedures.

- The ethical standards and quality control procedures which apply to audit work also apply to this kind of engagement.

- The engagements are regulated by various international standards on reporting engagements. Engagements to perform agreed-upon procedures are governed by ISRS 4400 '*Engagements to Perform Agreed-upon Procedures Regarding Financial Information*'. Engagements to compile financial information are governed by ISRS 4410 '*Engagements to Compile Financial Information*' and ISAE 3400 '*The Examination of Prospective Financial Information*' governs the accountants' review of forecasts and projections.

- Students do not have to be able to write reports for these types of engagements but should be familiar with the different types of assignment and on which ones they will give limited assurance and on which ones will give no assurance.

ASSURANCE ENGAGEMENTS

Introduction

Assurance engagements performed by professional accountants are intended to enhance the credibility of information about a subject matter by evaluating whether the subject matter conforms in all material respects with suitable criteria, thereby improving the likelihood that the information will meet the needs of an intended user.

The objective of an assurance engagement is for a professional accountant to:

- evaluate or measure a subject matter;
- that is the responsibility of another party;
- against identified suitable criteria,

and to express a conclusion that provides the intended user with a level of assurance about that subject matter.

The level of assurance provided by the professional accountant's conclusion conveys the degree of confidence that the intended user may place in the credibility of the subject matter. An audit is a specific form of assurance assignment.

Apart from audits such assignments can include:

- reports on internal controls;
- value for money reviews;
- performance development reviews;
- environmental or corporate social responsibility audits;
- risk evaluations;
- compliance reviews;
  . . . etc.

Companies often want to report on these issues to shareholders or demonstrate assurances that they are complying with regulations or best practice and the accountants' role is to add credibility to the statements made.

It is not practicable to look at every type of assurance engagement in detail. Instead the principles contained in this section should be applied to the specific engagement. We will, however, look at one or two types of review specifically as these offer guidance on the general approach.

Approach

The applicable reporting standard is the International Standard on Assurance Engagements (ISAE) 3000 'Assurance Engagements other than Audits or Reviews of Historical Financial Information' produced by the IAASB.

This applies to all assurance engagements, other than audits, but not reviews of financial information or prospective financial information, which we looked at earlier, which are covered by the various International Standards on Review Engagements (ISREs).

It doesn't cover any assignments where the accountants are not giving assurances or opinions so it doesn't apply to attestation, compilation or agreed-upon procedures type of assignments, nor does it apply to consultancy work or assignments to prepare tax computations where no opinion or conclusion is expressed.

The standard distinguishes between:

- reasonable assurance engagements; and
- limited assurance engagements.

We will look at these in more detail later.

The standard requires the accountant to comply with the appropriate ethical code and to have implemented quality control procedures applicable to the individual engagement.

There are two key points:

- The accountants should consider any request to change the assignment, before it is completed from an assurance engagement to a non-assurance engagement, or from a reasonable assurance engagement to a limited assurance engagement and should not agree to any change without reasonable justification.

- The accountants should plan and perform the engagement with an attitude of professional scepticism recognising that circumstances may exist where information may be materially misstated. Students will recognise parallels in the wording with that of ISA 240 – 'The Auditors' Responsibility to Consider Fraud in an Audit of Financial Statements'.

The key components of this type of a review are:

1 The bodies involved in this type of assignment, i.e.:

- The reporting accountants (called 'the practitioner' in the ISAE).
- The responsible party (i.e. a company, a public body, etc.)
- The intended user (i.e. members of the public, a regulatory body, etc.).

2 The subject matter, e.g. set of accounts, an environmental report, the operations of a department, etc.
3 The suitable criteria – e.g. benchmark data, IASs, etc.
4 The process of completing the engagement – in many ways very similar to the approach adopted when undertaking a statutory audit.
5 The conclusion and report.

The simplest way of thinking about this is to use the audit as an example.

In an audit, which is a form of assurance assignment, the reporting accountants (the auditors) report to the intended user (the shareholders) on the subject matter, i.e. information which is the responsibility of the responsible party (the accounts prepared by the directors) as to compliance with against suitable criteria, i.e. the Companies Act 2006 and the accounting standards.

Assignment risk

Every assignment carries with it some element of risk. The risk is that the reporting accountants will give an incorrect conclusion in their report, i.e. that they will positively confirm that X information complies with Y criteria when it doesn't or alternatively that it doesn't comply when it does.

Students will recall that the main components of this risk, which relates only to the reporting accountant, are:

- Inherent risk;
- Control risk;
- Detection risk.

Remember also however that there is another type of risk – business risk which relates to the risks faced by the entity itself. We looked at this in Chapter 14.

Only those risks which relate to the assignment are relevant but the reporting accountants must not only satisfy themselves that they can reduce assignment risk to an acceptable level but also that the organisation's risk management processes are sufficient to identify and manage business risk so that it will not adversely affect their report and its conclusion.

The process

The ISAE sets out the basis on which the reporting accountants should approach the assignment. Much of it is familiar territory as it basically follows the same steps as the planning and completion of a statutory audit assignment so there is no need to go into detail about each aspect of the approach.

Students should be familiar with each of the steps in the process:

- The accountants should obtain an understanding of the subject matter and other engagement circumstances, sufficient to identify and assess the risks of the subject matter information being materially misstated, and sufficient to design and perform further evidence-gathering procedures.
- The accountants should plan the engagement so that it will be performed effectively.

  Examples of the main matters to be considered include:

  - The terms of the engagement. These should be evidenced by an Engagement Letter.
  - The characteristics of the subject matter and the identified criteria.
  - The engagement process and possible sources of evidence.
  - The accountants' understanding of the entity and its environment, including the risks that the subject matter information may be materially misstated.
  - Identification of intended users and their needs, and consideration of materiality and the components of assurance engagement risk.
  - Personnel and expertise requirements, including the nature and extent of any experts' involvement.

- The accountants should assess the appropriateness of the subject matter. The reasons for this are:
  - Accountants should not take on an assignment where the subject matter is outside their competence to such an extent that they cannot properly assess the assignment risk – i.e. the risk of giving an incorrect or inappropriate report. If the assignment is of specialised nature the accountants should decline it.
  - Accountants should consider the risk of being unable to gather sufficient, appropriate evidence about the subject matter in order to validate their conclusions.
- The practitioner should assess the suitability of the criteria to evaluate or measure the subject matter.

  Criteria can either be established or specifically developed. In many cases this may not be easy. Suitable benchmark criteria may be difficult to find whereas in the case of an assignment to evaluate compliance with regulations, etc. the criteria are usually much more precise. Clearly if suitable criteria cannot be found the assurance cannot be given.
- The accountants should consider materiality and assurance engagement risk when planning and performing an assurance engagements. The accountants should reduce assurance engagement risk to an acceptably low level in the circumstances of the engagement. Assignment risk has the same components as audit risk.
- The accountants should consider the use of experts as appropriate. Remember that the reporting accountant remains responsible for identifying a suitably qualified and experienced expert and cannot delegate any responsibility for the report's conclusions to the expert. The accountants are responsible for the totality of their report.
- The accountants should obtain representations from the responsible party, as appropriate. Written confirmation of oral representations reduces the possibility of misunderstandings.
- The accountants should consider the effect on the subject matter information and on the assurance report of events up to the date of the assurance report – i.e. perform a subsequent events review.
- The accountants should document matters that are significant in providing evidence that supports the assurance report and that the engagement was performed in accordance with ISAEs.
- The accountants should conclude whether sufficient appropriate evidence has been obtained to support the conclusion expressed in the assurance report. In developing the conclusion, the accountants must consider all relevant evidence obtained, regardless of whether it appears to corroborate or to contradict the subject matter information.
- The assurance report should be in writing and should contain a clear expression of the practitioner's conclusion about the subject matter information.

  The report can either relate to the responsible parties assertions about the subject matter or the subject matter itself in a form similar to the assertion made by the responsible party.

Assurance report content

The assurance report should include the following basic elements:

(a) *A title*

The report should have a title that clearly indicates the report is an independent assurance report. An appropriate title helps to identify the nature of the assurance report, and to distinguish it from reports issued by others, such as those who do not have to comply with the same ethical requirements as the reporting accountants.

(b) *An addressee*

An addressee identifies the party or parties to whom the assurance report is directed. Whenever practical the assurance report is addressed to all the intended users.

(c) *An identification and description of the subject matter*

This includes, for example:

- the point in time or period of time to which the evaluation or measurement of the subject matter relates;
- where applicable, the name of the entity or component of the entity to which the subject matter relates; and
- an explanation of those characteristics of the subject matter or the subject matter information of which the intended users should be aware, and how such characteristics may influence the precision of the evaluation or measurement of the subject matter against the identified criteria, or the persuasiveness of available evidence.
  For example:

  - The degree to which the subject matter information is qualitative versus quantitative, objective versus subjective, or historical versus prospective.
  - Changes in the subject matter or other engagement circumstances that affect the comparability of the subject matter information from one period to the next.

(d) *Identification of the criteria*

The assurance report identifies the criteria against which the subject matter is evaluated or measured so the intended users can understand the basis for the accountants' conclusion.

The assurance report may include the criteria, or simply refer to them if they are contained in an assertion prepared by the responsible party which is available to the intended users or, if they are otherwise available, from a readily accessible source. The users must be able to evaluate the benchmark criteria for themselves.

The accountants should consider whether it is relevant to the circumstances, to disclose:

- the source of the criteria;
- measurement methods used when the criteria allow for choice between a number of methods;
- any significant interpretations made in applying the criteria in the engagement circumstances; and
- whether there have been any changes in the measurement methods used.

(e) *Where appropriate, a description of any significant inherent limitations associated with the evaluation or measurement of the subject matter against the criteria*

While, in some cases, inherent limitations can be expected to be well understood by readers of an assurance report, in other cases it may be appropriate to make explicit reference in the assurance report.
For example:

- In an assurance report related to the effectiveness of internal control, it may be appropriate to note that the historic evaluation of effectiveness of controls is not necessarily relevant to future periods due to the risk that internal control may become inadequate because of changes in conditions, or that the degree of compliance with policies or procedures may deteriorate.

(f) *When the criteria used to evaluate or measure the subject matter are available only to specific intended users, or are relevant only to a specific purpose, a statement restricting the use of the assurance report to those intended users or that purpose*

Whenever the assurance report is intended only for specific intended users or a specific purpose, the accountants should consider stating this fact in the assurance report. The reason for this is that if the report is made available to parties who do not have access to the relevant criteria their understanding of the full implications of any conclusions or points made in the report may be flawed.

(g) *A statement to identify the responsible party and to describe the responsible party's and the accountant's respective responsibilities*

This informs the intended users that the responsible party is responsible for the subject or the subject matter information and that the practitioner's role is to independently express a conclusion.

(h) *A statement that the engagement was performed in accordance with ISAEs*

Where there is a subject matter-specific ISAE, that ISAE may require that the assurance report refers specifically to it.

(i) *A summary of the work performed*

The summary will help the intended users understand the nature of the assurance conveyed by the assurance report.

(j) *The conclusion*

Where the subject matter information is made up of a number of aspects, separate conclusions may be provided on each aspect.

While not all such conclusions need to relate to the same level of evidence-gathering procedures, each conclusion is expressed in the form that is appropriate to either a reasonable assurance or a limited assurance engagement.

Where appropriate, the conclusion should inform the intended users of the context in which the practitioner's conclusion is to be read: the practitioner's conclusion may, for example, include wording such as:

'This conclusion has been formed on the basis of, and is subject to the inherent limitations outlined elsewhere in this independent assurance report.'

This would be appropriate, for example, when the report includes an explanation of particular characteristics of the subject matter of which the intended users should be aware.

(k) *The assurance report date*

This informs the intended users that the accountants have considered the effect on the subject matter information and on the assurance report of events that occurred up to that date but no further.

(l) *The name of the firm and a specific location*

Which ordinarily is the city where the practitioner maintains the office that has responsibility for the engagement. This informs the intended users of the individual or firm assuming responsibility for the engagement.

LEVELS OF ASSURANCE

It is possible to give 'reasonable assurance' or 'limited assurance'.

Reasonable assurance

'Reasonable assurance' is less than absolute assurance but more than limited assurance.

The objective of a reasonable assurance assignment is to reduce assignment risk to an acceptably low level so the reporting accountant can give a *positive* opinion.

Again if the analogy of the audit is used the reporting auditor gives a positive opinion – *'the financial statements present a true and fair view, etc.'* and can do this only within the bounds of an acceptable level of audit risk.

As with audit risk, reducing assurance engagement risk to zero is very rarely attainable, or cost beneficial, as a result of factors such as the following:

- the use of selective testing;
- the inherent limitations of internal control;
- the fact that much of the evidence available to the practitioner is persuasive rather than conclusive;
- the use of judgement in gathering and evaluating evidence and forming conclusions based on that evidence;
- in some cases, the characteristics of the subject matter.

In a reasonable assurance engagement, the conclusion should be expressed in the *positive* form:

Example

'In our opinion internal control is effective, in all material respects, based on XYZ criteria.' or:
'In our opinion the responsible party's assertion that internal control is effective, in all material respects, based on XYZ criteria, is fairly stated.'

Remember that the conclusion can either relate to the subject matter itself or to the responsible party's assertions about the subject matter.

Clearly reasonable assurance can only be given if the subject matter is:

- the responsibility of a third party;
- is in a form which is clearly identifiable and which can be subjected to evidence-gathering procedures;
- and the accountants are not aware of any circumstances where reasonable assurance, based on suitable criteria if such can be found, cannot be given.

Note however, in some cases, the evidence-gathering procedures may be difficult or expensive. If the accountants, for example, are required to report on local procurement policies for a multinational company this might involve a lot of staff and a lot of overseas travel. Cost or other such difficulties should not be a barrier to giving reasonable assurance if that is what is required, but the client must be aware of this before the engagement commences.

Limited assurance

Limited assurance requirements will result in a *negative assurance* opinion and will be based on much more limited evidence gathering procedures.

The objective of a limited assurance assignment is to reduce assignment risk to an acceptable level so a negative expression of opinion can be given.

In a limited assurance engagement, the conclusion should be expressed in the *negative* form:

Example

'Based on our work described in this report, nothing has come to our attention that causes us to believe that internal control is not effective, in all material respects, based on XYZ criteria.'
or:

'Based on our work described in this report, nothing has come to our attention that causes us to believe that the responsible party's assertion that internal control is effective, in all material respects, based on XYZ criteria, is not fairly stated.'

Qualified conclusions, adverse conclusions and disclaimers of conclusion

Where the accountants express a qualified conclusion, the assurance report should contain a clear description of all the reasons.

The reporting accountants should not express an unqualified conclusion when the following circumstances exist and, in their opinion, the effect of the matter is or may be material:

- There is a limitation on the scope of the accountants' work.

  That means, circumstances prevent, or the responsible party or the engaging party imposes a restriction, that prevents the accountants from obtaining evidence required to reduce assurance engagement risk to the appropriate level.

  The accountants should express a qualified conclusion (*except for*) or a *disclaimer* of conclusion;

- In those cases where:

  - the reporting accountants conclusion is worded in terms of the responsible party's assertion, and that assertion is not fairly stated, in all material respects; or
  - the practitioner's conclusion is worded directly in terms of the subject matter and the criteria, and the subject matter information is materially misstated,

  the accountants should express a qualified or (*except for*) adverse conclusion.

When it is discovered, after the engagement has been accepted, that the criteria are unsuitable or the subject matter is not appropriate for an assurance engagement. The practitioner should express:

- a qualified conclusion or adverse conclusion when the unsuitable criteria or inappropriate subject matter is likely to mislead the intended users; or
- a qualified conclusion or a disclaimer of conclusion in other cases.

The practitioner should express a qualified conclusion when the effect of a matter is not so material or pervasive as to require an adverse conclusion or a disclaimer of conclusion.

A qualified conclusion is expressed as being *'except for'* the effects of the matter to which the qualification relates.

Both reasonable assurance and limited assurance engagements require the application of assurance skills and techniques and the gathering of sufficient, appropriate evidence as part of an iterative, systematic engagement process that includes obtaining an understanding of the subject matter and other engagement circumstances.

The nature, timing and extent of procedures for gathering sufficient appropriate evidence in a limited assurance engagement are, however, deliberately limited relative to a reasonable assurance engagement.

For some subject matters, there may be specific ISAEs to provide guidance on procedures for gathering sufficient appropriate evidence for a limited assurance engagement. In the absence of a specific ISAE, the procedures for gathering sufficient appropriate evidence will vary with the circumstances of the engagement, in particular the subject matter and the needs of the intended users and the engaging party, including relevant time and cost constraints.

The next chapter looks in detail at some specific types of non-audit assurance assignments.

Summary

- The objective is to measure the subject matter, which is another party's responsibility, against suitable criteria and to report.
- Assurance assignments may give 'reasonable assurance' or 'limited assurance'.
- Assignments must be evidenced with a letter of engagement.
- ISAE 3000 is the reporting standard.
- The reporting accountants must consider the level of assurance risk.
- They must gather sufficient, appropriate evidence to validate their conclusions.
- The report should identify the criteria used and the work done to validate or otherwise the subject matter against those criteria.
- The conclusions may be positively worded in the case of reasonable assurance or negatively worded in the case of limited assurance.

Points to note

- Firms of accountants are commercial enterprises as well as professional practices. They continually seek new work and new areas of application of their expertise. The demand for various forms of assurance and attesting is increasing.
- Assurance engagements are governed internationally by the International Standard on Assurance Engagements 3000. An assurance engagement is one where a professional accountant is engaged to evaluate or measure a subject matter that is the responsibility of another party against identified suitable criteria, and to express a conclusion that provides the intended user with a level of assurance about that subject matter.
- This includes attest and direct reporting engagements but excludes agreed-upon procedures and compilation engagements.

Case Study 1

Tickitt & Run are the auditors of BigBoy PLC and have been asked as a special-purpose audit engagement to express an opinion on the present liquidity of the company and, in particular, the ability of the company to repay some proposed loan finance. The report is required by the Unlikely Bank PLC in connection with a large loan for new premises and equipment.

Discussion
What work should the accountants do in connection with the assignment?
   Produce an accountants' report on the basis that:

(a) All is well and there are no apparent difficulties in repaying the loan based on management's forecasts of the benefits of the new assets to the business.

(b) Present liquidity is adequate but could be problematic if some debts are not recovered in full and the assumptions underlying the forecast of ability to repay the loan are very optimistic.

Case Study 2

The directors of Dunbar Holdings are seeking to win an award for business excellence. As part of the award process reporting accountants have to assess the business performance against a set of predetermined criteria set out in the award documentation. This covers such matters as HR policy, staff morale, financial solvency, customer satisfaction and compliance with environmental regulations.

The assessment has to be performed by independent reporting accountants who will give an assurance as to compliance with the award rules.

Tickitt & Run are to investigate and report.

During the course of their work they discover that staff morale in some parts of the business is very low after some compulsory redundancies, the business was recently fined for illegal dumping of toxic materials and one of their new products is attracting a lot of complaints because it doesn't work very well. However, Dunbar is a large company and these issues are only a relatively minor part of their operations which are generally good.

Discussion

- What type of assurance is being sought?
- How will the reporting accountants deal with the issues they have uncovered in the context of their report?
- How will the report be worded?

Student self-testing questions

Questions with answers apparent from the text

a) List the procedures that should be adopted in compiling financial statements.
b) State the objectives of an assurance engagement.
c) What is an attest function?
d) What is due diligence and when is it performed?
e) What is a direct reporting engagement – give an example.
f) How should a direct reporting engagement be carried out?
g) What is negative assurance and when is it appropriate?
h) What should an accountant do if the prospective financial information is based on unrealistic assumptions?
i) What should appear in a direct reporting engagement report?
j) What are the three criteria for assurance assignments?
k) What is the role of the responsible party?
l) To whom are the accountants reporting?
m) What approach will the accountants take?
n) What two forms of reporting are there?

o) What is the difference between them in terms of the accountants' approach to the assignment?

p) When should accountants give a limited conclusion and what form will it take?

Examination question

Imperiol, a limited liability company, manufactures and distributes electrical and telecommunications accessories, household durables (e.g. sink and shower units) and building systems (e.g. air-conditioning, solar heating, security systems). The company has undergone several business restructurings in recent years. Finance is to be sought from both a bank and a venture capitalist in order to implement the board's latest restructuring proposals.

You are a manager in Hal Falcon, a firm of Chartered Certified Accountants. You have been approached by Paulo Gandalf, the chief finance officer of Imperiol, to provide a report on the company's business plan for the year to 31 December 20X7.

From a brief telephone conversation with Paulo Gandalf you have ascertained that the proposed restructuring will involve discontinuing all operations except for building systems, where the greatest opportunity for increasing product innovation is believed to lie. Imperiol's strategy is to become the market leader in providing 'total building system solutions' using new fibre optic technology to link building systems. A major benefit of the restructuring is expected to be a lower ongoing cost base. As part of the restructuring it is likely that certain of the accounting functions, including internal audit, will be outsourced.

You have obtained a copy of Imperiol's Interim Report for the six months to 30 June 20X6 in which the company's auditors, Discorpio, provide a conclusion giving negative assurance. The following information has been extracted from the Interim Financial Report:

(1) Chairman's statement

    The economic climate is less certain than it was a few months ago and performance has been affected by a severe decline in the electrical accessories market. Management's response will be to gain market share and reduce the cost base.

(2) Balance sheet

	30 June 20x6 (unaudited)	31 December 20x5
	$m	$m
Intangible assets	83·5	72·6
Tangible non-current assets	69·6	63·8
Inventory	25·2	20·8
Receivables	59·9	50·2
Cash	8·3	23·8
Total assets	246·5	231·2
Issued capital	30·4	30·4
Reserves	6·0	9·1
Accumulated profits	89·1	89·0
	125·5	128·5
Interest bearing borrowings	65·4	45·7
Current liabilities	55·6	57·0
Total equity and liabilities	246·5	231·2

(3) Continuing and discontinuing operations

	Six months to 30 June 20x6 (unaudited)	Year to 31 December 20x5
	$m	$m
Turnover		
Continuing operations		
Electrical		
and telecommunication accessories	55·3	118·9
Household durables	37·9	77·0
Building systems	53·7	94·9
Total continuing	146·9	290·8
Discontinued	–	65·3
Total turnover	146·9	356·1
Operating profit before interest and		
taxation – continuing operations	13·4	32·2

Required:

(a) Explain the matters Hal Falcon should consider before accepting the engagement to report on Imperiol's prospective financial information.

(b) Describe the procedures that a professional accountant should undertake in order to provide a report on a profit forecast and forecast balance sheet for Imperiol for the year to 31 December 20x7.

(ACCA)

33

Value for money, performance evaluation, environmental reporting and corporate social responsibility reporting assignments

INTRODUCTION

Following on from Chapter 32 we can look at some specific assurance-type assignments which are not immediately obvious as being within the type of work auditors normally carry out, but with which audit firms are becoming increasingly involved.

As stated in the introduction to the previous chapter, assurance assignments can be many and varied and the practitioner has to follow the principles laid down in the previous chapters, including those relevant to carrying out audit work, in order to complete such assignments satisfactorily.

However, there are some types of assignment which have specific characteristics and it is appropriate to single these out for special comment.

These are:

- performance reporting;
- value for money; and
- environmental reporting.

Accounting firms are actively engaged in this type of work and are becoming increasingly involved, particularly in the public sector but also in the private sector, in evaluating the performance of an organisation against agreed criteria or best practice.

VALUE FOR MONEY

Value for money (VFM) auditing is an audit methodology in which auditors are either required to, or exercise discretionary power to, satisfy themselves, by examination of the accounts and otherwise, that the organisation has made proper arrangements for securing *economy, efficiency and effectiveness* in the use of resources.

This is very common in the public sector, where public money raised through taxation has to be accounted for and the public are understandably anxious to ensure that it isn't being wasted.

However, it is also applicable to some private sector bodies and to organisations such as charities who may want to obtain best use of limited funds

ECONOMY, EFFICIENCY AND EFFECTIVENESS

These terms, known as the 'three Es', are fundamental to an understanding of VFM audit approaches and the concepts involved should be explored more deeply than these definitions.

Economy is '*acquiring resources of appropriate quality and quantity at the lowest cost – the measure of input*'.

The most important thing to note is that, while obtaining low prices is certainly important, it is not the only consideration when obtaining resources. Achieving true economy also entails a consideration of qualitative aspects, such as whether the resources purchased are fit for purpose.

For example, it would clearly be uneconomical to buy very cheap but poorly made equipment which would require regular replacement.

Efficiency is '*maximising the useful output from the resources used, or minimising the level of work in producing a given level of input*'.

The main VFM consideration is whether the resources obtained are put to good use and whether the processes and working practices in use represent best practice.

Effectiveness is '*ensuring that the output from any given activity is achieving the desired result*'.

VFM does take a 'process-driven' approach, considering whether economically obtained resources are put to efficient use to generate outputs, however, it must also consider whether these outputs are useful and whether they are actually achieving the objective.

Areas for review

Common areas VFM auditors will consider as being involved in value for money initiatives within an organisation include:

- The systems of budgeting, controlling revenue and capital expenditure and income, and for allocating scarce resources. A sound budget-setting and monitoring process is essential for identifying and correcting poor economy and efficiency – if this is not present management will be unable to achieve its VFM goals.
- The quality and robustness of strategic and business planning and forecasting.
- The monitoring of tendering arrangements for large capital, service or supply contracts.
- Personnel management, including arrangements for deciding and reviewing staffing levels and for recruiting, training, rewarding and otherwise motivating employees.
- Arrangements concerned with the proper management of all the assets of the organisation to ensure they are all contributing to the efficiency of operations. This might include the introduction of energy efficiency policies and the disposal of inefficient or high-maintenance equipment which does not pay its way.
- Arrangements designed to take advantage of economies of scale or skill, particularly in the purchasing of goods and services.

- The quality and accuracy of management and performance information.
- Clear understanding of responsibilities, authority and accountability throughout the organisation's structure.
- Clear communication of policy objectives throughout the organisation.
- Monitoring results against predetermined performance objectives and standards, to ensure that outstanding performance is encouraged and unacceptable performance corrected.
- The use of comparative data or benchmarking arrangements with suitable comparator organisations.
- Mechanisms for consulting with, and responding to, the needs of customers.

Approach

When reviewing VFM performance, accountants should also consider a wider set of indicators or information, such as:

- Key performance indicators as selected by management or as determined by investigating accountants based on experience in comparable organisations.
- Investigations in obtaining a detailed knowledge of the audited body, i.e. systems reviews, flow charting, discussions with staff and line management.
- The existence of standards such as ISO 9000 or Investors in People and the outcome of standard reviews.
- Analytical procedures – fluctuating or increasing levels of expenditure might highlight risk factors.
- Comparison with other bodies or similar parts of the same organisation (e.g. other subsidiaries) to identify areas where performance appears to be weak.
- Discussions with management and staff.
- Board and other committee minutes – minutes of staff meetings might be more relevant.
- The effect on the organisation or parts of the organisation which has been through rapid change.
- Information from outside sources: market research, customer complaints, press, Internet comment.

Auditors should be alert to:

- Structural weaknesses, for example:
  - no clearly defined corporate strategy for the longer term;
  - poorly defined and badly communicated objectives;
  - use of outmoded or top heavy business structures;
  - failure to consider outsourcing opportunities or more efficient ways of achieving objectives;
  - poorly trained or inexperienced management;
  - duplication of effort within the business structure;
  - poorly defined responsibility allocation.
- Waste, for example:
  - errors (overpayments, failure to take discounts);
  - poor communications (ordering goods not required); inefficiencies (high wastage rates of material); poorly performing, old or obsolete technology;

- Extravagance, for example:

  - overstaffing;
  - high rates of pay for poor productivity;
  - excessive specifications;
  - excessive quantity of purchases/inventory;

- Weak management information systems, for example:

  - large overspends against budget indicative of poor monitoring or bad budgeting;
  - prestigious projects with little economic justification;
  - poor prioritisation of work leading to inefficient use of resources;
  - lack of client consultation or market research;
  - lack of key performance indicators.

PERFORMANCE EVALUATION

For most organisations the primary consideration of performance is measured by the financial statements, e.g. the profit for the year, the return on capital, the cash flow generated – in short any one of a host of financial measures.

However, other measures can be employed to evaluate the performance of the organisation as it affects other stakeholders, for example, customers, suppliers and staff.

Operational performance

As we have seen in the section above there are a range of measures to evaluate operational performance from the point of view of economy, efficiency and effectiveness.

This is particularly relevant in service-based organisations such as public sector bodies or charities where the criteria for measuring performance are not financial. Such measures as:

- Hospital waiting lists;

- School league tables;

- Train delays, etc.

have all provided indicators of performance efficiency.

Assessing operational performance

The organisation should develop its own measures for assessing its performance against clearly defined targets or key performance indicators (KPIs).

There are various methodologies organisations can adopt and it is outside the scope of this book to discuss them in detail.

From a reporting accountants' perspective there are three key considerations:

- The applicability of the KPI – is it a reliable indicator? It may be that one indicator is not sufficient or that, of itself, it is not a true indicator of underlying performance.

- The ability of the management information system to provide information in order to measure actual performance against it. The KPI may be a desirable measure but, in practice, it may be too costly or time-consuming to collect the data or it is susceptible to misrepresentation or distortion in order to paint a false picture.

- The amount of sufficient, appropriate evidence the accountants can obtain in order to give the assurance required.

The report of investigating accountants can be used to give credibility to management assertions about performance and accountants have to be very careful that they follow the precepts of the reporting standards and carry out their work with a due level of scepticism and professionalism.

ENVIRONMENTAL REPORTING

Introduction

All enterprises in the twenty-first century face a climate of rapid change and escalating regulatory requirements. Amongst the major changes occurring are environmental obligations both legal and moral (known as constructive obligations). In recent years there has been an exponential growth in the awareness of environmental issues which has resulted in increased pressures on business and other organisations to respond to very public issues including:

- climate change;
- a need for waste management;
- a need to avoid polluting the earth, water and air;
- a need for recycling;
- a need for a safe and clean environment.

The importance of environmental matters has affected auditors in that environmental matters can constitute considerable risks to some audit clients and environmental matters can, in some circumstances, lead to the risk of material misstatement in financial statements.

The professional bodies consider that, as environmental considerations increase in importance, there will be a growth in the investigation of and reporting of environmental matters.

This will probably mean more opportunities for professional firms in auditing environmental statements.

There are two aspects to environmental considerations as they affect auditors.

- The effect of environmental issues on financial statements and the risk of a material misstatement.
- Environmental reporting as an assurance assignment.

Environmental issues and financial accounts

Some major considerations are:

- Material environmental matters can present major risks to some clients and can lead to possible misstatements in the financial statements. Auditors should incorporate consideration of these risks specifically in their planning processes. Clients particularly at risk include mining and extraction companies, chemical companies, airlines, waste management companies, water companies and utilities and construction companies, etc.
- Responsibility for environmental matters, their recognition, measurement and disclosure, lies with the management.

The main possibilities for misstatement in financial statements include:

- The introduction of environmental laws and regulations which may involve impairment of asset values due to obsolescence.
- Failure to comply with legal requirements may require accrual of remediation, compensation or legal costs.
- Fines, damages and legal costs may need to be accrued for violations including contingent liabilities for pending legal actions.
- Some companies (including waste management companies, chemical manufacturers, etc.) may incur environmental obligations as a direct result of their core operations, e.g. site restoration costs.
- Products may have to be redesigned or may no longer be capable of being sold.
- Constructive obligations may occur from publicly stated environmental policies. These may not be legal obligations but may be just as binding.
- Contingent liabilities may need to be disclosed in some circumstances.
- Initiatives to abate environmental damage may cost a great deal but may not enhance the value of fixed assets.

The auditors are required by ISA 315 '*Understanding the Entity and Its Environment and Assessing the Risks of Material Misstatement*' to consider all aspects of the business, its operations and the environment in which it operates.

These environmental concerns should, therefore, be taken into account when considering the risks to, and the factors which, affect the business and its operations.

Laws and regulations

The auditor has to be aware of the relevant laws and regulations which affect the organisation.

It is the management's responsibility to ensure adherence to laws and regulations but as environmental matters connected with laws and regulations may cause misstatements in financial statements, the auditors also need to be aware of any potential for misstatement.

The auditor's approach here may be:

- to use their existing knowledge of the business;
- enquire of management as to policies and procedures on environmental matters;
- enquire of management as to environmental laws and regulations that may have a fundamental effect on the entity and its financial statements;
- discuss with management the policies or procedures adopted for identifying, evaluating and accounting for litigation, claims and assessments.

Operational issues

The auditors need to be aware of the possible impact that the organisation's processes and operations may have on the environment, including the possible effects caused by pollution and contamination and the hazards to employees and the immediate environs of the premises from which the operations are conducted.

Asset values

Environmental legislation may have the effect of impairing asset values. Auditors need to be aware of the provisions of IAS 36 '*Impairment of Assets*'. Non-current assets must be written down to their recoverable amount, which is the lower of net realisable value and the value in use. If the organisation is the proud owner of, say, contaminated land, the value may be nil as it is unsaleable, or the costs of decontaminating it may be prohibitive.

Third parties

Auditors also need to be aware of major customers or significant suppliers who might be affected by environmental matters and consider the effect on the company as part of the consideration of business risk (see Chapter 14).

ENVIRONMENTAL REPORTING ASSIGNMENT

Audit firms are increasingly becoming involved in separate environmental reporting assignments as part of an organisation's demonstration of its wider sense of corporate responsibility.

This is, quite rightly, often the preserve of experts in environmental issues but the experience of auditors in evaluating evidence against benchmark criteria and in pulling together information to provide a coherent reporting framework is often seen as a key skill in an organisation's environmental reporting framework.

An environmental audit is a method used to obtain accurate, comprehensive and meaningful information on the environmental impact of a company from which management decisions can be based.

The benefits of carrying out environmental audits include:

- ensuring compliance with legislation;;
- reducing waste costs;
- reducing water and energy costs;
- good public relations (if the results are published).

There is a lot of legislation in this area but some of the most important legal rules are contained in:

- Environmental Protection Act 1990.
- Management Licensing Regulations 1994 (as amended).
- Environmental Protection (Duty of Care) Regulations 1991.

The relevant British Standard is ISO 14004, '*Environmental Management Systems – General Guidelines on Principles*' and the complementary auditing standard is ISO 19011 '*Guidelines for Quality and Environmental Management Systems Auditing*'. It is outside the scope of this book to do anything other than outline the basic principles, but students and others interested in this topic will find a wealth of information on the Internet and through bodies such as the British Standards Group (BSI).

In addition to ISO 14001 there is an EC approved scheme called EMAS – the Eco-Management and Audit Scheme. This is a voluntary initiative designed to improve companies' environmental performance.

Its aim is to 'recognise and reward' those organisations that go beyond minimum legal compliance and continuously improve their environmental performance. In addition, it is a requirement of the scheme that participating organisations regularly produce a public environmental statement that reports on their environmental performance. EMAS, the accrediting body, claims that it is this voluntary publication of environmental information, whose accuracy and reliability has been independently checked by an environmental verifier, that gives EMAS and those organisations that participate enhanced credibility and recognition.

Types of environmental audit

Environmental audits can be undertaken for a variety of reasons. They can be specific to a particular subject, i.e. water use, or more general such as initial reviews. Audits are also undertaken to accredit companies to environmental management systems (EMS) such as those under ISO 14001 and EMAS.

There are several different approaches to environmental audit and review. Audits may be carried out as part of an organisation's routine processes to increase efficiency, in connection with an acquisition or as part of a larger compliance review.

They are often performed 'in house' by experts employed by the organisation and it may well be part of the Internal Audit function to collate and review these internal reports.

Other audits will be carried out by external experts, including external audit firms.

Apart from specific anti-pollution type legislation much of the compliance work carried out is at the behest of the organisation, there is no statutory compulsion. Organisations do not have to accredit themselves to a particular standard or develop an environmental management system so all the work carried out by the auditors is on an assignment basis.

Environmental review (environmental audit)

This is a general term usually referring to a basic audit that looks at a range of environmental factors. This type of audit provides valuable management information regarding the environmental situation on a site, and can be used to signpost areas of concern or where further investigative work may be required.

An environmental review would normally involve looking at the site as a whole to determine impacts on the local environment, e.g. location of nearby rivers, location of any local housing, etc. External areas would then be examined looking at areas where waste was stored, location of drainage systems, etc. The internal areas are often broken down into manageable units such as office, canteen, process areas, etc. then, within each area, environmental issues such as storage, waste, lighting, heating, air emissions, and water emissions are noted.

Certain documents are normally inspected as part of this type of audit, particularly waste management documentation, pollution control authorisations, discharge consents from water companies, Environment Agency, etc. Company plans of the site can be used to mark areas of interest such as waste storage areas, surface water drains, etc.

Environmental reviews are also carried out as a first stage towards an environmental management system (EMS). They are used to identify the company's impact on the environment and to create a register of impacts and aspects.

Waste audit

These audits are often linked with environmental reviews and usually form the first step in any waste minimisation exercise. The audit is concerned with waste production and handling at a site. The first concern is to ensure that wastes are being handled and stored in a safe, environmentally acceptable manner at a reasonable cost. Once this is determined then quantities of wastes are noted along with their origin and reason for production. 'Hidden' wastes should also be considered such as waste raw materials, energy and water, and wasted time, etc.

It is also important that adequate records are kept as proof of good waste management. A record-keeping system would typically include a file of consignment notes including special wastes, records of waste produced by a particular department and storage records highlighting any problem wastes which may be stored for a long period. The type of records kept will depend on the company's structure, activities, and type of waste produced. Performance may be audited against legal requirements or against company policy.

The results of a waste audit should show any gaps in information or poor waste management practice. It is important to take action after the audit and look at possible ways to minimise waste production, saving the company money and helping the environment.

Waste disposal site audits

These audits cover the transport and disposal of wastes by a disposal contractor. They are often undertaken as part of compliance with Duty of Care Regulations, to ensure a company's waste is being handled correctly. They are usually carried out internally, and involve a questionnaire-type approach covering issues such as how waste is stored, and general housekeeping on the site. Transport issues are usually covered but can be dealt with separately, especially if the company that owns the waste site is different from the company that transports the waste.

Waste management documentation is checked during the audit, including Waste Management Licences, Waste Carriers Licences and Duty of Care Documentation. This can also be checked with the Environment Agency.

Water audit

These audits are similar to waste audits in that they are often linked with environmental reviews and usually form the first step in any water reduction exercise. The audit is concerned with water use on a site and wastewater production. Water usage on the site is examined and quantified where possible to determine the areas of greatest usage. Wastewater is also quantified if possible, and areas of greatest production identified.

The result of the audit is a water mass balance where a company can identify water going into a site and water leaving the site; any large discrepancies can be investigated as this may indicate leakage or another problem on the site. Another benefit of the audit is that once identified, areas of high water usage or wastage can be investigated and savings made.

Compliance audit

This type of audit is usually done 'in house' to assess compliance with environmental legislation or company procedures. This can be either one aspect of it, e.g. Duty of Care audit, or more generally, all environmental legislation. This type of audit is rarely carried out in isolation, and will normally form part of a general environmental review or EMS audit.

Environmental management system (EMS) audit

These audits form a key element of the environmental management systems established under ISO 14001 and the EC's Eco-Management and Audit Scheme (EMAS). These audits can be carried out by either internal or external auditors and there are set criteria to which audits must comply. The audit will have to be verified by an accredited person who is independent of the site's auditors to receive certification. These audits should not be confused with environmental reviews which are also carried out as part of an EMS (see above).

Acquisition audit

This can be pre- or post-acquisition and concentrates on any potential claims or liabilities for environmental damage, or the costs of installing pollution control equipment, which may affect the viability of purchasing a new site.

Potential for contaminated land is of particular importance; often this type of audit will recommend a more detailed study to investigate any potential contamination. A phased approach is often used, with a Phase 1 audit being an initial appraisal of the site, looking for potential liabilities, e.g. underground storage tanks and also looking at the geography, geology, hydrogeology, site history and the environmental setting.

A Phase 2 audit is then recommended if a certain area needs further investigation. This may involve more elaborate procedures such as borehole samples being taken of soil and ground water. Phase 3 is a phrase also used sometimes; this generally tends to be once the results of Phase 2 are received and some remedial action is required.

This type of audit tends to be undertaken by specialist consultants, often employed by the potential purchaser of the site. However, in some cases it is carried out by the site owner prior to putting the property on the market, to assist with the valuation. Phase 1 audits can be carried out 'in house' as long as time is set aside for doing the necessary research. However, Phase 2 and 3 audits need to be carried out by trained personnel to ensure boreholes are taken according to recognised methods, and that samples are analysed for the correct determinants.

Due diligence audit

This type of audit is normally carried out on behalf of potential investors in a company for similar reasons to the acquisition audits. It is a particularly comprehensive audit and will usually involve a team of professional auditors visiting a site over a period of several days. A wide range of environmental and other factors such as health and safety and fire risk assessments are included, as well as comprehensive site history and legislative reviews.

Audit tools

Each of the types of audit mentioned above use similar techniques adapted to a particular situation. Audit teams, whether internal or external, usually develop their own structure and approach for a particular study. Tools comprise:

- Checklists – useful in providing pointers to the type of information being sought. Also can be used to check compliance with certain procedures, where 'yes or no' answers can be given.
- Questionnaires – these are useful for straightforward situations or when audits are repeated as part of an ongoing programme. It is best to include open questions to allow for a full response rather than be restricted to 'yes or no' answers.
- Interviews – these can be undertaken to determine staff awareness on site of particular environmental issues such as contents of the Environmental Policy, or awareness of spillage procedures. Interviews are often used as a tool for EMS auditing to determine effectiveness of staff training.
- Observation – watching how a process is carried out can provide a more realistic picture of the extent of compliance with a specific procedure than could be obtained simply by asking an individual how a process is performed. However, this should never be used in isolation as it may not provide enough detail or may lead to incorrect assumptions if further investigations are not made.
- Discussion – at the start of an audit it is usual that a meeting is held with key personnel on the site to inform them of the audit activities and what is required of them. Depending on the scale of the audit, review meetings can be held during, but certainly after, the audit to allow for clarification of any points raised.

Reporting

Whatever the outcome of an audit, it is vital that it is recorded and that a report is produced. This report can be as detailed or as brief as the company requires. Phase 1 acquisition audits are often a 'tick sheet' type approach whilst due diligence audit reports can run into several volumes!

What is generally required is a description of the site and type of business, a breakdown of issues covered, results and an action plan for the way forward. A concise executive summary or action plan is often produced separately, as it can be used as an additional management tool. The audit team leader is responsible for preparing the report.

There is no specific format for a report but it could include:

- objectives;
- what was audited, including the organisation/area and scope;
- details of the audit client;
- audit team details and qualifications;
- dates and locations of the audit investigation;
- audit criteria;
- audit plan;
- people contacted within the auditee organisation;
- the audit process;
- problems encountered that may have an impact on the reliability of the results;
- achievement of the audit objectives;
- areas within the scope of the audit but not covered;
- audit findings;
- conclusions;
- improvement recommendations;
- follow-up plans and arrangements.

The audit report should be prepared, reviewed, approved and distributed within a defined time from the end of the investigation. ISO 19011 states that the report should be the property of the audit client (note that it is not, unless they are one and the same, the property of the auditee). The report should, of course, remain confidential.

Two things should be borne in mind:

- The auditors should bring to bear on this type of work the same qualities of skill and judgement that they would if this were a statutory audit under the Companies Act and the same criteria regarding independence, integrity and confidentiality need to be applied.
- Where the auditors are asked to give an opinion, as opposed to simply reporting facts, they should bear in mind the requirements regarding assurance assignments set out in Chapter 32 above. In most cases, unless there are suitable, independent, defined criteria against which environmental performance can be measured auditors should refrain from giving an opinion and simply report facts and make recommendations.

CORPORATE SOCIAL RESPONSIBILITY

Increasingly audit firms are becoming involved in the evaluation of the operations of client organisations against environmental and social criteria as part of their commitment to a wider Corporate Social Responsibility (CSR) programme. In these the organisation is endeavouring to demonstrate its commitment to environmentally and socially aware policies by attempting to measure them against some benchmark criteria and have that achievement audited.

This requires audit firms to look at operational aspects of their clients from a non-financial aspect and to identify suitable criteria against which their client can be assessed. This type of work is often the province of experts and it is beyond the scope of this book to give anything other than a general outline of the type of work carried out and how it is reported.

This is, however, an expanding area as, increasingly, organisations are becoming conscious of their public profile and are being made aware of their responsibilities not only to their share-holders, customers and staff but also to the environment and to the communities in which they operate. Society does not consider it acceptable for modern business organisations to ignore their wider social obligations in pursuit of profits and shareholder value, and it is now consid-ered good business practice to formulate corporate strategies taking social and environmental issues into account. Most large companies now have some form of ethical statement which will include recognition of the need for moral and ethical behaviour, compliance with all laws and regulations and recognition of the impact of their activities on the world around them.

Audit firms are now being asked, as independent arbitrators, to measure the achieve-ment of organisations against identified benchmarks and to report, not just to shareholders, but to the world at large as the organisation acknowledges its performance in these areas to a wider public.

We have looked at Environmental Reporting, which is one aspect of such a programme; the other aspect of it is the organisation's interaction with the community in which it oper-ates, its social performance.

Social audits

There are several definitions of a social audit but all, more or less, say the same thing.

A Social Audit is a process whereby an organisation can assess its social impact and eth-ical behaviour in relation to its aims and objectives, and also those of its stakeholders and the wider community. It is a process which involves a review of the organisation's ethical and moral behaviour against its own ethical code and against the values of the society in which it functions and which it tries to promote.

It does not involve financial considerations but includes such matters as:

- The development and monitoring of ethical and moral codes within the organisation.
- Support for charitable and community causes.
- Human resources policies for recruitment, training, remuneration and retention of staff.
- Maintenance of ethical standards in areas where the organisation may not be required to do so, e.g. the use of child labour in developing countries or the avoidance of pollution where anti-pollution legislation does not exist.
- Information and transparency.
- Observance of human rights and ethical treatment of animals.

Advantages and disadvantages

Organisations which have carried out social audits have reported benefits from the audit process such as:

- Improved knowledge about the operations of the organisation both internally and as they affect stakeholders, which leads to business process improvements.

- Enhanced reputation and credibility in the marketplace and improved customer relations.

- Improved staff relations and human resources policies which helps motivate existing staff and improves the calibre of applicants for jobs.

- Improved strategic planning as goals are more clearly defined.

However, there are two significant drawbacks:

- The process requires honesty and acceptance from everyone in the organisation from the board of directors downward. One of the features of social auditing is improved transparency and communication in the organisation and managers must be prepared to accept and deal with any performance issues thrown up by the audit.

- It is costly and resource-intensive. It requires a considerable time commitment from staff and often requires the company to buy in outside expertise. The benefits of carrying out the social audit must be evaluated in terms of the costs of carrying it out.

Audit methodology

Clearly with such a wide remit, and as every organisation is different, there are no standard tests which social auditors can carry out. Instead each organisation must develop its own methodology and its own form of reporting.

One approach is:

- To identify all the stakeholders, all those affected by the company's actions.

- From this a number of stakeholder groups are selected to be questioned in detail, either in person or through written questionnaires.

- The key questions that would be of interest to each stakeholder group are then identified, normally in consultation with members of that group.

- Attempts to insert market research questions that would be of interest to the organisation, but not to the stakeholders, should be resisted.

Auditors can be involved in the selection and design process, advising the organisation on the process. They can then 'audit' the results to ensure that the process has been carried out honestly and fairly.

Conclusions and recommendations for improvement can be drawn and an action plan developed.

Note that this need not be an annual process. The organisation might carry out a comprehensive review, or design a rolling programme, taking into account cost and resource availability. However, it should not be a 'one-off' exercise – it is part of a continuous improvement programme.

Summary

- VFM involves consideration of economy, efficiency and effectiveness issues.
- Environmental and social matters have become very important in daily life and, for some companies, can lead to misstatements in financial statements.
- Management are responsible for dealing with and reporting on environmental matters.
- There are many opportunities for environmental matters to lead to misstatements in financial statements.
- Auditors need to consider the impact of environmental matters on items in the financial statements.
- Environmental audits are increasingly being developed as part of social responsibility programmes and to lead to compliance and process improvements.
- Environmental and social audits are carried out internally with involvement of internal audit but increasingly with assistance from external audit firms.
- These are assurance assignments and, generally, are confined to reporting facts, no opinion being given.
- Social issues are increasingly important and organisations are increasingly reviewing their non-financial performance in ethical and stakeholder matters.

Points to note

- The government in the UK and in other countries have introduced much legislation to assist in improving or conserving the environmental and many agencies and regulatory bodies now have statutory powers to require companies to take action.
- Environmental audits are not just an investigation into the interaction of a company with its environment and with legal requirements but rather an investigation into policies and systems and how well practices and procedures fulfil policies.
- Some public companies include information on environmental matters in their annual reports.
- Auditors need to be very alert to environmental factors in audits.
- Some legislation imposes personal liabilities on directors and managers in the case of infringement of environmental legislation.
- The public now expects ever-rising standards of corporate behaviour and this will affect both auditing and the auditors.
- It is important to realise that ISO 14001 is not a set of environmental performance guidelines. Rather it is a standard framework for management activities in the environmental area.
- Environmental auditing or verification as a set of procedures is not very different from the audit of financial statements.

Case Study

Diggitup PLC are a quoted company heavily engaged in the waste disposal industry and engage also in some open cast mining in land reclamation projects. The company sees itself as performing an unpleasant duty which the rest of the public are unwilling to do for itself. The company has inevitably acquired a reputation for being environmentally unfriendly and has noticed that the share price has fallen despite good profits and excellent prospects.

They operate from their old freehold factory and offices on a site in a manufacturing estate in Wolverhampton which dates back to the nineteenth century.

Their plant is relatively old but is regularly maintained to a good standard. They have certification under ISO 9000 but not under BS 7750. The auditors are Tickitt & Run who are aware that the company has asked for a loan from the bank to be secured on the freehold premises.

Discussion

- Suggest factors which may have caused the company's reputation and fall in share price.
- Suggest an action programme for improving the company's public image.
- What possible misstatements may occur in the financial statements as a result of environmental factors?
- How might the auditor approach the audit?
- Indicate some green policies the company may adopt.
- What environmental factors may affect the audit?
- How might Tickitt & Run incorporate environmental factors in their audit?

Student self-testing questions

Questions with answers apparent from the text

a) List some major considerations re environmental factors and the audit.

b) What are the major environmental standards?

c) How might environmental issues affect the audit opinion?

d) What internal control issues concern environmental matters?

e) What substantive procedures may an auditor adopt?

f) How are auditors involved in corporate social responsibility issues?

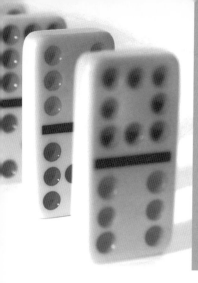

34

Current issues

INTRODUCTION

Auditing is a changing discipline and this chapter is about issues that are currently exercising the profession.

By definition 'current issues' frequently go out of date quite quickly so this chapter contains only brief indicators of the issues facing the profession at the time of writing. Having said that, some issues, such as auditor independence, have been around almost as long as the profession!

In practice it is important for students to read the professional press and student periodicals to ensure they keep up to date with current issues as these often form the basis of examination questions.

AUDITING ISSUES

At the time of writing the Companies Act 2006 has not been fully implemented. The impact of new rules on restriction of auditor liability and the deregulation of private companies has yet to be felt and these will no doubt continue to be of interest.

The government is proposing a further increase in the audit exemption limit, which will take more SMEs out of the full audit requirement. This may have an impact on the SMEs themselves, but it is also likely to affect the smaller audit firms as well.

APB and IAASB Statements of Auditing Standards and other guidance on auditing matters are being issued regularly. Currently they are much exercised by issues around ethics and quality control, topics we will return to later.

The Accounting Standards Board and the IASB issue new material frequently and the Urgent Issues Task Force (UITF) also make pronouncements. All these need to be known by auditors. The latest buzz word is convergence whereby UK and international accounting and auditing standards will be brought together for the purposes of consistency in financial reporting internationally. Students should ensure they are up to date on financial reporting matters.

The professional bodies make new pronouncements and issue new guidance on many issues, particularly ethical and auditing issues. The professional bodies are particularly concerned about the maintenance of auditing standards and the Professional Oversight Board will look at any cases where larger audits are involved to ensure that standards are maintained in even the largest audit firms.

The fall out from the Enron saga continues. The Securities and Exchange Commission in the USA has recently pronounced on professional independence and this has led to a debate on the issue which may have repercussions for some time. The Sarbanes Oxley (Sarbox) legislation has severely restricted the ability of audit firms to cross sell client services as this was seen as compromising auditor independence, however, the US regulators appear to be relaxing their grip and recent pronouncements indicate that they are interested in exploring more of a principles-based approach as opposed to the heavily regulated one currently adopted.

The costs of auditing and the international nature of many large clients have led to concentration amongst audit firms, particularly those below the 'Big 4'. Larger second rank firms are merging and are concerned about the domination of the Big 4 (PwC, Ernst, Deloitte and KPMG) in auditing FTSE 100 companies. They are trying to break the stranglehold of the big firms on this lucrative market.

The rise of the public sector, in auditing terms, continues to grow and, increasingly, private sector firms are being involved in carrying out Performance Evaluation work, often in conjunction with other regulatory authorities such as the Social Services Inspectorate (SSI) or the education standards watchdog, OFSTED. This opens up new areas for the audit profession and creates the requirement for professionals with different skills to their corporate auditor colleagues.

As described in Chapter 33, new opportunities for non-financial assurance work have developed. These include environmental and social auditing, value for money auditing and performance reporting.

AUDIT CHALLENGES

New challenges are being posed to auditors arising from the increased use of Internet and other electronic forms of trading. Auditing practices have to remain flexible to accommodate new forms of corporate activity. The increased use of risk-based auditing methods means that the calibre and experience of audit staff has to be maintained. In addition the requirement for technical computer skills is growing and the auditing profession is now heavily computerised, both in preparing audit working papers and in carrying out audit testing.

The rise in new forms of retailing, particularly Internet-based trading, presents new challenges to the auditing profession, challenges which have not yet fully matured. Consider the challenge posed to the auditor of a client who is an Internet-based retailer, with computers and offices in the UK, distribution warehouses in Germany and France, and a head office in the USA which carries out all its activities electronically using paperless systems. Systems-based audit testing is not going to work! Audit processes and procedures cannot afford to lag behind the trading methods of the client.

This is particularly relevant at a time when reports indicate that fraud is on the increase. This is not only fraud resulting from external attack, hackers, etc., but internal 'high flyer' fraud. Research indicates that the most likely culprit is a male senior manager with more than two years' experience in the organisation, in other words the very person the auditor comes to for information and explanations.

Research into new forms of auditing involving such arcane areas such as Game Theory are being talked about in academic circles as a way of designing audit procedures in such a way as to improve the chances of detecting fraudsters, but this is very much in its infancy at the moment.

INDEPENDENCE

As was apparent from Chapter 6 it is important for auditors not only to independent but to appear to be independent. In recent years auditing firms have seen auditing almost as a loss leader, and they have seen auditing as giving access to a client so that the client can be sold all manner of additional services, all of which are seen as being the really lucrative part of the profession.

However, since the spectacular collapses of corporate behemoths Enron and WorldCom in the USA, whose towering financial performance turned out to be founded on shifting sand, the auditing profession has moved out of the cupboard and is now seen as very much at the forefront of the accounting world. Suddenly everyone wants a clean certificate from a respected firm of auditors. However, this has once again brought to the forefront of the debate the old question of audit firms cross selling other services to their audit clients.

The financial scandals in the USA have concentrated the minds of American regulators and auditor independence is now seen as a key plank of the Corporate Governance structure (Chapter 2).

Four key principles of auditor independence have been suggested. These are:

- An auditor may not have a mutual or conflicting interest with the client.
- An auditor may not audit his own firm's work.
- An auditor may not function as management or as an employee of the audit client.
- An auditor may not act as an advocate for the audit client.

There are obvious advantages to auditors carrying out other work for audit clients, such as the fact that their knowledge of the client will enable the auditors to offer services to their client in a context which they already understand. However, consider the principles of agency theory outlined in Chapter 1. The auditors act for the shareholders to monitor the activities of their agents, the directors. How can those self-same auditors profess to be independent when those directors are handing out lucrative consultancy contracts to those auditors, or at least to the same firm if not the same individuals?

The audit firms would appear to be conflicted. This dilemma has yet to be resolved satisfactorily, possibly because it is not, really, in the interests, at least in the UK, of the larger firms to resolve it quickly. The Sarbox regulations in the USA decided the issue quite simply for the profession there.

From time to time the idea is floated that the audit profession should become an arm of the government, a sort of financial inspectorate, and not be part of the private sector accountancy profession. This idea has not been greeted with any enthusiasm from any party but it remains an option.

ETHICS AND QUALITY ISSUES

The professional bodies require strict adherence to the ethical codes and have considerable enforcement mechanisms. Necessarily ethical codes should be obeyed in the spirit as well as the letter but sometimes aren't in the face of commercial pressures. The use of aggressive accounting practices in order to maintain profits (and often, coincidentally, bonus payments), can put auditors under severe pressure. No firm is willing to lose a large client and the temptation must be to bend and stretch the rules as far as possible to accommodate the client.

This is not to say that audit firms succumb to pressure, but the reality is that the audit world is very competitive and results have to be maintained. The increased use of risk management approaches must not so change ethical behaviour so that the truth stops being truth and starts becoming the fact that no one found out you lied.

The profession had a severe shock following the destruction of the giant auditing firm of Arthur Andersen, post-Enron, and it is that which prompted the regulators to look closely at quality control and to ensure that lapses in ethical behaviour are punished.

The regulation of the profession has moved away from the RSBs, but whether this will result in the public's having any greater perception of the independence of the profession remains to be seen.

Research indicates that the 'perception gap', the difference between what auditors actually do and what the public think they do, is still a real issue. The question of trust remains vital. A major loss of trust by the investing public could result in a severe shock to the financial world and the role of the independent, ethically sound, technically competent auditor remains central to that trust. Whilst companies are undoubtedly responding to the rise in Corporate Social Responsibility their primary function is to create wealth and increase shareholder value, so their ethical progress may well be corralled within financial realities.

CORPORATE GOVERNANCE

The UK continues to adopt a 'substance over form' approach and has resisted the US way of regulation. The rise of non-executive directors in the maintenance of corporate governance standards within companies has been and continues to be significant. The growth of audit and remuneration committees has been a good thing for the audit profession generally. With them has come the development of the internal audit function as an arm of quality control.

Internal auditors no longer see themselves as a corporate police force but as an arm of management and the development of that aspect of the profession is assisting the work of external auditors and helping to maintain ethical standards within organisations and to deter fraud and malpractice.

NEW OPPORTUNITIES, NEW PROBLEMS

Apart from the new opportunities in the area of CSR already mentioned and the increasing technical demands on individual auditors, new opportunities are arising in the developing world.

Predictions made by Goldman Sachs in 1999 were that, by 2025, India would have the third largest economy in the world behind China and the USA, in that order.

The rise of the economies of India and the Far East has not, as yet, been matched by a rise in the level of financial regulation. Overseas investors in those countries have expressed doubts about the quality of financial information being presented to them. Companies involved in joint ventures or partnerships are finding it increasingly difficult to rely on the results without inserting their own financial resources in an effort to ensure the probity of the information. This means that audit firms based in countries with a higher level of regulation are able to sell services into these countries. In addition there are training and development opportunities for training the vast numbers of auditors and accountants required to service these new economies.

Summary

- Auditing is a dynamic discipline and change is now rapid.
- New material emanates from statutes, the ASB and IASB, the APB and IFAC, UITF, corporate governance, professional bodies, regulation and technological change.
- Quality control of audit work is important in order to maintain public confidence.
- Independence is an important topic especially in relation to other work.
- Audit automation and new audit techniques such as risk analysis are current issues.
- The audit profession has to stay abreast of new forms of trading, particularly Internet-based operations.
- New opportunities have arisen in the fields of CSR and also in the developing world.

Points to note

- Auditing is a surprisingly dynamic discipline. Students are advised to keep up to date by reading the professional press and the business pages of the newspapers can help as can reading annual reports and accounts, either in manually signed format or electronic format.
- The question of auditor independence is a difficult one due to the conflicting professional and commercial instincts of auditors. Regulators want more independence (= not doing other work) and auditors want more work other than auditing. The use of business risk assessment methods is now becoming central to audit work.
- Computers and the Internet are changing the face of auditing.

Case Study

Megablast Inc. trades internationally as a manufacturer and distributor of electrical goods ranging from consumer goods (TV's, washing machines, etc.), to electrical equipment and electronic components. Its shares are currently listed on the New York Stock Exchange and it is subject to the Sarbanes Oxley legislation and lots of other listing rules.

The CEO, Lindsey Lovely, has been considering moving the operation to London and transferring the business to a new holding company listed on the UK Stock Exchange. There are many tax and accounting issues but the main one Lindsey is concerned about is the regulatory regime in America.

The auditors, international accounting firm Tickitt & Run, quite approve of the move to London and are helping Lindsey with the decision.

Discussion
- Why would Tickitt & Run be so keen to see Megablast relocate?
- What benefits would it bring to Megablast to do so?
- What ethical issues are involved?

Student self-testing questions

Questions with answers apparent from the text

a) List some influences for change in auditing.

b) Where do new audit regulations come from?

c) List advantages and disadvantages of auditors' taking other work from audit clients.

d) What approach to regulation has been taken by the USA?

e) How does it differ from the UK approach?

f) How can the audit profession benefit from the developing world?

Appendix I

Example of an Audit Engagement Letter

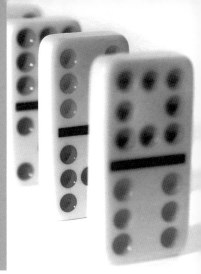

Note this is an example of an Engagement Letter prepared by the Auditing Practices Board and relating to the provision of audit services.

It is written by the auditor to the client and the client is required to sign a copy of it and return it to the auditor as confirmation that the terms of the engagement have been accepted. This forms the contract between the parties.

Additional services to be provided by the auditors such as preparation of tax computations etc., would have to be included in the letter or subject to a separate letter

Dear Sirs

The following letter is for use as a guide in conjunction with the considerations outlined in this ISA and will need to be varied according to individual requirements and circumstances.

To the Board of Directors or the appropriate representative of senior management:

You have requested that we audit the balance sheet of . . . . as of . . . ., and the related statements of income and cash flows for the year then ending. We are pleased to confirm our acceptance and our understanding of this engagement by means of this letter. Our audit will be made with the objective of our expressing an opinion on the financial statements.

We will conduct our audit in accordance with International Standards on Auditing (or refer to relevant national standards or practices). Those Standards require that we plan and perform the audit to obtain reasonable assurance about whether the financial statements are free of material misstatements. An audit includes examining, on a test basis, evidence supporting the amounts and disclosures in the financial statements. An audit also includes assessing the accounting principles used and significant estimates made by management, as well as evaluating the overall financial statement presentation.

Because of the test nature and other inherent limitations of an audit, together with the inherent limitations of any accounting and internal control system, there is an unavoidable risk that even some material misstatements may remain undiscovered.

In addition to our report on the financial statements, we expect to provide you with a separate letter concerning any material weaknesses in accounting and internal control systems which come to our notice.

We remind you that the responsibility for the preparation of financial statements including adequate disclosure is that of the management of the company. This includes the maintenance of adequate accounting records and internal controls, the selection and application of accounting policies, and the safeguarding of the assets of the company.

As part of our audit process, we will request from management written confirmation concerning representations made to us in connection with the audit.

We look forward to full cooperation with your staff and we trust that they will make available to us whatever records, documentation and other information are requested in connection with our audit.

Our fees, which will be billed as work progresses, are based on the time required by the individuals assigned to the engagement plus out-of-pocket expenses. Individual hourly rates vary according to the degree of responsibility involved and the experience and skill required.

This letter will be effective for future years unless it is terminated, amended or superseded.

Please sign and return the attached copy of this letter to indicate that it is in accordance with your understanding of the arrangements for our audit of the financial statements.

Tickett & Run

Acknowledged on behalf of

ABC Company by

(signed)

. . . .

Name and Title

Date

Appendix II
Audit Planning Memorandum

Prepared by: _____ Date: _____ Reviewed by: _____ Date: _____		
Timetable	Planned	Actual
Provisional dates		
Planning meeting with client		
Dates — interim audit		
Date Final audit		
Accounts sign		
AGM		
Changes since previous audit	Comments/Notes	
Client's trade or business		
Operations		
Key management and staff		
Accounting system		
Financing		
Professional advisors		
Legal and regulatory		
Audit strategy: Reliance to be placed on Internal controls (Yes/No)	Comments/Notes	
Sales and Receivables		
Purchases and payables		
Stock		
Work in Progress		
Salaries and Wages		
Bank receipts and payments		
Cash control		
Non current assets (detail)		
Other (detail)		
Evaluation of internal audit function – effective (Yes/No – details)		
Areas where significant errors discovered in previous visits		
Areas where material error or misstatement most likely		
Likelihood of fraud (including senior management fraud)		
Conclusion on audit strategy		
Risk based		
Systems based		
Substantive (Justify)		

Approved by audit partner (Sign/date) Audit Programme reviewed by Audit partner (Audit partner to sign off prior to commencement of audit work)	
Systems evaluation – *Create update systems notes and flowcharts for:* *Carry out walkthrough tests for:* *Update Permanent File for:*	Comments/Notes
Specific planning points *Changes to audit programme from previous period* *Specialist external assistance required* *Use of CAATs (detail)* *IT assistance required*	Comments/Notes
Detail schedules to be prepared by client *Schedules/dates* *Final accounts drafted*	Comments/Notes
Dates of relevant Audit Committee meetings *Do final accounts have to be approved by Audit committee before finalisation?*	Comments/Notes

Liaison with Internal Audit
To what extent are we to reduce our work by relying on work of IA?
Set preliminary dates for IA meetings
   Planning
   Interim
   Final
	Comments/Notes

Detail other services to be provided by client and responsibility *Tax computations* *VAT compliance* *Final accounts drafting* *Other (detail)*	Comments/Notes
Audit team *Date* *Specific staff requirements* *Date of briefing meeting* *Points to raise at briefing meeting* *Specific audit staff responsibilities*	
Supervision and review *Responsibility for audit team supervision and review* *Specific areas to be reviewed by* *Audit manager* *Audit partner* *Hot review required?* *Details*	Comments/Notes
Analytical review *Detail relevant financial ratios* *Conclusions from analytical review*	
Time and cost budget *Consider variations from previous year time budget and cost to actual charge*	
Comments and points not covered above	Comments/Notes

Clearly this is meant to be indicative only and is designed to illustrate the sorts of issues which would be taken into account at the planning stage.

It would be prepared by the Audit manager and approved by the Audit partner prior to the commencement of the audit work.

INDEX